p	Probability		X	of an interval
Q	The statistic for the Cochran test		$\bar{X}$	Sample mean
Q	Quartile deviation		fX	Product of f and X
r	Pearson product-moment correlation coefficient		χ^2	Chi square test statistic
ρ	Spearman rank correlation coefficient		x	Deviation score
			χ_r^2	Statistic for the Friedman test
S.E.M.	Standard error of the mean		z	Standard score
s	Sample standard deviation		$!$	Factorial
Σ	Sum of		$\mid \ \mid$	Absolute value
ΣX	Sum of the scores		$<$	Less than
$(\Sigma X)^2$	Square of the sum		$>$	Greater than
ΣX^2	Sum of the squares		$\geq$	Equal to or greater than
t	The statistic for the Student's t		$\leq$	Equal to or less than
T	The smaller sum of the ranks for either ΣR^+ or ΣR^- (used in the Wilcoxon test)		$\neq$	Not equal
			$\sqrt{\ }$	Square root
U	The statistic for the Mann-Whitney U test			

4-6 *Quartile Deviation*

$$Q = \frac{Q_3 - Q_1}{2}$$

4-7 Q_3 *Formula*

$$Q_3 = LL + \frac{(\frac{3}{4}N - cf)}{fw} i$$

4-8 Q_1 *Formula*

$$Q_1 = LL + \frac{(\frac{1}{4}N - cf)}{fw} i$$

4-9 *Range Formula*

$$\text{Range} = X_H - X_L$$

7-1 *Binomial Formula*

$$p(x) = \binom{N}{x} P^x Q^{N-x}$$

7-2 *Chi-Square Formula*

$$\chi^2 = \Sigma \frac{(O - E)^2}{E}$$

7-3 *McNemar Test*

$$\chi^2 = \frac{(|A - D| - 1)^2}{A + D}$$

7-4 *Cochran Q Test*

$$Q = \frac{(k - 1)(k \Sigma C^2 - T^2)}{kT - \Sigma R^2}$$

(continued inside back cover)

STATISTICS
for the Social Sciences

Vicki F. Sharp

California State University, Northridge

Statistics
FOR THE SOCIAL SCIENCES

Little, Brown and Company

Boston Toronto

To Dick

Library of Congress Catalog Card No. 78–70849

First Printing

Published simultaneously in Canada
by Little, Brown & Company (Canada) Limited

Printed in the United States of America

PREFACE

This book is designed for undergraduate and graduate students who need a clear, concise introduction to applied statistics. The text can be used effectively in introductory courses in statistics, research, or tests and measurement; or it can be used as a practical statistics handbook for research. The student-centered, activity-oriented approach makes it appropriate for use either as a course text or for self-paced, individualized instruction.

The ten chapters are presented in a sequence that enables the reader to grasp the material easily. Chapters 1 and 2 provide the necessary, practical knowledge. Chapters 3 and 4 discuss measures of central tendency and variability. Chapter 5 includes a play that helps the student become familiar with concepts that are important in statistical research. Chapter 6 demonstrates how to choose the right statistical test by means of an easy to follow map. Chapters 7, 8, and 9 present the most commonly used nominal, ordinal, and interval tests. Chapter 10 discusses correlation.

The book contains some special features. At the beginning of each chapter the objectives are listed. Practice problems, with answers immediately following, are given throughout each chapter. A self-test with questions keyed to the text is included at the end of each chapter, so the student can refer back to the explanation if necessary. Answers follow the self-tests for immediate reinforcement. Formulas and statistical test requirements and summaries are set apart to highlight them. The book is made more enjoyable by motivational devices such as the play, a statistical road map, flowcharts, and simple, down to earth examples and illustrations. The numbers used in the examples are intentionally small to reduce computational drudgery. There are no mathematical derivations. The statistical tests are explained in an easy to follow, step-by-step manner. For the student's convenience, the appendix provides tables and references; and in addition, formulas and a glossary of symbols are listed on the inside covers of the text. The instructor's manual that accompanies the text contains work sheets and test items, both with answers. Questions for both are keyed to the

v

text pages for easy review. Pages are perforated to facilitate duplication for classroom review and tests.

Sincere appreciation is given to the authors and publishers who gave permission to use the tables. Among them, I am grateful to the Literary Executor of the late Sir Ronald A. Fisher, F.R.S., to Dr. Frank Yates, F.R.S., and to Longman Group Ltd., London, for permission to reprint Table 2.1 and Appendix tables B, E, O, and Q from their book *Statistical Tables for Biological, Agricultural and Medical Research* (6th edition, 1974).

Many individuals have contributed to this book. My students field-tested the material, and Elaine Barth did the outstanding technical typing. A special thanks is given to the staff at Little, Brown for their dedication to this endeavor. Invaluable assistance and direction were provided by Mylan Jaixen, editor; Betsy Foote, editorial assistant; Cynthia Chapin, book editor; and Robert Lentz, copy editor. I wish to thank Carmine A. Yengo, Trenton State College, for his excellent suggestions and worthwhile criticism at each stage of writing. His suggestions were extremely helpful, and many are incorporated in the book. My appreciation is extended also to Ralph Howard, a Ph.D. candidate at Cal Tech; John A. Lindlof, University of Maine at Orono; Keith E. Meredith, University of Arizona; and Alan R. Hartke, The American College Testing Program, who also read and critiqued all chapters. I was encouraged to continue working on this project by Sy Metzner, a friend, and Bobbie and Paul Friedman, my parents.

Finally, thanks to my loving husband, Dick, for his support and criticisms of the manuscript.

CONTENTS

SELF-TEST FOR ASSESSING MATH ABILITY

Test Instructions: Statistics is fun? Research is exciting? Yes — they can be, depending upon one's approach. The approach in this book is a practical one. Chapter 1 reviews the basic mathematics you need in order to understand the statistics and research presented in this book. The review should help to remove perhaps the major obstacle to your enjoying statistics and research.

Before you start reading Chapter 1, take the following self-test. After you have taken this test, you will be able to decide which material in the chapter you need to review. Do not feel discouraged if you have forgotten some of the math.

pp. 1–5   **1.** Solve the following problems:

(a) $\frac{1}{8} + \frac{1}{9} = $ _____   (c) $\frac{1}{4} \times \frac{2}{8} \times \frac{6}{12} \times \frac{2}{4} = $ _____

(b) $\frac{2}{3} - \frac{1}{9} = $ _____   (d) $\frac{4}{8} \div \frac{2}{3} = $ _____

pp. 5–6   **2.** Solve the following problems using decimals:

(a)   5.21
        24.10
        34.10
      + 1.6

(c) $\frac{.0009}{.003} = $ _____

(b)   674.2
     − 12.0

(d)   3.56
     × 2.4

p. 6   **3.** Round these numbers to the nearest tenth:
   (a) 13.456 _____   (c) 1.445 _____
   (b) 12.465 _____   (d) 1.222 _____

pp. 6–7   **4.** Solve these problems:
   (a) $8946824.1 \times 0 = $ _____   (c) $643 \times 0 = $ _____

   (b) $\frac{0}{9} = $ _____   (d) $8 + 0 = $ _____

p. 7   **5.** What shortcuts would you use to solve the following problems? After you state your answer, solve the problems.

   (a) $80 \times 40 = $ _____   (c) $674 \times .01 = $ _____
   (b) $368 \times 100 = $ _____   (d) $833 \times .001 = $ _____

p. 8

6. A group of 75 students took a math test. Seven received A's, 10 received B's, 40 received C's, 10 received D's, and 8 received F's. Find the proportion of students receiving A's, D's, and F's. Change this proportion to decimal form, then convert it to a percent. Round to the nearest hundredth.
   (a) Students receiving A's _____
   (b) Students receiving D's _____
   (c) Students receiving F's _____

p. 9

7. Solve the following problems:
   (a) $4^2 =$ _____   (c) $6^2 =$ _____
   (b) $3^3 =$ _____   (d) $2^4 =$ _____

pp. 9–10

8. Using Table A, find the square roots of the following numbers:
   (a) 16 _____   (d) 21.2521 _____
   (b) 11,236 _____   (e) 5.5696 _____
   (c) 13.6489 _____   (f) 100 _____

pp. 10–12

9. Complete the following operations with sign numbers:
   (a) $(-2) + (-5) =$ _____
   (b) $(-6) + 6 =$ _____
   (c) $(-5) + (-8) + (-6) + 5 + 2 + 1 =$ _____
   (d) $15 - 2 =$ _____
   (e) $15 - (-2) =$ _____
   (f) $(-4) \times (-8) =$ _____
   (g) $(-2) \times 3 =$ _____
   (h) $\dfrac{40}{4} =$ _____
   (i) $\dfrac{-20}{5} =$ _____
   (j) $\dfrac{-10}{-5} =$ _____

pp. 12–13

10. Taking into account the order of arithmetic operations, solve the following problems:
    (a) $6 + 7 \times 2 - 20 \div 2 =$ _____
    (b) $(6 \times 3) + 12 \div 2 =$ _____
    (c) $3^2 + 20 \div 2^2 + 5\sqrt{25} =$ _____
    (d) $(6 \times 5) + 6 \div 2 =$ _____

pp. 13–14

11. What do these symbols mean?
    (a) $6 < 9$ _____
    (b) $\overline{X}$ _____
    (c) $\sqrt{N}$ _____
    (d) s _____

pp. 13–14

12. For the following raw scores, 2, 3, 4, 5, 2, 1, find:
    (a) $\Sigma X =$ _____   (c) $(\Sigma X)^2 =$ _____
    (b) $\Sigma X^2 =$ _____   (d) $N =$ _____

pp. 14–16

13. Using the formula $s = \dfrac{1}{N}\sqrt{N \Sigma X^2 - (\Sigma X)^2}$, find the standard deviation for the following raw scores: 1, 2, 2, 2, 2, 1, 1, 10, 10, 3
    (a) $N =$ _____   (c) $\Sigma X^2 =$ _____
    (b) $\Sigma X =$ _____   (d) $s =$ _____

ANSWERS TO SELF-TEST FOR ASSESSING MATH ABILITY

1. (a) $\frac{17}{72}$ (c) $\frac{1}{64}$

   (b) $\frac{5}{9}$ (d) $\frac{3}{4}$

2. (a) 65.01   (c) .3
   (b) 662.2   (d) 8.544

3. (a) 13.5   (c) 1.4
   (b) 12.5   (d) 1.2

4. (a) 0   (c) 0
   (b) 0   (d) 8

5. (a) 3200   (c) 6.74
   (b) 36,800   (d) .833

6. (a) $\frac{7}{75} = .0933$ or 9.33%

   (b) $\frac{10}{75} = .1333$ or 13.33%

   (c) $\frac{8}{75} = .1067$ or 10.67%

7. (a) 16   (c) 36
   (b) 27   (d) 16

8. (a) 4   (d) 4.61
   (b) 106   (e) 2.36
   (c) 3.69   (f) 10

9. (a) -7 (f) 32
   (b) 0   (g) -6
   (c) -11 (h) 10
   (d) 13   (i) -4
   (e) 17   (j) 2

10. (a) *Solution:* Multiply and divide first, then add and subtract.

$$6 + 7 \times 2 - 20 \div 2 = 6 + 14 - 10$$
$$= 10$$

(b) *Solution:* Parentheses first, division next, then addition.

$$(6 \times 3) + 12 \div 2 = 18 + 12 \div 2$$
$$= 18 + 6$$
$$= 24$$

(c) *Solution:* Square root, then square; multiply, then divide, add, and subtract.

$$3^2 + 20 \div 2^2 + 5\sqrt{25} = 9 + 20 \div 4 + 5 \times 5$$
$$= 9 + 5 + 25$$
$$= 39$$

(d) *Solution:* Parentheses first, divide, then add.

$$(6 \times 5) + 6 \div 2 = 30 + 6 \div 2$$
$$= 30 + 3$$
$$= 33$$

11. (a) 6 is less than 9.
    (b) The mean or arithmetic average.
    (c) Square root of a number.
    (d) The standard deviation.

12. (a) $\Sigma X = 17$ $(2 + 3 + 4 + 5 + 2 + 1)$
    (b) $\Sigma X^2 = 59$ $(4 + 9 + 16 + 25 + 4 + 1)$
    (c) $(\Sigma X)^2 = 289$ $(17)^2$
    (d) $N = 6$

13. (a) $N = 10$
    (b) $\Sigma X = 34$
    (c) $\Sigma X^2 = 228$
    (d) $s = 3.4$ *Solution:*

$$s = \frac{1}{10} \sqrt{(10)228 - (34)^2}$$

$$= \frac{1}{10} \sqrt{2280 - 1156}$$

$$= \frac{1}{10} \sqrt{1124}$$

$$= \frac{1}{10} (34)$$

$$= 3.4$$

BASIC MATH
FOR STATISTICS

1

In the following paragraphs you will learn how to interpret statistical symbols, read a statistical formula, and review such topics as fractions and decimals. At the end of the chapter a self-test will show you how well you have learned the material.

SYMBOLS FOR ARITHMETIC

Addition is represented by a plus $(+)$ sign as in $(3+4)$.

Subtraction is represented by a minus $(-)$ sign as in $(4-3)$.

Multiplication is shown four ways:

1. Cross $(\times)$ as in (8×5)
2. Parentheses $(\quad)$ as in $8(5)$ or $(8)(5)$
3. Dot $(\cdot)$ as in $8 \cdot 5$
4. Juxtaposition of two statistical symbols as in fx

Division is shown four ways:

1. Division sign $(\div)$ as in $(20 \div 10)$
2. Horizontal bar $(—)$ as in $\dfrac{20}{10}$
3. Slanted line $(\;/\;)$ as in $20/10$
4. The traditional form $10\overline{)20}$

FRACTIONS
Addition of Fractions

When fractions are to be added with the same denominator (bottom numbers), $\dfrac{1}{4}+\dfrac{1}{4}$, simply add the numerators (top numbers) and place the answer over the common denominator, $\dfrac{1}{4}+\dfrac{1}{4}=\dfrac{2}{4}$. A problem occurs when the fractions do not have the same denominators. A criss-cross method is used to add fractions with different denominators. For example, to add $\dfrac{1}{4}+\dfrac{3}{5}$:

1. Multiply the first numerator (1) by the second denominator (5), $1 \times 5 = 5$:

$$\frac{①}{4}+\frac{3}{⑤}.$$

2. Multiply the second numerator (3) by the first denominator (4), $3 \times 4 = 12$:

$$\frac{1}{④} + \frac{③}{5}.$$

3. Add the two products, $5 + 12$, and write their sum, 17, as the numerator in the new fraction, $\frac{17}{?}$.

4. Multiply the first denominator (4) by the second denominator (5) and write this product as the denominator in the new fraction, $\frac{17}{20}$.

Following these steps you can see that

$$\frac{1}{4} + \frac{3}{5} = \frac{(1 \times 5) + (3 \times 4)}{4 \times 5} = \frac{17}{20}$$

Subtraction of Fractions

Subtraction of fractions follows the same rules as addition of fractions. If the denominators are the same, $\frac{2}{4} - \frac{1}{4}$, simply subtract the numerators, $2 - 1$, and place the answer over the common denominator, $\frac{2}{4} - \frac{1}{4} = \frac{1}{4}$. If the fractions do not have the same denominators, use the criss-cross method. For the problem $\frac{2}{5} - \frac{1}{10}$:

1. Multiply the first numerator (2) by the second denominator (10), $2 \times 10 = 20$:

$$\frac{②}{5} - \frac{1}{⑩}.$$

2. Multiply the second numerator (1) by the first denominator (5), $1 \times 5 = 5$:

$$\frac{2}{⑤} - \frac{①}{10}.$$

3. Subtract the two products, $20 - 5$, and write their difference, 15, as the numerator in the new fraction, $\frac{15}{?}$.

4. Multiply the first denominator (5) by the second denominator (10), $5 \times 10 = 50$, and write this product as denominator in the new fraction, $\frac{15}{50}$. Following

these steps, you can see that

$$\frac{2}{5} - \frac{1}{10} = \frac{(2 \times 10) - (1 \times 5)}{5 \times 10} = \frac{15}{50}$$

The fraction $\frac{15}{50}$ is reduced to $\frac{3}{10}$. (A short explanation on reducing is given below.)

Multiplication of Fractions

In multiplying fractions such as $\frac{1}{2} \times \frac{1}{3} \times \frac{2}{6} \times \frac{4}{8}$, multiply the numerators, $1 \times 1 \times 2 \times 4 = 8$, then the denominators, $2 \times 3 \times 6 \times 8 = 288$. The answer is $\frac{8}{288}$, which can be reduced to $\frac{1}{36}$. Reduce a fraction by dividing its numerator and denominator by the same number.[1] Eight divided by eight is equal to one, $8\overline{)8}^{\,1}$, while 288 divided by eight equals 36, $8\overline{)288}^{\,36}$; therefore, $\frac{8}{288}$ reduces to $\frac{1}{36}$.

Multiplication of fractions is often long and involved. For example, the following numbers might be encountered: $\frac{1}{3} \times \frac{8}{12} \times \frac{6}{24} = \frac{48}{864}$ or $\frac{1}{18}$. These figures may seem difficult to handle; however, the problem can be simplified. We can shortcut by reducing the numbers before multiplying them. This shortcut is often referred to as canceling. Before you multiply fractions, examine the numerators and denominators to see if they can be evenly divided by the same number. Cross out any numerator and any denominator that can be divided by the same number. Next perform these divisions and place the correct answers above and below the crossed-out numbers.

In the preceding example the canceled fractions look like this:

$$\frac{1}{3} \times \frac{\overset{1}{\cancel{8}}}{\underset{2}{\cancel{12}}} \times \frac{\overset{1}{\cancel{6}}}{\underset{3}{\cancel{24}}}$$

First you cancel the 8 in the second numerator with the 24 in the third denominator, since both numbers can be evenly divided by 8; 8 divided by 8 equals 1 and 24 divided by 8 equals 3. Next cancel the 6 in the third numerator with the 12 in the

---

[1] Reduction does not change the value of the fraction. Often it is not possible to reduce a fraction.

second denominator, since both numbers can be evenly divided by 6: 6 divided by 6 equals 1 and 12 divided by 6 equals 2. Now you have $1 \times 1 \times 1$ in the numerator and $3 \times 2 \times 3$ in the denominator. Multiply these numbers; the answer is the same as before: $\frac{1}{18}$.

Division of Fractions

To divide a fraction by a fraction, simply invert (reverse) the numerator and denominator of the divisor (the second fraction) and multiply.[2] Therefore, $\frac{5}{8} \div \frac{2}{3}$ becomes $\frac{5}{8} \times \frac{3}{2} = \frac{15}{16}$, and $\frac{2}{3} \div \frac{3}{4}$ becomes $\frac{2}{3} \times \frac{4}{3} = \frac{8}{9}$.

DECIMALS
Adding or Subtracting Decimals

When adding or subtracting decimals, make sure the decimal point of one number is directly below the decimal point of another; then proceed as usual.

$$
\begin{array}{r}
4.094 \\
35.02 \\
1.02 \\
+\ \ 5.1 \\
\hline
45.234
\end{array}
\qquad
\begin{array}{r}
343.2 \\
-\ \ 23.1 \\
\hline
320.1
\end{array}
$$

Multiplying Decimals

When multiplying decimals, you have to place a decimal point in the product (answer). Let's take 3.407×2.3 as our example.

1. Multiply 3.407 by 2.3, getting the product 78361 before the decimal point is placed.
2. Count the number of decimal places in each factor.[3] In the first factor, 3.407,

---

[2] A divisor is the number by which you divide; here, it is the second fraction.

[3] A *factor* is any one of two numbers that is used in multiplication to form an answer or product.

there are three decimal places, and in the second factor, 2.3, one decimal place. Add the number of decimal places, $3 + 1$, to obtain the sum of 4.
3. Using this sum, start at the right of your product 78361 and count off four places, 7.8361. Place the decimal point between the 7 and the 8 as follows: 7.8361.

Dividing Decimals

Before dividing decimals, you must make the divisor[4] into a whole number by moving its decimal point to the right of the last number. For example, $.02\overline{)\,.008}$ becomes $.02\overline{)\,.008}$. Next move the decimal point in the dividend as many places as you moved the decimal point in the divisor—in this case, two places: $02.\overline{)\,.008}$. Divide normally and place the decimal point in the quotient directly above the new decimal point in the dividend, $2\overline{)\,.8}$, to get the answer, .4.

Rounding Decimals

When you round a number[5] to the nearest decimal place, you find the place in the number where it is to be rounded. Next you rewrite as many numbers as you need and eliminate the rest. If the first number you drop is less than 5, you do nothing to its preceding number. When you round 6.824 to the tenth place, the number 2 is the first number dropped, and it is less than 5; therefore the answer is rounded to 6.8. If the first number you drop is 5 or more, raise the preceding number by 1. When you round 9.784 to the tenth place, the number 8 is the first number dropped, and it is more than 5; therefore the 7 is raised to 8, and the rounded number becomes 9.8.

RULES OF ZERO

1. When a number is multiplied by a zero, the answer is always zero ($617.3 \times 0 = 0$, or $0 \times 617.3 = 0$).
2. When a zero is divided by another number, the answer is always zero $\left(\dfrac{0}{8} = 0\right)$.

---

[4] The number you divide by is called the *divisor,* the number you divide is called the *dividend,* and the answer is called the *quotient.*

[5] In this book we will express our answers to the nearest tenth or hundredth place. Generally we will carry all operations through in terms of hundredths and round to the nearest tenth in the last step.

3. Division by zero is not a legal operation.
4. When a number is added to zero, the sum is the number itself $(8 + 0 = 8)$.
5. When a zero is subtracted from a number, the remainder is the number itself $(8 - 0 = 8)$.

SHORTCUTS WITH ZEROS

Here are a few math shortcuts to make your work easier.

Multiplying by Numbers That End in Zero

When you multiply numbers that end in zero, disregard the zeros and multiply the numbers $(30 \times 40 = 12\_\_)$. After completing the multiplication, add the number of zeros in the original numbers to the answer. In this case you would add two zeros to get 1200.

Multiplying by 10s, 100s, 1000s *move to the right*

When you multiply a number by 10, 100, or 1000, you simply move the decimal point in the multiplicand [6] to the right as many places as there are zeros, and each time you move it you add a zero. It is understood that, even though it is not visible, a decimal point is at the end of each of these numbers. For example, 386 multiplied by 10 becomes 3860, because you move the decimal one place to the right and add one zero. If you multiply 386 by 100, you get 38,600 by moving the decimal two places to the right and adding two zeros.

Multiplying by .1, .01, .001 *move to the left*

The rule above is reversed when you multiply by .1, .01, and .001. When you multiply by .1, .01, or .001, move the decimal point in the multiplicand to the left as many places as there are decimal places in the multiplier. For example, 4 multiplied by .1 becomes .4; you move one decimal place to the left. Likewise, 4 multiplied by .01 becomes .04, since you move two decimal places to the left.

[6] To refresh your memory in multiplication, a *multiplicand* is the number that you multiply, the *multiplier* is the number that you use to multiply, and the *product* is the answer. For example, in the problem $324 \times 2 = 648$, the multiplicand is 324, the multiplier is 2, and the product is 648.

PROPORTIONS

A *proportion* is the comparison of a part to its whole. For example, if you cut a chocolate cake into four equal pieces, each piece is a proportion of the total cake and can be written as the proportion $\frac{1}{4}$. The numerator is the part; the denominator is the whole. You can change this proportion to decimal form by dividing the numerator by the denominator—that is, the 1 by 4, which equals .25:

$$4\overline{)1.00}^{\,.25}$$

Convert the value into a percentage by multiplying it by 100—that is, by moving the decimal point two places to the right—as follows: $.25 \times 100 = 25\%$. If you wish to convert a percent to a decimal, simply reverse this procedure. For instance, to convert 5% to a decimal you divide 5 by 100, which is .05. In effect you move the decimal point two places to the left.

Problem

As another example let's consider a group of 50 students taking a statistics test. Three received A's, five received B's, 35 received C's, five received D's, and two received F's. Can you find the proportion of students receiving each grade? After finding these proportions, convert each to decimal form, then to a percentage. Let's begin by finding the proportion of students receiving A's. The part is three, and that is written as the numerator; the whole is 50, and that is written as the denominator. The proportion is $\frac{3}{50}$. To change $\frac{3}{50}$ to a decimal, you divide 3 by 50; the decimal is .06. Next, convert .06 to a percentage by multiplying it by 100. That is, move two places to the right, as follows: $.06 \times 100 = 6\%$. Work out the remainder of the problem yourself; then consult the answers that follow.

Answers

Grades	Proportions	Decimals	Percentages
A	$\frac{3}{50}$	.06	6%
B	$\frac{5}{50}$	.1	10%
C	$\frac{35}{50}$	.7	70%
D	$\frac{5}{50}$	.1	10%
F	$\frac{2}{50}$	.04	4%

EXPONENTS

Factors that are equal can be written in exponential form. Two equal factors such as 6×6 are written in exponential form as 6^2; three equal factors such as $8 \times 8 \times 8$ are written as 8^3. The small number written in the right-hand corner is called an *exponent*. It tells you how many times to repeat the factor. The factor is called the *base*. For example, in the expression 4^2 the exponent is the ^{2}; it tells you to multiply the base 4 two times. In other words, 4^2 is the same as 4×4, which equals 16. Whenever we multiply a number by itself we *square* it. As another example, if you have a base of 5 and an exponent of 3—that is, 5^3—you multiply the 5 three times (called cubing) to get $5 \times 5 \times 5$, which equals 125.

SQUARE ROOTS

The *square root* of a given number is a number that, when multiplied by itself, yields the given number. The square root of 25 is 5, since 5 multiplied by itself (5×5) produces the original 25. Checking square roots is easy: you simply multiply your square root by itself to see if you end up with the original number. Table A in the Appendix contains the square roots of the whole numbers from 1 to 1000. In order to find the square root of a number, say 35, simply look down the N column until you find 35, then run your fingers across the table until you are under the $\sqrt{N}$ column, where you will find the answer, 5.9161.

To find the square root of decimals or numbers over 1000, use the N^2 column of 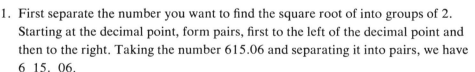 Table A to approximate the answer. Follow these steps:

1. First separate the number you want to find the square root of into groups of 2. Starting at the decimal point, form pairs, first to the left of the decimal point and then to the right. Taking the number 615.06 and separating it into pairs, we have 6 15. 06.
2. If there is an *incomplete pair* preceding the decimal point, like the 6 in 6̲ 15. 06, you will be looking up a *five-digit number* in the N^2 column of Table A. However, if the pair of numbers to the left of the decimal point is *complete* (16̲ 15. 06), you will be looking up a *six-digit number* in the N^2 column. Since the pair of numbers in our example 6 15. 06 is incomplete, you will be looking up a *five-digit number* in the N^2 column.[7]
3. If you can't find the number in the N^2 column, choose the number that comes

[7] The reason we use five- and six-digit sections of Table A instead of other sections is that we want as much accuracy as possible.

closest. In this case the closest number to 615.06 is 615.04. Starting at 615.04, run your fingers across the page until you are under the *N* column. You now have the number 248. This number will be your square root, once you find where to place the decimal point.

4. In order to find where the decimal point belongs, place 248 over the original number, 615.06. Place only one number over each pair or incomplete pair, putting the new decimal point directly above the decimal point in the original number:

2   4.   8
6 15. 06

The approximate square root of 615.06 is 24.8.

5. A pair of zeros in the original number will yield one 0 in the square root. In the number .0025 there are two 0's. The square root of .0025 is .05.

Below are three examples of numbers that have been paired and their square roots found:

Number	Pairing	Square root
84679	8 46 79	291
846.79	8 46. 79	29.1
84.679	84. 67 90	9.20

NEGATIVE AND POSITIVE NUMBERS

What are positive and negative numbers? Let's look at a number line. Zero is the starting point on this measuring scale, which goes in both directions.

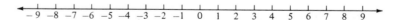

$-9 \quad -8 \quad -7 \quad -6 \quad -5 \quad -4 \quad -3 \quad -2 \quad -1 \quad 0 \quad 1 \quad 2 \quad 3 \quad 4 \quad 5 \quad 6 \quad 7 \quad 8 \quad 9$

The numbers to the left of zero are negative and have a negative sign. Those to the right of zero are positive and have a positive sign (which usually is omitted). The sign of a number indicates the direction, whether the number falls to the right or left of 0 on a number line. The size of the number indicates its distance from 0. For example, the number +6 tells you that this number is 6 units to the right of 0.

Below are the rules for computation with sign numbers. Don't worry if you find it difficult to remember these rules; they will always be in this book for you to refer to.

Addition of Sign Numbers

1. When you add numbers with the *same* sign, such as $(5 + 4)$ or $(-2) + (-3)$, add the numbers and put their sign on the sum. That is, $5 + 4 = 9$ and $(-2) + (-3) = -5$.

2. When you add numbers with different signs, such as $(-6) + 2$ or $5 + (-4)$, subtract the smaller number from the larger and put the sign of the larger number on the difference.[8] For instance, $(-6) + 2 = -4$, because the sign of the larger number is negative, while $5 + (-4) = 1$, because the sign of the larger number is positive.

3. When you add a series of numbers with positive and negative signs, such as $-4 + -6 + -7 + 6 + 4 + 2$, add all the positive numbers, $6 + 4 + 2 = 12$, then add all the negative numbers, $-4 + -6 + -7 = -17$, and combine the results following rule 2 $(-17 + 12 = -5)$. Remember, the sign of the larger number is negative; that is why the answer is negative.

Subtraction of Sign Numbers

4. When you subtract sign numbers, such as $15 - (-8)$, change the sign of the second number (subtrahend), and change the sign of the operation to addition: $15 - (-8) = 15 + (+8)$. Following rule 1 for addition, add 15 to 8 to get 23. To solve the problem $15 - (8)$, change the sign of the 8 to a negative 8 and change the sign of the operation: $15 - (8) = 15 + (-8)$. Following rule 2 for addition, subtract the smaller number (8) from the larger (15) and put the sign of the larger number on the difference $(+7)$.

Multiplication of Sign Numbers

5. The multiplication of numbers with the *same* sign, such as 6×2 or $(-4) \times (-5)$, gives a product with a *positive* sign: $6 \times 2 = 12$ and $(-4) \times (-5) = 20$.

6. The multiplication of numbers with *unlike* signs, such as $(-6) \times (2)$, gives a product with a *negative* sign: $(-6) \times (2) = -12$.

Division of Sign Numbers

7. Division follows the same rule as multiplication. When you divide numbers with

[8] The answer in subtraction is called the *difference*.

the same sign, such as $\frac{8}{4}$ or $\frac{-6}{-3}$, the division will give a positive answer (quotient):

$\frac{8}{4} = 2$ and $\frac{-6}{-3} = 2$.

8. When you divide numbers with unlike signs, such as $\frac{-6}{2}$, the quotient will have

   a negative sign: $\frac{-6}{2} = -3$, and likewise $\frac{6}{-2} = -3$.

ORDER OF ARITHMETIC OPERATIONS

For the problem $3 \times 4 + 12 \div 2$, what is the correct answer: 12, 24, 18, or 30?

1. Do you multiply 3×4, then add 12, and finally divide by 2 to get 12?
2. Do you add $4 + 12$, multiply by 3, then divide by 2 to get an answer of 24?
3. Do you multiply 3×4 and get 12, divide 12 by 2 and get 6, then add these two results together, $12 + 6$, to get the final answer of 18?
4. Do you divide 12 by 2, add the answer to 4, then multiply by 3 to get an answer of 30?

To avoid confusion in problems involving several operations, mathematicians have agreed upon certain rules of order.

1. Any operations inside parentheses, brackets, or braces take priority over all other operations.
2. Operations involving exponents (squares and square roots) come next.
3. After performing these operations, do all multiplications and divisions, then additions and subtractions.

The initials of the phrase, "My Dear Aunt Sally," which suggest multiply and divide before you add or subtract, may help you remember the proper order of the last four operations.

Let's solve the sample problem $\sqrt{25} + 5 + 8 \times 2 - 16 \div 4 + (6 - 3)$.

1. Working with the numbers inside the parentheses first, we get $6 - 3 = 3$; this gives us $\sqrt{25} + 5 + 8 \times 2 - 16 \div 4 + 3$.
2. Next we find the square root of $\sqrt{25}$, which is 5. (Note there is no number that has to be squared.) We now have $5 + 5 + 8 \times 2 - 16 \div 4 + 3$.
3. a. Multiplication and division come next: $8 \times 2 = 16$; $16 \div 4 = 4$. This leaves us with $5 + 5 + 16 - 4 + 3$.

b. Add the remaining numbers: $5 + 5 + 16 + 3 = 29$. Now subtract $29 - 4$; the answer is 25.

Returning to our original problem, $3 \times 4 + 12 \div 2$, we find that the answer is 18, because you:

1. First do the multiplications and divisions of the numbers as indicated: $3 \times 4 = 12$; $12 \div 2 = 6$. You have $\underline{12} + \underline{6}$.
2. Next do the additions and subtractions indicated: add $12 + 6$; the answer is 18.

USING STATISTICAL SYMBOLS

Mathematical symbols are a short way of saying things. Learning mathematical symbols is like learning a new language. The chart below will help you review some symbols. Other symbols will be presented as we proceed.

Symbol	Meaning
Σ (sigma)	The sum of (add all the values)
X	Raw score
$\sqrt{N}$	Square root of a number (the square root of N)
$=$	Is equal to
$\neq$	Is not equal to
$>$	Is greater than
$<$	Is less than
$\geq$	Is equal to or greater than
$\leq$	Is equal to or less than
N	The total number of scores or individuals in a group
s	The standard deviation of a sample: the square root of variance[9]
$\overline{X}$	The mean or arithmetic average of a sample

Now let us perform a few operations on 3, 4, 5, and 2, using what you have just learned.

1. Find ΣX. This means find the sum of the raw scores. In this case we add $3 + 4 + 5 + 2$, and the $\Sigma X = 14$.
2. Find ΣX^2. This means find the sum of the squares of the individual scores. To do this:
   a. Square each score (multiply the score by itself):

   $$(3)^2 + (4)^2 + (5)^2 + (2)^2 = 9 + 16 + 25 + 4$$

[9] This definition will be explained in Chapter 4.

b. Add the squared scores to obtain a sum:

$$9 + 16 + 25 + 4 = 54$$

c. $\Sigma X^2 = 54$.

3. Find $(\Sigma X)^2$. This tells you to find the sum of all the individual scores, then square the sum. Note that this is quite different from ΣX^2.
   a. Performing the operation inside the parentheses, first sum all the X's (scores):

   $$(3 + 4 + 5 + 2) = 14$$

   b. Next square the sum: $14^2 = (14 \times 14) = 196$. Therefore, $(\Sigma X)^2 = 196$.

After using these symbols to perform operations, you will find it relatively easy to learn to read a statistical formula.

HOW TO READ AND COMPUTE A STATISTICAL FORMULA

In this section you are going to learn how to read and compute a statistical formula. For now, you are not interested in the meaning of this formula. Usually in a statistical formula the problem is stated to the left of the equal sign while the directions are stated to the right. In the formula for the mean, $\overline{X} = \dfrac{\Sigma X}{N}$, the problem is to find the $\overline{X}$. The directions are $\dfrac{\Sigma X}{N}$. In order to follow these directions you should:

1. Know what each symbol in the equation means.
2. Perform the operations on these numbers according to the arithmetic rules of order.

Translating the problem into an answer is now a simple task. As an example, let's take the raw-score formula for the standard deviation:

$$s = \frac{1}{N} \sqrt{N \Sigma X^2 - (\Sigma X)^2}$$

In this example certain liberties have been taken. The scores are very small, so that long computations can be avoided. The raw scores (X's) for this problem are: 3, 4, 5, 2, and 10.

1. Let's substitute the appropriate numbers for the symbols in the formula. The N represents the total number of scores in the group. There are five, so we put a 5 wherever there is an N in the formula:

$$s = \frac{1}{5} \sqrt{5 \Sigma X^2 - (\Sigma X)^2}$$

The ΣX means the sum of all the individual scores. We add the individual scores, $3 + 4 + 5 + 2 + 10$, obtaining the sum of 24. Wherever there is a ΣX we now are able to put a 24:

$$s = \frac{1}{N} \sqrt{N \Sigma X^2 - (24)^2}$$

Finally we find ΣX^2, the sum of the individual scores squared. We square the individual scores, $(3)^2 + (4)^2 + (5)^2 + (2)^2 + (10)^2$, and obtain $9 + 16 + 25 + 4 + 100$. Adding these squared numbers, we obtain 154. Wherever there is a ΣX^2 we substitute 154:

$$s = \frac{1}{N} \sqrt{(N)154 - (\Sigma X)^2}$$

In substituting these numbers, be sure to put the parentheses, exponents, and radicals where they belong. If we have done this correctly,

$$s = \frac{1}{N} \sqrt{N \Sigma X^2 - (\Sigma X)^2} \quad \text{now becomes} \quad s = \frac{1}{5} \sqrt{(5)154 - (24)^2}$$

2. Next, we do the mathematical calculations necessary to find the standard deviation. Using your knowledge of the arithmetic rules of order, go directly to the numbers inside the square root. Square the number in the parentheses; 24 squared is 576. Then multiply 154 by 5 to get 770. Our problem now looks like this:

$$s = \frac{1}{5} \sqrt{770 - 576}$$

3. Subtract $770 - 576$, which gives us 194. Our problem now looks like this:

$$s = \frac{1}{5} \sqrt{194}$$

4. Find the square root of 194. Looking up 194 in the table under $\sqrt{N}$, we get 13.9284, which we round to 13.93.

5. The last step consists of dividing 13.93 by 5 and rounding the answer: $13.93 \div 5 = 2.79$ or, when rounded to the tenth place, 2.8. The standard deviation for this set of numbers is 2.8.

The above steps are summarized below.

$$s = \frac{1}{N} \sqrt{N \Sigma X^2 - (\Sigma X)^2}$$

(1) $s = \frac{1}{5} \sqrt{(5)154 - (24)^2}$

(2) $s = \frac{1}{5} \sqrt{770 - 576}$

(3) $s = \frac{1}{5} \sqrt{194}$

(4) $s = \frac{1}{5} (13.93)$

(5) $s = 2.8$

To check yourself and find out how well you know this material, take the following mastery test. The answers are supplied at the end of the chapter.

If you do not do sufficiently well to continue to Chapter 2, study the sections that troubled you. After you feel comfortable with the material, retake the original assessment test.

SELF-TEST FOR MASTERY

If you have trouble working a problem, reread the explanation on the page listed.

p. 2

1. Solve the following problems:

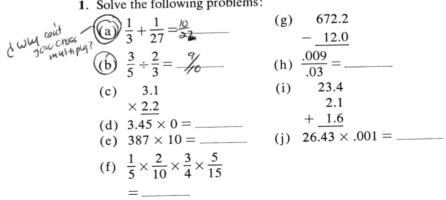

d why can't you cross multiply?

(a) $\frac{1}{3} + \frac{1}{27} = \frac{10}{27}$

(b) $\frac{3}{5} \div \frac{2}{3} = \frac{9}{10}$

(c)   3.1
       $\times$ 2.2

(d) $3.45 \times 0 = $ _____

(e) $387 \times 10 = $ _____

(f) $\frac{1}{5} \times \frac{2}{10} \times \frac{3}{4} \times \frac{5}{15}$

= _____

(g)   672.2
       $- \underline{12.0}$

(h) $\frac{.009}{.03} = $ _____

(i)   23.4
         2.1
       $+ \underline{1.6}$

(j) $26.43 \times .001 = $ _____

p. 6

2. Round the following numbers to the tenth place:

(a) 2.561 _____

(b) 2.3210 _____

(c) 1.20 _____   (e) .0954 _____

(d) 98.643 _____   (f) 9.85 _____

p. 6

3. Solve these problems:

(a) $8943.1 \times 0 =$ _____   (e) $324 \times .01 =$ _____

(b) $\dfrac{0}{6} =$ _____   (f) $394 \times 100 =$ _____

(g) $8^2 =$ _____

(c) $6 - 0 =$ _____   (h) $3^4 =$ _____

(d) $60 \times 40 =$ _____

p. 8

4. Refer to problem 6 on the Self-Test for Assessing Math Ability. Find the proportions of students receiving B's and C's on the math test.

     Remember that 75 students took this math test; 10 received B's and 40 received C's. After you have found these proportions, change to decimal form, then convert them to a percent. Round to the nearest hundredth.

(a) B's _____   (b) C's _____

p. 9

5. Using Table A in the Appendix find the square root of:

(a) 11,233 _____   (c) 23.445 _____

(b) 5.567 _____   (d) 38 _____

p. 10

6. Complete the following operations:

(a) $(-2) + (-9) =$ _____

(b) $\dfrac{-15}{5} =$ _____

(c) $-8 + -9 + -7 + 10 + 15 + 8 =$ _____

(d) $\dfrac{-25}{-5} =$ _____

p. 12

7. Solve these problems:

(a) $4^2 + 12 \div 2^2 - 5\sqrt{100} =$ _____

(b) $4^3 + 20 \div 10 - 5 =$ _____

(c) $5 \times 5 + 6 \div 2 =$ _____

p. 13

8. What do the following math symbols mean?

(a) $6 > 3$ (c) Σ *Sum of*

(b) $2 < 4$ _____   (d) X *raw score*

p. 14

9. Find the standard deviation for the following raw scores:

2, 2, 5, 6, 10, 10, 1, 1, 2, 2 _____   *memorize formula*

ANSWERS TO SELF-TEST

1. (a) $\dfrac{10}{27}$ (d) 0   (h) .3

(b) $\dfrac{9}{10}$ (e) 3870   (i) 27.1

(f) $\dfrac{1}{100}$ (j) .02643

(c) 6.82   (g) 660.2

2. (a) 2.6
   (b) 2.3
   (c) 1.2

   (d) 98.6
   (e) .1
   (f) 9.9

3. (a) 0
   (b) 0
   (c) 6
   (d) 2400

   (e) 3.24
   (f) 39400
   (g) 64
   (h) 81

4. (a) $\dfrac{10}{75} = .133$ or 13%

   (b) $\dfrac{40}{75} = .5333$ or 53%

5. (a) 106
   (b) 2.36

   (c) 4.84
   (d) 6.1644

6. (a) -11
   (b) -3

   (c) 9
   (d) 5

7. (a) *Solution:* Square root, then square, multiply and divide, add and subtract.

$$4^2 + 12 \div 2^2 - 5\sqrt{100} = 16 + 12 \div 4 - 5 \cdot 10$$
$$= 16 + 3 - 50$$
$$= -31$$

   (b) *Solution:* Cube first, divide, add and subtract.

$$4^3 + 20 \div 10 - 5 = 64 + 20 \div 10 - 5$$
$$= 64 + 2 \ - 5$$
$$= 61$$

   (c) *Solution:* Multiply and divide, add.

$$5 \times 5 + 6 \div 2 = 25 + 3$$
$$= 28$$

8. (a) 6 is greater than 3.
   (b) 2 is less than 4.

   (c) Sum of.
   (d) Raw score.

9. $s = 3.33$. *Solution:*

$$s = \frac{1}{10} \sqrt{(10)279 - (41)^2}$$
$$= \frac{1}{10} \sqrt{2790 - 1681}$$
$$= \frac{1}{10} \sqrt{1109}$$
$$= \frac{1}{10} 33.30$$
$$= 3.33$$

THINGS YOU SHOULD KNOW

2

Chapter 2 gives you a reprieve, so that the math you reviewed in Chapter 1 has time to become part of you. Chapter 2 also will be your appetizer for the entrée to come, giving you something to digest without overwhelming you. The philosophy here is that it's better to know five topics well than be confused by ten topics. Your assignment is:

1. To understand the difference between *descriptive* and *inferential* statistics.
2. To know what you are talking about when you bring up the terms *population* and *sample*.
3. To become acquainted with *sampling techniques,* so that you know how to use them to choose a sample.
4. To obtain a mental grasp of the term *variable*.
5. To understand the four different *levels of measurement*.

If these topics sound hard, don't worry. Take your time and read the material carefully. If you have trouble, reread it a day later. If you still have problems, be sure to consult your teacher. Remember, none of us are geniuses.

DESCRIPTIVE AND INFERENTIAL STATISTICS

In the past the statistics field has been divided into two conceptual branches—descriptive and inferential. After you have finished reading this book, you will see a great deal of overlap between these branches. However, for the present it is advantageous to make a distinction between them, because they are used for different purposes.

Descriptive Statistics

Statistical methods concerned with describing or giving a clearer picture of the data are called *descriptive statistics*. Statistical techniques such as the mean, median, standard deviation, range, Spearman rank correlation, and Pearson product-moment correlation are used for organizing and summarizing information about observations. As a fifth-grade teacher looking at your class's scores on a math test, for example, you need some way to make sense out of this mass of numbers. You arrange the scores from highest to lowest and then use some of the techniques listed above. First, you might find out what the average score in the group is by using a measure such as the mean. Next, you might want to find out whether the students are from different mathematical backgrounds, so that you can allow for individual differences when teaching. You can find out about the variability of the scores by using a measure of variability such as the standard deviation. Finally, you might want to find out whether the fifth-grade students who do well in math also do well in reading. You take reading and math scores of each student in the group and use measures such as the Pearson product-moment correlation to see if there is a relationship between math and reading.

Inferential Statistics

Statistical methods concerned with inferring beyond the data are called *inferential statistics*. These methods attempt to draw conclusions about a population of things on the basis of observations of only a portion of the population. The researcher uses a small group to obtain data, then draws inferences about the larger group, attempting to make reasonable decisions with incomplete information. As a teacher of the same fifth-grade class you are not at this time interested in just your class, but all fifth-grade classes in your county, state, or country. When you draw conclusions from studying your own class, you generalize these conclusions to all fifth-grade classes in your county, state, or country.

Statistical inference is primarily concerned with two types of problems:

1. An estimation of what the population is like. For example, in a sampling poll you may take a percentage of the voters in a gubernatorial election in order to predict the winner.
2. Testing hypotheses about a population. For example, you might want to determine whether Amtex, a gasoline substitute, is superior to gasoline in improving mileage in cars.

Some of the statistical techniques used to treat these types of problems are the *t*-test, the chi-square test, the Kolmogorov-Smirnov test, and the Friedman test.

We have been talking about arriving at inferences about a population from a sample. Let us look more closely now at what is meant by *population* and *sample*.

SYMBOLS FOR POPULATION AND SAMPLES

Statisticians have thought the distinction between population and sample so important that they have given each term its own set of mathematical symbols. The numbers obtained from samples are called *statistics* and the mathematical symbols used are generally Roman. The measures obtained from populations are called *parameters* and the mathematical symbols used are generally Greek. A few of these symbols are listed below for easy reference.

Terms	(Sample) statistic	(Population) parameter
Mean	$\overline{X}$	μ
Standard deviation	s	σ
Pearson product-moment	r	ρ
Number of scores	N	n

POPULATION

A *population* is a well-defined group of animals, people, plants, or objects that have something in common.

You may define a population, for example, as the freshman psychology students at California State University, Northridge, in 1990 or the maple trees on Benefit Street in Sherman Oaks, California, in 1990. By these definitions you are limiting the group to include certain items and exclude others. You are not interested in the freshman English students at Stanford, nor in the palm trees on Beta Street in Florida.

For all our studies it would be nice to use the entire population and forget about ever taking a sample. We would not need a discussion on samples, and life would be less complicated. Unfortunately, it is often difficult if not impossible to deal with an entire population for reasons of time, expense, and inconvenience. In some instances it is literally impossible to examine every member of a population, such as the grains of sand on the beaches in California during the month of January or the number of words printed during the month of December. Because of these problems, it becomes necessary to use a smaller group called a sample.

SAMPLING

A *sample* is a subgroup selected from the entire population. It can be small or large. Many samples are taken every day, such as those used in the Neilsen ratings and the Harris polls. These are supposed to indicate the taste of the entire population of people who watch television or vote during an election.

Since a great deal of research is done with samples, it is of utmost importance that each sample be truly a slice out of the pie called population. If a sample does not have the same ingredients on a smaller scale as the original population, the sample is *biased* and the study is no longer valid.

A prime example of a biased sample occurred in 1936. On the basis of polls it conducted, a popular national magazine, *The Literary Digest,* predicted that Alfred Landon, the Republican candidate, would defeat Franklin Roosevelt, the Democratic candidate, in the presidential election that year. However, Roosevelt won a landslide victory, capturing the electoral vote of 46 of the 48 states. The reputation of *The Literary Digest* as a pollster suffered considerable damage. The mistake the magazine made was to choose its sample from telephone subscribers and car owners. These people were not representative of the entire voting population, since they were richer and most of them, as it turned out, were Republicans.

As you can see from this example, you must insure that the sample of the population drawn for the study has the same characteristics as the entire population. In other words, that slice of pie cannot differ from the whole pie.

We shall examine three different methods for trying to choose a random sample:[1] simple random sampling, cluster sampling, and stratified sampling.

Simple Random Sampling

In *simple random sampling* every element of the population is listed. Next a random selection is made of a number of the elements in the population, and the result of this selection is the sample. As an illustration, a psychiatrist may want a sample of 103 mentally disturbed patients at Alpha Mental Hospital. He first lists all 1000 patients in the population, and from this list he randomly selects 103 for his sample.

In the process of drawing a random sample there are two concerns:

1. Every individual has an equal chance of being selected.
2. The selection of one person in the sample is independent of the selection of another. The selection of a wife must not depend upon the selection of her husband. If men and women are to be used in a sample, they must be listed as individuals.

How do you draw a random sample? There are numerous ways of insuring randomness, such as a table of random numbers, a lottery, or a fair roulette wheel.

One of the most useful devices for this purpose is the table of random numbers.

[1] A sample is defined as random when each member of the population had the same opportunity to be selected.

Table 2-1: Random Numbers

	1	2	3	4	5
1	53 74 23 99 67 63 38 06 86 54 35 30 58 21 46 63 43 36 82 69 98 25 37 55 26	61 32 28 69 84 99 00 65 26 94 06 72 17 10 94 65 51 18 37 88 01 91 82 81 46	94 62 67 86 24 02 82 90 23 07 25 21 31 75 96 61 38 44 12 45 74 71 12 94 97	98 33 41 19 95 79 62 67 80 60 49 28 24 00 49 32 92 85 88 65 24 02 71 37 07	47 53 53 38 09 75 91 12 81 19 55 65 79 78 07 54 34 81 85 35 03 92 18 66 75
2	02 63 21 17 69 64 55 22 21 82 85 07 26 13 89 58 54 16 24 15 34 85 27 84 87	71 50 80 89 56 48 22 28 06 00 01 10 07 82 04 51 54 44 82 00 61 48 64 56 26	38 15 70 11 48 61 54 13 43 91 59 63 69 36 03 62 61 65 04 69 90 18 48 13 26	43 40 45 86 98 82 78 12 23 29 69 11 15 83 80 38 18 65 18 97 37 70 15 42 57	00 83 26 91 03 06 66 24 12 27 13 29 54 19 28 85 72 13 49 21 65 65 80 39 07
3	03 92 18 27 46 62 95 30 27 59 08 45 93 15 22 07 08 55 18 40 01 85 89 95 66	57 99 16 96 56 37 75 41 66 48 60 21 75 46 91 45 44 75 13 90 51 10 19 34 88	30 33 72 85 22 86 97 80 61 45 98 77 27 85 42 24 94 96 61 02 15 84 97 19 75	84 64 38 56 98 23 53 04 01 63 28 88 61 08 84 57 55 66 83 15 12 76 39 43 78	99 01 30 98 64 45 76 08 64 27 69 62 03 42 73 73 42 37 11 61 64 63 91 08 25
4	72 84 71 14 35 88 78 28 16 84 45 17 75 65 57 96 76 28 12 54 43 31 67 72 30	19 11 58 49 26 13 52 53 94 53 28 40 19 72 12 22 01 11 94 25 24 02 94 08 63	50 11 17 17 76 75 45 69 30 96 25 12 74 75 67 71 96 16 16 88 38 32 36 66 02	86 31 57 20 18 73 89 65 70 31 60 40 60 81 19 68 64 36 74 45 69 36 38 25 39	95 60 78 46 75 99 17 43 48 76 24 62 01 61 16 19 59 50 88 92 48 03 45 15 22
5	50 44 66 44 21 22 66 22 15 86 96 24 40 14 51 31 73 91 61 19 78 60 73 99 84	66 06 58 05 62 26 63 75 41 99 23 22 30 88 57 60 20 72 93 48 43 89 94 36 45	68 15 54 35 02 58 42 36 72 24 95 67 47 29 83 98 57 07 23 69 56 69 47 07 41	42 35 48 96 32 58 37 52 18 51 94 69 40 06 07 65 95 39 69 58 90 22 91 07 12	14 52 41 52 48 03 37 18 39 11 18 16 36 78 86 56 80 30 19 44 78 35 34 08 72
6	84 37 90 61 56 36 67 10 08 23 07 28 59 07 48 10 15 83 87 60 55 19 68 97 65	70 10 23 98 05 98 93 35 08 86 89 64 58 89 75 79 24 31 66 56 03 73 52 16 56	85 11 34 76 60 99 29 76 29 81 83 85 62 27 89 21 48 24 06 93 00 53 55 90 27	76 48 45 34 60 33 34 91 58 93 30 14 78 56 27 91 98 94 05 49 33 42 29 38 87	01 64 18 39 96 63 14 52 32 52 86 63 59 80 02 01 47 59 38 00 22 13 88 83 34
7	53 81 29 13 39 51 86 32 68 92 35 91 70 29 13 37 71 67 95 13 93 66 13 83 27	35 01 20 71 34 33 98 74 66 99 80 03 54 07 27 20 02 44 95 94 92 79 64 64 72	62 33 74 82 14 40 14 71 94 58 96 94 78 32 66 64 85 04 05 72 28 54 96 53 84	53 73 19 09 03 45 94 19 38 81 50 95 52 74 33 01 32 90 76 14 48 14 52 98 94	56 54 29 56 93 14 44 99 81 07 13 80 55 62 54 53 89 74 60 41 56 07 93 89 30
8	02 96 08 45 65 49 83 43 48 35 84 60 71 62 46 18 17 30 88 71 79 69 10 61 78	13 05 00 41 84 82 88 33 69 96 40 80 81 30 37 44 91 14 88 47 71 32 76 95 62	93 07 54 72 59 72 36 04 19 76 34 39 23 05 38 89 23 30 63 15 87 00 22 58 40	21 45 57 09 77 47 45 15 18 60 25 15 35 71 30 56 34 20 47 89 92 54 01 75 25	19 48 56 27 44 82 11 08 95 97 88 12 57 21 77 99 82 93 24 98 43 11 71 99 31
9	75 93 36 57 83 38 30 92 29 03 51 29 50 10 34 21 31 38 86 24 29 01 23 87 88	56 20 14 82 11 06 28 81 39 38 31 57 75 95 80 37 79 81 53 74 58 02 39 37 67	74 21 97 90 65 62 25 06 84 63 51 97 02 74 77 73 24 16 10 33 42 10 14 20 92	96 42 68 63 86 61 29 08 93 67 76 15 48 49 44 52 83 90 94 76 16 55 23 42 45	74 54 13 26 94 04 32 92 08 00 18 55 63 77 09 70 47 14 54 36 54 96 09 11 06
10	95 33 95 22 00 90 84 60 79 80 46 40 62 98 82 20 31 89 03 43 71 59 73 05 50	18 74 72 00 18 24 36 59 87 38 54 97 20 56 95 38 46 82 68 72 08 22 23 71 77	38 79 58 69 32 82 07 53 89 35 15 74 80 08 32 32 14 82 99 70 91 01 93 20 49	81 76 80 26 92 96 35 23 79 18 16 46 70 50 80 80 60 47 18 97 82 96 59 26 94	82 80 84 25 39 05 98 90 07 35 67 72 16 42 79 63 49 30 21 30 66 39 67 98 60

SOURCE: Tables are taken from Tables XXXIII of Fisher and Yates: *Statistical Tables for Biological, Agricultural and Medical Research,* published by Longman Group Ltd., London (previously published by Oliver and Boyd, Edinburgh), and by permission of the authors and publishers.

It is constructed so that each number has an equal chance of appearing independently of any other number. Step by step let's learn how to use a random number table.

Assume you have a population of 50 students and you want 25 in your sample. Note, generally speaking, that if you are dealing with a small population, say 100, you should use 50% of your population size for a sample. As the population increases, smaller proportions are adequate. For example, if you had a population of 10,000, 10% would be sufficient for a sample.

Assign each subject in your population a number by a systematic method. For example, you might list the names in alphabetical order, then assign the first person in the list the number 1, the second person the number 2, and so on until 50 individuals are assigned numbers from 1 to 50.

Now look at Table 2-1, a table of random numbers, which we have numbered like a grid. Before you enter the table, you need to have a predetermined method of entry. For instance, you might decide to use your social security number, 486-45-3682. You select the first two digits, 4 and 8. Enter the table of random numbers by first finding the 4 across the top of the page, then counting down 8 squares to the starting square (the intersection of across 4 and down 8).

Starting Square

㉑	45	57	09	77
47	45	15	18	60
25	15	35	71	30
56	34	20	47	89
92	54	01	75	25

Starting with the upper left-hand number in the square (21), work downward in this column until you reach the last number (82). The numbers you will encounter as you descend in this column are 21, 47, 25, 56, 92, 96, 61, 76, 52, 16, 81, 96, 16, 80, and 82. Numbers such as 56, 92, 96 will not apply to your sample because you assigned only from 1 to 50. The numbers that will apply are 21, 47, 25, 16, and 16. Whenever you encounter a number that *repeats* an earlier one (16) or a number for which you have *no person* (96, 76, and so on), you completely disregard it and continue counting downward.[2] So far you have only four numbers for your sample; therefore, you must continue to use the table. Return to the starting number (21) and go upward in the same column (48, 01, 50, 45, 53, . . .), adding

----

[2] This technique is referred to as sampling without replacement. It allows any member of the population to appear only one time in the sample.

to your sample the numbers that are applicable: 48, 01, 50, 45, 33, 30, 42, 12, 28, 23, 37, 38, 43, 24, 32, 49. You now have 20 numbers; you need 25, so you must continue. Return again to the starting number (21) and go to the number on its immediate right, 45. The number 45 becomes your new starting number. Do with 45 the same thing you did with 21 until you have 25 numbers between 1 and 50. The students who have these numbers are members of the sample you will use in your study.[3]

When a table of random numbers is not handy, many people use the lottery technique. Again, the population is arranged in a sequential order. A number is assigned to each person, and pieces of paper bearing these numbers are placed in a revolving drum. The numbers in the drum are tossed and mixed well. Then, without looking, the researcher selects a number from the drum. He records this number. He continues drawing until a sample of 25, the desired number of people for the sample, is selected.

Another device for selecting a random sample is the roulette wheel. Every person in the sample is given a number from the wheel in some orderly sequence. A spin of the wheel determines the person to be selected for the sample. The researcher continues this process until the sample has been chosen. If the same number is spun more than once, the repetitions are disregarded. Since the roulette wheel contains only 38 numbers, it can be used only for small samples.

Although simple random sampling is important in inferential statistics, many studies are not based upon simple random samples. The reason is that in order to draw a simple random sample you must first list every element in the population. For many large populations it is not feasible or practical to do this. Other large populations are in a state of change with people moving, dying, and being born, so that publications such as telephone directories and mailing lists, which might be considered as population lists, are not accurate. If for any reason you cannot obtain a list of the elements of the population ahead of time, do not use simple random sampling; instead, use some other sampling technique, such as cluster sampling.

Cluster Sampling

Cluster sampling, a variation of simple random sampling, does not require that every element in the population be listed ahead of time. Cluster sampling is multistep simple random sampling. That is, the population is divided into clusters and a simple random sample of these clusters is drawn. Then these

[3] A table of random numbers is found in the appendix, Table B.

sample clusters are themselves divided into subclusters and a simple random sample is taken of the subclusters. This procedure continues to smaller and smaller units until the researcher wishes to stop.

Suppose, for example, you want to find out whom the people prefer for president in 1980, and you decide to use cluster sampling. Step one finds you looking at a map of fifty states or clusters. Using a random sampling technique, such as a table of random numbers, you choose certain states for your sample. In step two you divide these chosen states into congressional districts and draw a random sample of congressional districts. In step three you divide these chosen congressional districts into voting precincts and draw a random sample of the voting precincts. In step four you obtain a list of all the voters in these sample precincts and ask them your questions. Notice it is only now that you need a list of the names of the voters. Remember, in simple random sampling you need a complete list of people from the beginning.

Stratified Sampling

A *stratified sample* is another variation of a simple random sample. There are two major reasons for the use of stratified sampling: (1) you want to make comparisons among different subgroups of the population; (2) you want to reduce your sampling error—that is, ensure that the sample is more representative of the total population. The stratified sample has two requirements: (1) a list of the elements of the population, and (2) additional information on the relevant variable(s) in the population.[4]

The stratified sampling technique is used when it is important to ensure that the different characteristics in the population, such as sex, age, ethnic background, and party affiliation, are taken into consideration. Simple random sampling may or may not accomplish this. If these variables are not accounted for, the sample you choose will probably not be representative (it will be a biased sample), and this will affect the outcome of your study. When you stratify a sample, you divide the population into homogeneous groups or strata based on relevant variables such as ethnic background, sex, and so on. Each group or stratum has distinguishing characteristics that set it apart from the other group. An illustration of a stratified sample follows.

Dick Anderson, a sociologist, is interested in the voting preferences of the students at X University. He wants to know whom they will vote for in the coming

---

[4] An explanation of the term *variable* will be given shortly; for now, think of a variable as a characteristic.

election for student body president. He feels that certain characteristics or factors will affect the voting for the only female honor roll candidate, Gail Sands. These characteristics are grade-point average and sex. Because of their possible influence, he feels that the proportion of these factors in the overall population must be represented in the sample. In order to do this he divides the total population of 1000 into four subgroups based on grade-point average and sex.

   I: Male students with a G.P.A. of 3.0 or above
  II: Female students with a G.P.A. of 3.0 or above
III: Male students with a G.P.A. of under 3.0
IV: Female students with a G.P.A. of under 3.0

He figures the percentage of each subgroup that is in the population. He then chooses a number for his sample. Using the number chosen, he draws from each subgroup so that the size of each subgroup in the sample is proportionate to its size in the total population. In the end he has a sample that has all the important characteristics of the population.[5]

    Figure 2-1 shows the steps involved in doing a proportionally stratified sample.

1. The total population represented by the different subgroups is shown. There are 1000 individuals in the population.
2. a. Group I has <u>150</u> individuals or 15% of the total population; that is, 150/1000 = .15 or 15%.
   b. Group II has <u>250</u> individuals or 25% of the total population; that is, 250/1000 = .25 or 25%.
   c. Group III has <u>350</u> individuals or 35% of the total population; that is, 350/1000 = .35 or 35%.
   d. Group IV has <u>250</u> individuals or 25% of the total population; that is, 250/1000 = .25 or 25%.
3. The number for the sample is arbitrarily chosen—in this case, 120.

    Using the number chosen, 120, you have drawn from each subgroup the exact percentage of individuals that are found in the real population. Group I has 15% representation; 15% of 120 is <u>18</u> individuals. Eighteen individuals are drawn from Group I. Group II has 25% representation; 25% of 120 equals <u>30</u> individuals. Thirty individuals are drawn from Group II. Group III has 35% representation; 35% of 120 is <u>42</u> individuals. Forty-two individuals are drawn from Group III.

                [5] The type of sampling technique illustrated is proportionate; there will be no discussion of the disproportionate stratified sampling.

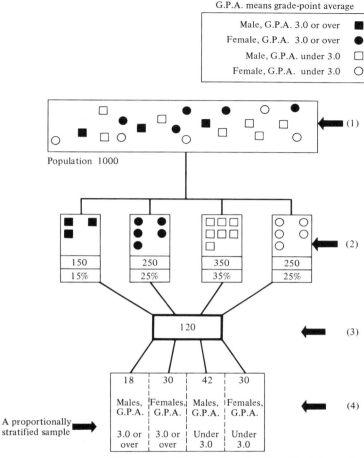

Figure 2-1: Proportionally Stratified Sample

Finally, Group IV has 25% representation; 25% of 120 is <u>30</u> individuals. Thirty individuals are drawn from Group IV. These values, as shown in Figure 2-1, represent the sample that will be used in the study.

Stratifying the population reduces sampling error and also reduces the size of the sample needed. The stratified sample, though smaller than the simple random sample, has a sampling error of the same magnitude. Stratifying a large sample, however, such as one on a nationwide basis, is usually difficult. The cost in time and money of doing a study would be immense. You must also be aware ahead of time of the specific characteristics in the population that you want to study. Select only those variables that are relevant or important. When you have a large population and are not sure of the relevant characteristics, it is wiser to use other sampling techniques.

Concluding Thoughts on Sampling

By now you may have concluded that the larger the sample size, the greater the chances of its representing the real population. This is a correct assumption. However, no matter what sampling technique you employ, you will never be absolutely certain that the sample and the population are alike.

Why have we devoted so much time to a discussion of sampling? The reason is that many students who are conducting research projects have *biased* samples— samples that have systematic errors. The results based on a biased sample may be worthless, no matter how beautifully the study is written and how sophisticated the statistics.

For further information on sampling you are referred to the book by Snedecor listed in References at the end of this volume.

VARIABLES

Experimental studies always focus on a group of people, animals, cars, airplanes, or the like. Each group is observed on the basis of one or more characteristics that are of experimental interest. For instance, a sociologist who is teaching monkeys sign language is interested in vocabulary achievement as measured by a standardized test. Therefore, he scores each monkey on this characteristic. A characteristic such as vocabulary achievement is known as a *variable*. Variables are defined as characteristics that vary from one subject to another. In the monkey study not all monkeys will obtain the same score on the vocabulary achievement test. Scores will vary from monkey to monkey. Some monkeys will know more vocabulary than others. Other examples of variables used in studies are statistics test scores, age, hair color, income, eye color, and political party membership.

Variables can be classified as quantitative or qualitative. *Quantitative variables* are ones that vary in quantity, such as test scores, income, and age. These variables can be ordered. That is, a person earning $75,000 a year is certainly higher on the income scale than a person earning $25,000. *Qualitative variables* are ones that vary in nature, not size, such as political party membership, eye color, hair color. They cannot be ordered.

A characteristic that is a variable in one study may be held constant in another, or it may not be relevant at all. For example, age may vary in one study, but in another the subjects may be of the same age, so the variable age is held constant. In another case, age may not be a factor under consideration.

Variables that are related to one another so that one variable depends on the other are said to be *functions* of each other. In discussing variables that have a functional relationship, we distinguish between the independent and the dependent variable. An *independent variable* is one that the researcher manipulates to see what changes occur as a consequence in another variable. A *dependent variable* varies with the value of the independent variable. It is always some sort of response. If we are studying the effectiveness of a new method of teaching vocabulary to monkeys, the method of teaching is the independent variable and the monkeys' vocabulary achievement or response is the dependent variable.

MEASUREMENT

For years now you have been dealing with numbers. You have been balancing that check book, counting your change, and tabulating your golf score. You have performed all sorts of arithmetic operations—adding, subtracting, multiplying, and dividing—and usually getting the right answer. However, in order to be able to perform operations with numbers in a meaningful way, you have to know what these numbers represent. Adding $2 + 3 + 4 + 6 + 7 + 5 + 4 + 8 + 2$, for example, is only an abstract exercise, but it becomes meaningful when you know that the results will give you a golf score for nine holes.

In the field of measurement it is essential to know what the numbers represent. Measurement is the assignment of numbers to objects or events according to rules. Once this assignment is made, the numbers are not just numbers; they have certain properties and represent certain characteristics that determine which arithmetic operations can be performed. The numerals assigned to football uniforms are no longer just numerals; they identify the players. The numbers on the uniforms are labels that cannot be added, subtracted, multiplied, or divided. As you can see, after numbers are assigned to objects or events they are treated differently. Those numbers on the football uniform are different from the numbers used to show gem hardness, which in turn are different from the numbers on test scores or the numbers on a measuring scale.

Measurement has been usefully classified into four scales: nominal, ordinal, interval, and ratio (Stevens, 1968). Each scale is a way of assigning numbers to objects, and each has its own limitations and degree of precision. We shall discuss the scales in order of precision, from the lowest to the highest.

Nominal Scale

Nominal is the weakest level of measurement. At this level numbers are assigned to identify, label, or classify individuals or objects. In life you are constantly categorizing or distinguishing items from one another. Even when you go to a football game this labeling occurs. Paul and Karen Shaw, for example, recently went to a football game to watch their son, Dick, play. Unfortunately, because of car trouble they arrived late and were seated in the top row of the stadium. They were so far away from the players they could not recognize any of their faces. The only way they could find Dick was by looking for blue jersey number 38. The numbers on the uniforms were important only for identifying players; they could not serve any other mathematical function. Player number 33 could not be added to player number 38 to make player 71.

When you use nominal data you classify your people, objects and so on into categories. Then, under the different category headings, you list the number of objects or people there are. For example, according to political preference in Sedona County, each individual is placed in four categories as shown in Table 2-2. Democrat, Republican, Undecided, and Independent. The number of individuals in each category has been noted. Since the categories are independent of each other, a person can be placed in only one category. The list of categories covers every political preference that exists in Sedona County. Therefore, every person in the sample is listed. Finally, the order in which these categories are listed has no significance. As a matter of convenience in display, the categories with more members are listed first—but they need not be, and nothing is implied about their relative merits. The numbers are assigned to the categories for identification only. The arithmetic operations you perform on any of these numbers are only a matter of counting.

Table 2-2: Political Preference of People of Sedona County

Political preference	Number of people
Democrat	25
Republican	15
Undecided	6
Independent	9

Other examples using nominal measurement are classification by religion (Protestant, Jewish, Catholic, and so on) and by gender (male, female).

Ordinal Scale

The next higher level of measurement is *ordinal*. Ordinal measurement, in addition to distinguishing individuals or objects from one another, is concerned with arranging them in some kind of rank or order. You use numbers this way every day. A prime example occurs at most universities every year around promotion time. At the annual personnel meeting at a university in California a dreadful argument arose about six candidates for professorship. Victor Black, a young professor, was quite upset about the way personnel decisions were being made; he felt they were based on gossip, innuendoes, and personal biases. He wanted a drastic change in these policies. Victor suggested that on the basis of important criteria such as student evaluations, publications, committee work, research, and participation in organizations, the six candidates should be ranked from the highest to the lowest and the three best chosen. This would presume that the candidate receiving 1 was better than the candidate receiving 2, the candidate receiving 2 was better than the candidate receiving 3, and so on. Even Victor's superb method, however, did not reveal whether the same differences existed between the candidates. Candidate 1 might be slightly better than candidate 2, while candidate 2 might be way above candidate 3. Despite this lack of precision, Victor felt that ranking the candidates was more equitable than what had been done in the past.

In our society numbers are used to rank people, objects, or events every day. Candidates in a beauty contest, scholarship applicants, military service personnel, gems, racing cars, and earthquakes all are subjected to this procedure. The arithmetic operations permissible at this level are counting and ranking.

Interval Scale

In discussing ordinal data we noted that we could not state the exact differences between the candidates being ranked. Candidate A might have been ten times better than candidate B; there was no way of making this judgment using the ordinal measurement. To obtain more precision we must use the interval level. At this level measurement is broken down on a scale of equal units. The same distance exists between, say, 50 and 55 as between 60 and 65.

Consider, for example, a math test given by a college professor. The scores are such numbers as 98, 95, 90, 50, and 25. The professor, looking at these test scores, can say John's 98 is three points higher than Bill's 95. What she cannot say is that Jan's score of 50 represents twice as much knowledge of math as Bill's score of 25. In making this statement the professor would assume that a zero on the test represented zero knowledge in math. Of course, a student can score zero on this math test, but it does not represent a complete absence of any knowledge of math. All this zero says is that on this particular test the person could not answer any of the math problems.

Other examples of interval measurement are those of temperature on Fahrenheit and Celsius scales and of time on our calendar.

The arithmetic operations permissible on an interval scale are addition and subtraction, but not multiplication and division. In our example, you can add the five test scores to get an average, but you cannot divide 50 by 25 and say that Jan knows twice as much as Bill. Multiplication and division require a scale with an absolute zero.

Ratio Scale

Ratio is the strongest level of measurement. Every day you use it to measure height, weight, or volume. Ratio has an absolute zero, which permits multiplication and division. The Kelvin scale used in physics has a zero point that represents a complete absence of temperature. When you go to the supermarket to buy meat, the butcher uses a ratio scale; if he puts nothing on this scale, it will show zero or an absence of weight. If he puts 227 grams of meat on the scale, removes it, and then later puts 454 grams of meat on the scale, it will properly register each weight. The 227 grams of meat on the scale will weigh half as much as the 454 grams of meat. The butcher can legitimately say that the 227 grams is one-half as much meat. The ratio can be shown as $\frac{227 \text{ grams}}{454 \text{ grams}}$, equaling one-half.

Many of the studies in social sciences do not use the ratio level of measurement, because they are not measuring some physical trait. In the physical sciences the studies often use the ratio level of measurement, because they are measuring such physical traits as height, weight, and volume. All arithmetic operations are permissible at this level.

Concluding Remarks on Measurement

All your data might not fall this neatly into these categories. However, if you bear in mind that most do, you will find it much simpler to choose a statistical test. Level of measurement is one of the criteria used in selecting a statistical test to analyze your data.

Table 2-3 summarizes the four levels of measurement just covered.

Table 2-3: Quick Reference Chart

Levels	Arithmetic	Features	Examples
Nominal	Counting	1. Categorizes	Social security numbers
Ordinal	Counting Ranking	1. Categorizes 2. Ranks	Hardness of gems
Interval	Counting Ranking Addition Subtraction	1. Categorizes 2. Ranks 3. Has equal units	Test scores
Ratio	Counting Ranking Addition Subtraction Multiplication Division	1. Categorizes 2. Ranks 3. Has equal units 4. Has absolute zero	Bathroom scale

CAPSULE REVIEW OF THE CHAPTER

Statistics has two major divisions: descriptive and inferential.

Descriptive statistics are methods that give a clearer picture of the data. They are used for organizing and summarizing information about observations. Among the techniques are the median and Spearman rank correlation.

Inferential statistics are methods concerned with inferring beyond the data. They attempt to draw conclusions on the basis of observations of only a sample of the population. Among the techniques are the chi-square test and *t*-test. Since inferential statistics draw inferences about a population on the basis of a sample, we need to know what the terms *population* and *sample* mean.

A population is a well-defined group of animals, people, plants, or objects that have something in common. A sample is merely a smaller group selected from this population. In other words, a sample is a subset or portion of the population. Because sampling becomes such an important issue in research, the sample selected must be representative of the population. Some of the techniques used to insure the representativeness of the sample are simple random sampling, cluster sampling, and stratified sampling.

Simple random sampling draws a small group of individuals from the population. This method insures that every individual has an equal chance of being selected, and that the selection of one person in the sample is independent of the selection of another. Cluster sampling is multistep random sampling. The population is divided into clusters, and a simple random sample of the clusters is drawn. Stratified sampling divides the population into homogeneous groups. It is used when you want to reduce sampling error.

Experimental studies always focus on a group of people, objects, events, or the like. You observe the group in terms of one or more characteristics known as variables. Variables are characteristics that vary.

When, having gathered these data from the sample, you want to analyze them by using some statistical procedure, you must know the level of measurement. Nominal, the lowest level, categorizes the data; ordinal, the next level, ranks the data; interval, the third level, compares the data by addition or subtraction; and ratio, the highest level, compares the data by multiplication or division.

Now is the time to take the second mastery test. Answer the questions carefully. The page numbers given at the end of each question show where the material appears in the text.

SELF-TEST FOR MASTERY

If you have trouble working a problem, reread the explanation on the page listed.

pp. 22, 23

1. WHY ARE MANY POLITICIANS LIKE LOBSTERS? In order to answer this question you must match every lettered item on the left with its correct phrase on the right. Then, in the space preceding the lettered item, write the parenthesized word that follows the correct phrase. The first one is done for you.

Because	(a)	Nominal	A subgroup of the population. (*change*)
_____	(b)	Parameter	A multistep random sample. (*turn*)
_____	(c)	Sample	Ruth was born in 1925, and Bobbie was born in 1930. (*into*)
_____	(d)	Statistic	Karen weighs 40.82 kilograms. (*water*)
_____	(e)	Descriptive statistics	Sy is the third most popular writer in the class. (*they*)

——— (f) Ordinal   Numbers used to identify, such as a telephone number. (*Because*)

——— (g) Inferential statistics   A table of random numbers. (*cold*)

——— (h) Interval   Statistics that are useful in organizing and summarizing the data on hand. (*when*)

——— (i) Population   The mean. (*green*)

——— (j) Ratio   Mathematical symbols that describe populations. (*they*)

Statistics that enable a person to go beyond the data from a sample. (*get*)

Mathematical symbols that describe samples. (*color*)

A defined group of people or objects that have something in common. (*hot*)

p. 21   **2.** A watch repair service wants to see if its 1000 customers are satisfied. The customer relations representative draws a simple random sample of 100 clients by using a table of random numbers.
(a) What is the population?
(b) What is the sample?
(c) Why should sampling be done in the first place?

p. 23   **3.** Students at a nursery school were assigned numbers from 1 to 90. Using the table of random numbers in this chapter, choose 25 students for a random sample. Use the numbers 4 and 6 to find your starting square. Remember, 4 over and 6 down.

p. 22   **4.** What is the difference between a sample and a population?

p. 23   **5.** What is the difference between simple random sampling and cluster sampling?

p. 27   **6.** What is stratified sampling?

7. Thinking in terms of level of measurement, which statements below are Reasonable (R) and which are Unreasonable (U)? Circle R or U.

p. 33   (a) Ruth scored 80 on her math test. She knows twice as much as Jeff, who scored 40. R or U

p. 32   (b) There are 20 males and 26 females in David's class. R or U

p. 34   (c) Jeff weighs 140 lb., twice as much as Andrew's 70 lb. R or U

p. 33   (d) Dick ranked first in the class and Vince ranked second. We conclude that Dick is ten times better than Vince. R or U

8. Which statements below are about descriptive statistics and which about inferential statistics?

p. 20
   (a) Jim had the highest score on the math test, while Ben had the lowest. _____

p. 21
   (b) To save time Bob decided to have every fifth student on the list of entering high school freshmen take a math test in order to see how well these freshmen do in math. _____

p. 21
   (c) A graduate study committee sent a questionnaire to a random sample of former graduates to see if they were employed. _____

p. 30
9. A variable is _____.

p. 31
10. A camp counselor was interested in studying the effect free time had on a child's expenditure on recreational items such as games, balls, baseball bats and gloves. In this study the amount of money spent on the recreational items would be the (a) _____ variable, and the free time a child was allowed would be the (b) _____.

ANSWERS TO SELF-TEST

Score yourself by adding up the points for each correct answer and write the total in the Evaluation form.

3 points each
1. Because they change color when they get into hot water.

5 points each
2. (a) 1000 customers.
   (b) 100 clients.
   (c) Because it is less expensive and would take less time. Anyway, 100 people are enough to determine satisfaction.

3. 76, 33, 30, 53, 45, 50, 01, 48, 21, 47, 25, 56, 61, 52, 16, 81, 80, 82, 90, 65, 58, 42, 69, 68, 60. *Scoring:* Perfect score = 7 points; 10 correct = 3 points; less than 10 = 0 points.

9 points
4. Population is the entire group of people or objects that have something in common. A sample is a subgroup of the population.

9 points
5. Simple random sampling draws a small group of individuals from the population, whereas cluster sampling divides the population into clusters and takes simple random samples of the clusters.

10 points
6. Stratified sampling occurs when the population is broken down into homogeneous groups. Then the sample is randomly drawn from each subgroup.

3 points each

7. (a) U. Ruth's score of 80 is interval, so multiplication and division are not allowed.
(b) R. For nominal level of measurement, counting cases within categories is reasonable.
(c) R. Since the level of measurement is ratio, multiplication and division are allowed.
(d) U. Since the level of measurement is ordinal, this is unreasonable because the distance between the ranks is not equal.

2 points each

8. (a) Descriptive statistics.
(b) Inferential statistics.
(c) Inferential statistics.

1 point

9. A characteristic that varies.

2 points each

10. (a) Dependent variable.
(b) Independent variable.

Evaluation

Rating	Score
100 = Champ	
85–99 = Heavyweight	
70–84 = Lightweight	
0–69 = Featherweight	

MEASURES OF CENTRAL TENDENCY

3

In Chapter 3 we have five major objectives:

1. To understand the terms mean, median, and mode.
2. To be able to calculate the mean, median, and mode for ungrouped and grouped data.
3. To understand what a frequency distribution is.
4. To be able to set up a frequency distribution.
5. To be able to represent a frequency distribution on a graph.

We begin with a story that illustrates three of the most commonly used measures of central tendency.

During the fall of 1980 at Sand State College Professor Victor O'Shay came under criticism from his colleagues. The attack was led by Professor Ford, who felt that Victor's grades were too high in his seminar class. Accusing him of unprofessionalism and of lowering the high standards of Sand College, she brought her charges to the department chairman, Dr. Lyons. The grades Victor gave that semester were based on the following final test scores: 98, 92, 92, 92, 83, 80, 78, 75, 65, 48, 17. Victor felt that this group was best represented by the middle score, 80. This grade of 80 is high, but not unreasonably high. Dr. Ford, however, felt that Victor's grades were best represented by 92, the most frequently occurring score. Dr. Ford said that Victor gave an average grade of 92, which was too high. Dr. Lyons, the department chairman, computed the average as 74.55, and he would have liked to fire Dr. Ford for being so unreasonable.

The numbers chosen by the professors to represent Victor's class scores are in fact different measures of central tendency. A *measure of central tendency* is a single score that is used to describe a group of scores. It is a typical or average score that describes the group in general. Dr. O'Shay used the median, 80; Dr. Lyons used the mean, 74.55; and Dr. Ford used the mode, 92. Each of these measures has a different way of interpreting what the average score is. The situation determines which measure is appropriate. In this situation, which of these measures of central tendency best represents Victor's group of scores? Is it the mean, median, or mode?

In the pages that follow, we shall discuss these three widely used measures of central tendency—the arithmetic mean, the median, and the mode. In reading these pages you will come to an undertanding of why the median (80) best represents Professor O'Shay's group of scores.

MEAN FOR UNGROUPED DATA

The *mean* or *arithmetic average* is the most frequently used measure of central tendency. It is the one most easily understood, and it can be used at the interval or ratio level.

From the day you are born to the day you die you are confronted with this insidious measure. Your height, weight, temperature, test scores, and athletic prowess are laid bare with this single score, which compares you with others. By the time you have finished elementary school you know all about the mean. You are cognizant that you are above or below it. In fact, on many occasions you use it to find out information that deeply concerns you.

Suppose an experimental psychologist wants to know the average score for the mice running through a maze he designed. He selects a small sample of mice and records their scores: 7, 5, 5, 4, 2, 1. Looking at this information, he ask himself, "What is the mean?" He answers this question by finding the sum of the scores and dividing it by the number of scores. Expressed symbolically, the formula for this sample mean is:

Formula 3-1   *Mean for Ungrouped Data*

$$\overline{X} = \frac{\Sigma\ X}{N}$$

Expressed in words, the formula says the mean ($\overline{X}$) is equal to the sum[1] of the scores ($\Sigma\ X$) divided by the number of scores (N). The sum of the scores ($\Sigma\ X$) is equal to 24; that is, $7 + 5 + 5 + 4 + 2 + 1$ equals 24. The number of scores (N) equals 6: there are six mice running through the maze. Substituting these values in the formula, you have

$$\frac{\Sigma\ X}{N} = \frac{24}{6}$$

Dividing 24 by 6, you get 4. The psychologist knows that the average score or mean for his sample of mice is 4. He also knows that any mouse with a score more than 4 is better than an average mouse in its ability to run through the maze, and any mouse below 4 is not as good as the average mouse in its ability to run through the maze.

As practice, solve the following problem.

Problem   Find the mean for the following scores: 8, 9, 10, 6, 4, 3.

Answer   The mean is 6.7.

$$\overline{X} = \frac{\Sigma\ X}{N} = \frac{8 + 9 + 10 + 6 + 4 + 3}{6} = \frac{40}{6} = 6.7$$

In finding the mean for the preceding problem, we used every score just as we

---

[1] Remember, the symbol Σ means to add up the scores.

found it, and the numbers were not grouped or summarized in a table; that is why the formula is called the *mean for ungrouped data* or the *raw-score formula for the mean*. Most people solve all their mathematical problems by using ungrouped data. Nevertheless, at times you will need to summarize your data in a table called a *frequency distribution*. If you have 15 or more scores and you want to see whether any pattern exists, a frequency distribution will give you a clearer picture of the data.

For example, suppose you were faced with the following set of raw scores: 46, 60, 87, 77, 51, 51, 47, 72, 91, 71, 69, 61, 68, 63, 62, 60, 61, 76, 83, 52, 58, 57, 67, 56, 66. How would you make sense out of them? The only thing that can be said about these scores is that some are greater than others. By putting these data in a frequency distribution you can then make other statements about them.

The simplest type of frequency distribution is an arrangement of the scores in order of size, with the frequency of each score indicated in a column labeled frequency (f). Table 3-1 shows this type of frequency distribution. This summary table is more useful than the original array of scores. By inspection you can see that the scores range from 46 to 91 and you can identify those that occur most frequently (51, 60, 61). When there are few scores to work with, this simple frequency distribution is all that you need to construct. When there are many scores, however, not only is listing every score tedious and time-consuming, but you may also lose sight of any pattern that exists. In this situation it is useful to group the scores into *class intervals*, such as 20–24, 25–29, and so on, until every score in the distribution has been included in an interval. If, for example, you have the raw scores 21, 26, 36, 37, 41, 41, 42, 42, 42, 46, 46, 47, 48, 48, 51, 51, 51, 52, 52, 53, 53, 56, 57, 57, 58, 61, 62, 63, 66, 67, 77, and you set them in a grouped frequency distribution with an interval size of 5, you have Table 3-2.

The class intervals listed in Table 3-2 represent all the originally recorded scores. For example, in the interval 20–24 the score 21 is found. In the interval

Table 3-1: A Simple Frequency Distribution

Scores	f	Scores	f
91	1	63	1
87	1	62	1
83	1	61	2
77	1	60	2
76	1	58	1
72	1	57	1
71	1	56	1
69	1	52	1
68	1	51	2
67	1	47	1
66	1	46	1

Table 3-2: A Grouped Frequency
Distribution with an
Interval Size of 5

Class interval	f
75–79	1
70–74	0
65–69	2
60–64	3
55–59	4
50–54	7
45–49	5
40–44	5
35–39	2
30–34	0
25–29	1
20–24	1

55–59 the scores 56, 57, 57, 58 are found. Notice there are 12 intervals in the frequency distribution. A common practice is to have from 10 to 20 class intervals. If you have less than ten intervals, you might get an inaccurate description of your distribution, and if you have more than 20, any pattern that might exist may be distorted, and the work involved will be excessive.

For each interval in Table 3-2 the number of raw scores in that interval is recorded in the frequency column. For example, in the interval 45–49 a frequency of 5 is recorded. This 5 represents five raw scores that lie in that interval. In the interval 75–79 a frequency of 1 is recorded, representing one raw score that lies in that interval. When the scores are grouped in this manner, the exact scores of an individual are completely lost. You do not know where the scores are in an interval; you just know how many scores there are. In the interval 45–49 all you know is there are five scores in that interval. In order to find out what these scores are, you must look at the original list, where you find 46, 46, 47, 48, 48.

In order to understand frequency distributions you should be familiar with the terms discrete and continuous data, real limits, interval size, and midpoint.

DISCRETE AND CONTINUOUS DATA

Data may be classified as discrete or continuous. Whenever you see *discrete data,* they are reported as whole units, such as the number of cars on a parking lot or the number of children in a family. For example, there are either 100 cars in the lot or 101; there can't be 100.4 cars or 100.5 cars. No fractional value is reported.

Whenever you see *continuous data,* the numbers can take on any value within a range. Reporting a person's weight is continuous, because the possible values can be reported as whole numbers of pounds plus fractional values. An individual can be described as weighing 111.2 pounds and being $15\frac{1}{2}$ years old. Measurement using continuous data approximates the true value. Usually continuous numbers are measured to their nearest whole unit. For instance, when a person first enters a doctor's office, the nurse records his weight. She records, let's say, 145 pounds. In most cases this number 145 represents a weight that has been rounded off to 145 pounds. Weight measured in pounds is regarded as ranging from .5 units below the number to .5 units above the number. Therefore, a weight of 145 pounds would be considered to represent an interval from 144.5 to 145.5, reported for convenience as 145.

REAL LIMITS

The *real limits* of a number obtained from continuous measurement are one-half unit (.5) below the number and one-half unit (.5) above the number. The real limits of 33 are 32.5 to 33.5. On a frequency distribution, data are treated as continuous. Referring again to Table 3-2, the *lower real limit* of any interval is the number .5 units below the lowest number in that interval, while the *upper real limit* of the interval is the number .5 units above the highest number in that interval. For example, the lower real limit of the interval 45–49 is 44.5, and the *upper real limit* of the same interval is 49.5.

Problem   Find the real limits for each interval in Table 3-2.

Answers

(a)	19.5–24.5	(e)	39.5–44.5	(i)	59.5–64.5
(b)	24.5–29.5	(f)	44.5–49.5	(j)	64.5–69.5
(c)	29.5–34.5	(g)	49.5–54.5	(k)	69.5–74.5
(d)	34.5–39.5	(h)	54.5–59.5	(l)	74.5–79.5

INTERVAL SIZE

If you want to find out the *interval size* on an already formed frequency distribution, you subtract the *lower real limit* of the interval from the *upper real limit.* Look again at the frequency distribution in Table 3-2. If you only subtract the actual numbers that are recorded for each interval, the size of each interval appears to be only 4. For instance, if you take the interval 45–49 and subtract 45 from 49, the answer appears to be 4. But of course this is not the true interval size. To get the true interval you must subtract the lower real limits from the upper real limits. For the interval 45–49, subtract 44.5 from 49.5; you will find that the interval size is 5. Figure 3-1 shows the lower and upper real limits of this interval.

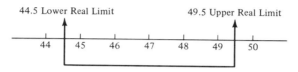

Figure 3-1: Real Limits of the Interval 45–49

MIDPOINTS

The *midpoint* of an interval is the score that best represents the scores for that interval. The midpoint is one-half the distance between the lower and the upper real limits. We find it by adding the lower real limit to the upper real limit of the interval, then dividing by 2. That is,

$$\frac{\text{lower real limit} + \text{upper real limit}}{2}$$

Look again at Table 3-2. The interval 70–74 has a lower real limit of 69.5 and an upper real limit of 74.5. Substituting in the formula, you have

$$\frac{69.5 + 74.5}{2} = \frac{144}{2} = 72$$

Adding, 69.5 + 74.5 = 144. Dividing 144 by 2, you get 72, the midpoint. Figure 3-2 shows the midpoint for this interval.

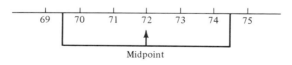

Figure 3-2: Midpoint for the Interval 70–74

Problem   As practice, find the midpoints for the following intervals:

(a) 50–52	(c) 63–65	(e) 140–149
(b) 50–59	(d) 45–49	(f) 45–47

Answers

(a) 51	(c) 64	(e) 144.5
(b) 54.5	(d) 47	(f) 46

Now that you have an understanding of discrete and continuous data, real limits, interval size, and midpoint, you will have no trouble in setting up a frequency distribution with class intervals. First, we shall set up a distribution of this type, step by step, using the raw scores 68, 21, 46, 46, 48, 47, 63, 41, 41, 41, 42, 43, 31, 32, 36, 37, 56, 58, 52, 53, 33, 36, 37, 53, 54, 41, 42, 43, 27, 57, 26, 47, 62. The directions below show you how to form the columns on the worksheet and set up the table.

PROCEDURE

Worksheet for the Frequency Distribution

Class interval	f
65–69	1
60–64	2
55–59	3
50–54	4
45–49	5
40–44	8
35–39	4
30–34	3
25–29	2
20–24	1

$$\Sigma f = 33$$

Directions for Setting Up a Frequency Distribution

1. Arrange the following raw scores, 68, 21, 46, 46, 48, . . . , 62, in order of size. That is: 21, 26, 27, 31, 32, . . . , 68.
2. Find the range of the scores for this frequency distribution. Subtract the lowest raw score in the distribution from the highest raw score. That is, subtract $68 - 21 = 47$. Write the answer, 47, in the blank: Range = ___.

Range = <u>47</u>

3. Determine the size of your class intervals (i).
   a. Divide the range (47) by the number 10.[2]
   b. Round the answer to the nearest whole number. That is, round 4.7 to 5.0.
   c. If your answer for interval size is an even number, to avoid having a decimal midpoint pick the closest odd number. Since 5.0 is odd, write 5 in the blank: $i =$ ___.

$i = \underline{5}$

4. Determine the place to begin your lowest class interval. This interval must include the lowest number, 21. You can select a number as low as 17 as your starting number. For convenience choose a number between 21 and 17 that is a multiple of your interval size. (You determined your interval size in step 3.) In this case your interval size is 5, and since 20 is a multiple of 5, this is your starting number.

5. Create your class intervals with an interval size of 5. Starting with 20, make the class intervals 20–24, 25–29, 30–34, 35–39, . . . , 65–69. Each class interval begins with the number following the maximum score of the interval below it. The maximum score of the interval 20–24 is 24, so the next interval begins with the number following it, 25. Keep creating intervals until the highest raw score, 68, has been included.

6. Form the f column. Count the number of scores in every class interval and write each number opposite its class interval in the column labeled frequency (f). For example, in the class interval 30–34 there are three scores, so write 3 in the frequency column.

7. Find the Σf. Add the numbers in the frequency column, $1 + 2 + 3 + 4 + \ldots + 1$, and write the answer, 33, opposite the Σf.[3]

For practice solve the following problem.

Problem

Use the raw scores 28, 31, 32, 34, 34, 34, 36, 36, 37, 37, 38, 40, 40, 40, 40, 40, 41, 41, 41, 42, 42, 43, 43, 43, 45, 45, 45, 46, 46, 48, 48, 51, 51, 51, 52, 52, 55 to form a frequency distribution.

[2] You can divide by any arbitrary number from 10 to 20, depending on how many class intervals you want. The convention of having ten to 20 class intervals gives you balance between excessive detail and necessary condensation.

[3] This is a check on your work; the Σf should equal the number of original raw scores.

Answer

Frequency Distribution

Class intervals	f
54–56	1
51–53	5
48–50	2
45–47	5
42–44	5
39–41	8
36–38	5
33–35	3
30–32	2
27–29	1

$$\Sigma f = 37$$

GRAPHING

In order to allow visual interpretation of a frequency distribution, it is common practice to draw a graph. To represent values on a graph you use two axes; the vertical axis is labeled Y and the horizontal axis, X. The two axes meet at a right angle, as shown in Figure 3-3. The X axis is usually longer than the Y axis, a ratio of 3 to 2. If the X axis is 6 inches, the Y axis would be 4 inches. Both of the axes must be uniformly numbered.

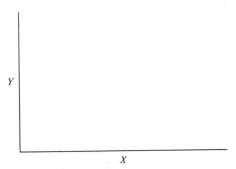

Figure 3-3: Graph Axes and Labels

There are many possible ways to represent data in graph form. In this section you will learn about two common methods: the histogram and the frequency polygon.[4]

[4] For a more complete treatment of graphing consult Hays (1973).

Histogram

The *histogram* is a bar graph. On a histogram the frequencies appear on the Y axis and the class intervals on the X axis. If an interval has zero cases, a space is left to represent the frequency of zero. An example of a histogram is shown in Figure 3-4.

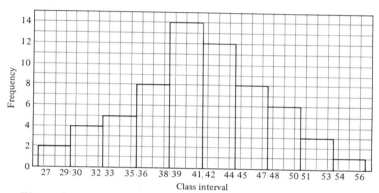

Figure 3-4: Histogram

Notice that the bar for each interval is drawn from the *real limits* of the interval. For example, the bar for the interval 27–29 begins at 26.5 and ends at 29.5. The frequency of each class interval is shown by the height of the bar. For instance, the interval 27–29 has a frequency of two; it is not as tall as the interval 30–32, which has a frequency of four.

Frequency Polygon

If you plot the midpoints of each bar in the histogram in Figure 3-4, you will have the frequency polygon in Figure 3-5.

A frequency polygon has each class interval plotted as a point above the midpoint of the interval; the points are connected with straight lines. The frequency of each interval is shown by the height of the dot. Conventionally, so as not to have this drawing floating in the air, intervals are added below and above, and these intervals are given a frequency of zero. In Figure 3-5 the interval 24–26 (midpoint 25) and interval 57–59 (midpoint 58) were added and given a frequency of 0.

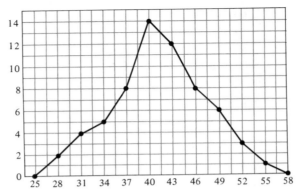

Figure 3-5: Frequency Polygon

You may notice that the drawings for Figures 3-4 and 3-5 have a similar shape. All curves have a characteristic shape, depending upon how the data are distributed. Some common shapes of distribution are shown in Figure 3-6.

In a symmetrical distribution such as the normal or bell-shaped curve (a) in Figure 3-6, the scores are concentrated in the center of the distribution; the right half of the curve is the mirror image of the left half. Many number traits approximate this curve. We will discuss the characteristics of this particular curve in more detail in Chapter 4. Curves (b) and (c) can be described in terms of their skewness. They lack symmetry; the majority of scores are on the right or left side of the distribution. Curve (b) is negatively skewed; its tail extends to the left. In this situation there would be many high scores and few low scores; that is, the scores are concentrated at the upper end of the distribution. Curve (c) is positively skewed; its tail is to the right. In this situation there would be many low and few high scores; the scores are concentrated at the lower end of the distribution. Curves (d) and (e) of Figure 3-6 can be described in terms of their peakedness or kurtosis. These curves are symmetrical, but they differ in height in the middle part of the distribution. Curve (d) is a flat or platykurtic curve and is not as peaked as curve (e). In curve (d) the scores are mostly concentrated in the center, and there is an even spread of scores away from the center. Curve (e) is a high arching or leptokurtic curve. In this figure there is an extreme concentration of scores in the center of the distribution. Finally, curve (f) is a symmetrical curve which is not normal. It has a high concentration of scores in two different points or modes of the distribution and thus is called a bimodal curve. It indicates that two separate populations are represented on one graph.

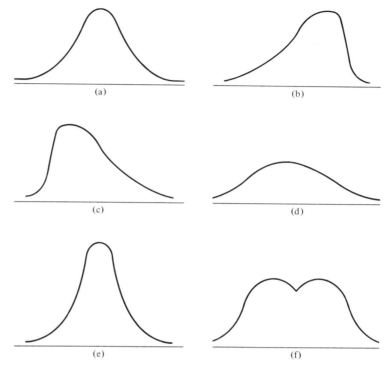

Figure 3-6: Some Common Types of Distributions

How do you find the mean if your data are in a frequency distribution? The following paragraphs should answer this question.

MEAN FOR GROUPED DATA

When you try to find a mean from a frequency distribution, you do not use the raw scores. Instead, you use the midpoint of each interval to represent the raw scores in that interval. Thus all scores that fall in the interval 19.5–24.5 would be assigned the score of 22, the midpoint of the interval. The midpoint is symbolized by a capital X.[5] To compute the mean from a frequency distribution you have to add each midpoint as many times as it occurs. For example, in Table 3-2

---

[5] Notice that the raw scores are also assigned the capital X symbol.

the interval 35–39 has a frequency of 2 and a midpoint of 37. The midpoint would be added two times (37 + 37) in computing the mean. Adding a score two times is equivalent to multiplying it by 2—that is, multiplying it by the frequency. The same logic applies to all class intervals in a frequency distribution. Therefore, to find the mean it would be easier to find the sum of the products of the frequency times the midpoint or $\Sigma(fX)$ and divide this by the number of scores (N). The formula for the mean is then symbolized as follows:

Formula 3-2   *Mean for Grouped Data*

$$\overline{X} = \frac{\Sigma(fX)}{N}$$

Since you replaced each measure by its class interval's midpoint, this formula is a little different from the one for finding the mean for the original scores. It is really only an approximation of the true mean. The meanings of the symbols are spelled out below.

Symbol	Meaning
Σ	Sum of
f	Frequency
X	Midpoint[6]
fX	Product of f and X
N	Number of scores

PROCEDURE

The formula for the mean for grouped data

$$\overline{X} = \frac{\Sigma(fX)}{N}$$

tells you to multiply each frequency by the midpoint in the class interval, sum the results, and then divide by the number of scores in the group. You are now ready to use this formula and find the mean. First set up a worksheet, using the data in the following frequency distribution.

---

[6] In this formula X stands not for the raw score, but for the midpoint of the interval.

Frequency Distribution

Class intervals	Frequency
50–54	1
45–49	0
40–44	1
35–39	2
30–34	3
25–29	5
20–24	10
15–19	4
10–14	3
5–9	2

After the worksheet is set up, follow directions 1 through 5, make substitutions in the formula, and solve it.

Worksheet for the Mean for Grouped Data

Class intervals	Midpoint X	Frequency f	fX
50–54	52	1	52
45–49	47	0	0
40–44	42	1	42
35–39	37	2	74
30–34	32	3	96
25–29	27	5	135
20–24	22	10	220
15–19	17	4	68
10–14	12	3	36
5–9	7	2	14
		$N = 31$	$\Sigma(fX) = 737$

Directions for Finding the Mean for Grouped Data

1. Find the midpoint of each interval and enter it in the column labeled X.
2. Set up your fX column by multiplying the frequency of each interval by its midpoint. The frequency of interval 5–9 is 2, and its midpoint is 7. If you multiply 2×7, you find an fX for this interval of 14. The frequency for interval 10–14 is 3, and its midpoint is 12. If you multiply 3×12, you find an

ƒX of 36. Continue the same procedure for each interval until the ƒX column is completed.

3. Find $\Sigma(fX)$. Add all the numbers in the ƒX column. Starting from the top of the ƒX column, you add $52 + 0 + 42 + 74 + 96 + 135 + 220 + 68 + 36 + 14$. Write the sum 737 opposite the $\Sigma(fX) = $ _____.

$\Sigma(fX) = \underline{737}$

4. Find N. Add the numbers in the frequency column. You add $1 + 0 + 1 + 2 + 3 + 5 + 10 + 4 + 3 + 2$. Write the sum 31 opposite the $N = $ _____.

$N = \underline{31}$

5. Find the $\overline{X}$ from this frequency distribution by substituting in the formula $\Sigma(fX)/N$. Divide the number found in step 3 (737) by the number found in step 4 (31), and write the answer opposite $\overline{X} = $ _____. Dividing 737 by 31 gives 23.8, which is the mean.

$\overline{X} = \underline{23.8}$

Finding the Mean for Grouped Data

1. Find the midpoint of each interval, and enter it in column X.
2. Form the ƒX column by multiplying the frequency of each interval by its midpoint.
3. Find $\Sigma(fX)$ by adding all the numbers in the ƒX column.
4. Find N by adding all the numbers in the frequency column.
5. Find the mean: divide the sum found in step 3 by the sum found in step 4.

Problem

As practice, find the mean for the following frequency distribution.

Class interval	Frequency
32–34	1
29–31	1
26–28	2
23–25	3
20–22	4
17–19	10
14–16	4
11–13	3
8–10	2
5–7	1

Answer

$$\overline{X} = \frac{\Sigma(fX)}{N} = \frac{573}{31} = 18.5$$

A FEW FACTS ABOUT THE MEAN

Now you will learn some interesting things about the mean. The mean is the most popular measure of central tendency. It is affected by the value of every single score in the distribution. For example, if you are finding the mean for the raw scores 10, 4, 3, 4, 2, you add all these scores together and divide by 5. Every score affects the results. Because it is affected by every score, the mean is amenable to more advanced statistical procedures. The mean is used to analyze data that are at the interval or ratio level of measurement.

Unfortunately, just because the mean is dependent upon each score in the distribution, a fluctuation in one score can have a big impact if the distribution is small. This was especially the case when six children were telling how many candy bars they won at a carnival. They reported their winnings as 36, 5, 4, 4, 2, 1. The mean was found to be 8 ($52 \div 6 = 8.67$). However, when a parent told the children they had won on the average eight candy bars, they thought he was a dope. After all, five of the six children had won less than eight candy bars. The children were more right than the parent. In this situation the parent should not have used the mean. The median would have been a more appropriate measure, because it is not influenced by extreme scores.

The mean is a very stable measure of central tendency. But how can this be so, after what we have just observed? What kind of stability are we referring to? The mean is stable when we draw several samples from a population. We would expect the sample means to differ slightly from one another owing to chance. However, it has been found that the means of samples drawn from a population will fluctuate only very slightly. The sample means are more similar to each other (stable) than are the sample medians or sample modes.

The mean cannot be computed from a distribution that has open-ended intervals. For some frequency distributions, especially ones involving the variable of income, the lower real limit of the lowest interval or the upper real limit of the highest interval is eliminated. This is done to keep down the number of intervals. For example, you might have class intervals of monthly income and make the highest interval open-ended by labeling it 20,000 and above. Because of the incompleteness of the information in the last interval, it is impossible to find the midpoint for this interval and the mean cannot be found for this distribution. In these situations either the median or mode is used. Neither of these measures would be affected by the lack of information in this interval.

MEDIAN FOR UNGROUPED DATA

The *median* is the *point* in the distribution of scores where 50% of the scores fall below it, and 50% fall above it. The median is used to analyze data that are at the ordinal level of measurement. In order to find the median for an odd number of raw scores, you arrange these scores in order of magnitude from the lowest to the highest. For example, you arrange 3, 1, 7, 8, 5, 6, 9 from the lowest to highest as follows: 1, 3, 5, 6, 7, 8, 9. Next you count until you reach the point where 50% of the scores fall below it and 50% above it. For this problem that point is 6: three scores fall above 6 and three scores fall below 6. If you are finding the median for an even number of raw scores, this problem is a little different. The median will fall between the two middle scores. You will take the average of these two scores. In finding the median for 3, 4, 6, 7, 8, 19, the median falls between 6 and 7. Add the middle scores together (6 + 7 = 13), then divide the answer (13) by 2, which equals 6.5, the median. The median 6.5 represents the point in the distribution that has 50% of the scores falling above it and 50% falling below it.

Problem   Find the median for 3, 8, 9, 13, 14, 18.

Answer   Median = 11.

To find the median for the practice problem was a simple matter. However, when the data are presented in a frequency distribution, or when tied raw scores affect the median, you compute the median in a different manner.

First let's look at Table 3-3 and find the median for data in a frequency distribution. Then we will be able to compute a median for tied raw scores.

Table 3-3: Clay High School French Test Scores

	Score intervals	f
Calculating	68–70	1
a Median	65–67	1
	62–64	2
	59–61	3
	56–58	6
	53–55	4
	50–52	4
	47–49	2
	44–46	2
	41–43	2
		$N = 27$

First determine how many scores are in the distribution by adding the number of frequencies. In this case you have 27 scores. Since the median is the point above and below which 50% of these scores fall, you know that you are now looking for the point above and below which 13.5 of the scores fall (one-half of 27 = 13.5). Start at the bottom of the frequency column in Table 3-3 and add frequencies, coming as close to 13.5 as you can without exceeding it. Adding 2 + 2 + 2 + 4, you reach 10. For this frequency distribution you find that the 13.5 score lies somewhere in the 52.5–55.5 interval. You know now that the median point is somewhere between 52.5 and 55.5 How do you find it? To find the median you use Formula 3-3.

Formula 3-3   *Median for Grouped Data*

$$\text{Median} = LL + \left(\frac{\frac{1}{2}N - cf}{fw} \right) i$$

The meanings of the symbols are given below.

Symbol	Meaning
LL	Lower real limit of the interval that contains $\frac{1}{2}N$
$\frac{1}{2}N$	One-half the number of scores
cf	Cumulative frequencies (sum of scores up to the interval containing the median)
i	Interval size
fw	Frequency of the number of scores within the interval containing the median

PROCEDURE

The worksheet and the direction sheet for finding the median follow. Together we will find the median for the French test scores.

Preparing the Worksheet

$N = \underline{27}$

1. Find N. Add all the numbers in the column headed f—that is, $1 + 1 + 2 + 3 + 6 + 4 + 4 + 2 + 2 + 2 = 27$. Write the sum 27 opposite the $N = $ ___.

$\frac{1}{2}N = \underline{13.5}$

2. Find $\frac{1}{2}N$. Multiply $\frac{1}{2} \times 27$ and write the answer 13.5 opposite the $\frac{1}{2}N = $ _____.

3. Find cf. Starting at the bottom number in the column headed f, add the numbers until you come as close as possible to $\frac{1}{2}N$ without exceeding it—that is, $2 + 2 + 2 + 4 = 10$. Write the

$cf = \underline{10}$

sum 10 opposite the $cf = $ ___.

4. Find fw. Still in the column headed f, the number following the last number used to complete your sum from step 3 is

$fw = \underline{4}$

$LL = \underline{52.5}$

$i = \underline{3}$

your *fw* number. Write the number 4 opposite the $fw = \underline{\hspace{1cm}}$.
5. Find *LL*. Take the lower limit of the interval on the same line where your *fw* number is located. Write 52.5 opposite
$LL = \underline{\hspace{1cm}}$.
6. Determine *i*. Determine the size of an interval. (See pp. 46–47). Write the interval size (3) opposite the $i = \underline{\hspace{1cm}}$.

Worksheet for Calculating
the Median

Score intervals	*f*
68–70	1
65–67	1
62–64	2
59–61	3
56–58	6
53–55	4
50–52	4
47–49	2
44–46	2
41–43	2
	$N = 27$

Substituting in the Formula

Make the appropriate substitutions by replacing each step with its corresponding number.

A. $\text{Median} = LL + \left(\dfrac{\frac{1}{2}N - cf}{fw} \right) i$

B. $M = \text{step 5} + \left(\dfrac{\text{step 2} - \text{step 3}}{\text{step 4}} \right) \times \text{step 6}$

C. $M = 52.5 + \left(\dfrac{13.5 - 10}{4} \right) \times 3$

Solving the Formula for the Median

A. $M = 52.5 + \left(\dfrac{13.5 - 10}{4} \right) \times 3$

B. Working inside the parentheses, subtract 10 from 13.5, then divide the answer by 4; that is, $13.5 - 10 = 3.5$ and $4\overline{)3.5} = .88$

C. Multiply $.88 \times 3 = 2.64$

D. Add 52.5 + 2.64 and enclose the answer or median in a box

$$M = 52.5 + .88 \times 3$$
$$M = 52.5 + 2.64$$
$$M = \boxed{55.14}$$

The median is 55.14. This step-by-step procedure for calculating the median is summarized below:

Step-by-Step Procedure for Calculating the Median

1. $\frac{1}{2}N$	13.5
2. cf	10
3. fw	4
4. LL	52.5
5. i	3

6. Calculate $M = LL + \left(\dfrac{\frac{1}{2}N - cf}{fw} \right) i$

(a) $M = 52.5 + \left(\dfrac{13.5 - 10}{4} \right) 3$

Parentheses first
(b) $M = 52.5 + (.88)3$
Multiply
(c) $M = 52.5 + 2.64$
Add
(d) $M = \boxed{55.14}$

Problem

As practice, find the median for the following frequency distribution.

Frequency Distribution

Class intervals	f
105–109	1
100–104	3
95–99	4
90–94	5
85–89	10
80–84	5
75–79	4
70–74	2
65–69	1
60–64	1

Answer

The median is 87.0.

Step-by-Step Procedure

1. $\frac{1}{2}N$ 18
2. cf 13
3. fw 10
4. LL 84.5
5. i 5

Finding the Median for Tied Raw Scores

Now that you have computed the median for scores in a frequency distribution, you will use the procedure just learned to compute a median for tied raw scores. When there are scores that are tied in the middle of the distribution, you set up a frequency distribution with an interval size of 1 and use the same formula to find the median as for grouped data,

$$M = LL \left(\frac{\frac{1}{2}N - cf}{fw} \right) i$$

The reason is that, if instead you used the counting procedure you used for ungrouped data, you would not be able to finish the problem. For example, the tied scores 1, 2, 3, 4, 4, 4, 5, 5, 5, 6 represent ten policemen's target scores on the rifle range Monday morning. If you found the median by counting, you would start at the bottom, and when you attempted to find the point where 50% of the cases fall above and 50% fall below, you would encounter three 4's, which would make it impossible to find the answer. Therefore, you must put these scores in a frequency distribution with an interval size of 1. Run the scores from lowest to highest. When you have a score that is tied, record the number of times the score occurs in the frequency column. The policemen's rifle-range scores are shown in frequency distribution in Table 3-4.

Table 3-4: Ten Policemen's Scores
on a Rifle Range

	Score intervals	f
Tied Scores	6	1
	5	3
	4	3
	3	1
	2	1
	1	1
		$N = 10$

The stepwise procedure for solving this problem is summarized in the accompanying table. If you have any question about how the values were reached, review the direction sheet for finding the median for grouped data on p. 59.

Steps in Calculating the Median for Tied Scores

1. $\frac{1}{2}N$ 5
2. cf 3
3. fw 3
4. LL 3.5
5. i 1

6. Calculate $M = LL + \left(\dfrac{\frac{1}{2}N - cf}{fw} \right) i$:

    (a) $M = 3.5 + \left(\dfrac{5 - 3}{3} \right) 1$

    (b) $M = 3.5 + \dfrac{2}{3}$

    (c) $M = 3.5 + .67$

    (d) $M = 4.17$

Problem

Find the median for the following tied raw scores: 7, 8, 9, 10, 10, 11, 11, 11, 12.

Answer

The median is 10.25.

Procedure

1. $\frac{1}{2}N$ 4.5
2. cf 3
3. fw 2
4. LL 9.5
5. i 1

Frequency Distribution, Tied Raw Scores

Score intervals	f
12	1
11	3
10	2
9	1
8	1
7	1

A FEW REMARKS ABOUT THE MEDIAN

The median is affected by the number of observations, not the size of each score, as the mean is. For example, examine Group A and Group B, as listed below. The medians are the same (6), but the means are different. The mean for Group A is 12.7 and for Group B is 6.3. The mean for Group A is larger because of the extremely large score of 67, which pulls the mean upward. Note that if the score of 67 were 1000, the median would still be 6, but the mean would be very high: 116.3.

Group A: 2, 3, 4, 5, 6, 8, 9, 10, 67
Group B: 2, 3, 4, 5, 6, 8, 9, 10, 10

The median can be used in an open type of frequency distribution where the top interval might be, say, "50,000 or over," whereas the mean cannot, because you cannot find the midpoint of this open-ended interval.

The median is not a score but a point; it cannot be used in further calculation. It is used to analyze data that are at the ordinal level of measurement.

MODE FOR UNGROUPED DATA

The *mode* is the simplest, but the least precise, measure of central tendency. It can be used with nominal data. In ungrouped data the mode is defined as the score that occurs the most frequently. The mode is 2 for the following scores of ten high-schoolers during a basketball game: 10, 9, 9, 9, 9, 2, 2, 2, 2, 2. But this mode will change if it is discovered that Billy and Johnny stepped over the line when they made their shots for the basket. If you rescore the game and count Johnny's and Billy's scores as 1's instead of 2's, the scores now look like this: 10, 9, 9, 9, 9, 2, 2, 2, 1, 1—and the mode changes from 2 to 9. The large discrepancy between 2 and 9 makes the mode a rather unstable measure. Regardless of this limitation, you can see it is easy to find the scores that occur the most often. But there are problems here, too, if you have scores such as the following: 7, 7, 7, 5, 5, 5, 4, 3, 2, 1. There are two modes, 5 and 7. Which mode is the more representative of the group of scores? An even more difficult situation arises when there is no mode at all.

MODE FOR GROUPED DATA

The mode for grouped data is defined as the midpoint of the interval with highest frequency. The interval with the highest frequency in Table 3-5 is 20–24; it has a frequency of 5. The midpoint of this interval, the mode, is 22.

Unless the data are such that there is a highest frequency, do not assign a mode to a distribution.

As the foregoing discussion makes evident, the mode has serious limitations as a precise measure. Merely changing the interval size from 3 to 5, for example, could change the mode. The mode's chief value, where a more precise measure is not needed, is that it is easy to find.

Table 3-5: *Spelling Test for*
Fifth-Grade Class

Finding the Mode

Score intervals	f	X
40–44	3	42
35–39	1	37
30–34	1	32
25–29	2	27
20–24	5	22
15–19	4	17
10–14	3	12
5–9	4	7
0–4	1	2

ADVANTAGES AND DISADVANTAGES OF THE MEAN, MEDIAN, AND MODE

Discussions throughout the chapter have pointed out the advantages and disadvantages of the measures of central tendency. Table 3-6 highlights the major points.

Table 3-6: *A Comparison of the Measures of Central Tendency*

	Mean	Median	Mode
Advantages	1. Used for interval or ratio data 2. Most stable measure 3. Considers every score	1. Used for ordinal data 2. Insensitive to extreme score 3. Used in an incomplete distribution	1. Used for nominal data 2. Locates highest concentration of scores 3. Quickest estimate
Disadvantages	1. Affected by extreme scores 2. Cannot be used in an incomplete distribution	1. Amenable to only a few math operations 2. Less stable than the mean	1. Least stable measure 2. Cannot be used in math computations

Whenever you need to find an average and don't know which measure to use, refer to this table. The measure of central tendency you choose will always depend upon your purpose. If you are a buyer of dresses and you want to buy the ones that sold the most, you will be interested in the mode. If you want to know the average income of people from a small town and you are afraid your scores will be influenced by a billionaire's score, choose the median. If you want to find the average score of several samples from the population and you are concerned about the stability of the measure, use the mean.

It should be clear now that the best measure of central tendency depends upon the situation. Returning to the story that opened this chapter, we can see why Dr. O'Shay's use of the median was correct. Since he had few scores to work with and some were extreme, the median in this situation was the best measure of central tendency.

WHAT HAVE YOU LEARNED?

Let's review briefly what you have learned about the measures of central tendency and the frequency distribution.

You first encountered the mean. You found out the mean is the sum of all the scores divided by the number of scores. You were taught how to find the mean for ungrouped data using Formula 3-1, $\overline{X} = \dfrac{\Sigma X}{N}$. You then learned how to group data in a frequency distribution, and from this distribution you were able to draw a picture that represented the data. You were taught how to compute the mean for grouped data using Formula 3-2, $\overline{X} = \dfrac{\Sigma(fX)}{N}$.

Next you learned about the median. You found out that the median was the point above which and below which 50% of the scores fall. You were taught how to find the median by counting when you had an odd number of scores and how to take the value in the middle when you had an even number of scores. You were given Formula 3-3,

$$\text{Median} = LL + \left(\frac{\frac{1}{2}N - cf}{fw}\right) i$$

for finding the median for grouped data and tied scores.

Finally, you were shown the mode. The mode was defined as the most frequently occurring score. You were told that in order to find a mode in a frequency distribution, you must find the midpoint of the interval where the greatest number of frequencies was found.

As you learned the meaning of the mean, median, and mode, and also how to calculate them, you learned about their advantages and disadvantages, which were summarized in Table 3-6 for your future reference.

SELF-TEST FOR MASTERY

If you have trouble working a problem, reread the explanation on the page listed.

1. This is a self-correcting exercise. Each word or phrase beneath the square refers to the mean, median, or mode. Match each item by putting a 1, 2, or 3 in its corresponding box in the square. If it refers to the mean, put a 1; a median, 2; and a mode, 3. The first item has been done for you. When you have completed placing the numbers in the lettered boxes, add each row and column. If you matched correctly, you should get the same number everywhere.

(b) p. 42; (e) p. 58;
(h) p. 64; all
others, p. 65

(a) 2	(b)	(c)	_____
(d)	(e)	(f)	_____
(g)	(h)	(i)	_____

_____ _____ _____

(a) ordinal scale (data)
(b) arithmetic average
(c) nominal scale (data)
(d) least stable measure
(e) middle point
(f) interval scale (data)
(g) measure used in advanced statistics
(h) most frequently occurring score
(i) unaffected by extremely high or low scores

2. The following scores are the weekly wages of 47 factory workers in a foreign country: 48, 47, 50, 53, 45, 49, 47, 56, 54, 51, 60, 46, 61, 51, 60, 50, 56, 52, 44, 49, 51, 40, 46, 54, 50, 55, 47, 48, 50, 50, 51, 47, 54, 43, 53, 55, 55, 50, 53, 57, 57, 55, 59, 45, 44, 64, 67

p. 48
(a) Put the data in a frequency table with a class interval of 3.

p. 51
(b) Draw a frequency polygon for this frequency distribution.

p. 52
3. Draw the following curves:
(a) A normal curve
(b) A curve that is skewed to the right
(c) A peaked curve

p. 43
4. What is the mean for the following scores?
(a) 10, 10, 6, 4, 3, 2, 1 _____

(b) 3, 4, 10, 5, 6, 7, 8 ⎯⎯⎯

(c) 5, 6, 29, 32, 4, 6 ⎯⎯⎯

p. 58
5. What is the median for the following scores?

(a) 3, 7, 5, 5, 5, 5, 6, 6, 6, 6, 6, 7 ⎯⎯⎯

(b) 10, 9, 8, 7, 9, 6, 5, 5, 4, 9 ⎯⎯⎯

(c) 4, 5, 7, 10, 11, 6 ⎯⎯⎯

p. 64
6. Find the mode for these scores:

(a) 4, 5, 6, 8, 9, 10, 11, 9 ⎯⎯⎯

(b) 4, 10, 9, 8, 8, 7, 6, 5, 5 ⎯⎯⎯

(c) 4, 5, 6, 7, 10, 11 ⎯⎯⎯

7. Using the scores reported in the table below, compute the mean, median, and mode.

Algebra Test Scores for S High

Score intervals	f
80–84	1
75–79	2
70–74	4
65–69	8
60–64	10
55–59	2
50–54	3
45–49	1
40–44	0
35–39	1

p. 54
(a) Mean = ⎯⎯⎯
p. 59
(b) Median = ⎯⎯⎯
p. 64
(c) Mode = ⎯⎯⎯

8. Tell what is wrong with the measures of central tendency used in the following situations:

p. 58
(a) A professor knew the median for her four statistics classes. There were 70, 85, 90, 95. She averaged the scores and reported the median score for all her students as 85.

p. 57
(b) A child received $2 a week for allowance. He wanted to know the average amount given his friends for allowance. The children were given $1, $1, $1, $1, $1, $2, $2, and $15. He figured the mean and told his mother he wanted more money.

p. 58
(c) A nurse heard that the mean salary for all nurses in St. Louis was $10,000. She wrote her mother that half of the nurses received more than $10,000 per year.

ANSWERS TO SELF-TEST

Score yourself by adding up the points for each correct answer and write the total in the Evaluation form.

2 points each   **1.** Each row, column, and diagonal add up to 6.

2	1	3
3	2	1
1	3	2

9 points   **2.** (a)

Class intervals	f
66–68	1
63–65	1
60–62	3
57–59	3
54–56	9
51–53	8
48–50	10
45–47	8
42–44	3
39–41	1

9 points   (b)

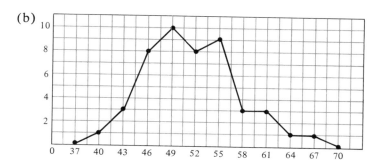

1 point each   **3.**

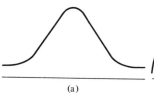

(a)

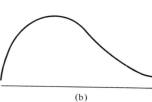

(b)

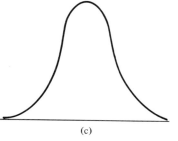

(c)

4. (a) 5.14; (b) 6.14; (c) 13.67

5. (a) 5.7: $M = LL + \left(\dfrac{\frac{1}{2}N - cf}{fw}\right) i$

$$= 5.5 + \left(\frac{6-5}{5}\right) 1$$

$$= 5.5 + \frac{1}{5}$$

$$= 5.6$$

(b) 7.5; (c) 6.5

6. (a) 9

(b) There are two modes, 5 and 8.

(c) No mode

7. (a) Mean = 63.6: $\bar{X} = \dfrac{\Sigma(fX)}{N} = \dfrac{2034}{32} = 63.6$

(b) Median = 64:

(1) $M = LL + \left(\dfrac{\frac{1}{2}N - cf}{fw}\right) i$

(2) $M = 59.5 + \left(\dfrac{16 - 7}{10}\right) 5$

(3) $M = 59.5 + (.9)5$

(4) $M = 59.5 + 4.5$

(5) $M = 64.0$

(c) Mode = 62

8. (a) The medians for separate groups of scores cannot be added together. You would have to put all the scores in one big distribution and compute the median.

(b) The $15 makes it inadvisable to use the mean, which is affected by extreme scores.

(c) The reported salary was the mean, not the median.

Evaluation

Rating	Score
120 = Champ	
100–119 = Heavyweight	
70–99 = Lightweight	
0–69 = Featherweight	

MEASURES OF VARIABILITY

4

Measures of central tendency, which we discussed in Chapter 3, are very popular and simple ways of organizing data to make them more meaningful to us. The idea of *averaging* that is behind these measures was familiar to us long before we read Chapter 3. We are accustomed to reading in the newspapers that the average income among workers in the United States is such and such or that the average amount of sugar consumption per person comes to such and such. If we are sports enthusiasts, we are bombarded with averages (measures of central tendency) all the time: batting averages for individual players and for entire teams, average number of touchdowns by a team per game, average number of basketball throws by players and teams per game. Sometimes it seems our society sees everything in terms of averages—which is unfortunate, because an average provides only one kind of information, and to stop there is to gain an incomplete description that may leave us with erroneous notions about individuals and groups.

As an example of these erroneous notions, consider Tom, a sociology major, who constantly spouted averages describing the relative standings of individuals and groups, much to the annoyance of those who had to listen to him. The only way he seemed to know to make the world meaningful was to sum it all up in terms of measures of central tendency. Bored beyond endurance, Jane and George, two friends of his, decided to strike back. Pretending they needed his help on a research study, they flattered Tom by showing him the scores of two groups on a test they had administered and asking him whether he agreed with their conclusion that Group B had done better, because higher scores had been achieved by members of that group. The scores for Group A were 5, 4, 5, 5, 5, 4, 6, 5, 6, 5, and those for Group B were 9, 2, 7, 2, 2, 9, 2, 5, 3, 9. Tom took a quick look at the scores and agreed with their conclusions immediately. Then, in his usual braggadocio manner, he proceeded to show them how such a conclusion could receive statistical support by computing the means of the two groups. Tom's calculations are shown in Table 4-1.

Imagine his surprise when he discovered the groups had identical means of 5. With all those 9's, Group B looked so much better! Tom did not realize that to describe groups only by way of a measure of central tendency was insufficient. These two groups had the same mean, but there was no denying that they were different. The difference was in the variation among the scores to be found in each group.

Figure 4-1 shows these two distributions visually. The dark squares represent the scores in the distribution. Group A's scores are clustered around the mean of 5, with the lowest being 4 and the highest 6. Group B's scores are scattered more away from the mean of 5 in either direction, with the lowest being 2 and the highest 9. As you can see, the groups are different in regard to scatter or spread. Group A shows

Table 4-1: Means of Two Distributions

Group A	Group B
5	9
4	2
5	7
5	2
5	2
4	9
6	2
5	5
6	3
5	9
$\Sigma X = 50$	$\Sigma X = 50$
$N = 10$	$N = 10$
$\overline{X} = 5$	$\overline{X} = 5$

small variability while B shows larger variability, even though both distributions have identical means and the same number of scores.

Even though Tom had found out that measures of central tendency were not the end-all in describing groups, he did not give up on statistical measures. He had a new problem now: he needed to find out how the amount of variation within a group could be indicated by a single value, just as the central tendency of the group was indicated by a single value. He needed a measure that would indicate whether the numbers in a distribution were spread apart or clustered together around the mean. Tom was now ready for Chapter 4 of this book.

The next section will discuss four measures of variability: the standard deviation, and variance, the quartile deviation, and the range. You will (1) learn how to

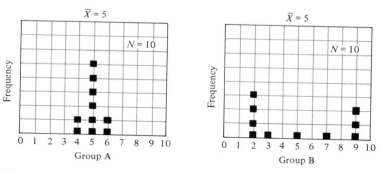

Figure 4-1: Two Distributions with the Same Mean

compute these measures of variability, (2) find out how to apply them, and (3) discover their advantages and disadvantages. You will also explore the standard deviation in greater depth. You will see how it is used in conjunction with the mean to determine different sections of the normal curve. Further, you will examine how standard scores shed light on the relationship of the standard deviation and the normal curve. You will learn what the standard error of the mean is and how to compute it.

The measures of variability tell you the extent to which scores vary about a measure of central tendency. Variance and the standard deviation are concerned with the extent to which scores deviate from the mean.

VARIANCE AND THE STANDARD DEVIATION

Variance is the mean of the squared deviations, often referred to as the *mean squared* (M.S.). A widely used measure in inferential statistics, it takes into account every score in a distribution. The variance is the extent to which the scores tend to cluster around or scatter away from the mean of the distribution. To find the extent to which each score deviates from the mean, you subtract the mean from each score $(X - \bar{X})$ and obtain a deviation score (x).

As an illustration, Nancy earned the following scores in a vocabulary test: 9, 8, 5, 8, 5. The mean for this distribution of scores is 7 $(35 \div 5)$. If you subtract the mean of 7 from each score, you obtain a deviation score (x). This subtraction is done in Table 4-2.

Table 4-2: Nancy's Scores

$X - \bar{X} = x$
$9 - 7 = 2$
$8 - 7 = 1$
$5 - 7 = -2$
$8 - 7 = 1$
$5 - 7 = -2$

As you can see, subtracting 7 from 9 gives a deviation score of 2, and subtracting 7 from 8 gives a deviation score of 1. Notice that a positive deviation score indicates the raw score is above the mean, and a negative deviation score indicates the raw score is below the mean. Also, when your deviation score has a value of 0, this indicates the raw score is at the mean. The "x" or deviation score gives you more information about an individual's standing in a distribution than the "X" raw scores did.

For example, Nancy's raw score of 9 really tells us little about Nancy, because we know nothing about the distribution. But if we report her "x" deviation from the mean as 2, we know that Nancy stands 2 points above the mean, whatever that is.

We now have the deviation of each raw score from the mean: 2, 1, -2, 1, -2. The idea is to add up these scores and divide by the number of scores in the distribution to get the average of the deviations. In other words, instead of getting a measure of central tendency of the raw scores, we are getting a measure of central tendency of the deviation of the scores from the mean. In short, we are finding the average of the deviations and using that as a measure of variation. It tells us how, on the average, the raw scores vary from the mean. An obstacle to this very good idea is the fact that if we add up the column of x, we always get zero.[1] One way to overcome this obstacle and pursue our idea is to square all the x's, as follows:

x	x^2
2	4
1	1
-2	4
1	1
-2	4

Now we add up the deviations squared (x^2), getting a value called the *sum of squares* ($\Sigma \, x^2$). Adding up $4 + 1 + 4 + 1 + 4$ gives us the sum of 14. Next we divide this sum of squares, $\Sigma \, x^2$, by the number of scores in our distribution. Dividing 14 by 5, we have 2.8. This 2.8 is the *variance* or the *average of the squared deviations*. The variance of 2.8 tells us that on the average the square of the deviation from the mean is 2.8. It is hard to give an intuitive meaning to variance; nonetheless, this statistic is quite useful.

When we square the deviation scores, we are changing the original units of measurement to square units of measurement. When we were dealing with vocabulary words, we squared Nancy's scores, which changed the original units of measurement, vocabulary words, to square units of measurement, squared vocabulary words. Therefore, we ended up with a variance of 2.8 squared vocabulary words, which in common-sense terms is ridiculous. When we use variance, our numbers are always in square units. In many situations it is desirable that the numbers describing the distribution be in the original units. Variance does not satisfy this requirement, but the standard deviation does.

[1] By definition the mean is the point at which the sum of the deviations is equal to zero. Then the sum of the deviations will always equal zero.

Standard deviation is defined as the square root of variance or the square root of the mean of the squared deviation scores. This is symbolized by Formula 4-1.

Formula 4-1   *Standard Deviation*

$$s = \sqrt{\frac{\Sigma (X - \bar{X})^2}{N}}$$

What we are doing is nothing more than taking the square root of the value found for variance. For example, to find the standard deviation of the previous example we take the square root of the variance, 2.8, which is 1.7, and this gives us the standard deviation for this group of scores.

Using Formula 4-1 is quite easy when the mean is a whole number. When it is not, the computations take considerably more time, and the formula ceases to be practical. For instance, if we were to subtract the mean of 7.86 from the scores 8.93, 9.93, 7.36, 10.54, and 3.44, we would have to be concerned about rounding errors, and the computations would take more time than subtracting the mean of 9 from 10, 9, 8, 7, and 3.

Fortunately, it is possible to compute the standard deviation directly from the raw scores without calculating each deviation. This mathematically equivalent formula—our operational formula— is given as Formula 4-2.

Formula 4-2   *Operational Formula for Standard Deviation*

$$s = \frac{1}{N} \sqrt{(N) \, \Sigma X^2 - (\Sigma X)^2}$$

The terms in this formula are explained briefly below:

Symbol	Meaning
ΣX	Find the sum of the scores
$(\Sigma X)^2$	Square the sum of the scores
ΣX^2	Square each score and then find the sum of the squares
N	The number of scores

PROCEDURE

Let's find the standard deviation by using this formula on the following example. In a clinic for autistic children two psychologists were recording the number of correct responses given by a sample of five children in a half-hour interval. The scores for these children were 2, 5, 4, 1, 3.[2] The mean for these scores was 3.0. Next the psychologists wanted to find the standard deviation for these ungrouped data. In order to do so, we are going to (1) set up a worksheet, (2) make substitutions, and (3) solve the formula. We may call this the ABC method.

Standard Deviation Worksheet

X	X^2
2	4
5	25
4	16
1	1
3	9
$\Sigma X = 15$	

C. $\Sigma X^2 = 55$

A. $(\Sigma X)^2 = 225$

B. $N = 5$

Directions for Setting Up the Worksheet

1. Write each score in any order in the column headed X.
2. Square each score and write it in the column headed X^2.
3. Add all the scores in the column headed X. Write their sum opposite the ΣX equal sign.
4. Square the sum found in step 3 and write it in box A.
5. Count the number of scores in the column headed X. Write this number in box B.
6. Add all the numbers in the column headed X^2. Write their sum in box C.

Substitutions

We are ready to make our substitutions using the numbers in boxes A, B, and C. These will be step-by-step substitutions in the standard deviation formula:

$$s = \frac{1}{N} \sqrt{(N) \Sigma X^2 - (\Sigma X)^2}$$

A. Substitute the number 225 in box A for $(\Sigma X)^2$

$$s = \frac{1}{N} \sqrt{(N) \Sigma X^2 - 225}$$

[2] For computational ease we are using an extremely small sample size.

B. Substitute the number 5 in box B for the N's

$$s = \tfrac{1}{5}\sqrt{(5)\ \Sigma\ X^2 - 225}$$

C. Substitute the number 55 in box C for $\Sigma\ X^2$

$$s = \tfrac{1}{5}\sqrt{(5)55 - 225}$$

Solving the Formula

Now we can solve the formula $s = \tfrac{1}{5}\sqrt{(5)55 - 225}$, performing the following computations:

A. Multiply 5 times 55 (275)

$$s = \tfrac{1}{5}\sqrt{275 - 225}$$

B. Subtract 225 from 275 (50)

$$s = \tfrac{1}{5}\sqrt{50}$$

C. Find the square root of 50 (7.07)

$$s = \tfrac{1}{5}(7.07)$$

D. Find one-fifth of 7.07 by dividing 7.07 by 5 (1.41) to obtain the standard deviation

$$s = 1.41$$

Now prove to yourself how easy it is to find a standard deviation (the formula that causes students to pull out their hair). The practice problem concerns a business student, Sol Brown, who had to do a quick market survey for a class. He did an analysis on the movie-going habits of a sample of male students living in the college dorms, finding out the number of movies per month these seven men attended: 6, 4, 6, 3, 1, 3, 2. He found the mean was 3.57, and he wanted to know how much the students varied from the mean. To help Sol out, calculate the standard deviation for him.

Problem   Using Sol's information about the number of times each student attended movies, find the standard deviation by completing the worksheet.

Sol's Worksheet

X	X²

$\Sigma X = \overline{}$

A. $(\Sigma X)^2 =$

B. $N =$

C. $\Sigma X^2 = \overline{}$

Answer

X	X²
6	36
4	16
6	36
3	9
1	1
3	9
2	4

$\Sigma X = 25$

C. $\Sigma X^2 = 111$

A. $(\Sigma X)^2 = 625$

B. $N = 7$

$$s = \frac{1}{N} \sqrt{(N) \, \Sigma X^2 - (\Sigma X)^2}$$

$$s = \frac{1}{7} \sqrt{(7) 111 - 625}$$

$$s = 1.76$$

Quick Check on Your Work

Before you compute the standard deviation, there is a quick way you can approximate it if your distribution is normal. Find the range of your sample; that is, subtract the smallest number from the largest number. Next, divide the range by 6 if your sample size is 500 or more, by 5 if it is less than 500, or by 3 if it is less than 50.[3] For example, let's say you have a distribution of 600 scores, of which the highest is 80 and the lowest is 40. Your range is 40 (80 − 40 = 40). Since you have 600 scores in your distribution, you divide 40 by 6 and get an approximate standard deviation of 6.7. Now if you compute the standard deviation and obtain 50, you know something is wrong with your work.

Additional Information about the Standard Deviation

If you have two groups with the same means, their composition may be entirely different, depending on their standard deviations. For example, if the standard deviation is small for one group, the scores will be clustered around the mean; it is a more homogeneous group. If the standard deviation is relatively large for the other group, the scores will be more scattered around the mean; it is a more heterogeneous group. We can quickly see this point in terms of the two groups Tom was concerned about at the beginning of the chapter. The mean and standard deviation for Groups A and B are shown in Table 4-3.

Table 4-3: Mean and Standard Deviation for Two Groups

Group A	Group B
5	9
4	2
5	7
5	2
5	2
4	9
6	2
5	5
6	3
5	9
$\Sigma X = 50$	$\Sigma X = 50$
$\overline{X} = 5$	$\overline{X} = 5$
$s = .6$	$s = 3.0$

Notice that the groups have the same means but different standard deviations. Group A's standard deviation is .6 and Group B's is 3.0—five times as large. Group

[3] For an approximate normal distribution it can be shown that the standard deviation should be about one-sixth of the range. When you have 50 or 100 scores, the standard deviation should be about one-fourth or one-fifth of the range, and when the sample size is less than 50, the standard deviation will be roughly one-third of the range.

A with its small standard deviation of .6 has scores very close to the mean, while Group B with its relatively large standard deviation of 3.0 has scores that are more scattered around the mean. (Refer back to Figure 4-1 for a graphic representation.) However, we are still in the dark about the meaning of the magnitude of these standard deviations. Suppose the values for the standard deviations had been 2 for Group A and 10 for Group B; you would again have said the value for Group B's standard deviation was five times greater than for Group A's. Later, we shall give meaning to the size of the standard deviation for a set of data from a normal population. But first let us take a look at another way of calculating the standard deviation.

STANDARD DEVIATION FOR GROUPED DATA

The procedure used for finding a standard deviation from grouped data is basically the same as for ungrouped data. The real difference is that you are working with midpoints and frequencies. The midpoint of the interval, symbolized as X, represents the raw scores found in that interval. The frequency, f, for each interval tells you how many raw scores are in that interval. The formula for the standard deviation for grouped data follows.

Formula 4-3   *Standard Deviation for Grouped Data*

$$s = \frac{1}{N} \sqrt{(N) \, \Sigma \, fX^2 - (\Sigma \, fX)^2}$$

Since Formula 4-3 requires the use of larger numbers, the problems we will look at have been simplified, so that you will not become bogged down with the numbers and lose sight of the procedure. Ordinarily a frequency distribution has at least ten intervals, but some of the problems you will be solving will have fewer.

Table 4-4: Frequency Distribution of Test Scores for a Special Education Class

Score interval	f
13–15	1
10–12	0
7–9	4
4–6	2
1–3	1

Our first problem concerns eight students from a special education class, who were given a test in sign language. Their scores are recorded in Table 4-4. These scores gave a mean of 7.25. What is their standard deviation? Use the formula for grouped data:

$$\frac{1}{N} \sqrt{(N) \, \Sigma \, fX^2 - (\Sigma \, fX)^2}$$

The terms in this formula are explained below.

Symbol	Meaning
Σ	Sum of
f	Number of scores in the interval
X	Midpoint score for the interval
fX	Frequency times the midpoint
N	Sum of the frequencies

PROCEDURE

Again we proceed with the ABC method and set up a worksheet, make substitutions, and solve the formula.

The Standard Deviation Worksheet for Grouped Data

PART I

Score interval	f	X	fX
13–15	1	14	14
10–12	0	11	0
7–9	4	8	32
4–6	2	5	10
1–3	1	2	2
			$\Sigma \, fX = 58$

A. $N = 8$ B. $(\Sigma \, fX)^2 = 3364$

PART II

f	X^2	fX^2
1	196	196
0	121	0
4	64	256
2	25	50
1	4	4

C. $\Sigma \, fX^2 = 506$

Setting Up the Worksheet

These directions have two parts. Be sure to work through Part I before proceeding to Part II.

PART I

1. Set up your frequency distribution for the data you are going to use.
2. Add all the scores in the column headed f. Write their sum in box A opposite $N = $ _____.
3. Find the midpoint of each interval and put this number in the column headed X.
4. Form your fX column: multiply the numbers found in the frequency (f) column by the corresponding numbers found in the midpoint (X) column.
5. Add all the numbers in the column headed fX. Write their sum opposite the $\Sigma\ fX = $ _____.
6. Square the sum you found in step 5 and write it in box B opposite $(\Sigma\ fX)^2 = $ _____.

PART II

7. Recopy your frequency column.
8. Square each midpoint (X) and write it in the same order in the column headed X^2.
9. Form your fX^2 column. Multiply the numbers found in the frequency (f) column by the corresponding numbers found in the midpoint-squared (X^2) column.
10. Add all the numbers in the column headed fX^2. Write their sum in box C opposite $\Sigma\ fX^2 = $ _____.

Substitutions

We are ready to make our substitutions, using the numbers in boxes A, B, and C. Again, these will be step-by-step substitutions in the formula:

$$s = 1/N\sqrt{(N)\ \Sigma\ fX^2 - (\Sigma\ fX)^2}$$

A. Substitute the number (8) in box A for N

$$s = \tfrac{1}{8}\sqrt{(8)\ \Sigma\ fX^2 - (\Sigma\ fX)^2}$$

B. Substitute the number (3364) in box B for $(\Sigma\ fX)^2$

$$s = \tfrac{1}{8}\sqrt{(8)\ \Sigma\ fX^2 - 3364}$$

C. Substitute the number (506) in box C for $\Sigma\ fX^2$

$$s = \tfrac{1}{8}\sqrt{(8)\ 506 - 3364}$$

Solving the Formula

Now we can solve the formula $S = \frac{1}{8}\sqrt{(8)\ 506 - 3364}$ with the following computations:

A. Multiply 8 times 506 (4048)

$$s = \frac{1}{8}\sqrt{4048 - 3364}$$

B. Subtract 3364 from 4048 (684)

$$s = \frac{1}{8}\sqrt{684}$$

C. Find the square root of 684 (26.15)

$$s = \frac{1}{8}\ (26.15)$$

D. Find one-eighth of 26.15 by dividing 26.15 by 8 (3.27). This is the standard deviation

$$s = 3.27$$

Now, let's see whether you can do a standard deviation formula for grouped data by yourself. It is no more complicated than the last problem you did. A little practice now should make you more secure. It is best not to defer this practice till the end of the chapter; by that time too many distractions may have intervened.

Problem

Nancy Bee, a flight instructor, gave a test to her students. She figured out the mean but did not have time to figure out the standard deviation. The test scores were set up in a frequency distribution. Fill in the incomplete worksheet below and find the standard deviation.

Worksheet

PART I

Score interval	f	X	fX
16–18	1		
13–15	1		
10–12	4		
7–9	2		
4–6	1		
	___	___	$\Sigma\ fX =$ ___
	A. $N =$		B. $(\Sigma\ fx)^2 =$

PART II

f	X^2	fX^2
—	—	
		C. $\Sigma fX^2 =$

Answer

PART I

f	X	fX
1	17	17
1	14	14
4	11	44
2	8	16
1	5	5
		$\Sigma fX = 96$

A. $N = 9$ B. $(\Sigma fX)^2 = 9216$

PART II

f	X^2	fX^2
1	289	289
1	196	196
4	121	484
2	64	128
1	25	25
		C. $\Sigma fX^2 = 1122$

$$s = \frac{1}{N}\sqrt{(N)\ \Sigma fX^2 - (\Sigma fX)^2}$$

$$s = \frac{1}{9}\sqrt{(9)1122 - 9216}$$

$$s = 3.30$$

STANDARD DEVIATION AND NORMAL CURVE

The *normal curve* gets a lot of attention in a school setting because of its tie-in with grades. Professors often give grades according to a person's standing on the normal curve—also referred to as the bell-shaped curve, the Gaussian curve, the DeMoivre's curve, or the curve of error. (In addition, some students have given it other, more colorful names.) The normal curve looks like Figure 4-2.

Figure 4-2: The Normal Curve

Measurements such as height, weight, and IQ aptitude scores are usually distributed in the population in such a way that, when drawn graphically, they look like this curve. In fact, most of the data in the social sciences approximate this curve. Scores on various tests are typically concentrated in the middle with fewer at the ends. For example, if this curve represented variation in the weights of American women, you would find the greatest number of women to be concentrated around the mean weight of 125 lb, which would be in the middle of the curve. The fewest women would be found around the very low weight of 85 lb and around the very high weight of 200 lb.

A more complete picture of the normal curve is given in Figure 4-3. The curve here has been divided into sections. The line that divides it into two equal parts is labeled $\overline{X}$ (the mean). The lines labeled $\overline{X} + 1s$, $\overline{X} + 2s$, $\overline{X} - 1s$, $\overline{X} - 2s$, and so on represent standard deviation units; they tell you how many units you are away from the mean. To see how this works, suppose you have calculated the mean of a distribution of scores to be 86 and, using the formula you have just learned, you calculate the standard deviation to be 14. If you apply these numbers to the curve, you will place the raw score of 86 at the point of the mean. Adding a standard devi-

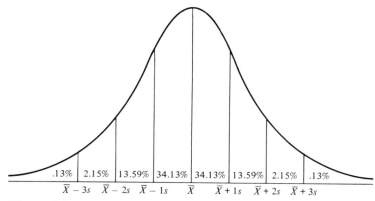

.13% | 2.15% | 13.59% | 34.13% | 34.13% | 13.59% | 2.15% | .13%

$\overline{X} - 3s$ $\overline{X} - 2s$ $\overline{X} - 1s$ $\overline{X}$ $\overline{X} + 1s$ $\overline{X} + 2s$ $\overline{X} + 3s$

Figure 4-3: The Normal Curve Subdivided

ation unit of 14 to the mean ($86 + 14 = 100$) shows you that the raw score of 100 is at the point of $\overline{X} + 1s$ (or one standard deviation above the mean). Subtracting a standard deviation unit of 14 from the mean tells you that the raw score of 72 is at the point of $\overline{X} - 1s$ (or one standard deviation below the mean). Accordingly, if you add another standard deviation unit of 14 to the raw score of 100, you will find that a raw score of 114 falls at the point of $\overline{X} + 2s$, and if you add another standard deviation unit of 14 to that raw score of 114 you will find that a raw score of 128 falls at the point of $\overline{X} + 3s$. Likewise, subtracting a standard deviation unit of 14 from the raw score of 72 tells you that a raw score of 58 falls at $\overline{X} - 2s$, and subtracting still another standard deviation unit from the score tells you that a raw score of 44 falls at the point of $\overline{X} - 3s$. To sum up: if, in this distribution of scores that has a mean of 86 and a standard deviation of 14, Susan has a score of 114, you know that Susan is two standard deviations above the mean. If Sharon has a score of 72, you know that she is one standard deviation below the mean. Figure 4-4 illustrates this example.

Later we shall see how all this is applied. Before we do, however, look once again at Figure 4-4. Notice in the area under the normal curve that each section has numbers, such as .13, 2.15, 13.59. These numbers are percentages; they tell you the percentage of cases that fall in a particular section. For example, if you add all the numbers above the mean ($.13 + 2.15 + 13.59 + 34.13$), the sum is 50. This means that 50% of the total number of cases or scores are above the mean. If you add all the numbers below the mean, the answer again is 50; 50% of the total number of

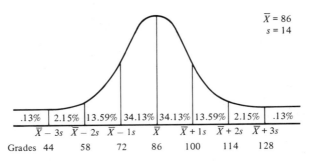

Figure 4-4: Standard Deviations Applied to a
Distribution of Scores

cases or scores in the distribution fall below the mean. The total percentage adds up, of course, to 100%.

If, now, you add the percentages of cases or scores between +1s and −1s (34.13 + 34.13), you will find that 68.26% or approximately 68% of the scores fall in this section. For instance, if you had 3000 scores in your distribution, you would expect roughly 68% of them—2040—to fall between −1s and 1s. If you had 5000 scores in a distribution, approximately 68% of them—3400—would fall between −1s and 1s.

Relating this to what we said about raw scores and using the same example ($\overline{X} = 86; s = 14; N = 3000$), we find that roughly 68% of the population taking this test (that is, 2040 persons) will have raw scores between 72 (−1s) and 100 (1s).

One final and very important note. The percentages in the various sections always remain the same. This is what makes the normal curve so useful in statistical analysis. What will change, depending upon what is being measured and how it is being measured, are the numerical values of the raw scores along the baseline. Obviously, not all distributions will have a mean of 86 and a standard deviation of 14. But, regardless of what the mean and standard deviation of a distribution are, the percentage of scores falling between the mean and 1s is always 34.13. The same holds true of all the other sections of the curve.

Study the normal curve in Figure 4-3 and then see if you can answer the following questions.

Questions   1. If there were roughly 6000 scores from a normal population, how many scores fall between +1 standard deviation above the mean and −1 standard deviation below the mean?

2. If your raw score on a test falls at the point 1*s* above the mean, what is the percentage of cases underneath you?
3. If your raw score falls at the point 3*s* above the mean, what is the percentage of cases underneath you?
4. If your raw score falls at the point $\overline{X} - 2s$, what is the percentage of cases underneath you?
5. If there are roughly 4000 scores from a normal population of scores, how many scores fall between +2 S.D. above the mean and −2 S.D. below the mean?

Answers

To find the answers to questions 2 through 4 simply add the area under the curve.
1. 4095.6 scores (68.26 × 6000)
2. 84.13% (50% + 34.13)
3. 99.87% (50% = 34.13 + 13.59 + 2.15)
4. 2.28% (.13 + 2.15). You need to take the exam when you are feeling better.
5. 3817.60 (95.44 × 4000)

You now are able to see clearly that scoring +3 S.D. above the mean is wonderful and that scoring −2 S.D. below the mean is something you want to avoid.

z SCORES

Now that you are fairly comfortable with the normal curve, let's investigate some useful scores based upon it: z scores or standard scores. We can readily see their usefulness in terms of an example.

Tom, a college student, took three examinations one day. A week later he found out that his raw scores were: chemistry, 85; psychology, 70; and sociology, 86. Now suppose we ask what seems to be a ridiculous question: On which exam did Tom do best and on which did he do worst? With the raw scores before us, the answer seems obvious. But we are looking only at the absolute value of the raw scores; we are not taking into consideration that, unless the means and standard deviations of the distributions of scores of the three examinations are the same, Tom's place in each distribution may be different.

To see what this means, suppose you calculated the mean and standard deviation of the distribution of scores for each of the three exams and summarized the results, together with Tom's scores, as in Table 4-5. As you can see, the mean and standard deviation are different for each raw score. How, then, can you compare these raw scores when the distributions are different? This is like asking how you can compare someone 54 inches tall with someone 6 feet tall. In order to compare these measure-

Table 4-5: Tom's Scores

Subject	X	$\overline{X}$	s
Chemistry	85	75	5
Psychology	70	60	4
Sociology	86	83	6

ments, you must convert them to the same scale, which you can do by converting 6 feet to 72 inches. Now you can compare 72 inches with 54 inches and say that the 72-inch person is 25% taller than the 54-inch person ($54/72 = 3/4 = 75\%$).

Looking at Tom's original raw scores, you encounter a similar problem. In order to compare these raw scores you must convert them to the same scale. In this case you transform the raw scores to z scores. The z scores can be compared because they have equal units of measurement. The z score tells you how far above or below the mean an individual stands in a normal distribution; it shows you immediately what percentage of the group he or she surpasses. When a score has been converted to a z score, the mean will be 0 and the standard deviation 1, as illustrated in Figure 4-5.

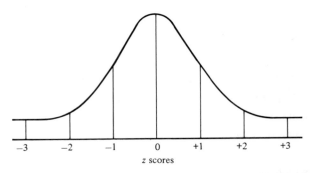

z scores

Figure 4-5: Mean and Standard Deviation of z Scores

A z score is defined as the deviation of the raw score from the mean divided by the standard deviation. The formula for the z score is:

Formula 4-4   *z-Score Formula*

$$z = \frac{X - \overline{X}}{s}$$

The meanings of the symbols are as follows:

Symbol	Meaning
X	Raw score
$\bar{X}$	Mean
s	Standard deviation

Returning to our original problem, let us convert Tom's raw scores to z scores in order to compare them. We begin by taking the formula $z = (X - \bar{X})/s$ and using it for the chemistry score. The mean of 75 is subtracted from the score of 85, which gives 10. The 10 is then divided by the standard deviation of 5, which gives a z of 2.0. Now let's look at the position of this value on a normal curve. In Figure 4-6 the chemistry score is represented by a dot. As you can see, a z of $+2.0$ is two standard deviations above the mean.

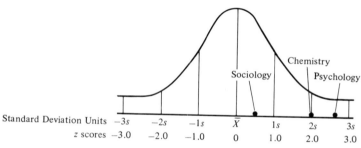

Figure 4-6: Tom's z Scores

We convert the psychology score to a z score using the same formula. The work is shown below.

$$z = \frac{X - \bar{X}}{s}$$

$$z = \frac{70 - 60}{4}$$

$$z = \frac{10}{4}$$

$$z = +2.5$$

In this case we have a z score that is $+2.5$ standard deviations above the mean. This z score is represented by a dot in Figure 4-6.

Finally, using the same formula, we convert the sociology score of 86 to a z score. The work is shown below.

$$z = \frac{X - \bar{X}}{s} = \frac{86 - 83}{6} = \frac{3}{6} = .5$$

In this case a z of .5 is one-half standard deviation above the mean. This is represented by a dot in Figure 4-6.

Looking at our results, we find that, as far as relative position in the three distributions is concerned, Tom actually performed better on the psychology examination (2.5 standard deviation units above the mean) than on the other two exams. Using the percentages of the normal curve that you learned previously, you can see that with his raw score of 70, Tom surpassed more than 99.38% of the students taking the psychology exam. In chemistry he surpassed 97.72% of the other students, and in sociology he surpassed only 69.15% of the students taking that test[4]— even though his raw score for sociology, 86, was higher than the 85 in chemistry and the 70 in psychology.

So you have learned that raw scores by themselves do not give a true picture of an individual's standing in a group as compared to other members of the group or as compared to his or her standing in other groups; therein rests the value of the z score. A raw score of 42 can be slightly above, far above, somewhat below, or far below the mean of a distribution, depending upon what the mean and the standard deviation of that distribution happen to be. But a particular z is always found at the same point in any distribution, regardless of the numerical value of the mean and standard deviation. Once you have converted your raw scores to z scores, you know how far above or below the mean an individual stands in a distribution; you can tell immediately what percentage of the group the individual surpasses.

Use of z Scores in Testing

Because some people are frightened at working with negative or decimal numbers, they often transform the z score into another type of standard score, such as those listed in Figure 4-7. The T scores used for Armed Forces testing have a mean of 50 and standard deviation of 10. The College Entrance Examination Board and the Graduate Record Exam use a mean of 500 and standard deviation of

[4] The exact percentages of the area found below the z scores can be figured from Table C. For the purposes of this text it is enough to realize that a person with a z of 2.5 has surpassed 97.72% of the population and that a person with a z of .5 has not surpassed 84% of the population.

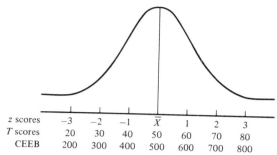

z scores   −3   −2   −1 $\bar{X}$ 1   2   3
T scores   20   30   40   50   60   70   80
CEEB   200   300   400   500   600   700   800

Figure 4-7: Standard Scores

100. However, these scores are directly related to the z score. All of them tell you how far any score deviates from the mean. In order to interpret the location of these scores, you use the z-score formula. If, for example, you wish to know how many standard deviations from the mean a score of 550 is on the College Entrance Examination Board, you apply the z formula:

$$z = \frac{X - \bar{X}}{s}, \qquad \frac{550 - 500}{100}, \qquad z = .5$$

Now you know that the score 550 is one-half the standard deviation from the mean.

More can be said about z scores, but it would take us beyond the purpose of this discussion. The emphasis here has been on the application of the standard deviation to the normal curve. Now, let us use the standard deviation to compute the standard error of the mean and learn what this measure is.

STANDARD ERROR OF THE MEAN

The *standard error of the mean* (S.E.M.) is an estimate of how much the sample mean would be expected to deviate from the population mean. When you draw random samples from a sampling distribution, you can expect the means of these samples to vary from one another. For instance, if you give a math test to two randomly drawn samples of 30 college freshmen at Cal College, their means will almost certainly be different. One sample mean might be 94 while the other might be 92. This difference of two points is simply an error in our sampling. Sampling errors are the results of dealing with the sample and not the whole population. If you continue to draw samples of the same size from the same population and compute the mean and standard deviation for, say, 1000 samples, the means will form a sampling distribution, the mean of which provides a good estimate of the population mean. The variability among these sample means is described as the standard error of the mean.

If a population is given and we take a random sample out of it and if N, the sample size, is large enough (which for most samples means larger than 30), the sampling distribution of means is very close to a normal distribution. The larger N is made, the closer the sampling distribution comes to a normal distribution. This procedure of drawing samples is a painstaking method for finding the standard error of the mean. Fortunately, mathematicians have a formula whereby the standard error of the mean can be estimated from one sample (Formula 4-5):

Formula 4-5   *Standard Error of the Mean*

$$\text{S.E.M.} = \frac{s}{\sqrt{N}}$$

The meanings of the terms are as follows:

Symbol	Meaning
s	Standard deviation
N	Number of scores in each sample

This formula is used only when the sampling distribution is normal or for a Student t-distribution. If you are working with a chi-square distribution, knowing the standard error of the mean is not relevant. The S.E.M. is important, then, for some but not all sampling distributions.

Problem   Find the standard error of the mean for a sample of 25 college freshmen's psychology test scores. The mean for this sample is 90 and the standard deviation is 5.

Answer $\text{S.E.M.} = s/\sqrt{N}$. The standard deviation is 5 and the number of scores is 25, so $\text{S.E.M.} = 5/\sqrt{25} = 5/5 = 1$.

You have found that the standard error of the mean is 1. How important is this fact? What understanding does it give you? Looking at this information on a normal curve, you can find out more about your sample mean. Let's examine Figure 4-8 together.

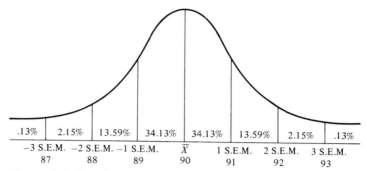

| .13% | 2.15% | 13.59% | 34.13% | 34.13% | 13.59% | 2.15% | .13% |

−3 S.E.M. −2 S.E.M. −1 S.E.M. $\overline{X}$ 1 S.E.M. 2 S.E.M. 3 S.E.M.
  87   88   89   90   91   92   93

Figure 4-8: Standard Error of the Mean on a Normal Curve

The standard error of the mean is thought of as a standard deviation of sample means. Since the mean is equal to 90, we place 90 below the $\overline{X}$ in the drawing. Adding to the mean a standard error of the mean of 1 shows you that the score of 91 is at the point of 1 S.E.M. (or one standard error of the mean above the mean). Subtracting from the mean a standard error of the mean of 1 tells you that the score of 89 is at the point of −1 S.E.M. (one standard error of the mean below the mean). Accordingly, if you add to the score of 91 another standard error of the mean of 1, you find that the score of 92 falls at the point of 2 S.E.M., and if you add to that score of 92 another standard error of the mean of 1, you find that a score of 93 falls at the point of 3 S.E.M. Likewise, subtracting from the score of 89 a standard error of the mean of 1 tells you that the score of 88 falls at −2 S.E.M., and subtracting still another standard error of the mean tells you that 87 falls at −3 S.E.M. Placing these values on the curve now tells you the probability of selecting any particular mean value. Remember, you know the percentages of the scores that fall in the different sections of the normal curve. For example, the probability of obtaining a sample with a mean value of 91 is 84.13% (50 + 34.13). The probability of obtaining a sample mean between 89 and 91 is 68.13%. (Review the previous section.)

Since the standard deviation is a very important measure of variability, let's make some further observations about it.

COMMENTS ON THE STANDARD DEVIATION

The standard deviation (s) is the most widely used measure of variability in research. It takes into account the value of every score in the distribution. It is used in advanced statistical computations.

The standard deviation is the most stable measure of variability from sample to sample. To illustrate this point, take two or three fairly large random samples from the same population and compute the standard deviation for each one. The values you obtain will vary less from sample to sample than would any other measure of variability.

In certain situations it is not desirable to use the standard deviation. For example, it cannot be calculated for an open-ended frequency distribution, because you cannot find the midpoint of the open-ended interval. (Refer to Chapter 3 for discussion of open-ended distributions.)

The standard deviation is influenced by extreme scores. In such situations it is desirable to use the quartile deviation.

QUARTILE DEVIATION

The *quartile deviation* (Q), also referred to as the *semi-interquartile range,* is used along with the median at the ordinal level of measurement. The population is divided into four equal subgroups by three quartiles. The first quartile (Q_1) is the point below which 25% of the cases fall and the point above which 75% of the cases fall. The second quartile (Q_2) is the point below which 50% of the cases fall and above which 50% of the cases fall. Think, now: have you heard those words before? Yes—in Chapter 3 in our discussion of the median. Q_2 is the median. Finally, the third quartile (Q_3) is the point below which 75% of the cases fall and above which 25% of the cases fall.

The quartile deviation is defined as one-half the distance between Q_3 and Q_1. Formula 4-6 expresses this definition.

Formula 4-6   *Quartile Deviation*

$$Q = \frac{Q_3 - Q_1}{2}$$

PROCEDURE

The use of this formula with ungrouped data is relatively easy. Let us do this for Manuel, who is interested in the number of blue jeans his college chums have. He finds that some of his friends have only two pairs of blue jeans, which they wear to death, while others have as many as eight pairs. The number of blue jeans his friends have certainly varies. He finds that the median for this distribution is 5.5. He now wants to know what the quartile deviation is. In order to find Q, follow the directions below. The scores are arranged in order and displayed in the left-hand column.

Directions for Finding Q (Ungrouped Data)

Number of blue jeans

8
7
—————— Q_3
6
6
5
3
—————— Q_1
2
1

1. Find Q_3. You find 3/4 of 8 scores, which equals 6. Then count to find the point where 6 scores fall below and 2 scores fall above. You count up 6 scores from the bottom and see that the point Q_3 lies between the scores of 6 and 7; therefore, Q_3 equals 6.5.[5]
2. Find Q_1. You find 1/4 of 8 scores, which equals 2. Then count to find the point where 2 scores fall below and 6 scores fall above. In counting, you see that the point Q_1 lies between scores 2 and 3; therefore, Q_1 equals 2.5.
3. Finally, you substitute the values you found in steps 1 and 2 in the formula. $(Q_3 - Q_1)/2$ becomes $(6.5 - 2.5)/2$.

$$Q = \frac{6.5 - 2.5}{2}$$

A. Subtract 2.5 from 6.5 and get 4

$$Q = \frac{4}{2}$$

B. Divide 4 by 2 and get 2

$$Q = 2$$

C. The quartile deviation is 2

The number of blue jeans varies on the average by 2 from the median.

Finding Q for Grouped Data

The formula for grouped data is the same as for ungrouped: $(Q_3 - Q_1)/2$. However, to find Q_3 and Q_1 you must use a different procedure. This procedure is almost identical to the one used for the median, except that instead of finding 1/2 of N, you are finding 3/4 of N (Q_3) and 1/4 of N (Q_1).

In finding the quartile deviation for grouped data you first find Q_3 by using Formula 4-7. Second, you find Q_1, using Formula 4-8.

[5] If Q_3 fell between scores 6 and 8, you would take the average of these two scores, and Q_3 would be 7.

Formula 4-7	Q_3 Formula
	$$Q_3 = LL + \frac{(\frac{3}{4}N - cf)}{fw} i$$

Formula 4-8	Q_1 Formula
	$$Q_1 = LL + \frac{(\frac{1}{4}N - cf)}{fw} i$$

Finally, you take the values you have found and substitute them in Formula 4-6, $(Q_3 - Q_1)/2$, and solve. The symbols for the formulas are explained below:

Symbol	Meaning
LL	Lower real limit of the interval that contains $\frac{3}{4}N$ or $\frac{1}{4}N$
$\frac{1}{4}N$	One-fourth the number of scores
$\frac{3}{4}N$	Three-fourths the number of scores
cf	Cumulative frequencies are the number of scores up to the interval containing the quartile
i	Interval size
fw	Frequency of scores within the interval containing the quartile

Situation

Let's find the quartile deviation for a sample problem. A member of the finance committee of a small college wanted to justify the expenditure of money for a new library facility. He surveyed a group of 28 students studying for a B.A. degree and found out how many hours they used the library during a week. From these data he set up the frequency distribution shown in Table 4-6.

The median of this frequency table was found to be 19.9. He next wanted to find out the quartile deviation. Follow the directions for finding Q_3, then Q_1, and finally Q.

PROCEDURE

Directions for Finding Q_3 (Grouped Data)

$N = \underline{28}$
$\frac{3}{4}N = \underline{21}$

1. Find N. Add all the numbers in the column headed f. Write this number (28) in the blank for N.
2. Find $\frac{3}{4}N$. Multiply $\frac{3}{4} \times 28$. Replace $\frac{3}{4}N$ with 21.
3. Find cf. Again, starting at the bottom number in the column headed f, add the numbers until you come as close as possible

Table 4-6: Frequency Distribution: Number of Hours Students Use the Library

Score interval	f
30–32	1
27–29	0
24–26	2
21–23	10
18–20	5
15–17	1
12–14	1
9–11	5
6–8	2
3–5	1
	$N = 28$

$cf = \underline{15}$

to $\frac{3}{4}N$ (that is, to 21) without exceeding it. Write this sum for cf, which is 15 $(1 + 2 + 5 + 1 + 1 + 5 = 15)$.[6]

4. Find fw. Still in the column headed f, the number following the last number used to complete your sum from step 3 is your fw number. Write 10 in the blank.

$fw = \underline{10}$

5. Find LL. Take the lower real limit of the interval on the same line where your fw number is located. Write 20.5 for LL (see p. 46).

$LL = \underline{20.5}$

6. Determine i. Determine the size of the interval. Write 3 in the blank for i (see pp. 46–47).

$i = \underline{3}$

Substitutions for Q_3

Make the appropriate substitutions by replacing each step with its corresponding number.

A. $Q_3 = LL + \left(\dfrac{\frac{3}{4}N - cf}{fw} \right) \times i =$

B. $Q_3 = \text{step 5} + \left(\dfrac{\text{step 2} - \text{step 3}}{\text{step 4}} \right) \times \text{step 6}$

C. $Q_3 = 20.5 + \left(\dfrac{21 - 15}{10} \right) \times 3$

[6] Traditionally the cf column is formed separately. If it is easier for you to do so, by all means set up a separate column and call it cf.

Solving the Formula for Q_3

$$Q_3 = 20.5 + \left(\frac{21 - 15}{10}\right) \times 3$$

A. Subtract 15 from 21 (6)

$$Q_3 = 20.5 + \frac{6}{10} \times 3$$

B. Multiply $\frac{6}{10}$ by 3 $\left(\frac{18}{10}\right)$

$$Q_3 = 20.5 + \frac{18}{10}$$

C. Divide 18 by 10 (1.8)

$$Q_3 = 20.5 + 1.8$$

D. Add $20.5 + 1.8$ (22.3) and enclose Q_3 in a box

$$\boxed{Q_3 = 22.3}$$

Directions for Finding Q_1 (Grouped Data)

$N = \underline{28}$
$\tfrac{1}{4}N = \underline{7}$

1. Find N. Write it in the blank.
2. Find $\tfrac{1}{4}N$. Multiply $\tfrac{1}{4} \times 28$. Replace $\tfrac{1}{4}N$ with 7.
3. Find cf. Starting at the bottom number in the column headed f, add the numbers until you come as close as possible to $\tfrac{1}{4}N$ (that is, to 7) without exceeding it. In the blank for cf write

$cf = \underline{3}$

   this sum, which is 3 $(1 + 2 = 3)$.
4. Find fw. Still in the column headed f, the number following the last number used to complete your sum from step 3 is

$fw = \underline{5}$

   your fw number. Write 5 in the fw blank.
5. Find LL. Take the lower limit of the interval on the same line

$LL = \underline{8.5}$
$i = \underline{3}$

   where your fw number is located. Write 8.5 for LL.
6. Determine i. Determine the size of the interval. Write 3 in the blank for i.

Substitutions for Q_1

Make the appropriate substitutions by replacing each step with its corresponding number.

A. $Q = LL + \left(\dfrac{\tfrac{1}{4}N - cf}{fw}\right) \times i =$

B. Step 5 $+ \left(\dfrac{\text{step 2} - \text{step 3}}{\text{step 4}}\right) \times \text{step 6}$

C. $Q_1 = 8.5 + \left(\dfrac{7-3}{5}\right) \times 3$

Solving the Formula for Q_1

$$Q_1 = 8.5 + \left(\dfrac{7-3}{5}\right) \times 3$$

A. Subtract 3 from 7 (4)

$$Q_1 = 8.5 + \dfrac{4}{5} \times 3$$

B. Multiply 4/5 times 3 (12/5)

$$Q_1 = 8.5 + \dfrac{12}{5}$$

C. Divide 12 by 5 (2.4)

$$Q_1 = 8.5 + 2.4$$

D. Add 8.5 + 2.4 (10.9) and enclose Q_1 in a box

$$\boxed{Q_1 = 10.9}$$

Finding Q

SUBSTITUTING IN THE FORMULA FOR Q

A. $\dfrac{Q_3 - Q_1}{2} =$

B. $\dfrac{\text{step D }(Q_3) - \text{step D }(Q_1)}{2} =$

SOLVING THE FORMULA FOR Q

$$\dfrac{22.3 - 10.9}{2}$$

A. Subtract 10.9 from 22.3 (11.4)

$$\dfrac{11.4}{2}$$

B. Divide 11.4 by 2 (5.7) to obtain the quartile deviation

$$Q = 5.7$$

With help, you have found Q to be 5.7. Now, let's see if you can find a quartile deviation on your own.

Problem   Find Q, using the following frequency distribution.

Score interval	f
85–89	10
80–84	2
75–79	2
70–74	2
65–69	4
60–64	9
55–59	2
50–54	1

$$N =$$

Answer $$Q = \frac{Q_3 - Q_1}{2} = \frac{85.5 - 62.28}{2} = 11.61$$

$Q_3 = 85.5$		$Q_1 = 62.28$	
$\frac{3}{4}N$	24	$\frac{1}{4}N$	8
cf	22	cf	3
fw	10	fw	9
LL	84.5	LL	59.5
i	5	i	5

Comments on the Quartile Deviation

The quartile deviation is not as influenced as other measures of variability by extreme scores, because it is based on the spread of scores in the center. If the scores are closely concentrated around the median, you will notice that the value for Q is smaller than if the spread of scores is greater around the median. Unlike the standard deviation, the quartile deviation does not take into consideration the value of each score in the distribution. The quartile deviation is not as stable as the standard deviation from sample to sample, nor can it be used in more advanced statistical computations like the standard deviation. The quartile deviation is used with ordinal data. It can be used in open type of frequency distribution—for example, where the top interval is "25,000 or over"—whereas the standard deviation cannot be used in this type of distribution. The quartile deviation as a measure of variability is used in conjunction with the median.

RANGE

The final measure of variability to be covered in this chapter is the *range*, defined as the distance between the lowest and the highest score in a distribution. The formula is:

Formula 4-9 *Range Formula*

$$\text{Range} = X_H - X_L$$

To find the range you subtract the lowest score in the distribution from the highest score. For example, for the following distribution of numbers, 9, 4, 2, 3, 3, 3, 2, 2, 2, 2, you would subtract the lowest score 2 (X_L) from the highest score 9 (X_H); the range equals 7.[7] The range is used quite often in meterology and for quality control in industry, because it is so easy to compute. It is certainly easier to find the largest score and the smallest and subtract them than to find the standard deviation. However, the range does have certain drawbacks.

Drawback one is that the range increases in size as the sample size becomes larger. The larger the sample, the more chance one has of drawing an extreme score and increasing the size of the range. The smaller the sample, the less extreme the highest and lowest scores are apt to be. For instance, the range of heights of eight businessmen would be smaller than the range of heights of 75 businessmen.[8]

Drawback two is that the range, because it is based on two extreme scores, is unable to reflect the variation in the intermediate scores. We can easily see this by looking at an example. Suppose you have two sets of scores—one set representing the individual weights of seven women on a college tennis team (89, 125, 120, 129, 120, 125, and 130 lb), the other set the individual weights of seven men on the men's college tennis team (150, 191, 155, 191, 191, 154, and 187 lb). You are to figure the range for each group. When you subtract 89 from 130, the range for the women's tennis team is 41. When you subtract 150 from 191, the range for the men's tennis team also is 41. Something is very strange here. Both ranges are the same, but these two groups are certainly different. Through simple observation you

[7] The range defined by some statisticians is the difference between the highest and lowest scores plus one. In this instance the authors take into account the lower real limit of the lowest score and the upper real limit of the highest score. For the example above the range would be $9.5 - 1.5 = 8$.

[8] By the use of fancy formulas it is possible to adjust the range for the growth in size, but then it is no longer simple to compute.

can see that the majority of women weigh the same, excepting the lightweight woman of 89 lb. However, half the men weigh about 150 lb, while the other half weigh about 180 lb. The patterns of variability for these two groups differ considerably, but the range of 41 does not reflect this.

Drawback three concerns the way in which the range is determined. As you know, the range is determined by only two scores, therefore it is very much affected by extreme scores. A fluctuation in just one of the scores can greatly change the value of the range. As an example, look again at the women's tennis team weights two months later and determine the range. This time one score has changed drastically. The light girl who weighed 89 lb is now at 120 lb. The first time she was weighed she was suffering from a broken romance. In the interim she regained her weight. The effect of this one score on the range is considerable: if you subtract 120 lb from 130 lb, your range now is 10, not 41.

The fourth drawback in using the range is that it is unstable from sample to sample. In choosing two samples from the same population, you might pick one sample with an extreme value and another with no particular extreme. The range for these two samples would differ considerably, even though they were from the same population.

These properties of the range point up the need to take into account all scores in a distribution if we are to get a reliable measure of variability. This is one of the reasons for using the standard deviation.

ADVANTAGES AND DISADVANTAGES OF THE STANDARD DEVIATION, QUARTILE DEVIATION, AND RANGE

In this chapter you have seen that each measure of variability has advantages as well as disadvantages. You have found also that each measure of variability is closely associated with a particular measure of central tendency. The median and quartile deviation, the mean and standard deviation, are used in pairs to describe the data. You have observed that the measures of variability have advantages and disadvantages similar to those of their respective measures of central tendency. The measure of variability you choose, then, will depend upon the situation.

Table 4-7 summarizes the major weaknesses and strengths of each measure. Whenever you find yourself in a predicament, not knowing which measure of variability to use, refer to this table. It will help you select the right measure for the situation.

Table 4-7: Comparison of the Measures of Variability

	Standard deviation	Quartile deviation	Range
Advantages	1. Interval or ratio level 2. Most stable measure 3. Considers every score	1. Ordinal data 2. Insensitive to extreme scores 3. Used in an incomplete distribution	1. Quick estimate
Disadvantages	1. Affected by extreme scores 2. Cannot be used in an incomplete distribution	1. Amenable to only a few mathematical operations 2. Less stable than standard deviation	1. Least stable 2. Cannot be used in mathematical computation

It is time now to review the new material. At this point you should find things getting easier for you. The measures of variability are no harder to learn than the measures of central tendency.

SUMMARY

In this chapter you learned that you need the measures of variability as well as the central tendency measures in order to describe a distribution of scores. The measure of variability describes how the scores are clustered around the mean, median, or mode. The measures of variability explained were the standard deviation, the quartile deviation, and the range.

The standard deviation, one of the most widely used measures of variability, was discussed, and you learned how to compute it. You learned how, in conjunction with the mean, it is used to determine different sections of the normal curve and the percentage of cases that will fall between any two particular raw scores, or the percentages of cases that will fall above and below a particular raw score. You learned how this information enabled you to convert raw scores into standard scores, such as z, which always mean the same thing from one distribution to another regardless of the numerical value of the mean and standard deviation. You learned how to use the standard deviation to compute the standard error of the mean.

The quartile deviation was explained next, and you learned how to compute and use it. You saw that this was the measure to be used in conjunction with the median.

Finally the range, a very quick and easy measure of variability, was explained. It is based on the highest and lowest score in any distribution. The range has many weaknesses, four of which we examined.

The advantages and disadvantages of the standard deviation, quartile deviation, and range were summarized in Table 4-6. By looking at this summary you should be able to pick the right measure of variability for each occasion.

Now it is time for the self-test on these measures of dispersion (variability).

SELF-TEST FOR MASTERY

If you have trouble working a problem, reread the explanation on the page listed.

1. Fill in the accompanying crossword puzzle by supplying the key words.

Across

p. 90
    1. Johnny scores a 75 on a test that has a mean of 80 and a standard deviation of 5. He is one standard deviation _____ the mean.

p. 103
    2. The range is the most influenced by _____ scores.

p. 105
    3. The measure of variability best suited for an open distribution is the _____ deviation.

p. 103
    4. When you compute the range, you use _____ scores.

p. 72
    5. Ms. Sherrin's class and Mr. Jackson's class have identical means on an English test. Chances are that the

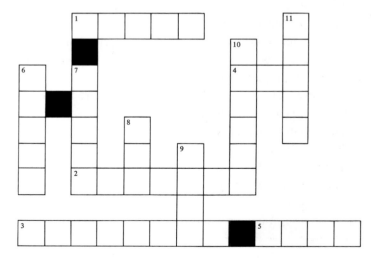

standard deviations found for each class will not be the _____ .

Down

p. 105 6. The _____ varies the most from sample to sample.

p. 105 7. The standard deviation takes into account the _____ of every score.

p. 105 8. The quartile deviation is _____ sensitive to extreme scores.

p. 86 9. The normal curve is sometimes referred to as the _____-shaped curve.

p. 105 10. The standard deviation is the most _____ from sample to sample.

p. 90 11. On a normal curve a z score of 1.0 is _____ the mean.

p. 76 **2.** What is the standard deviation for the following scores?
   (a) 3, 6, 2, 1, 7, 6 _____
   (b) 6, 7, 4, 3, 2 _____
   (c) 4, 3, 2, 1, 1 _____

p. 96 **3.** What is the quartile deviation for the following scores?
   (a) 8, 7, 6, 5, 2, 3, 1, 9 _____
   (b) 4, 10, 3, 2, 1, 8, 5, 11 _____
   (c) 15, 10, 11, 12 _____

p. 103 **4.** Find the range for these scores:
   (a) 4, 5, 8, 15, 2, 11 _____
   (b) 6, 4, 8, 2, 5, 8, 6, 9 _____
   (c) 1, 2, 3, 6, 1, 4 _____

p. 81 **5.** Using the scores reported below, compute the standard deviation.

Manual Dexterity Test

Score intervals	f
16–18	1
13–15	2
10–12	4
7–9	2
4–6	1
1–3	1

Standard deviation = _____

p. 96 **6.** Using the scores reported below, compute the quartile deviation.

Archery Test

Score interval	f
55–59	3
50–54	0
45–49	15
40–44	10
35–39	1
30–34	6
25–29	3
20–24	2
	$N =$

Quartile deviation = _____

p. 89
7. Doug earned an 80 in chemistry. The mean on his chemistry test was 70 and the standard deviation was 8. He then received an 85 in sociology. The mean on the sociology test was 80 and the standard deviation was 15.
  (a) Is Doug better in chemistry or in sociology? _____
  (b) Where is Doug's score for chemistry on the normal curve? How many standard deviations is it above or below the mean? _____
  (c) Where is Doug's score for sociology on the normal curve? How many standard deviations is it above or below the mean?

8. Using the raw scores 3, 2, 1, 5:
p. 90
  (a) Calculate the z-score equivalents.
     [*Hint:* Calculate the mean and standard deviation first.]
     3 = _____ 2 = _____ 1 = _____ 5 = _____
p. 90
  (b) Which of the four people scored above the mean on this test? _____
p. 90
  (c) Rank these four people from lowest to highest according to their z scores. _____ _____ _____ _____

p. 88
9. Between a +1 standard deviation and a −1 standard deviation approximately _____% of the cases fall.

p. 87
10. If you scored three standard deviations above the mean, approximately what percentage of cases are underneath you? _____

p. 94
11. A scientist takes one sample of 100 airplane pilots and gives them a math test. The mean from this test is 80 and the standard deviation is 8. The standard error, rounded to the tenth place, is _____.

p. 95
12. If the standard error of the mean is 2 and the mean is 90,

what percentage of scores would be expected to fall:
(a) below 94 _____
(b) between 88 and 92 _____
(c) below 96 _____

ANSWER TO SELF-TEST

Score yourself by adding up the points for each correct answer and write the total in the Evaluation form.

1 point for each word

1.

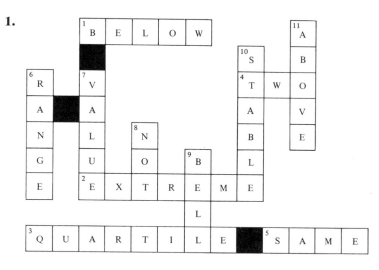

5 points each **2.** (a) $s = 2.27$; (b) $s = 1.85$; (c) $s = 1.17$

4 points each **3.** (a) $Q = 2.5$; (b) $Q = 3.25$;

(c) $Q = 1.5$; $Q_3 = \dfrac{15 + 12}{2} = 13.5$

3 points each **4.** (a) Range $(R) = 13$; (b) $R = 7$; (c) $R = 5$

15 points **5.**
$$s = \frac{1}{N} \sqrt{(N)\, \Sigma fX^2 - (\Sigma fX)^2}$$

$$= \frac{1}{11} \sqrt{(11)\,1322 - 12{,}544}$$

$$\boxed{= 4.06}$$

14 points **6.** $Q = \dfrac{Q_3 - Q_1}{2}$ $\qquad$ $Q_3 = LL + \left(\dfrac{\frac{3}{4}N - cf}{fw}\right) i$

$\qquad = \dfrac{47.17 - 33.67}{2}$ $\qquad = 44.5 + \left(\dfrac{30 - 22}{15}\right) 5$

$\qquad = 6.75$ $\qquad\qquad = 47.17$

$$Q_1 = LL + \left(\frac{\frac{1}{4}N - cf}{fw}\right) i$$

$$= 29.5 + \left(\frac{10 - 5}{6}\right) 5$$

$$= 33.67$$

8 points

7. (a) Chemistry. (b) It is between $+1s$ and $+2s$. $(1.25s)$
(c) Between the mean and $\overline{X} + 1s$ $(.33s)$

8 points for (a), 2
points each for (b)
and (c)

8. (a) $3 = z$ score of $.17$
$2 = z$ score of $\overline{-.51}$
$1 = z$ score of $\overline{-1.18}$
$5 = z$ score of $\overline{1.52}$

The data have an $\overline{X} = 2.75$, an $s = 1.48$

(b) The people with scores of $\underline{3}$ and $\underline{5}$
(c) The scores are ranked $-1.18, -.51, .17, 1.52$

1 point   **9.** 68.26%

1 point   **10.** 99.87%

1 point   **11.** .8

1 point each   **12.** (a) 97.72; (b) 68.26; (c) 99.87

Evaluation

Rating	Score
102 = Champ	
90–101 = Heavyweight	
74–89 = Lightweight	
0–73 = Featherweight	

You may be exhausted from working out the self-test problems. If you have used a calculator to make it easier on yourself, fatigue may have set in toward the end of these problems, and you may unknowingly have pushed the wrong button. Unless you have a printout on paper, the only way to avoid this problem is to double-check your work. (If your answers differ slightly from the book's answers, the small difference is due to rounding; don't worry about it.)

If you have completed the self-test without much trouble, you are ready for Chapters 5 and 6. These chapters will finish the background you need for the remainder of the book. Read them very carefully.

RESEARCH TERMINOLOGY

5

In Chapter 2 we distinguished between descriptive and inferential statistics. In Chapters 3 and 4 we used descriptive statistics, measures that describe and summarize information. To refresh your memory, examples of these measures are given below.

1. The *average* IQ at Cal College is 115.
2. The scores on the last history exam *ranged* from 70 to 95.
3. The T.V. Neilsen ratings report that 80 *percent* of those interviewed watched the tennis match on Monday night.

In this chapter we are going to begin our study of inferential statistics. *Inferential statistics* is concerned with making generalizations from a sample about the population. We often infer from a sample without statistical techniques. Every day of our lives we make decisions without having all the information at our disposal. For instance, Miriam was interested in buying a calculator. She had three friends who recently had bought brand X calculators. They had experienced considerable trouble with their machines. They told Miriam that the calculators worked infrequently and that the rechargeable batteries did not hold a charge for the guaranteed length of time. On the basis of her friends' experience with this small sample of brand X calculators, Miriam made a judgment about all brand X calculators and decided not to purchase one. By doing this, she inferred with incomplete information that all brand X calculators are unreliable. This seems like a logical conclusion; however, it might be that Miriam's friends by pure chance bought the only three lemons that this calculator company ever produced. The reports that Miriam heard about this company's calculators may not be truly representative of their quality. Her inference might be in error.

The techniques of statistical inference help us lessen the possibilities of making such errors in judgment. These statistical techniques provide us with a measure of how good our decisions really are. That is, they give us a basis for evaluating the chance of error in a hypothesis. In Miriam's situation, we could take a random sample of brand X calculators, make a decision about their effectiveness, and use statistical techniques to calculate the risk of error involved in making this decision.

This chapter and the next give you the background to handle the statistical tests for decision making. The new terms you encounter in these chapters will be used throughout the book.

In the present chapter you will learn the steps involved in doing research by reading a play about a mythical island called Clayton. In Clayton you will follow the progress of an experimental study,[1] where you will find out about:

1. Hypothesis testing: null hypothesis and the alternative hypothesis.
2. Probability and the level of significance.
3. Type I and Type II error.
4. Sampling distribution.

As you read the play and learn about a statistical concept, a footnote will refer you to a section in this chapter that will give you a clearer understanding of the statistical concept. If you desire, you can ignore these sections until you have read the entire play without interruptions. The play is meant to be enjoyable and informative, while at the same time it helps you develop an appreciation of what is involved in doing research.

The characters in the play are

Narrator	A person who explains the story and gives insight into the characters.
King Vic	A kind ruler, though at times arrogant and toughminded.
Sam	A timid, faithful servant.
Ralph	The King's most loyal palace guard.
Hector	The King's treacherous brother.
Soothsayer Sal	A woman of wisdom and energy.
Max	The court statistician.

THE ROYAL SPRING WATER

Narrator	Once upon a time there lived on the tropical island of Clayton a wise and noble king named Vic. He was a very rich and powerful leader, but a kind man with integrity. He was very happily married and had a wonderful wife and children. Everything seemed perfect for our hero until one overcast winter day. As the play begins, Vic is sitting on his royal throne when his head servant, Sam, comes running into the room out of breath.
Sam	(*gasping*) Your Majesty, your Majesty.
Vic	(*puzzled*) What is it, Sam?
Sam	(*upset*) Your wife and her friends have become ill after drinking the Royal Spring Water; five people are dead.
Vic	Oh, my God! How is my wife? Did you send for a doctor?
Sam	I sent for the royal doctor; your wife is going to be fine.

[1] An experimental study is one which investigates cause-and-effect relationships. Two or more groups are in the same situation except for the varying of the independent variable.

Vic	(*relieved*) Sam, are you sure the Royal Spring Water caused this catastrophe?
Sam	I am not sure the Royal Spring Water caused the problem. However, I have brought in your most trusted palace guard, Ralph, who says he has information that might shed some light on the situation.
Vic	Send him in immediately, you fool!
Narrator	Ralph rushes into the room holding a strange-looking red vial.
Vic	(*with authority*) What is it that you know? I command you to tell me.
Ralph	I saw your brother throw some liquid from this red vial into the Royal Spring Water today at dawn.
Vic	How did you manage to seize the vial?
Ralph	Before your brother left he hid it in a tree. Because he had acted so strangely, I took it from its hiding place and brought it to you.
Vic	You acted very wisely. What is in the vial?
Ralph	I don't know, your Majesty.
Vic	Thank you. Dismissed.
Narrator	The King sends for his brother, Hector, to get to the bottom of this matter. A few minutes later Hector arrives. He bows several times to his King.
Vic	Quit being so obsequious, Hector. Answer my question. Is this your red vial?
Hector	(*turning red*) Yes.
Vic	What is in this vial?
Hector	(*slyly*) The vial contains only some helpful minerals that I have already taken myself.
Vic	In that case let me give you a teaspoon of this liquid.
Hector	No, I will not take any; I think you have tampered with it.
Vic	Of course I have not tampered with it. I know you are using this as an excuse, because you attempted to poison all of us. Confess now, and I will show you mercy.
Hector	(*upset*) It is not true. It is not true. You have no proof that I am lying.
Vic	You are right. I am not sure of your guilt. For this reason you are going to be placed under palace arrest. Until I can get to the bottom of this business, you are confined to your quarters.
Narrator	The King sends for the palace guard to escort Hector to his quarters. Vic then sits down to think. He thinks for what seems like an eternity and then decides he needs the wise counsel of the village soothsayer. He dispatches a servant to fetch Soothsayer Sal. She arrives an hour later.
Sal	(*bowing*) Your Royal Majesty, of what service can I be to you?
Narrator	Soothsayer Sal has an air of authority that permeates the room.

	Although she bows courteously, she is still in full command.
Vic	(*humbly*) I need your help.
Sal	(*gently*) Tell me what bothers you, your Highness.
Narrator	Vic pours out the story. After hearing his tale, Sal replies thoughtfully.
Sal	Honorable ruler, I see the problem clearly. You want to know if the contents of the red vial thrown in the Royal Spring Water causes illness or death.
Vic	Exactly. But how do we find out?
Sal	We shall do an experimental study.
Vic	By all means, Sal, let's be scientific. What do we do first?
Sal	We draw two large samples of clear fresh water from the village well, because this has a history of being safe. We then pour the contents from the red vial into one sample and not the other.
Vic	Go on!
Sal	Next, we take two random samples of people. How many people do you want in each group, your Majesty?
Vic	(*feeling important*) I have decided upon 50 people in each group. Sal, from your knowledge, would this be a good number to choose?
Sal	Yes, your Majesty, 100 subjects, 50 in each group, is a very respectable sample size upon which we might draw conclusions about the red vial.
Vic	Now tell me, Sal, why do we have two groups?
Sal	One group of subjects will drink exclusively the village water with the contents from the red vial added, while the other group will drink exclusively the village water without any additives.
Vic	(*Very upset*) This is all well and good, but I don't want to kill loyal subjects to find out whether the red vial contains poison. But, I must admit, I would love to force some Red Vial Water down Hector's gullet.
Sal	I understand your compassion and concern for the health of your subjects. However, this concern for their safety will no longer be an issue if we substitute the royal mice, which we know have been specially bred for years and have the same lineage.[2]
Vic	Yes, the royal mice are very valuable, but my people are a precious commodity.
Sal	Very insightful! Let's use mice. Now that we have decided on our subjects, I have a few questions. How much water do you think we should give the mice? When should we give the mice their water? How long should we run the experiment?

[2] In the play we are assuming that what poisons people poisons mice, which is a reasonable assumption.

Vic	I have decided we should give the mice eight tablespoons of water each day. We should give them the water as their only source of nourishment. They will receive four tablespoons of water at 6 o'clock in the morning and four tablespoons at 6 o'clock in the evening. We should do this every day for one whole week. Do my decisions seem reasonable according to your scientific mind?
Sal	Yes, very reasonable.
Vic	(*baffled*) Now, how do we begin?
Sal	We begin by using good standard statistical practices. We begin by stating the *null hypothesis*.
Vic	Hypothesis, null hypothesis? What in the devil is the null hypothesis?
Narrator	Vic is quite exasperated. After all, he doesn't want to appear ignorant, for he is the King.
Sal	(*soothing*) Don't worry, your Majesty. The null hypothesis is just a fancy phrase for a simple term.
Vic	(*unsure of himself*) What does it mean?
Sal	First let me tell you what a hypothesis is. A hypothesis is a statement that offers a solution to your problem. A hypothesis gives direction to your research. Looking at the question of whether the Red Vial Water differs from the Clear Water in its effect on your subjects, what are some of the assumptions or hypotheses you can make about this problem?
Vic	You mean, what are some of the possible solutions to this problem?
Sal	That is exactly what I mean.
Vic	I can say that probably the Red Vial Water is poisoned.
Sal	You are right. What are some other possibilities?
Vic	I can say it could be that the Clear Water is poisoned. I can say there is nothing wrong with either water; I can just say the two waters are different.
Sal	Now, that wasn't hard, was it?
Vic	No, Sal. Hypotheses are quite easy to formulate—but which of these hypotheses that I stated is the null?
Sal	The null hypothesis is the one that assumes there is no real difference between the Red Vial Water and the Clear Water.[3]
Vic	But . . . but . . . but . . . there is a difference. The two waters are not equal. Some people have died from drinking from the Royal Spring Water, which contained some of the red vial liquid.
Sal	You cannot be sure it was because of the red vial's contents that they died. Maybe something else in the water, perhaps a mysteri-

---

[3] You can stop reading if you wish and refer to an in-depth discussion of hypothesis testing in Section A, p. 124.

ous virus, is causing the illness or death of your people. Maybe there is no real difference between the two waters. The fact that these people died after drinking the Royal Spring Water could have been a matter of chance.

Vic   I never thought of looking at it that way. But what if I am right and there appears to be a real difference? What earthly good is the null hypothesis? Why state it at all?

Sal   You state the null hypothesis because, in theory, it is more convenient to test this type of hypothesis and apply statistical tests to it. In fact, your Majesty, you are already familiar with the logic surrounding the null.

Vic   How?

Sal   For example, when you try a prisoner in front of the Royal Court, the accused man is always assumed innocent unless we can prove him guilty beyond a reasonable doubt. Assuming the accused man is not guilty is a null hypothesis.

Vic   Now I understand! In order to be scientific we have to approach the problem with an open mind. We do this by assuming there is no difference between the two waters. That is why we begin by stating the null hypothesis. My question now is, when will we reject this null in favor of my own hypothesis, which claims there is a difference between the two waters?

Sal   At the end of the experiment, if it seems that there is a difference, you reject the null hypothesis in favor of your own hypothesis, which says there is a difference. Incidently, your own hypothesis is called the *alternative hypothesis*.[4]

Vic   My own hypothesis is the alternative hypothesis.

Sal   Are there any points about this discussion that are troubling you so far?

Vic   One thing bothers me. After we run this little experiment and get our results, how do we know when to get rid of our silly null? How many mice have to become ill or die?

Sal   You mean, when can we reject the null hypothesis?

Vic   Yes, I want to reject the null so I can say I am right. Then I can proclaim that the Royal Spring Water is dangerous because of the contents of the red vial and punish Hector appropriately.

Narrator   Sal looks at the King with disgust. She is now caught up in the pure joy of the experiment and hates to hear it put in such cold hard terms.

Sal   Your Majesty, you take my breath away with your brilliant question. To be objective, you have to decide in advance when you will reject the null hypothesis. You have the right to choose any

[4] For a more complete discussion of the alternative hypothesis refer to Section A, p. 124.

probability you desire. This probability is called a *level of significance.*[5] It is a value that can range from zero to one. For most experimental studies we choose .05 or .01.

Vic   This is simple enough. I have decided to choose .05 as my *level of significance.* Now, what does this .05 mean?

Sal   The .05 refers to your chances of being wrong by rejecting the null hypothesis when it is in fact true. You are willing to take the risk of being wrong in rejecting the null hypothesis five times out of 100.

Vic   Suppose I choose .01—does this mean I am willing to take the chance of wrongly rejecting the null hypothesis one time out of 100?

Sal   Correct. Now, let me ask you an even harder question. If you choose as your probability .0001, what is your chance of wrongly rejecting the null hypothesis?

Vic   That's easy. If I choose this number, my chance of being wrong is one time out of 10,000.

Sal   You understand it perfectly. If you choose .05 as your level of significance, you have a much greater chance of being wrong than if you choose .01.

Vic   Of course I understand. The smaller my probability number is, the less chance I have of being wrong. Sal, what determines whether I choose .05, .01, or .001 for our experiment? My risk seems to change by just changing a number.

Sal   It is determined by the problem. For example, let's say you want to see whether Saki has developed a better bow and arrow than Kiki's, the one currently used in the village. The null hypothesis states that Saki's bow and arrow is no different than Kiki's. The alternative hypothesis states that Saki's bow and arrow is better than Kiki's. In this example you would want to set the level of significance to reject the null hypothesis possibly at .001 or even smaller, say .000001.

Vic   Why that small?

Sal   Please give me the chance to explain.

Vic   Sorry. Continue.

Sal   Pretend, your Highness, for the sake of argument, you did not use .001. Instead, you set the level of significance at .05, a larger number. You are now willing to take the chance of being wrong in rejecting the null hypothesis five times out of 100. You carry through with your experiment using this .05 level of significance, and at the end of the experiment you reject the null hypothesis, which means that you accept the alternative

[5] For a more complete discussion of probability and level of significance, refer to Section B, p. 125.

hypothesis that Saki's bow and arrow is better than Kiki's. On this basis you then decide to use only Saki's bows and arrows. This means destroying all the bows and arrows you are presently using that were designed by Kiki. As a result you spend thousands of dollars for new weapons and you raise taxes. Everything you are doing is fine as long as you are right, but suppose you are wrong and there is really no difference in the effectiveness of Saki's weapons and Kiki's.

Vic   How could I be wrong?

Sal   The null hypothesis might have been true. The difference that occurred between the weapons might have been one that was occurring five times out of 100. Remember the risk we are taking is five times out of 100. So now the decision to adopt Saki's weapons results in wasting money that your royal treasury badly needs and overtaxing your people. Maybe this dilemma could have been avoided if you had not made the original decision to set your level of significance at .05.

Vic   How can my changing my level of significance from .05 to some other value prevent my wasting this money?

Sal   Well, if you had set your level of significance at .000001, a smaller number, you might *not* have rejected the null hypothesis. If you had not rejected the null hypothesis, you would not have made the decision to buy Saki's weapons. Since making this decision wrongly is so costly, you might not want to take the .05 chance of being wrong, and you might want instead to set your level of significance at .000001. You are willing to take the risk of being wrong 1 time out of 1,000,000, but not five times out of 100.

Vic   You are right, Sal. To avoid this type of error I would always set a very small level of significance, maybe as small as .000000000000000000000001, so I would have less chance of being wrong in rejecting the null hypothesis.

Sal   Your Majesty, this is true, but by doing this you might be increasing your chances of *not* rejecting the null hypothesis when it *should* be rejected.

Vic   If I set my level of significance too small, I might not reject the null when I should, and if I set it too large, I might reject the null when I shouldn't. It seems as if I can't win. I'm confused—what should I do?

Sal   It depends upon the nature of the problem and the consequences of your decision. The level of significance you choose depends on what kind of error you can afford to live with.

Vic   What do you mean?

Sal	Let's look at your problem with the red vial and examine the consequences of both types of error, and then you'll understand. If you set your level of significance at .05, you are increasing your chances of rejecting the null hypothesis wrongly, which means you would wrongly say there was a difference between the Red Vial Water and the Clear Water. You would act on this premise: you would wrongly forbid people to drink the Royal Spring Water and you would wrongly punish Hector. This type of error is called a *Type I error*.[6]
Vic	Ah! Ha! A Type I error would mean I would reject the null hypothesis wrongly.
Sal	Precisely the point.
Vic	And what are the consequences of *accepting* the null hypothesis when it should be *rejected?*
Sal	You mean what are the consequences of a Type II error? If you set your level of significance at .0001, this is the error you are increasing your chances of making. In accepting the null hypothesis wrongly you would wrongly state there was no difference between the Red Vial Water and the Clear Water. You would continue to have your subjects drink the Royal Spring Water. The consequences of your being wrong would be that many of your loyal subjects would die and Hector would go free to scheme again.
Vic	So I must decide which error I would be more willing to live with if I chose wrongly. I must set my level of significance accordingly.
Sal	That is right.
Vic	I would personally prefer to make a Type I error. Rejecting the null hypothesis wrongly would result in wrongly punishing my jealous brother and wrongly forbidding my subjects to drink from the Royal Spring. I definitely want to set my level of significance at .05 instead of a more stringent .0000001. I want to make it easier to reject the null.
Sal	Now that we have planned all the preliminaries—that is, drawn our samples, stated our null and alternative hypotheses, and set our level of significance—we must choose a statistical test.[7]
Vic	What is a statistical test? Why use it?
Sal	A statistical test is a method for testing your hypothesis. After we run our experiment and collect our data, we calculate this sta-

---

[6] For a more detailed discussion of Type I and Type II errors see Section C, pp. 127–128.

[7] Chapter 6 will give you the basis for selecting the proper statistical test. At the present time you are not expected to know this.

tistic. Then you use it to enter a table that helps you decide whether to reject or accept the null hypothesis.

Vic   What is the name of the test or statistic we will use?

Sal   The *chi-square test.*[8] Chi square is defined by the formula

$$\chi^2 = \Sigma \frac{(O - E)^2}{E}$$

Vic   It seems a little hazy; give me a few more details. Start with what happens next week.

Sal   Next week we will run our experiment. At the end of the week we will record data. That is, I will put down the number in the Red Vial group that die and that stay alive, and I also will record the number in the Clear Water group that die and that stay alive.

Vic   I understand that, but what happens after the data are recorded?

Sal   We will then examine the data and try to find out whether there is a real difference between these two groups.

Vic   I can tell you right off whether there is a difference. For example, let's say 30 mice die in the Red Vial group and 20 die in the Clear Water group. Obviously there is a difference, and therefore there is something wrong with the water.

Sal   Being scientific, you can't do this. Of course there is a difference, but who is to say it is a significant difference? It could have occurred by chance. Since you are working with samples, there is bound to be a difference, even if the samples are from the same population.

Vic   What determines whether this difference is a real one and not just due to chance? What makes the difference significant?

Sal   The difference is significant if it leads us to reject the null hypothesis at the level of significance we set. If the hypothesis is not rejected, the results are not significant.

Vic   You mean my results will be considered significant, and the null hypothesis rejected, if the probability of the results' occurring is .05 or less.

Sal   Yes. Your difference is then considered significant at the .05 level.

Vic   How do we find out this information from our data?

Sal   That is why we need a statistical test; we use it to analyze the data. In this case we will use the chi-square test. We compute a value for chi square using the numbers we recorded at the end of the experiment. If this value is equal to or greater than—but wait, let me not get ahead too fast. At this point I think it best to

---

[8] The chi-square test is used in this play because it is appropriate; it is also one of the most widely used statistical tests.

Narrator	consult Max, our Court Statistician. He has a magical way with figures, and he can best fill you in on the remaining details. Vic rings for a servant and tells him to run and fetch Max, who is visiting a distant village. Vic then orders dinner, and he and Sal continue their discussion. When Max arrives, Vic relates the events of the day—omitting, however, Sal's opinion on the type of statistical test to use in analyzing the data. Vic does this to determine Max's expertise. If Max fails to name the proper test, he will be banished from the island forever. Vic then asks Max to summarize what he has said.
Max	You have randomly selected two groups of mice. One group will be given exclusively eight tablespoons of Red Vial Water each day for a week—four tablespoons at 6 A.M. and four tablespoons at 6 P.M. each day. The other group will be given exclusively eight tablespoons of Clear Water each day for a week—four tablespoons at 6 A.M. and four tablespoons at 6 P.M. each day. You have stated in the null hypothesis that there is no difference between the Red Vial Water and the Clear Water. You intend to reject this hypothesis at the .05 level of significance. If you do reject it, you can accept the alternative hypothesis that the two waters are different with a .05 chance of being wrong.
Vic	Splendid. What happens now?
Max	It seems to me the way you designed this study you could use the chi-square test to analyze the data.
Vic	I agree, Max. I want you to work with Sal on this experiment.
Max	Be delighted to, most noble ruler. I feel we cannot afford to wait any longer. I would like to begin the study immediately.
Narrator	Everyone in the kingdom was excited to see what would happen in the week that followed. As the days went by, some mice in both groups became ill and some died. More mice in the Red Vial Water group were dying, but no one knew what these results meant. The difference might have been a chance occurrence. It seemed to most observers that the two waters were different and that the King's alternative hypothesis was acceptable. At the end of the week Sal and Vic were anxious for Max's opinion on the mystery.
Vic	Can you tell us your decision?
Narrator	Now that the great moment had arrived, Max was savoring it.
Max	Not quite yet; let's discuss this together. First I will fill you in on what I have accomplished thus far.
Vic	Proceed!
Max	First, I collected and organized my data from the study. Let me see. There were 25 dead who drank Red Vial Water and 8

	dead who drank Clear Water. The data show that more mice died from drinking Red Vial Water. This, of course, could happen by chance. I have to now find out whether this is a significant difference. That is why I plugged these findings into a chi-square formula. When I solved this formula, I obtained a chi-square value of 13.08.[9] Next, I enter a statistical table (Table E in the appendix).
Vic	Why do we use this table?
Max	(*haughty*) The table will tell me if the 13.08 represents a significant difference. I will find out if I can reject the null hypothesis at the .05 level of significance. The table is really a collection of chi-square distributions.[10]
Vic	(*irritated*) How does this table work?
Max	Different numbers of degrees of freedom[11] appear along the left-hand border of the table. Different levels of significance appear on the top border of the table. The chi-square values in the table are located by using a degree of freedom and a level of significance. For our particular problem the degree of freedom we use is 1 and the level of significance is .05. We simply run our fingers down the left-hand side of the table and find 1, then we run our fingers across this row until we are under the .05 level of significance. The number we find in the table is 3.84. We will use this value to make our decision.
Vic	What do you do with this table value of 3.84?
Max	You compare your computed chi-square value of 13.08 with this table value of 3.84. If your computed value of 13.08 is equal to or exceeds the table value, you reject the null hypothesis at the .05 level of significance. Then we say that this statistical difference is significant at the .05 level.
Vic	What if my computed value is less than my table value? What happens then?
Max	In that case, your Majesty, we would not be able to reject the null hypothesis. The difference would not be significant, and we would act as if the null hypothesis were true. We would act as if there were no difference between the Red Vial Water and the Clear Water.
Vic	Let's return to my problem! Can we reject the null hypothesis?

[9] Max's calculations for this chi square appear in Chapter 7, where there is a detailed discussion on the chi square.

[10] Refer to Section D, p. 128, for a more detailed discussion of sampling distributions.

[11] Degrees of freedom will be explained in Chapter 7. For now you need only realize that you need this information to enter Table E.

Max	Since the computed chi-square value of 13.08 exceeds the table value of 3.84, we can reject the null hypothesis. In doing this we can now accept the alternative hypothesis that the Red Vial Water is different from the clear water. We have determined that the likelihood of getting by chance alone a difference as large as the one we found between the two groups of mice is five or less than five times out of 100.
Vic	Thank you, Max, I now have evidence against my brother. After all, there was a significant difference between the two groups.
Narrator	Vic sends for his royal guard and issues orders. He declares that Hector, for his treachery, will have his head cut off. Furthermore, the Royal Spring is to be covered over with mud. The King then thanks Sal and Max, rewarding them with riches and each with his own palace. Everyone lives happily ever after except Hector and of course the mice who died from drinking the Red Vial Water.

THE END

SECTION A: HYPOTHESIS TESTING

The first step in decision making that the King uses is to state the *null hypothesis*. To state a hypothesis this way is a mathematical convenience. In theory it is more convenient to apply statistical tests to this type of hypothesis. The null hypothesis, referred to as H_0, proposes a solution to a problem by saying there is no difference between two distributions.[12] It says that the results in the study could be due to chance. Even when a sample is random, it is likely to be different from the population because it is smaller than the population. Drawing a random sample means everyone will have an equal opportunity to be drawn in the sample, but it does not guarantee the sample will reflect the population characteristics exactly.

In the play the null hypothesis stated there is no difference between the Red Vial Water and the Clear Water. It is really saying that any difference that is observed is due to chance. When stating the null hypothesis, usually a researcher thinks there is a difference and expects that the sample he has will contradict the null hypothesis. This hypothesis usually is formulated for the purpose of being rejected. When the null hypothesis is rejected, the researcher's alternative hypothesis (H_1), which is also stated at the beginning of the experiment, can now be accepted.

The *alternative hypothesis* is stated two ways: (1) by saying the two groups are unequal, or (2) by predicting the direction of the difference between the two groups.

---

[12] Conventionally the null hypothesis is restricted to a hypothesis of no difference (Ferguson, 1966).

The former is called a *nondirectional* hypothesis and the latter a *directional hypothesis*. For example, consider a problem involving the effectiveness of hearing aids. The null hypothesis states there is no difference between Group A's hearing aids and Group B's. Any one of three alternative hypotheses could be stated.

1. We could state that Group A's hearing aids and Group B's hearing aids are different (nondirectional).
2. We could state that Group A's hearing aids are superior to Group B's (directional).
3. We could state Group B's hearing aids are superior to Group A's (directional).

In stating a directional hypothesis, in order to reject the null hypothesis, you have to predict the correct direction ahead of time. For example, if you stated as your alternative hypothesis that Group A's hearing aids were superior to Group B's, and the results turned out to be the reverse—that is, Group B's hearing aids were superior to Group A's—you would not, if you followed good research practices, reject the null hypothesis.

In the play the King stated his alternative hypothesis when he said, "We shall reject this hypothesis in favor of my own, which claims there is a difference." His own hypothesis is the alternative hypothesis, which in this case is nondirectional, because it does not predict the direction of the difference.

SECTION B: PROBABILITY AND THE LEVEL OF SIGNIFICANCE

Let's consider the way probability enters our daily lives. As a gambler in Vegas, you are interested in the probability of rolling a certain number on the dice. As a weather forecaster, you are using probability to predict the amount of rainfall for tomorrow. As a doctor, you are inferring probability in predicting how fast your patient will recover. As a sociologist, you may ask: "What is the probability of successful marriage between people of different racial backgrounds?" As an insurance agent, the insurance premium you charge your client is determined by probability tables.

Probability values range from 0 to 1. The number 1 stands for absolute certainty and the 0 indicates no chance at all that an event will occur. As you know, there are few certainties in this world. Such proverbially inescapable events as death and taxes would qualify as having a probability of 1. You would use the 0 to indicate events that could never happen. The reader would agree that the following events could not happen:

1. A man's giving birth to a baby.
2. The author's being the heavyweight champion in 1908.
3. The reader's being the president of the United States in 1800.

Since most things in this life are relative, the probability of their occurrence falls between 0 and 1. You often see probabilities reported such as .5, .6, .65, .75. Of course, there are an infinite number of probabilities, ranking anywhere from 0 to 1.00.

When you are interested in probability, you are interested in the relative frequency of occurrence of an event over a number of trials. The formula for probability is $p = F/T$. That is, the probability is equal to the number of favorable outcomes (F) divided by the total number of possible outcomes (T). Whether an outcome is "favorable" depends on what is of experimental interest to the researcher. Let's take a few examples to illustrate this formula.

A high school sorority called the Sigmas met to decide whether Janice could become a member. They were very lukewarm about her joining, but according to the rules they had to give her a chance. They unanimously decided to let probability decide whether Janice would become a member of their sorority. They placed 30 marbles in a box, one of which was white. They then mixed the box of marbles well to approximate randomness. Next, they blindfolded Janice and allowed her to pick one marble from this box. In order for Janice to be allowed to join the Sigmas, she must pick the one white marble. What is the probability of Janice's joining this sorority? The total number of possible outcomes is represented by 30 marbles. The one favorable outcome, Janice's chance to join the Sigmas, is represented by the white marble. Substituting the numbers in the formula, we find the probability of Janice's drawing the white marble is 1/30 or one in 30 times.

As another example, suppose we find the probability of rolling a three on a die. A die has six faces bearing the numbers one through six. There is only one favorable outcome of rolling a three. There are a total of six possible outcomes. The probability is 1/6. Taking this sample a step further, if you roll the die a second time, what is the probability of rolling a three? For the second trial it would still be 1/6. What would be the probability of rolling a three on trial number eight? If you said 1/6 again, you are right. The probability remains the same for each separate trial. Notice that the chance of rolling a favorable outcome on a given trial does not increase as you take more rolls.

Just to see if you understand the examples so far, solve the following problem.

Problem   Dan has won two World Series tickets in a raffle. Now, he has to decide which of his five girlfriends will accompany him to the game. Will it be Gloria, Colleen, Maria, Vicki, or Marcia? He writes each girl's name on a slip of paper and puts it in a fish-bowl, mixing the slips well. He then blindfolds himself and draws a piece of paper from the bowl. What is the probability of Dan's drawing Colleen's name?

Answer   The probability of Dan's drawing Colleen's name is 1/5. That is, there are five slips of paper. The total number of possible out-comes then is five. However, only one outcome is favorable for Colleen. The number of favorable outcomes is one.

From the above examples you can see how important a concept probability is in our daily lives. In inferential statistics probability is the cornerstone. In order to make a decision about a statistical problem you must do so on the basis of probabil-ity. The decision to reject or accept the null hypothesis is based on a certain proba-bility, which is called the *level of significance*. We use probability because we are dealing with a sample, which only gives us incomplete information. Since we are dealing with this type of information, we cannot reach a decision with absolute certainty.

We first encountered probability in the play when we set our level of significance, often referred to as *alpha*. Alpha is the probability of rejecting the null hypothesis wrongly, if the null is in fact true. This level or alpha is chosen ahead of time by the researcher. That is, the researcher decides when he will reject the null hypothesis and say there is a significant difference, meaning that the results he obtains are not due to sampling error. The level of significance that is set depends on the research problem and serves as a guideline for decision making. In the social sciences it is usually set at .05 or .01. In the play the discussion revolves around what level of significance it would be best to set. The King makes a decision by looking at his own situation and the consequences of being wrong, and on this basis he chooses .05 as the level of significance. This means he is taking the chance of being wrong five out of 100 times.

SECTION C: TYPE I AND TYPE II ERROR

When we reject the null hypothesis, there is always some proba-bility that we are making a mistake. In the example used in the play there are five chances out of 100 that the King is wrong. At the end of the experiment, you do not know for certain whether the event you observed was really caused by poisoned water or whether it was due to chance alone, because you are working with samples. Why test the water at all, then, when you will not know the answer for sure? Think of it this way: no person can know the ultimate truth. We can only gain knowledge that allows us to make reasonable decisions.

In testing hypotheses you must be aware of the two types of errors that you could possibly make. They are summarized in Table 5-1. A Type I error rejects the null

Table 5-1: Types of Error in Hypothesis Testing

Type I error → reject null hypothesis → Wrong
Type II error → accept null hypothesis → Wrong

---

hypothesis when there is no difference; a Type II error fails to reject the null hypothesis when there is a difference. Note that the probability of making a Type I error is actually the level of significance. As you learned from the play, a lot depends upon the consequences—what error you can afford to live with. Vic would prefer making a Type I error, because the consequences would be closing down the Royal Spring Water and getting rid of a troublesome brother. In reality, you would rather make no errors at all, but in research you have to reach a compromise by which you balance the probability of each of these two errors against the acceptability of its consequences.

SECTION D: SAMPLING DISTRIBUTION

After Max's experiment is run, he takes his data and computes a value for chi square. He then refers to a table to find out if the value he computes is significant. This table is a family of sampling distributions for chi square. The properties of the sampling distribution are used to analyze the computed chi-square value.

What, then, is a sampling distribution? A *sampling distribution* for any statistic is a theoretical distribution that would occur if we randomly took all the possible samples of the same size from the population in question, computing a statistic for each sample. The statistics for these samples would form a distribution. Every statistical test has a sampling distribution. Some statistical tests use the same sampling distribution, so there are not as many sampling distributions as there are statistical tests. In the play the chi-square statistic has its own sampling distribution. What distinguishes the sampling distribution from other distributions is that what are being distributed are statistics rather than individual scores. Forming a sampling dis-

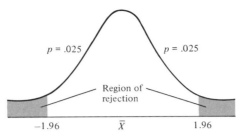

*Figure 5-1: Region of Rejection for Nondirectional
Alternative Hypothesis*

tribution for chi square (the statistic mentioned in the play) would mean computing a chi square for each randomly drawn sample; the chi squares would then form a sampling distribution of chi squares. In general, it is impossible to enumerate all possible samples and their statistics. Fortunately, mathematical theory provides us with sampling distributions of the statistics that might concern us. Mathematicians have provided us with tables from sampling distributions for numerous statistical tests. Examples are Tables E and P in the appendix.

Why is it so important to know the sampling distribution for your statistic? It allows you to make probability statements about the occurrence of a certain number for that statistic in the population by chance. By using the sampling distribution of chi square, Max was able to evaluate the probability of occurrence of his sample value of 13.08 and to reject the null hypothesis. By looking at the table, he was able to tell what the chances were of a chi-square value of 13.08 occurring in the population if the null hypothesis was in fact true. He rejected the null hypothesis, because his statistical test yielded a value that fell in the *region of rejection,* which is the same as the level of significance. The region of rejection is a part of the sampling distribution.

To graphically illustrate the region of rejection, let's use a statistical test that uses the normal distribution. As the experimenter, you set your level of significance at .05, which establishes your region of rejection; that is, this .05 defines values for which you would reject the null hypothesis. For this example, if your alternative hypothesis is nondirectional or two-tail,[13] the region is located at both ends of the curve, as shown in Figure 5-1. The total area in the region of rejection is .05

[13] Nondirectional tests often are called two-tail tests, because when the *t* distribution or normal distribution is used, two tails of the distribution are employed in the estimation of probabilities.

(.025 + .025). As you can see, the .05 is halved; .025 is placed at one end of the curve and .025 at the other. The normal distribution is used and the scores are translated into z values. Table D in the appendix shows you that .025 corresponds to a z of 1.96. The values of +1.96 and −1.96 are critical values, because they separate z values that will result in a decision to reject the null hypothesis. The shaded areas in Figure 5-1 define the region of rejection for the null hypothesis. If a z is less than or equal to −1.96 or greater than or equal to +1.96, you reject the null hypothesis. For example, −2.34 would be rejected because it is less than −1.96 and falls in the region of rejection. Also, +2.91 would be rejected because it is greater than +1.96 and falls in the region of rejection.

At times we wish to make a decision about the direction of the difference. Such tests are called directional or one-tail tests.[14] If your alternative hypothesis is directional, the region is located on the right or left end of the curve, depending upon the nature of the hypothesis. Figure 5-2 shows a normal distribution with .05 of the curve falling beyond −1.64, while Figure 5-3 shows a distribution with .05 of the curve falling beyond +1.64. Table D in the appendix shows you that .05 corresponds to a z of 1.64. The shaded areas in Figures 5-2 and 5-3 define the region of rejection

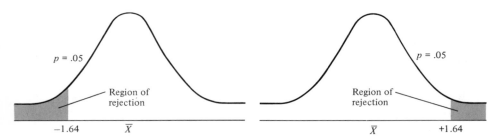

Figure 5-2: Region of Rejection on   *Figure 5-3: Region of Rejection on*
Left End of Curve   *Right End of Curve*

for the null hypothesis. In Figure 5-2 any value that is equal to or less than −1.64 is rejected. For example, −1.78 would be rejected because it is less than −1.64 and falls in the region of rejection. In Figure 5-3 any value that is equal to or greater than +1.64 is rejected. For example, +2.34 would be rejected because it is greater than +1.64 and falls in the region of rejection.

---

[14] Directional tests often are referred to as one-tail tests, because when the *t* distribution or normal distribution is used, two tails of the distribution are employed in the estimation of probabilities.

In these examples we have considered the normal distribution, but other theoretical distributions are employed in different contexts. In the play the .05 level of significance is used, but the sampling distribution was the chi square. If you graph this sampling distribution, it will resemble a chi square, because of the statistic you are using. The graph for the chi-square distribution looks like Figure 5-4. In this ex-

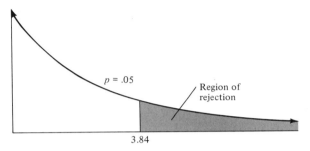

Figure 5-4: Chi-Square Curve with One Degree of Freedom

ample the critical value that results in the rejection of the null hypothesis is 3.84. Table E in the appendix shows you that .05 corresponds to the critical value of 3.84. The shaded area defines the region of rejection. If a chi-square value is equal to or greater than 3.84, you reject the null hypothesis.

SUMMARY

In this chapter you became acquainted with inferential statistics. You followed certain steps to test a statistical hypothesis. These steps were:

1. First you formulated the null hypothesis and your alternative hypothesis.
2. You decided upon your sample size and the procedure you would follow during the course of the study.
3. You selected a level of significance.
4. You selected a statistical test and its sampling distribution.
5. You decided on the region of rejection, which is determined by your statistical test, level of significance, and sampling distribution.
6. You collected data.
7. You calculated the value for your statistic.
8. You then decided whether the value for your statistic fell in the region of rejec-

tion. If it did, you rejected the null hypothesis, because the probability of obtaining such a value by chance was so small that you were *not* willing to attribute it to chance. If the value falls outside the region of rejection, we do not reject the null hypothesis because the difference is not large enough to be significant.

SELF-TEST FOR MASTERY

If you have trouble answering a question, reread the explanation on the page listed.

Complete each sentence by locating the missing word on the Word Search Sheet. The words are vertical, horizontal, and diagonal. Read the sentence, find the word on the Word Search Sheet, circle that word, and then fill in the blank. The first sentence has been done for you. The missing word *summarize* was located on the word search sheet and then placed in the blank to complete the sentence.

1. We use numbers to <u>summarize</u> information in descriptive statistics.

p. 112   **2.** Inferential statistics allows a person to draw reasonable conclusions from _____ information.

p. 120   **3.** In the play the King wanted to avoid making a Type _____ error.

p. 127   **4.** _____ tells you the probability of making a Type I error.

p. 120   **5.** Doctor X was testing a new operation on mice to be later used on human beings; he was very careful to avoid making a Type _____ error.

p. 121   **6.** When a researcher rejects the null hypothesis, he concludes the results are not due to _____ alone.

p. 131   **7.** You determine the level of significance _____ running your experiment.

p. 126   **8.** Suppose you bet $5 that you will be able to draw an ace from a deck of cards. The probability of your succeeding is one chance out of _____.

p. 129   **9.** Is this sentence true or false? A two-tail test should be used when an investigator wants to find out if the grade-point average of marijuana-smoking students differs significantly from that of nonsmoking students.

p. 128
10. The level of significance in an experiment is set at .05. In testing the null hypothesis, we find the difference between our two samples is so small that the probability of its occurring by chance is .30. We should _____ the null hypothesis.

p. 128
11. A sampling distribution consists of all the possible samples of the _____ size drawn _____ from the same population.

p. 120
12. You determine the alpha by weighing the _____ of the Type I and Type II errors.

p. 124
13. If you _____ the null hypothesis, you are saying that Group A is _____ different from Group B.

p. 130
14. In a normal distribution with alpha constant, the size of the region of rejection always remains the same, but the _____ can be different.

p. 126
15. Probability values range from 0 to _____.

p. 118
16. The _____ the level of significance, the larger the chance of a Type I error and the _____ the chance of a Type II error.

p. 124
17. The _____ hypothesis is formulated to be rejected.

```
Q F A L S E O P S I I O P R A N D O M L Y E S T S A M P L E O F
T R E J E C T C U R A N D O M L Y T L E V E P O P U L A T I O N
I N L E V E L N 0 4 5 6 M U R D E R I F O E P P S O M A N Y U P
N O L A B C O G F O L M D O G H A S E C C O N E O P A L P H A O
C S S E S E O E O D 9 1.7 8 1 3 N O C C D E C I S I O N I O L L
O C H A N C E T O O C L 6 1.6 8 N A A D E E 4 1 6.8 2 6 M N O P
M A D E C R E A S E D G U.8 6 8 7 2 N 6 V A V I J A L L A L O S
P E O K I N G K I N G H O 5 7 F O 2 U E I I N O T O O D O A A M
L I N C R E A S I N G U U O K 2 D O L T A A W O R K C O T R A A
E A S U M M A R I Z E F O N E I N I L H T S A M E A A S G G L L
T O D I C K O N O T E H I T T L A C D E I F G H I T T L E E N L
E O F B E F O R E A B S T H I I E U U O O O B I L I I Y O R E E
N O C O N S E Q U E N C E S N L N C O N N C I S O O O T H T E R
O T R E E T R O E S O S E T O P E G B A O S F I N D N H E W O R
S I G N I F I C A N T L Y O T M E S S T R U E R E W O R K N O T
```
Word Search Sheet

An investigator was concerned about the discrimination practiced against deaf men and women. He wanted to test in a controlled situation whether deaf teachers would be as effective in teaching children prespecified instructional objectives as would teachers with unimpaired hearing. The children to be taught had normal hearing, which made this an even more stringent task for deaf teachers, all of whom conducted their lessons with the aid of interpreters. In the experiment there were two groups of teachers; ten were deaf and ten had normal hearing. They were given two instructional objectives dealing with math and were told to prepare to teach four pupils on the campus of a high school in Los Angeles. Each teacher taught his students the same instructional objective at the same time. After 90 minutes of instruction a pupil test was administered by the investigator. A *t*-test [15] was used to determine the statistical significance of the difference. Answer the following questions.

p. 124	**1.** State the null hypothesis.
p. 124	**2.** State the alternative as a nondirectional hypothesis.
p. 124	**3.** State the alternative as a directional hypothesis.
p. 118	**4.** Set your level of significance at .001 and explain why you might prefer this to a .05 level when your alternative hypothesis is nondirectional.
p. 124	**5.** If you reject the null hypothesis and accept a nondirectional alternative hypothesis, what does this imply?
p. 124	**6.** If you reject the null hypothesis and accept a directional hypothesis, what does this imply?
p. 124	**7.** If you fail to reject the null hypothesis, what does this imply?

ANSWERS TO SELF-TEST

Score yourself by adding up the points for each correct answer and write the total in the Evaluation form.

SENTENCE COMPLETION

1 point for each word

1—Summarize; 2—Incomplete; 3—II; 4—Alpha; 5—I; 6—Chance; 7—Before; 8—13; 9—True; 10—Accept; 11—Same, Randomly; 12—Consequences; 13—Reject, Significantly; 14—Location; 15—1; 16—Larger, Smaller; 17—Null.

[15] The statistical test chosen for this situation will be explained in detail in Chapter 9.

Q F A L S E O P S I I O P R A N D O M L Y E S T S A M P L E O F

T R E J E C T C U R A N D O M L Y T L E V E P O P U L A T I O N

I N L E V E L N 0 4 5 6 M U R D E R I F O E P P S O M A N Y U P

N O L A B C O G F O L M D O G H A S E C C O N E O P A L P H A O

C S S E S E O E O D 9 1.7 8 1 3 N O C C D E C I S I O N I O L L

O C H A N C E T O O C L 6 1.6 8 N A A D E E 4 1 6.8 2 6 M N O P

M A D E C R E A S E D G U.8 6 8 7 2 N 6 V A V I J A L L A L O S

P E O K I N G K I N G H O 5 7 F O 2 U E I I N O T O O D O A A M

L I N C R E A S I N G U U O K 2 D O L T A A W O R K C O T R A A

E A S U M M A R I Z E F O N E I N I L H T S A M E A A S G G L L

T O D I C K O N O T E H I T T L A C D E I F G H I T T L E E N L

E O F B E F O R E A B S T H I I E U U O O O B I L I I Y O R E E

N O C O N S E Q U E N C E S N L N C O N N C I S O O O T H T E R

O T R E E T R O E S O S E T O P E G B A O S F I N D N H E W O R

S I G N I F I C A N T L Y O T M E S S T R U E R E W O R K N O T

Word Search Answer Sheet

TESTING TEACHERS

5 points
1. There is no significant difference between the deaf teachers and the teachers with unimpaired hearing in their ability to teach children prespecified instructional objectives.

5 points
2. There is a difference between the deaf teachers and the teachers with unimpaired hearing in their ability to teach children prespecified instructional objectives.

5 points
3. There are two alternative hypotheses; either one is acceptable. (a) Deaf teachers are better than unimpaired teachers in teaching children prespecified instructional objectives. (b) Unimpaired teachers are better than deaf teachers in teaching children prespecified instructional objectives.

5 points
4. You might prefer to make a Type II error. The consequences of a Type II error would be to accept the null hypothesis, which says there is no significant difference between deaf teachers and teachers with unimpaired hearing. In this case you would not discriminate against deaf teachers in hiring them.

5 points

5. This would imply there was a difference between deaf teachers and unimpaired teachers in their effectiveness.

5 points

6. This would imply that one group of teachers was superior to the other group of teachers.

5 points

7. There is no significant difference between deaf teachers and teachers with unimpaired hearing in teaching children prespecified objectives.

Evaluation

Rating	Score
49–51 = Champ	
41–48 = Heavyweight	
29–40 = Lightweight	
0–28 = Featherweight	

HOW TO CHOOSE A STATISTICAL TEST

6

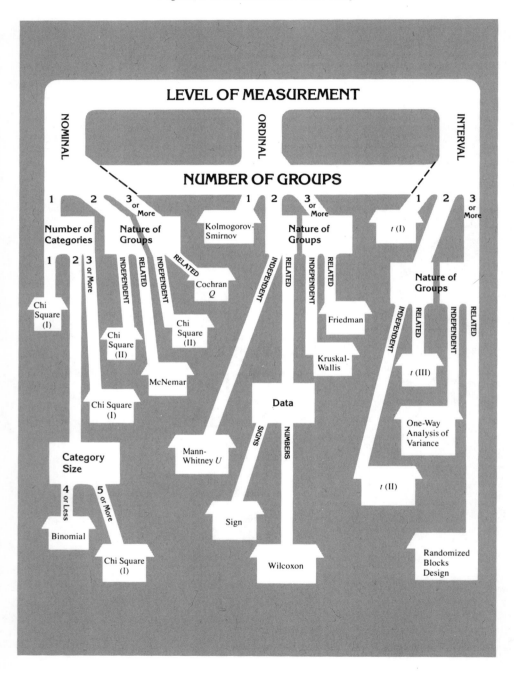

Figure 6-1: A Statistical Road Map

138

In research there are many different statistical tests of significance. Research studies differ in such things as the type of data collected, the kind of measurement used, and the number of groups used; these factors decide which statistical test is appropriate for a particular research study. If we do not know the reason for choosing one test over another, we may wind up using the wrong test, which could make our conclusions just as invalid as if we had not used any test at all. Of course, there is also the possibility that by chance we would use the right test. But choosing the correct test to satisfy the conditions of the study does not have to be guesswork, leaving us doubtful about the conclusions we draw from the data. There are reasons for choosing one test rather than another, and this chapter will explain these reasons.

The accompanying Statistical Road Map (Figure 6-1) gives the reader directions for finding 15 of the most widely used statistical tests. It takes into account the major requirements of each statistical test, which serve as directions for determining the appropriate test. The beauty of this map is that it is easy to understand and use.

When you look at the Statistical Road Map you'll see boulevards, intersections, avenues, streets, and houses. The boulevards are called "Level of Measurement" and "Number of Groups." The major function of the boulevards is to pose questions.

The intersections are small, rectangular islands called "Number of Categories," "Category Size," "Nature of Groups," and "Data." The intersections' major function, like the boulevards', is to pose questions.

The avenues, which run between the boulevards, are "Nominal," "Ordinal," and "Interval." The avenues' major function is to answer the questions posed by the "Level of Measurement" boulevard.

The streets branch off from the boulevards and intersections. Examples of streets on this map are "5 or More," "Independent," "Related," "Signs," and "Numbers." The streets provide answers to questions posed by the boulevards and intersections. The final destinations on the map are the houses in which the statistical tests are located. Examples of some statistical tests are chi square (I), Cochran Q, Mann-Whitney U, Friedman, t (I), and one-way analysis of variance.

Let's make use of the statistical road map. Shortly, we will learn the reason for choosing one path over another, but at the moment our main concern is how this map works. Place your finger on "Level of Measurement" boulevard. This boulevard asks, "What is the level of measurement?" You answer by traveling on "Nominal," "Ordinal," or "Interval" avenue. Let's say your data are ordinal, so you choose "Ordinal" avenue. After you have traveled on this avenue, the next boulevard you encounter is "Number of Groups," which poses the question, "How many groups are there?" You can answer by choosing "1," "2," or "3 or More" street. If you have three groups, you choose "3 or More" street. You then travel on this street until you reach the intersection "Nature of Groups." This intersection poses the question, "What is the nature of the groups?" You can answer by choosing "Independent" or "Related" street. If your groups are independent, you choose "Independent" street and travel on it until you come to a house for the Kruskal-Wallis test.

Before you continue reading, see if you can follow the directions in a practice problem.

Problem   What boulevard, avenue, streets, and intersections must you travel to reach the statistical test called Wilcoxon?

Answer   "Level of Measurement" boulevard, "Ordinal" avenue, "Number of Groups" boulevard, "2" street, "Nature of Groups" intersection, "Related" street, "Data" intersection, and "Numbers" street.

Now take a closer look at the Statistical Road Map. You will notice that it is really three maps in one. The avenues divide it into three sections. When you begin at Level of Measurement boulevard, you have a choice of going to the Nominal section, the Ordinal section, or the Interval section. Your avenue choice limits the houses to which you have access. For example, if you choose Nominal avenue, you can reach only the houses in this section of the map, where tests such as the binomial, McNemar, or Cochran Q are. If you choose Ordinal avenue, you can reach only the houses in this section of the map, where tests such as the Kolmogorov-Smirnov, sign, or Kruskal-Wallis are. Finally, if you choose Interval avenue, you can reach only the houses in the section where the tests such as t (I), t (II), and one-way analysis of variance are.

As you can see from examining this map, you must understand the meaning of each boulevard, intersection, avenue, and street in order to use it effectively. You must know what questions the boulevards and intersections are asking and what the appropriate answers to these questions are in order to make the proper choices of avenues and streets. In the following paragraphs each boulevard, avenue, street, and intersection will be fully explained. Read these explanations very carefully. After you understand the meanings of these terms, you will know which avenues and streets to travel to reach the right house, or the right statistical tests.

"LEVEL OF MEASUREMENT" BOULEVARD

The first boulevard you encounter on this map is "Level of Measurement." This boulevard asks, "What is your level of measurement?" This question concerns the nature of your data. There are three answers you can give, or three avenues you can travel according to the map: they are Nominal, Ordinal, or Interval.

"Nominal" avenue concerns itself with numbers that are assigned only to identify individuals or objects. Examples are social security and license plate numbers.

"Ordinal" avenue concerns itself with numbers that rank individuals or objects. Examples are gemstones ranked one to ten, and military status.

"Interval" avenue allows you to make comparisons between individuals or objects on a scale of equal units. Examples of interval measurement are scores on standardized tests and degrees on an ordinary thermometer.

You will notice there is no "Ratio" avenue. Most studies in the social sciences do not require the ratio level, because they are not measuring such physical traits as height, weight, and volume. Few statistical tests require this level of measurement.[1] After you have selected an avenue, the second boulevard that you encounter is "Number of Groups."

"NUMBER OF GROUPS" BOULEVARD

The "Number of Groups" boulevard poses the question, "How many groups are there in your study?"

If you take the "1" street, you are looking at a single group. You only want to find out whether this single group is representative of a specified population.

If your answer leads you to "2" street, you are interested in examining the difference between two groups. Did these two groups come from the same population? For two-group tests you can either have two separate groups or use the same group twice.

If you choose "3 or More" street, you are interested in the difference among three or *more* groups in the sample. Did these groups come from the same popula-

---

[1] Refer to Chapter 2 for a more complete explanation of levels of measurement.

tions? [2] Your choice of avenues and streets determines the intersections you encounter. The different intersections are explained next.

"NUMBER OF CATEGORIES" INTERSECTION

The "Number of Categories" intersection is reached only by traveling on "Level of Measurement" boulevard, "Nominal" avenue, and "1" street.

The "Number of Categories" intersection asks, "How many categories are there?" The number of categories for one-group samples refers to this one group's being broken down into subdivisions. For instance, one group of eighth-graders might be separated into two categories or subdivisions according to sex: male and female; or a group of college students may be divided into three categories according to marital status, such as married, divorced, and single.

There are three streets that you can travel at this intersection, "1," "2," or "3 or More."

Street "1" means you have one category; street "2," two categories; and street "3 or More," three or *more* categories. It is up to you to make the correct decision.

"CATEGORY SIZE" INTERSECTION

The "Category Size" intersection asks, "How many subjects or objects are in each of your categories?" You have a choice of two streets. You should choose the "4 or Less" street if you have four or less subjects in each category. If you have five or more subjects in each category, you should choose the "5 or More" street.

[2] If you have three or more groups, you must use the test that is right for three or more groups. Many people think you can use the two-group tests interchangeably with the three-or-more-group tests. This is not true. If you are dealing with six groups and you use a two-group test, you will be making 15 comparisons and you will not get the same answer for your research as when you use the three-or-more-group tests and make one comparison. Look at it this way: when you use a three-or-more group test, you have one chance to reject the null hypothesis, whereas when you use the two-group test you have 15 chances to reject the null hypothesis. By using a two-group test you are increasing your chance of rejecting the null hypothesis wrongly (Type I error).

"NATURE OF GROUPS" INTERSECTION

The "Nature of Groups" intersection asks, "What is the nature or character of your groups?" You answer by choosing "Independent" street or "Related" street.

"Independent" street refers to groups that have members in their samples that are not connected to members in the other sample(s). They are completely separate groups. The selection of a person in one sample in no way influences the selection of a person in the other. The independent groups may be random samples drawn from the same population or random samples drawn from different populations.

Let us consider an example where we have two independent groups drawn from the same population. For instance, if a researcher is interested in the effects of vitamins on teenage boys, he might randomly draw two samples from this population of teenage boys. He might then expose one group to vitamin A and the other to vitamin B. The researcher is using two independent groups because the choice of one male who uses vitamin A in no way affects the selection of another male who uses vitamin B.

Let us now look at an example involving randomly drawn samples from two different populations. An investigator might wish to test the difference in performance in math between men and women. The selection of men in this sample in no way influences the selection of women. They are independent, because knowing the female's score will not tell you a thing about the male's score.

"Related" street refers to groups that have members that are connected somehow to one another. There are two ways the individuals can be matched or connected. You can match a person with himself. That is, you can have the same person taking two different treatments. For example, a measurement might be made on a person's ability to shoot basketballs before a special drug is given. After the drug is given, another measure is taken to see how well he shoots baskets. The object is to find out if change has occurred as a result of the drug. The same person is being measured in two different situations.

Another way you can match is by pairing individuals in areas such as IQ, socioeconomic level, and ethnic background and then assigning them to each group. For instance, person A would be paired with person B, then person A would be randomly assigned to one class and his matched partner, B, would be assigned to the other class. In a study involving problem solving, subjects might be paired on the basis of their IQ scores; one member from each pair would then be randomly assigned to

Group I and the other to Group II. Because of this matching of IQ, you now have two groups that are alike in IQ's. Now any difference that you might have between the two groups on problem solving could not be attributed to the difference in IQ. As you can see, in order to match properly in this instance, it is very important that the subjects be matched on variables that are highly correlated with the dependent variables, in this case problem solving. The groups would not be related if you matched them on the basis of shoe size instead of the IQ tests.

Researchers frequently use matched pairs such as identical twins, husbands and wives, fathers and sons. Whatever the match, you would expect a relationship between measures from both groups.

"DATA" INTERSECTION

The "Data" intersection is reached by traveling on "Level of Measurement" boulevard, "Ordinal" avenue, "Number of Groups" boulevard, "2" street, "Nature of Groups" intersection, and "Related" street. The "Data" intersection asks, "How do you plan to use your data?" Two different answers are possible. If you travel on "Signs" street, the data you have are in the form of plus and minus signs. If you travel on "Numbers" street, the data are in the form of numbers, not signs.

PARAMETRIC AND NONPARAMETRIC TESTS

In research, statistical tests are referred to as either *parametric* or *nonparametric*. When you are choosing a statistical test using the Statistical Road Map, you are making a choice between a parametric or nonparametric test. The parametric tests listed on this map are *t* (I), *t* (II), *t* (III), one-way analysis of variance, and randomized blocks design.

What assumptions have to be met before you can use a parametric test? Four of the basic requirements are:

1. The groups in the samples are randomly drawn from the population. This is usually done by the use of a table of random numbers.
2. The data are at least the interval level of measurement.
3. The data are normally distributed. Most psychological and physical traits are normally distributed, and you really do not have to worry about this assumption unless you have a sample size that is extremely small.
4. The variances are equal. As a rough check on variance you could look at the

standard deviation of both samples; if one appeared two or three times larger, then you would question this assumption.[3]

Whenever these assumptions are met, use a parametric test, because it is more powerful than the nonparametric test. What we mean by *powerful* is that parametric tests have a higher probability of rejecting the null hypothesis when it should be rejected.

The rest of the tests on the map (chi square, binomial, Wilcoxon, and so on) are nonparametric tests. There are two reasons for the use of so many nonparametric tests.

1. Many of the advanced parametric tests, such as the analysis of covariance and Latin square, are too time-consuming to be done by hand and are more efficiently handled by a prerecorded program in the computer center.
2. In the social sciences, because of the nature of the data, the assumptions for a parametric test often are not met; therefore you have to choose a nonparametric test.

Nonparametric tests have fewer and less stringent assumptions. They meet the first requirement of a parametric test: the groups in the sample are randomly drawn. The other requirements of the parametric test are not met. The shape of the distribution does not have to be normal. They are distribution-free tests whose level of measurement is generally nominal or ordinal. When there is a very small sample size, six or fewer, you are forced to use a nonparametric test. As a rule, these tests are very easy to compute; however, they can become very laborious when the sample size is very large.

The parametric and nonparametric tests used on the map are listed in Table 6-1, together with the appropriate page numbers.

Now that you have a working knowledge of the map's composition, let's simulate research conditions and see if we can reach the house that contains the right statistical test with a minimum of trouble.

USING THE MAP

Youngblood worked for a large manufacturing company that produced hearing aids. He had the job of buying batteries for these hearing aids, and he had a choice between battery A and battery B at identical prices. He had no ex-

---

[3] Today most statisticians feel it is not worth the effort to test for homogeneity of variance (explained in Chapter 9).

Table 6-1: Tests Listed on the Statistical Road Map

Nonparametric tests	Page numbers	Parametric tests	Page numbers
Binomial	171	*t* (I)	267
Chi square (I)	181	*t* (II)	274
Chi square (II)	189	*t* (III)	282
McNemar	194	One-way	
Cochran *Q*	199	analysis of	
Kolmogorov-Smirnov	213	variance	289
Mann-Whitney *U*	220	Randomized [4]	
Sign	229	blocks	
Wilcoxon	235	design	
Kruskal-Wallis	241		
Friedman	249		

perience with either, but battery B had been applauded by many of his associates. Naturally, he wanted the battery that had the longer life. Taking random samples of 100 brand A batteries and 100 brand B batteries, he tested each group for battery life, recording the exact time each battery lasted. The null hypothesis stated there is no difference between the mean battery life of group A and the mean battery life of group B. Youngblood stated as his alternative hypothesis that brand B's battery life is longer than brand A's. Youngblood now wanted to select the statistical test that will effectively analyze the data and tell him whether the difference between the two groups was significant.

The first thing Youngblood did was look at the Statistical Road Map. He entered the map and traveled on the boulevard "Level of Measurement." He asked himself, "What is the level of measurement of my data?" He felt that since he was recording his data in minutes and seconds, this was ratio, and he could easily walk down "Interval" avenue. He traveled down "Interval" avenue until he came to the "Number of Groups" boulevard. He asked himself, "How many groups do I have?" Because he had chosen only two groups, he traveled on "2" street. The first intersection he came to was "Nature of Groups," which gave him the choice of "Independent" street or "Related" street. Since he had not matched these groups in any way or used the same group twice, he felt comfortable taking "Independent" street. He traveled on "Independent" street until he reached a house with the statistical test called *t* (II) inside. Youngblood's route is shown in the drawing.

[4] In order to complete the Statistical Road Map, the randomized blocks design was included. However, this parametric test is beyond the scope of this book. Refer to Hays (1973).

Level of
Measurement
Boulevard

Interval Avenue

Number of Groups
Boulevard

2 Street

Nature of Groups
Intersection

Independent Street

t (II)

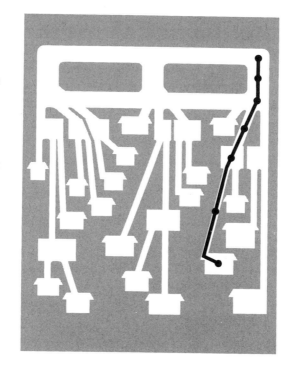

Now, let's test your skill and see if you really know how to use the map. You will be using it for the remainder of the chapter. In the following pages you will be presented with twelve situations. After you read each one, use the map to help you choose among three statistical tests. Underline the test that best fits the situation, then read the answer that follows. The right test will be named along with the correct route, and a short explanation will be given on why the other two tests were eliminated.

Situation I: The Delicious Hamburger

Mary has a fast-food restaurant that serves four types of hamburger: (A) hamburger with pickle and onion, (B) hamburger with tomato and pickle; (C) hamburger with chili, and (D) hamburger with relish and onion. She decides to reduce her costs by selling only one kind of hamburger. However, before she takes this drastic step, she wants to determine if the customers' choices of hamburger are equal. Her *null hypothesis* reads that in the sample of 100 customers, there is no difference in their preference among the four types of hamburger. She selects a random sample of 100 customers and asks each of them to indicate their hamburger preference. The results are shown in Table 6-2.

Table 6-2: Distribution of Choices of Four Hamburger Types for a Sample of 100 Customers

Hamburger preference	Frequency
A	45
B	20
C	17
D	18
	$N = 100$

Mary notices that hamburger A was chosen more often than hamburger B, C, or D. Is there a significant difference, or is this a case of sampling error? To arrive at whether the observed frequency is due to chance, you would apply the binomial, or chi square (I), or *t* (I) test. Underline the correct answer.

ANSWER

The answer for Situation I, The Delicious Hamburger, is the chi-square (I) test. The possible choices will be discussed in some detail for this first situation, providing a quick review of the thought processes involved in choosing an appropriate statistical test. The proper boulevards, avenues, intersections, and streets to travel are as shown.

You first go along "Level of Measurement" boulevard. The question is, "What is the level of measurement?" The answer chosen is "Nominal" avenue, because you are only recording preferences, which are frequencies; the customers were deciding on either A, B, C, or D. The second boulevard traveled is "Number of Groups." Since there is only one random sample of customers at Mary's restaurant, you choose to travel Street "1". The intersection you reach is "Number of Categories." You count the number of categories. Since you have four kinds of hamburgers, A, B, C, and D, there are four categories. You then travel on street "3 or More," which takes you to the house for the chi square (I) test. If you chose a *t* (I) test, you did not answer the question correctly at the "Level of Measurement" boulevard. The correct level of measurement is nominal. The *t* (I) requires an interval level of measurement.

If you chose a binomial test, you went wrong at the "Category" intersection. The binomial test requires only two categories, and this situation deals with four categories.

Level of
Measurement
Boulevard

Nominal Avenue

Number of Groups
Boulevard

1 Street

Number of
Categories
Intersection

3 or More Street

Chi square (I)

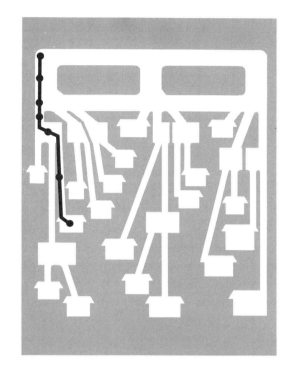

Situation II: The Beau Brummel Professors

Tom, Phil, and John, college instructors, were having a contest
to see who was the most fashionable in attire. The winner of this rather ridiculous
contest would be treated to a dinner by the losers. In order to fairly decide who was
the best dresser, they wanted some objective judges. Tom offered the list of students
who would be enrolled in the next semester's statistics course. They matched these
students three at a time according to their socioeconomic level and grades. That is,
students with similar grades and socioeconomic background formed a group of three,
or one matched triplet. Each student was assigned from a matched triplet to one of
three classrooms. The students were then asked to fill out a questionnaire on their
professors—a rating scale with 25 as the highest possible score. The *null hypothesis*
states that there is no significant difference between the ratings of the three classes.
The ratings are shown in Table 6-3.

Is there a significant difference in the students' rating of the instructors? Which
test should be used to analyze these data: the Kruskal-Wallis, Friedman, or *t* (III)?
Underline the correct answer.

Table 6-3: Dress Ratings for Three College Instructors

Matched triplet	Tom	Phil	John
A	20	25	10
B	21	24	15
C	22	20	16
D	18	20	22
E	16	20	25
F	16	20	25
G	14	23	15
H	17	24	13
I	14	23	13
J	18	22	10

ANSWER

The answer for Situation II, The Beau Brummel Professors, is the Friedman test. The correct route is as shown.

If you chose the Kruskal-Wallis test, you made a wrong turn at the intersection "Nature of Groups." The Kruskal-Wallis test is to be used with independently

Level of Measurement Boulevard

Ordinal Avenue

Number of Groups Boulevard

3 or More Street

Nature of Groups Intersection

Related Street

Friedman

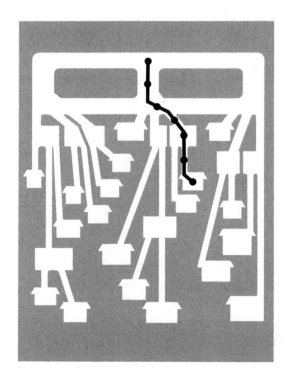

chosen groups. Remember, the groups in this example were matched according to socioeconomic status and grades.

If you chose the t (III), you first went wrong at "Level of Measurement" boulevard. The level of measurement for any t-test requires the interval, not the ordinal level.

Situation III: The Dedicated Researcher

A researcher who is working with autistic children is interested in determining the effects of two new methods of instruction. He randomly selects two groups of subjects. One group receives method A and the second group method B. After a six-month period the two samples are compared on a standardized reading achievement test. The *null hypothesis* states that there is no significant difference between the two groups of autistic children in their reading achievement. The results are shown in Table 6-4.

Table 6-4: Reading Achievement Test Scores for Two Groups of Autistic Children

Method A, group I	Method B, group II
2	3
3	3
2	2
1	1
1	1
2	2
3	3
2	2
2	3
	4

Find out whether there is a significant difference between method A and method B by comparing the reading achievement scores.[5] Apply the t (II), or Mann-Whitney U, or t (III) test to your data: underline the correct answer.

ANSWER

The answer to Situation III, The Dedicated Researcher, is the t (II) test. The correct route is as shown.

---

[5] Assume the reading scores are normally distributed.

Level of
Measurement
Boulevard

Interval Avenue

Number of Groups
Boulevard

2 Street

Nature of Groups
Intersection

Independent Street

t (II)

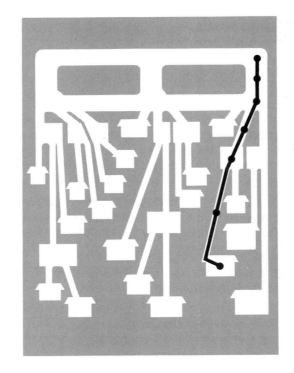

If you chose the Mann-Whitney U, you did not correctly answer the question concerning level of measurement. The level of measurement is not ordinal, but interval. Remember, you used a standardized achievement test.

If you chose the t (III), you went wrong at the intersection "Nature of Groups." The groups were not related; they were independently selected.

Situation IV: The Bubble Gum Children

Maria wants to find out which of her bubble gum formulas, Brand A, Brand B, or Brand C, produces the biggest bubbles. Success will earn her a big bonus from her company. She randomly selects three groups of children and gives each group a different brand of bubble gum. She asks each child to blow a bubble and has a panel of bubble gum enthusiasts rate each one on a nine-point scale. The *null hypothesis* states that there is no significant difference among the three groups in their ability to blow bubbles (and thus no difference in the bubble-producing properties of the three brands of gum). Scores for each child are shown in Table 6-5.

Table 6-5: Ratings on Bubble-Blowing Ability
for Three Groups of Children

Brand A	Brand B	Brand C
3	1	9
5	2	8
7	4	9
6		

Maria wants to know if a significant difference exists among the three brands of bubble gum. She uses a t (II), a Friedman, or a Kruskal-Wallis test to find out; underline the correct answer.

ANSWER

The answer to Situation IV, The Bubble Gum Children, is the Kruskal-Wallis test. The correct route is as shown.

If you chose the t (II) again, you forgot that the test was not to be used at the interval level of measurement.

Level of
Measurement
Boulevard

Ordinal Avenue

Number of Groups
Boulevard

3 or More Street

Nature of Groups
Intersection

Independent Street

Kruskal-
Wallis

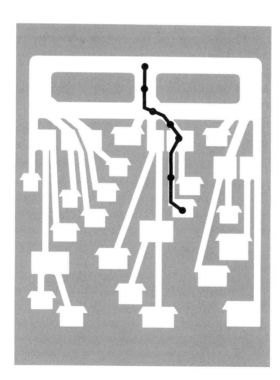

If you chose the Friedman, you answered the question about the nature of the groups wrongly. The Friedman test concerns itself with matched groups. These were independently selected.

Situation V: Rate a Teacher

Martin wanted to find out if there was a significant difference in how student teachers rated an experienced teacher's performance with children after they had taken a special teacher training course. He randomly selected two groups of future student teachers. One experimental group[6] of seven students took a special teacher training course, in which they were instructed to recognize the strengths and weaknesses of teachers. The control group of nine students took a regular course in teacher training, in which they studied great teachers in history and did not openly discuss what constitutes good teaching. When the courses ended, each group was shown a videotape of a teacher presenting material in front of a classroom. They were then asked to rate this teacher. The total rating possible was a 30. The *null hypothesis* states that there is no significant difference between the two groups in the scores they gave the experienced teacher. The data are shown in Table 6-6.

Table 6-6: A Teacher's Competency Rating

Experimental group scores	Control group scores
10	15
13	17
3	20
18	19
5	22
11	30
2	29
	4
	3

The ratings of the experimental group were compared to those of the control group. Was there a significant difference in the ratings of the two groups? Use a Wilcoxon, *t* (III), or Mann-Whitney *U* test; underline the correct answer.

---

[6] The experimental group is given the treatment; the control group is not given any treatment.

Level of
Measurement
Boulevard

Ordinal Avenue

Number of Groups
Boulevard

2 Street

Nature of Groups
Intersection

Independent Street

Mann-Whitney U

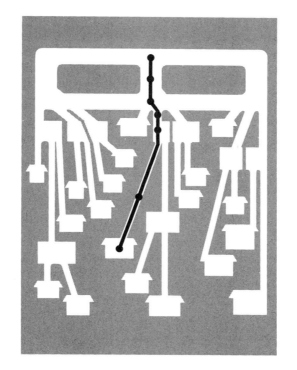

ANSWER

The answer to Situation V, Rate a Teacher, is the Mann-Whitney U. The correct route is as shown.

If you chose the Wilcoxon test, you need to review the nature of the groups, because this is a related test.

If you chose the t (III) test, you went wrong at "Level of Measurement" boulevard.

Situation VI: The Efficiency Expert

An efficiency expert was very dissatisfied with the back glass placement procedure in the Beta Automobile Plant.[7] He knew it needed to be made

[7] The procedure that assembly workers use to install glass on the back windows of cars. The workers place a piece of glass on a wooden table, apply sealer, allow it to partially dry, and then place the glass in the back window frame of a car.

easier. He had devised three new methods, but he did not know which one would be easier for the men. He randomly drew 30 men off the assembly line and matched them, three at a time, on their ability to install glass on the cars. He then assigned a person from each matched triplet to one of the three groups. Group I was shown method one, group II was shown method two, and group III was shown method three. Each group was asked to write a 1 if he believed his method was easy and a 0 if he believed his method was hard. The expert then analyzed the results. Five people in group I found method one easy, three people in group II found method two easy, and eight people in group III found method three easy. The *null hypothesis* states there is no significant difference among the three groups in their perceptions. The data are shown in Table 6-7.

Table 6-7: Results of Plant Workers' Survey

Method one, group I	Method two, group II	Method three, group III
1	1	1
0	1	1
0	0	0
1	1	1
0	0	0
1	0	1
0	0	1
1	0	1
1	0	1
0	0	1

Do these scores represent a significant difference among the three methods? Analyze these data using a Friedman, Cochran Q, or Kruskal-Wallis test; underline the correct answer.

ANSWER

The answer to Situation VI, The Efficiency Expert, is the Cochran Q test. The correct route is as shown.

If you chose the Friedman or the Kruskal-Wallis, you went wrong at "Level of Measurement" boulevard. The data are not ordinal, but nominal. The only arithmetic operation you are using is counting.

Level of
Measurement
Boulevard

Nominal Avenue

Number of Groups
Boulevard

3 or More Street

Nature of Groups
Intersection

Related Street

Cochran Q

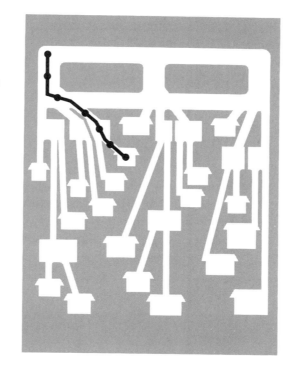

Situation VII: The New Discovery

Professor X had discovered a miraculous serum that could increase anyone's speed when running. The summer Olympics were approaching and the professor wanted to test his serum. He randomly assigned 20 individuals who were competing in the 32-kilometer race to four groups, five subjects in each group. Each group received a different gram dosage of the drug, and each then ran the 32-kilometer race. The times required to run the race are shown in Table 6-8.[8] The null hypothesis states there is no significant difference among the four groups in their ability to run 32 kilometers.

Is there a significant difference among the four groups in the speed with which they ran the 32-kilometer race? To find out, use the Friedman, one-way analysis of variance, or the chi-square (II) test; underline the right answer.

[8] This situation is a hyperbole. A person who ran 32 km in one minute would be going faster than sound.

Table 6-8: Number of Minutes to Run the 32-Kilometer Race

Group A	Group B	Group C	Group D
6	5	4	2
6	3	4	2
6	4	4	2
7	4	3	1
7	4	3	1

ANSWER

The answer to Situation VII, The New Discovery, is the one-way analysis of variance. The correct route is as shown.

If you chose the Friedman or chi-square (II) test, you went wrong at "Level of Measurement" boulevard. The data are not nominal or ordinal but ratio.

Level of
Measurement
Boulevard

Interval Avenue

Number of Groups
Boulevard

3 or More Street

Nature of Groups
Intersection

Independent Street

One-Way Analysis
of Variance

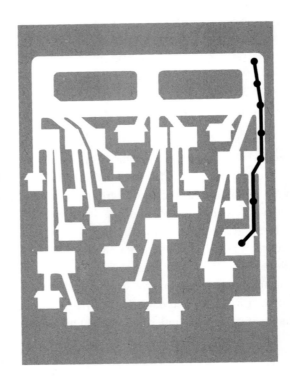

Situation VIII: The Dancing Coach

A choreographer, Pete Finely, has to choose between two dancing coaches who have opposite approaches. He decides to conduct a study to help him with this decision. He auditions 20 dancers, whom he then matches on their ability to do certain routines. One person from each matched pair is assigned to a dancing coach, and for 60 hours each coach teaches the dancers the same routine. At the end of this period the dancers are tested and rated from 1 to 30 on their ability to do this new routine. The results are given in Table 6-9. The *null hypothesis* states there is no significant difference between Group A and Group B in their ability to do this new dance routine.

Table 6-9: Ratings on Dancers Taught by Coach A and Coach B

Pair	Coach A	Coach B
A	30	20
B	10	5
C	29	24
D	20	18
E	16	20
F	23	23
G	21	16
H	26	25
I	23	20
J	23	20

Do these results indicate a significant difference between the two groups? Could the difference have arisen by chance? To arrive at the answer you would apply the sign, Mann-Whitney *U*, or Wilcoxon test; underline the correct answer.

ANSWER

The answer to Situation VIII, The Dancing Coach, is the Wilcoxon test. The correct route is as shown.

If you chose the sign test at the "Data" intersection, you made a wrong turn. The data you have are in the form of numbers, not in the form of plus and minus signs.

If you chose the Mann-Whitney *U* test, you made a wrong turn at the "Nature of Groups" intersection. Remember, the groups were matched on their ability to do certain dance routines.

Level of
Measurement
Boulevard

Ordinal Avenue

Number of Groups
Boulevard

2 Street

Nature of Groups
Intersection

Related Street

Data Intersection

Numbers Street

Wilcoxon

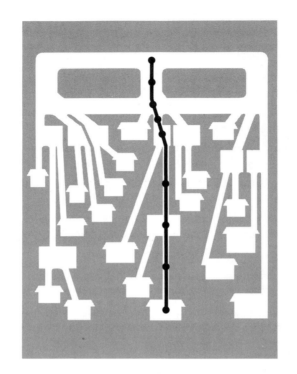

Situation IX: Politics as Usual

A political science student wanted to find out if moving from a rural to an urban area affected a person's voting preference. He believed that people moving from a farming area to an urban area were likely to change their political party. After these rural individuals had lived in the city a while, they had increasing contact with and were influenced by people from the city. He observed 27 randomly selected new residents on their first day of arrival in Chicago. He categorized them by their political party, Democrat or Republican. He then observed these same new residents one year later, after each had been exposed to the elements of the big city, and made the same categorization of the data. The numbers that he recorded are shown in Table 6-10. The *null hypothesis* states there is no significant difference between the two groups in their party affiliation.

Table 6-10: Change in Political Affiliation of New Residents after One Year in Chicago

First day	After one year	
	Democrats	*Republicans*
Republicans	15	4
Democrats	3	5

From these data the student attempted to find out if there was a significant difference in the change of party affiliation. He used a McNemar, sign, or chi-square (II) test to analyze his data; underline the correct answer.

ANSWER

The answer to Situation IX, Politics as Usual, is the McNemar test. The correct route is as shown.

Level of
Measurement
Boulevard

Nominal Avenue

Number of Groups
Boulevard

2 Street

Nature of Groups
Intersection

Related Street

McNemar

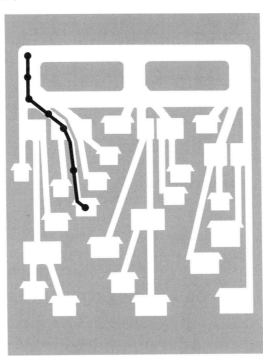

If you chose the sign test, you were wrong when you chose "Ordinal" avenue. The level of measurement is nominal.

If you chose the chi-square (II) test, the intersection that bothered you was "Nature of Groups." The groups are related; the same group was used twice.[9]

Situation X: The Wine Merchant

Alfredo, a purveyor of fine wines, wants to discern if the choice of white wine is determined by its dryness. To test this hypothesis he arranges to have five different varieties of white wine placed before a group of ten randomly selected wine buyers. The wines range from a very dry one, ranked as 1, to an extremely sweet one, ranked as 5. Each customer is then offered a choice among the five different types of wine; the customers' selections are shown in Table 6-11. The *null hypothesis* states that there is no significant difference in the ten customers' preferences among the five wines.

Table 6-11: Wine Selected by Customers

Ranks	1	2	3	4	5
Customer choice	2	2	5	0	1

Which test will you use to find out if there is a significant difference in the customer's choice of wine? Will you use the chi-square (I), McNemar, or Kolmogorov-Smirnov test? Underline the correct test.

ANSWER

The answer to Situation X, The Wine Merchants, is the Kolmogorov-Smirnov test. The correct route is as shown.

If you chose the chi-square (I) or the McNemar test, you made a wrong turn at "Level of Measurement" boulevard. The data are better than nominal. When you are concerned about ranking of wine, you are using numbers in an ordinal manner.

Situation XI: The Long-Ball Hitter

A high-school physical education instructor wants to compare the effectiveness of two methods of instruction in home-run hitting. He matches individuals trying out for his baseball team on the basis of their ability to hit the long

---

[9] Because the same group was used twice, there are two groups.

Level of
Measurement
Boulevard

Ordinal Avenue

Number of Groups
Boulevard

1 Street

Kolmogorov-
Smirnov

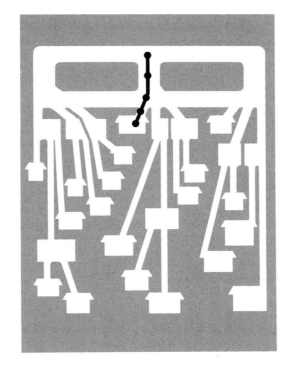

ball.[10] He assigns one member of each matched pair to Group A and the other to Group B, seven to each group. Group A now practices batting by using a pitching machine, while Group B practices batting with a major league hitter. At the end of six weeks each individual is given a slugging test, and the distance he hits the long ball is recorded, as shown in Table 6-12. The *null hypothesis* states there is no significant difference between Group A and Group B in their ability to hit the long ball.

Table 6-12: Long-Ball Hitters' Scores for Group A and Group B (in Meters)

Group A	Group B
76	120
90	130
100	130
75	140
120	140
100	135
70	140

[10] For this situation we are assuming the distribution is normal, even though conceivably it might be skewed.

Level of
Measurement
Boulevard

Interval Avenue

Number of Groups
Boulevard

2 Street

Nature of Groups
Intersection

Related Street

t (III)

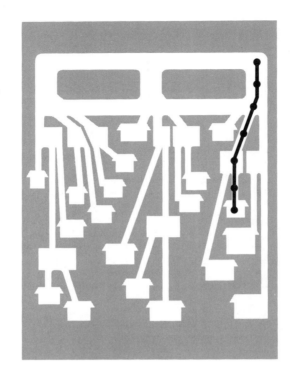

Do these results indicate a significant difference between the two methods of instruction? In order to analyze the data, you use the *t* (III), Mann-Whitney *U,* or Kruskal-Wallis test; underline the correct test.

ANSWER

The answer chosen for Situation XI, The Long-Ball Hitter, is the *t* (III) test. The correct route is as shown.

If you chose the Mann-Whitney *U* or the Kruskal-Wallis test, you missed out on the level of measurement. These data have a ratio level, and you should have taken "Interval" avenue.

Situation XII: Academic Freedom

The new chairman of the sociology department at Tibur College was very autocratic, and he wanted every teacher to give the same distribution of pass/fail grades in Sociology I. In order to check on his three instructors and make sure none was easier than any other, he did a little study. He made sure the students were randomly assigned at registration to each instructor's class. He stated as his *null hypothesis* that there is no significant difference between the three classes in the assignment of grades. At the end of the semester he recorded the instructors' grades, as shown in Table 6-13.

Table 6-13: Table of Instructors' Pass-Fail Grades

	Pass	Fail
Louis Fern	20	8
Donna Clay	11	13
Carl Perez	14	12

To find out if there was a difference in the grading of the three instructors, he analyzed these data using a binomial, chi-square (II), or Kruskal-Wallis test; underline the correct answer.

ANSWER

The answer to Situation XII, Academic Freedom, is the chi-square (II) test. The correct route is as shown.

Level of
Measurement
Boulevard

Nominal Avenue

Number of Groups
Boulevard

3 or More Street

Nature of Groups
Intersection

Independent Street

Chi square (II)

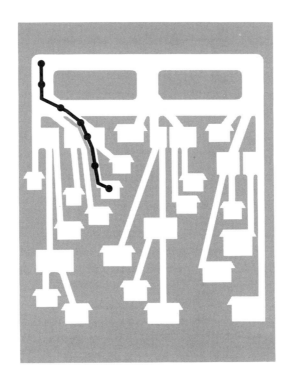

If you chose the binomial test, you went wrong at "Number of Groups" boulevard. There are three groups for this study.

If you chose the Kruskal-Wallis test, you selected incorrectly at Level of Measurement boulevard and gave your data credit for being ordinal instead of nominal.

SUMMARY

This chapter showed you how to choose a statistical test. You were given a Statistical Road Map as a tool to help you choose the appropriate test, and each term on the map was explained operationally. You learned how to use this map; then you practiced your skill by solving 12 situations.

Now test your knowledge: see if you can pass the next mastery test.

SELF-TEST FOR MASTERY

If you have trouble working a problem, reread the explanation on the page listed.

The eleven scrambled words listed below are the names of statistical tests. Unscramble each word and match it with its correct test description. (A word can be used more than once.) Place your answers in the space provided in the right-hand column. Use the Statistical Road Map to arrive at your decisions. The first example has been done for you.

Scrambled Words

hic reaqus (II)	lyssiaan fo riaavnec	estt *t* (III)	*Q* hccorna
edmfrian	eno yaw	moialnib	nooxcwil
estt *t* (II)	cm ramen	igsn	allisw surkkal

	Test descriptions	*Statistical tests*
p. 138	**1.** (a) ordinal (b) three groups (c) independent groups	<u>Kruskal-Wallis</u>

2. (a) nominal   _____
   (b) four groups
   (c) related groups

3. (a) ordinal   _____
   (b) two groups
   (c) related groups
   (d) plus and minus signs

4. (a) nominal   _____
   (b) one group
   (c) two categories, less than five in each category

5. (a) interval   _____
   (b) four groups
   (c) independent groups

6. (a) ordinal   _____
   (b) two groups
   (c) related groups
   (d) data recorded as numbers

7. (a) nominal   _____
   (b) two groups
   (c) independent groups

8. (a) ordinal   _____
   (b) four groups
   (c) related groups

9. (a) interval   _____
   (b) two groups
   (c) related groups

10. (a) nominal   _____
   (b) two groups
   (c) related groups

11. (a) nominal   _____
   (b) three groups
   (c) independent groups

ANSWERS TO SELF-TEST

Score yourself by adding up the points for each correct answer and write the total in the Evaluation form.

1 point each   1. (allisw surkkal) Kruskal-Wallis. 2. (*Q* hccorna) Cochran *Q*.
3. (igsn) Sign. 4. (moialnib) Binomial. 5. (lyssiaan fo riaavnec
eno yaw) One-way analysis of variance. 6. (nooxcwil) Wilcoxon 7. (hic reaqus (II)) Chi square (II). 8. (edmfrian)
Friedman. 9. (estt *t* (III)) *t* (III) test. 10. (cm ramen)
McNemar. 11. (hic reaqus (II)) Chi square (II).

Evaluation

Rating	Score
9–10 = Great	
7–8 = Fine	
6 = Satisfactory	
5 or less = Reread the chapter	

Next you will be reading Chapters 7, 8, and 9. The different sections of the
Statistical Road Map are covered by these chapters. If your level of measurement is
nominal, read Chapter 7 next. If your level of measurement is ordinal, turn to
Chapter 8. Finally, if your data are interval, refer to Chapter 9. Flowchart I
illustrates this referral process.

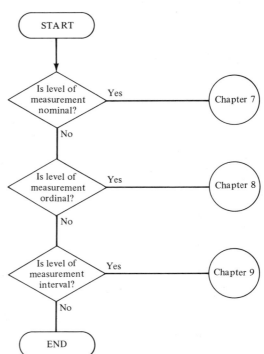

*Flowchart I: Determining the Level
of Measurement*

NOMINAL
TESTS

7

Figure 7-1: Nominal Tests

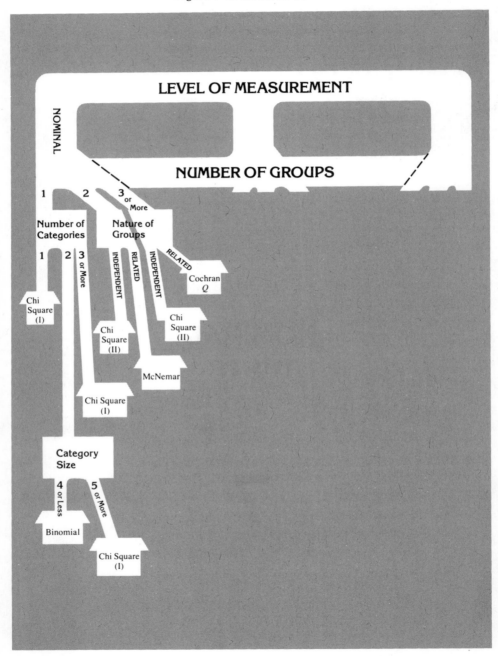

The next three chapters will cover the statistical tests that originate from the three avenues on the Statistical Road Map: Nominal, Ordinal, and Interval. Each test will be presented in the following manner:

1. Its purpose will be explained.
2. Its requirements will be listed.
3. A situation that warrants its use will be described.
4. The reader will be shown an easy-to-follow procedure to solve the formula for the test.
5. A practice problem will be provided to check the reader's grasp of the material.
6. The procedure will be summarized.

In this chapter we will discuss the tests reached by Nominal avenue, as shown on the map (Figure 7-1): binomial, chi square (I), chi square (II), McNemar, and the Cochran *Q*. Let's begin with the binomial test.

BINOMIAL TEST

Some of the statistical tests you will be studying are used to analyze data where there are many categories or outcomes. For instance, you might be concerned with marital status and break it down into four categories: divorced, widowed, single, or married. You might be interested in the six outcomes of rolling a die. You might be studying political party affiliation but be interested only in three major parties (categories): Republican, Democratic, and Independent. Finally, you might be concerned with grading by various instructors and break it down into five grading categories: A, B, C, D, and F. As you can see, these different subjects for research have more than two categories or outcomes.

The binomial test[1] is applicable only to data where there are two outcomes or categories. The two categories could be, for example:

1. Grades in a pass/fail course.
2. Party affiliation as broken down into either Republican or Democrat.
3. Outcome in tossing a coin heads or tails.
4. Outcome in rolling a six or not a six on a die.

The proportion of cases in one category is referred to as *P* and in the other category as *Q*. The value of *P* + *Q* always equals 1. If you know the value of *P*, you find *Q* by subtracting *P* from 1. The requirements for the binomial test are:

---

[1] The binomial test is called sometimes a *test of proportion*.

Binomial	1. Nominal data.
Requirements	2. One-group test.
	3. Two categories only.
	4. Sample size can be less than five.
	5. Independent observations.
	6. Simple random sample.
	7. Data in frequency form.

Let us start our discussion of the binomial test by talking about binomial probabilities.

Binomial Probabilities

You are working at an electronics firm, and your best friend Bobbie decides that she or you will buy lunch depending upon whether she flips a quarter heads or tails. Being sport-minded, you decide to go along with this game. Your "friend" then chooses heads and tells you to take tails. Over the next three days she tosses three heads, and you buy three lunches. These expensive results make you slightly suspicious about the coin. To ease your mind you want to find out the probability of a fair coin's coming up three heads in a row.

First let's look at the possible combinations that could occur for the three days. Table 7-1 shows these possibilities. For example, you could toss three heads, outcome 1, or three tails, outcome 2. The eight combinations shown in the table are all equally possible. Looking closely, now, you see there is only one chance out of eight that you could turn up with three heads. You then find the probability of getting three heads is equal to 1/8 or .125. There is a $12\frac{1}{2}$% chance of Bobbie's tossing three heads.

Table 7-1: Possible Combinations of Outcomes that Could Occur over a Three-Day Period

Outcome	First Day	Second Day	Third Day
1	H	H	H
2	T	T	T
3	H	T	T
4	H	H	T
5	H	T	H
6	T	H	H
7	T	T	H
8	T	H	T

Not only can you determine the probability of tossing three heads from Table 7-1, but also you can determine the probability of any outcome for a three-day period. You simply take the number of combinations that include the outcome in question and divide by the total number of possible outcomes. For example, if you wanted to know the probability of tossing exactly two heads in a three-day period, you would take the number of combinations that have two heads (that is, three: HHT, HTH, and THH) and divide by eight, the total number of possible outcomes. This gives you the probability of .375 or $37\frac{1}{2}\%$.

Working out all the possible combinations is simple enough for three days or trials, but as the number of trials increases, computation becomes very complex and laborious. The general formula for the binomial will help to resolve this difficulty. The formula is

---

Formula 7-1   *Binomial Formula*

$$p(x) = \binom{N}{x} P^x Q^{N-x}$$

The terms $\binom{N}{x}$ are binomial coefficients and are computed by the formula

$$\frac{N!}{x!\,(N-x)!}.$$

The meanings of the symbols are as follows:

Symbol	Meaning
!	Factorial [2]
N	Number of trials or sample size
x	Number of favorable outcomes for a series of trials
P	Probability of favorable outcome in a single trial [3]
$Q = (1 - P)$	Probability of unfavorable outcome in a single trial

Let's look at the same coin problem, but this time let's say it is two days later and the results are three heads and two tails. You now want to know the probability of tossing exactly three heads in five days, using Formula 7-1.

---

[2] The factorial of a positive number means the product of all the numbers from 1 to the number, inclusive. For example, $6! = 6 \times 5 \times 4 \times 3 \times 2 \times 1 = 720$ and $4! = 4 \times 3 \times 2 \times 1 = 24$. Table F gives factorials for numbers 0 through 20.

[3] Refer to Chapter 5, pp. 126–127 for a discussion of favorable outcomes.

PROCEDURE

Directions for Using the General Formula for the Binomial

Using the formula $p(x) = \begin{pmatrix} N \\ x \end{pmatrix} P^x Q^{N-x}$, find the probability

(p) of tossing three heads in five days.

$N = 5$

$x = 3$

$N - x = 2$

$\begin{pmatrix} N \\ x \end{pmatrix} = 10$

$P = 1/2$

$Q = 1/2$

1. Find N. Record the number of trials or the sample size. Since there are five days or trials, write the number 5 in the blank.
2. Find x. Record the number of favorable outcomes you desire for the series of trials. Since you are interested in the probability of three heads, write 3 in the blank.
3. Find $N - x$. Subtract the value found in step 2 (3) from the value found in step 1 (5). Write 2 in the blank.
4. Find $\begin{pmatrix} N \\ x \end{pmatrix}$. Refer to Table G.[4] Go down the N column until you find the number in step 1 (5). At this number run your fingers across the page until you are underneath the column with the x value found in step 2 (3). Record the value you have found in the table (10) in the blank.
5. Record P, the probability of your favorable outcome—tossing a head—in a single trial. Since two outcomes are possible (head, tail) and you are interested in only one of them (head), write 1/2 in the blank.
6. Find Q. Subtract the value found in step 5 (1/2) from 1. Write 1/2 in the blank.

Substitutions in the Formula

Make the appropriate substitutions by replacing each symbol with its corresponding number, as computed above in steps 1 through 6.

A. $p(x) = \begin{pmatrix} N \\ x \end{pmatrix} P^x Q^{N-x} =$

B. $p(3) = (\text{step 4}) \cdot \text{step 5}^{\text{raised to step 2}} \cdot \text{step 6}^{\text{raised to step 3}}$

C. $p(3) = 10 \cdot (\frac{1}{2})^3 \cdot (\frac{1}{2})^2$

[4] To make this formula easier to compute, Table G supplies you with all the binomial coefficients from 0 to 25. Having this table at your disposal makes it quite unnecessary to compute $\begin{pmatrix} N \\ x \end{pmatrix}$ for the binomial.

In other words, all you do is look up the value for $\begin{pmatrix} N \\ x \end{pmatrix}$ in Table G; you need not compute $\dfrac{N!}{x!(N-x)!}$.

Solving the Formula[5]

A. The term $(\frac{1}{2})^3$ means $\frac{1}{2} \cdot \frac{1}{2} \cdot \frac{1}{2}$ or $\frac{1}{8}$. The term $(\frac{1}{2})^2$ means $\frac{1}{2} \cdot \frac{1}{2}$ or $\frac{1}{4}$.

$$p(3) = 10 \cdot \frac{1}{8} \cdot \frac{1}{4}$$

B. Multiply $\frac{1}{8}$ times $\frac{1}{4}$ to get $\frac{1}{32}$.

$$p(3) = 10 \cdot \frac{1}{32}$$

C. Multiply 10 times $\frac{1}{32}$ to get $\frac{10}{32}$ and convert to a decimal (.3125).

$$p(3) = .3125$$

D. The probability of tossing three heads in five days is .3125 or roughly 31%.

Now let's see if you understand how to find binomial probabilities. Here is a practice problem that gives you an opportunity to use the binomial formula.

Problem   Vicki was taking an exam to get into a speech pathology program at Alpha University. She was finding six questions on the test very difficult to answer. Each question had three possible answers. She wanted to know the probability of getting five answers right out of six if she guessed at them. Table 7-2 shows the relevant part of the answer sheet before Vicki encircled her choices.

Table 7-2: Section of Answer Sheet

1. A B C	4. A B C
2. A B C	5. A B C
3. A B C	6. A B C

Answer   The probability of Vicki's getting five right out of six is .02.

$$p(x) = \binom{N}{x} P^x Q^{N-x}$$
$$p(5) = 6 \cdot \left(\frac{1}{3}\right)^5 \cdot \left(\frac{2}{3}\right)^1$$
$$p(5) = 6 \cdot \frac{1}{243} \cdot \frac{2}{3}$$
$$p(5) = 6 \cdot \frac{2}{729}$$
$$p(5) = \frac{12}{729} = \frac{4}{243} = .0164609 \text{ or } .02$$

[5] For a discussion of exponents refer to Chapter 1, p. 9.

As you can now attest, finding the probability of occurrence of certain outcomes using the binomial formula is not difficult. When we do research, however, we usually don't want to know just the probability of obtaining a specific value; more often we want to know the probability of obtaining that value and values more extreme.

For instance, you might ask the probability of obtaining two or fewer three's when you roll a die four times. In other words you want to know the probability of obtaining zero, one, or two three's. To get the answer you simply find the three separate probabilities, using the formula $p(x) = \binom{N}{x} P^x Q^{N-x}$, then add them together:[6]

$$p(0) = (1) \frac{1}{6}^0 \cdot \left(\frac{5}{6}\right)^4 = \frac{625}{1296} = .48$$

$$p(1) = (4) \left(\frac{1}{6}\right)^1 \cdot \left(\frac{5}{6}\right)^3 = \frac{500}{1296} = .39$$

$$p(2) = (6) \left(\frac{1}{6}\right)^2 \cdot \left(\frac{5}{6}\right)^2 = \frac{150}{1296} = .12$$

$$p = p(0) + p(1) + p(2) = .48 + .39 + .12 = .99$$

The probability for rolling two or fewer three's in four trials is .99. If you use a calculator, finding the answers to such problems is not a difficult task.

The Use of the Binomial Test

Up to this point we have been finding binomial probabilities and have not actually used the binomial test. The binomial test is an application of the binomial formula that we have been computing. Let us look now at a situation in which the binomial test is appropriate.

Situation

A high school teacher wants to test whether half the students in her class are Democrats. She feels that more than half are Democrats, so as her alternative hypothesis she states that more than half of the class are Democrats (one-tail test). The *null hypothesis* states that half of the children in her class are

---

[6] To compute $(1/6)^0$ in the first line of the solution, recall that any number to the zero power is equal to 1.

Democrats. She sets a .10 level of significance.[7] She chooses a random sample of ten students and asks them how they would vote in the 1980 presidential election. The would-be voters are classified as Republican or Democrat. The teacher learns that seven out of ten would vote as Democrats. Is this a significant difference?

The binomial test is appropriate in this situation because (1) the population is in two dichotomous categories, (2) the sample size is quite small, and (3) the data are nominal.

PROCEDURE

To test the statistical significance of her data the teacher uses the general binomial formula: $p(x) = \binom{N}{x} P^x Q^{N-x}$. She wants to find the probability that *seven or more* children are Democrats. Calculating only the probability of seven out of ten will not give her the correct answer. She calculates each of the separate binomial probabilities for seven out of ten; eight out of ten; nine out of ten; and ten out of ten; then she adds them to get one cumulative probability. Looking at the value for the cumulative probability, she can then decide to accept or reject the null hypothesis that her class is equally divided between Democrats and Republicans. Let's solve the teacher's problem and reach a decision. Check your work with that shown in Table 7-3. Adding the individual probabilities .001 + .010 + .044 + .117, you get the cumulative probability of .172.

Table 7-3: Computation of Binomial Probabilities for Binomial Test Situations

Probability of ten Democrats out of ten: $p(10) = \binom{10}{10} \left(\frac{1}{2}\right)^{10} \left(\frac{1}{2}\right)^{0} = .001$

Probability of nine Democrats out of ten: $p(9) = \binom{10}{9} \left(\frac{1}{2}\right)^{9} \left(\frac{1}{2}\right)^{1} = .010$

Probability of eight Democrats out of ten: $p(8) = \binom{10}{8} \left(\frac{1}{2}\right)^{8} \left(\frac{1}{2}\right)^{2} = .044$

Probability of seven Democrats out of ten: $p(7) = \binom{10}{7} \left(\frac{1}{2}\right)^{7} \left(\frac{1}{2}\right)^{3} = .117$

Statistical Decision

$p = .172$

1. Write the value for the cumulative probability. Place .172 in the blank to the left.

[7] For smaller samples, to decrease your chances of making a Type II error you set your level of significance at .10.

$\alpha = .10$

2. Write your level of significance.[8] Place .10 in the blank to the left.
3. If your cumulative probability, the number in step 1, is equal to or less than your level of significance, the number in step 2, you reject the null hypothesis. If your cumulative probability is greater than your level of significance, you do not reject the null hypothesis. In the present case you do not reject the null hypothesis, since your cumulative probability (.172) is greater than your level of significance (.10). Write *do not reject* in the blank to the left.

do not reject

We cannot reject the null hypothesis (at least not at the .10 level of significance). The political representations for Democrats and Republicans are the same for this teacher's class.

The tedium of computing these probabilities is enormous; therefore, statisticians have developed tables that can help when you are using the binomial test. Table H can be used for any sample size from 5 to 25 cases where the values for p and q are the same (both p and $q = 1/2$)—a situation that often occurs in practice. If you have situations that require different values for p and q, either compute the probabilities yourself or refer to more extensive tables, such as those found in the *Handbook of Tables for Probability and Statistics* published by the Chemical Rubber Company. When you want to use the binomial test and your sample size is larger than 25, which approximates the normal distribution, consult Siegel (1956) for the appropriate statistical procedure.

How to Use Table H

In this book Table H is presented for situations where p and q are the same; that is, p and $q = \frac{1}{2}$. Instead of computing the probability by using formula $p(x) = \binom{N}{x} P^x Q^{N-x}$, you can simply refer to Table H. How you use this table depends upon what your problem is.[9] If you are interested in the probability of getting x or fewer Democrats, you would use the table as is. For example, if you want to find out the probability that two or *fewer* students in a class of ten are Democrats, you enter Table H with a sample size of ten. You run your fingers down

---

[8] Level of significance is symbolized by the Greek letter alpha (α).

[9] The binomial distribution is symmetrical. This means that both tails of the distribution contain the same probabilities. In order to save space Table H contains only one half of the distribution. You can also use this table for the upper tail of the distribution by the simple modification explained below.

the left-hand column, labeled *N,* until you come to 10. Since you want to find the probability that two or fewer are Democrats, you run your fingers across this row until you are under an *x* of 2. You will find the table value of .055. Of course, the .055 can be determined by computing the probability of zero out of ten, plus the probability of one out of ten plus the probability of two out of ten.

Using Table H on problems such as this is a straightforward matter, but what about problems of finding the probability of getting *x* or more Democrats? In this case you can still use Table H, but you first have to modify its top border. Let's solve a problem by first modifying and then using Table H.

We will return to the problem above, the probability that seven or *more* students are Democrats. Working now with Table H:

1. Cross out the numbers at the top of the table in the row *x;* that is, cross out 0, 1, 2, 3, 4, ... 15.
2. Now replace the 0 you just eliminated with your sample size. The sample size always determines your starting point. For this problem 10 would be written above 0.
3. Next count backwards from your sample size until you reach 0, that is 9, 8, 7, 6, 5 . . . . . 0.
4. Write each of these above a crossed out number. 9 replaces 1, 8 replaces 2, 7 replaces 3 and so on until finally 0 replaces 10. See Figure 7-2.

Figure 7-2: Modified Table H

Now that you have modified the table, you are ready to use it. Run your fingers down the left-hand column labeled *N* until you come to your sample size of 10. Since you want to find the probability that seven or more students are Democrats, you next run your fingers across this row until you are under *x* of 7. You find a table value of .172 which is the same as the number you computed when you found the probability of seven out of ten, plus the probability of eight out of ten, plus the probability of nine out of ten, plus the probability of ten out of ten.

Now it is your turn to do an exercise to see if you understand how to use Table H.

Problem   Find the value in Table H when $x = 9$ or more and $N = 15$.

Answer   The value is .304.

In the high-school teacher situation a one-tail test was being used because you were predicting that one category would contain more Democrats. Table H shows these one-tail probabilities. If as your alternative hypothesis you simply stated that the two categories would differ, you would not be using a one-tail test but a two-tail. In this case you need two-tail probabilities.[10] If you want two-tail probabilities, you must double the value shown in these tables. For example, if the table value you found was .02, multiply this by 2 to get the two-tail probability value, .04.

Now solve a practice problem for the binomial test. Compute it yourself; then use the table to check your answer.

Problem   Marie Martinez, a sociologist, wants to test whether half the people in neighborhood A speak Spanish. She feels that more than half are Spanish-speaking. The *null hypothesis* states that half the people in neighborhood A speak Spanish; her *alternative hypothesis* states that more than half are Spanish-speaking. This is a one-tail test; Maria is predicting the direction of the results. She sets a .10 level of significance. She chooses a random sample of nine subjects, gives them a quick oral fluency quiz in Spanish, and then classifies them as Spanish-speaking or not. She learns that out of nine people seven speak Spanish. Using the binomial test, she tries to find out whether the null hypothesis can be rejected.

Answer   Reject the null hypothesis. Using Table H, she gets a value of .09, which is less than the .10 level of significance. Maria accepts the alternative hypothesis; she concludes that Spanish speakers are overrepresented in the population. The computation for this problem is shown below.

$$P(9) = \binom{9}{9} \left(\frac{1}{2}\right)^9 \left(\frac{1}{2}\right)^0 = .002$$

$$P(8) = \binom{9}{8} \left(\frac{1}{2}\right)^8 \left(\frac{1}{2}\right)^1 = .018$$

$$P(7) = \binom{9}{7} \left(\frac{1}{2}\right)^7 \left(\frac{1}{2}\right)^2 = .070$$

[10] The computation of a two-tail test is more involved. A more detailed discussion of the use of this test is given by Mood (1950, pp. 54–58).

Adding, $p(9) + p(8) + p(7) = .002 + .018 + .070 = .09$.
Note that this computed value is the same as the value found in
Table H.

The accompanying summary box shows you the steps to use when you solve a
problem using the binomial test.

Summary of the Binomial Test	**1.** Use the binomial formula (Formula 7-1): $$p(x) = \binom{N}{x} P^x Q^{N-x}$$ except in the following situations: (a) If your sample size is 25 or less and P and $Q = 1/2$, consult Table H. This table gives you one-tail probabilities. When your alternative hypothesis predicts the category with the smallest or largest frequencies, use this table. If you want two-tail probabilities, double the values in this table. (b) If P is not equal to Q, consult the CRC tables or use Formula 7-1; Table G gives you the $\binom{N}{x}$ part of the formula. For the computation of two-tail probabilities consult a more advanced statistical book. (c) If the sample size is larger than 25, consult Siegel (1956). **2.** Reject the null hypothesis if the probability found in the table is equal to or less than the predetermined level of significance.

Remarks on the Binomial Test

The binomial is a useful test because it computes exact probabilities in order to get the region of rejection, and you can use either a one- or
two-tail test. If the number in the sample is over 25, however, calculations of this
type become very cumbersome. The chi-square test and others like it do not compute
exact probabilities, but they are easier to calculate.

CHI-SQUARE (I) TEST

The chi-square (I) test is used to determine whether there is a
significant difference between the expected frequencies and the observed frequencies
in one or more categories. Do the number of individuals or objects that fall in each
category differ significantly from the number you would expect? Is this difference

between the expected and observed due to sampling error, or is it a real difference?

The requirements for the chi-square (I) test are:

Chi-Square
(I) Test
Requirements

1. Nominal data.
2. One-group test.
3. One or more categories.
4. Independent observations.
5. Adequate sample size.
   (a) The expected frequencies should be sufficiently large for two categories five or larger.
   (b) When there are more than two categories, no more than 20% should be smaller than five.
6. Simple random sample.
7. Data in frequency form.
8. All observations must be used.
9. Two-tail test only.[11]

Expected Frequencies

When you find the value for chi square (I),[12] you determine whether the observed frequencies differ significantly from the expected frequencies. You find the expected frequencies for chi square (I) in three ways.

1. You hypothesize that all the frequencies are equal in each category. For example, you might expect that half of the entering freshmen class of 200 at Tech College will be identified as women and half as men. You figure the expected frequencies by dividing the number in the sample by the number of categories. In this example, where there are 200 entering freshmen and two categories, male and female, you divide your sample of 200 by 2, the number of categories, to get 100 (expected frequencies) in each category.
2. You determine the expected frequencies on the basis of some prior knowledge. Let's use the Tech College example again, but this time pretend we have prior knowledge of the frequencies of men and women in each category from last year's entering class, when 60% of the freshmen were men and 40% were

---

[11] The chi-square cannot be used as a one-tail test. For directional testing you are forced to use another test.

[12] The chi square (I) is often called a "goodness-of-fit" test.

women. This year you might expected that 60% of the total would be men and 40% would be women. You find the expected frequencies by multiplying the sample size by each of the hypothesized population proportions. If the freshmen total is 200, you would expect 120 to be men (60% × 200) and 80 to be women (40% × 200).

3. You base the expected frequencies on some theory. An example would be Mendel's famous theory. Mendel was experimenting with two dihybrid garden pea plants whose parents were hybrids for both size and color. He discovered that when you crossed these two dihybrid garden pea plants, the ratio of 9:3:3:1 resulted; that is, 9/16 of the pea plants were tall and yellow, 3/16 were short and yellow, 3/16 were tall and green, and 1/16 were short and green. An agronomist decided to cross some of his own pea plants using dihybrid garden peas. He obtained 122 pea plants that were tall and yellow, 36 short and yellow, 40 tall and green, and 13 short and green. The expected frequencies are determined by multiplying the sample size by each of the probabilities. In this instance you would multiply 211 (sample size) by 9/16 to obtain[13] the expected frequency of 119 for tall yellow pea plants, multiply 211 by 3/16 to obtain the expected frequency of 40 for short yellow pea plants, multiply 211 by 3/16 to obtain the expected frequency of 40 for tall green pea plants, and multiply 211 by 1/16 to obtain the expected frequency of 13 for the short green pea plants.

Now let's take a situation, find the expected frequencies, and use the chi-square (1) test to solve the problem.

Situation

Paul, the manager of a car dealership, did not want to stock cars that were bought less frequently because of their unpopular color. The five colors that he ordered were red, yellow, green, blue, and white. According to Paul the expected frequencies or number of customers choosing each color should follow the percentages of last year. He felt 20% would choose yellow, 30% would choose red, 10% would choose green, 10% would choose blue, and 30% would choose white. He now took a random sample of 150 customers and asked them their color preferences. The results of this poll are shown in Table 7-4 under the column labeled "observed frequencies."

---

[13] Numbers are rounded to the nearest whole number.

Table 7-4: Color Preference for 150 Customers for Paul's Car Dealership

Category color	Observed frequencies	Expected frequencies
Yellow	35	30
Red	50	45
Green	30	15
Blue	10	15
White	25	45

The expected frequencies in Table 7-4 are figured from last year's percentages. Based on the percentages for last year we would expect 20% to choose yellow. We figure the expected frequencies for yellow by taking 20% of the 150 customers, getting an expected frequency of 30 people for this category. For the color red we would expect 30% out of 150 or 45 people to fall in this category. Using this method, Paul figured out the expected frequencies 30, 45, 15, 15, and 45. Obviously, there are discrepancies between the colors preferred by customers in the poll taken by Paul and the colors preferred by the customers who bought their cars last year. Most striking is the difference in the green and white colors. If Paul were to follow the results of his poll, he would stock twice as many green cars than if he were to follow the customer color preference for green based on last year's sales. In the case of white cars, he would stock half as many this year. What to do? Paul needs to know whether or not the discrepancies between last year's choices (expected frequencies) and this year's preferences on the basis of his poll (observed frequencies) demonstrate a real change in customer color preferences. It could be that the differences are simply a result of the random sample he *chanced* to select. If so, then the population of customers really has not changed from last year as far as color preferences go. The *null hypothesis* states that there is no significant difference between the expected and observed frequencies. The *alternative hypothesis* states they are different. (A two-tail test.) The level of significance is set at .05. The chi-square formula used on these data is

---

Formula 7-2   *Chi-Square Formula*

$$\chi^2 = \Sigma \frac{(O - E)^2}{E}$$

The symbols you will encounter in learning about the chi square (I) are explained below.

Symbol	Meaning
O	Observed frequencies in each category
E	Expected frequencies for the corresponding observed frequencies
Σ	Sum of
k	Number of categories
df	Degrees of freedom: number of categories minus one $(k - 1)$

PROCEDURE

Directions for Setting Up Worksheet for Chi Square (I)

We are now ready to use our formula for χ^2 and find out if there is a significant difference between the observed and expected frequencies for the customers in choosing cars. We will set up a worksheet; then you will follow the directions to form the columns and solve the formula.

Worksheet

Category	O	E	$(O - E)$	$(O - E)^2$	$\dfrac{(O - E)^2}{E}$
Yellow	35	30	5	25	.83
Red	50	45	5	25	.56
Green	30	15	15	225	15.00
Blue	10	15	-5	25	1.67
White	25	45	-20	400	8.89

$$\chi^2 = 26.95$$

Directions for Finding Chi Square (I)

1. Write the observed frequencies in the column labeled O.
2. By each observed frequency write its corresponding expected frequency in the E column. (See previous explanation.)
3. Subtract the numbers in the E column from the corresponding numbers in the O column; place the answers in the $(O - E)$ column.
4. Square each number in the $(O - E)$ column and put the results in a column labeled $(O - E)^2$.
5. Divide the numbers in the $(O - E)^2$ column by their respective E values and put the results in the column labeled $(O - E)^2/E$. For example, for the yellow cars, $25/30 = .83$.
6. Find chi square. Sum the numbers found in step 5—that is, the numbers found in the column labeled $(O - E)^2/E$. Add

$\chi^2 = 26.95$
_____

.83 + .56 + 15.00 + 1.67 + 8.89; write the sum, 26.95, in the blank.

7. Find *df*.[14] Subtract 1 from the number of categories. Write 4 in the blank.

$df = 4$
_____

8. Find the table value. Use the *df* found in step 7 to enter Table E. Run your fingers across the row until you are under the predetermined level of significance (.05). Write the value you find, 9.49, in the blank.

$T = 9.49$
_____

9. If your chi-square value (26.95) is equal to or greater than the table value (9.49), reject the null hypothesis. If not, do not reject it. Write *reject* in the blank.

reject
_____

In this situation, the rejection of the null hypothesis means that the differences between the expected frequencies (based upon last year's car sales) and the observed frequencies (based upon this year's poll taken by Paul) are not due to chance. That is, they are not due to chance variation in the sample Paul took; there is a real difference between them. Therefore, in deciding what color autos to stock, it would be to Paul's advantage to pay careful attention to the results of his poll.

In discussing chi square we referred to the term *degrees of freedom*. We learned how to find this value and use it to enter the sampling distribution table for chi square. Next we shall determine degrees of freedom and use it to enter sampling distributions for various other tests. It is wise at this point to gain an understanding of this term.

Degrees of Freedom

Degrees of freedom (*df*) refers to the number of values that are free to vary after restriction has been placed on the data. For instance, if you have four numbers with the restriction that their sum has to be 50, then three of these numbers can be anything, they are free to vary, but the fourth number definitely is restricted. For example, the first three numbers could be 15, 20, and 5, adding up to 40; then the fourth number has to be 10 in order that they sum to 50. The degrees of freedom for these values is then three. The degrees of freedom here is defined as $N - 1$, the number in the group minus one restriction ($4 - 1$). If two restrictions had been placed on the data and there were 20 numbers, degrees of freedom would be $N - 2$ or $20 - 2$. For example, the first restriction might say that the first five numbers must add to 20, and the second restriction might say that all 20 numbers must add to 60.

[14] Degrees of freedom (*df*) is explained in the next section. At this point just learn how to find it.

Return now to our car example, in which a single group of subjects selected among five categories. The degrees of freedom for the chi-square (I) test were defined by $k - 1$, the number of categories minus one; the degrees of freedom equaled four. When you established frequencies in four of the categories, the fifth one became fixed. Let's say the free-to-vary categories were 35, 50, 30, and 10; the fifth category would have to be 25 in order to yield a total of 150. This would, of course, hold true for any combination of categories. If you knew the red, green, blue and white category count, 50, 30, 10, and 25, the yellow count would have to be 35 in order to make 150.

Now that you understand degrees of freedom, let's solve a chi-square (I) problem in order to make sure you have a firm grasp of this procedure.

Problem   Let's return to Chapter 6, Situation I, The Delicious Hamburger, and use Table 6-1 to find the value for chi square (I). The *null hypothesis* states that the expected frequencies and the observed frequencies are actually the same and any difference between them is due to chance. Mary's alternative hypothesis states that they are different. The level of significance at which you would reject the null hypothesis is .05. Note that the frequencies for these various categories are expected to be equal.

Answer   The value found in the table is 7.82. Reject the null hypothesis, because chi square is equal to 21.52, which is greater than the table value. The customers do not all feel the same about the hamburger choices.

Hamburger preference	O	E	$(O - E)$	$(O - E)^2$	$\dfrac{(O - E)^2}{E}$
A	45	25	20	400	16
B	20	25	−5	25	1
C	17	25	−8	64	2.56
D	18	25	−7	49	1.96

$df = 4 - 1$
or 3 $\chi^2 = 21.52$

Comments on Chi Square (I)

If the value for chi square were zero, this would indicate perfect agreement between the observed frequencies and the expected frequencies. Since this is not the case, the bigger the value of chi square, the larger the difference between the observed and expected frequencies and the more likelihood that there is a significant experimental difference. In the hamburger situation the chi-square value was 21.52 and it was significant. This suggested that people's preferences in hamburgers were not all equal.

The steps in using the chi-square (I) test may be summarized as follows:

Chi-Square (I)
Test Summary

1. Write the observed frequencies in column O.
2. Figure the expected frequencies and write them in the E column.
3. Use Formula 7-2 to find the chi-square value:

$$\chi^2 = \Sigma \frac{(O - E)^2}{E}$$

4. Find df. Subtract 1 from the number of categories $(k - 1)$.
5. Find the table value (consult Table E).
6. If your chi-square value is equal to or greater than the table value, reject the null hypothesis.

Limitations of the Chi-Square (I) Test

Many statisticians endorse the rule that the expected frequencies in all the categories should be at least as large as five. Some even go so far as to recommend the combining of categories to meet this requirement. In many cases, however, this might not be wise. When you start combining after you see data, you might be doing something to the randomness of your sample; the manner in which the categories are combined may affect the inferences that you draw. This practice should be avoided if possible. In this book for more than two categories it is sufficient to have no more than 20% smaller than five.

Single Degree of Freedom

When you have a chi-square (I) problem that results in your having a single degree of freedom and less than ten for some of the expected frequencies, the chi square can be improved somewhat by using the correction formula of Pirie and Hamden (1972). When you have one degree of freedom, you must have a minimum of five as an expected frequency (actually, ten would be safer). Use the binomial test instead of the chi square (I) when the expected cells are less than five and you have but two categories.

CHI-SQUARE (II) TEST

In the last section we have been dealing with the chi square and its use with one group. However, chi square has wide application, and it can be used with two or more groups. To distinguish between the use of the chi square with one group and with two or more groups, we shall use the terms chi square (I) and chi square (II).

The question we ask in discussing chi square (II) is: do two or more groups differ in respect to some characteristics? In other words, do the number of frequencies that fall into each category for one group differ significantly from the number that fall into each category for another group or groups? For example, we might test whether the Republicans, Independents, or Democrats differ in their agreement or disagreement on abortion laws.

The requirements for chi square (II) are:

Chi-Square (II) Requirements

1. Nominal data.
2. Two or more groups.
3. Independent observation.
4. Adequate sample size:
   (a) No more than 20% of expected frequencies smaller than five.
   (b) When expected frequencies are very small, use the *Fisher exact probability* test (Siegel, 1956), not the chi square (II).
5. Two-tail test only.

The method for finding chi square (II) differs from that for chi square (I) in the way the expected frequencies are found. There is no prior basis for computing the expected frequencies, so they are derived from the data themselves. This involves setting up a contingency table. Let us take an example given in Chapter 6 and analyze the data using the chi square (II).

Situation

The chairman of the sociology department at Tibur College wanted to find out if there was a significant difference in the way his three instructors handed out pass/fail grades. He set a .05 level of significance. The data he had for his three instructors are recorded below.

Table 7-5: Table of Instructors'
Pass-Fail Grades

	Pass	Fail
Luis Fern	20	8
Donna Clay	11	13
Carl Perez	14	12

The *null hypothesis* states that the three classes were graded alike. The *alternative hypothesis* states the three instructors were not alike in the way they handed out grades. A two-tail test is being used.

PROCEDURE

The method for finding the expected frequencies for chi square (II) will be given in two parts. After you find expected frequencies, the third part will enable you to find chi square (II).

Part I: Setting Up Table A

Table A: Observed Frequencies

	Pass	Fail	Row totals
Luis Fern	20	8	_28_
Donna Clay	11	13	_24_
Carl Perez	14	12	_26_
			Grand total
Column totals	_45_	_33_	78

1. Find the row totals. Add the numbers in each row and place the sum on the dashed line to the right. For example, the row total for Luis Fern's scores is found by adding 20 + 8; the sum, 28, is placed on the dashed line.
2. Find the column totals. Add the numbers in each column and place the sum on the dashed line below. For example, for the pass grades the total is found by adding 20 + 11 + 14; the sum, 45, is placed on the dashed line.
3. The grand total is found by adding the row totals and placing their sum in the box. Add 28 + 24 + 26 and place 78 in this box.[15]

[15] You can also find the grand total by adding the numbers found in the column totals. If you add 45 + 33, you get a grand total of 78; this serves as a check on your work.

Part II: Setting Up Table B

Using the values you found in Table A, you are now able to find the expected frequency for each of the observed frequencies and record it in Table B.

Table B: Expected Frequencies

	Pass	Fail
Luis Fern	$\dfrac{28 \times 45}{78} = $ ⑯	$\dfrac{28 \times 33}{78} = $ ⑫
Donna Clay	$\dfrac{24 \times 45}{78} = $ ⑭	$\dfrac{24 \times 33}{78} = $ ⑩
Carl Perez	$\dfrac{26 \times 45}{78} = $ ⑮	$\dfrac{26 \times 33}{78} = $ ⑪

1. Multiply each observed frequency's row total by its column total and then divide by the grand total. For example, Luis Fern gave 20 pass grades; to find the expected frequency for this cell you multiply his row total, 28, by his column total, 45, and then divide by his grand total of 78. You get an expected frequency of 16 (rounded to the nearest whole number).
2. After you have found an expected frequency, record it in the appropriate cell in Table B and circle it.

Part III: Find Chi Square (II)

Now set up the same worksheet as for chi square (I) and find the correct value for chi square (II), using Formula 7-2, $\chi^2 = \Sigma \, (O - E)^2/E$.

Instructors' pass/fail grades	O	E	$(O - E)$	$(O - E)^2$	$\dfrac{(O - E)^2}{E}$
Luis's pass grades	20	16	4	16	1.00
Donna's pass grades	11	14	−3	9	.64
Carl's pass grades	14	15	−1	1	.07
Luis's fail grades	8	12	−4	16	1.33
Donna's fail grades	13	10	3	9	.90
Carl's fail grades	12	11	1	1	.09

$$\chi^2 = 4.03$$

1. Record the observed frequencies from Table A and place them in the column labeled O.

2. Record the corresponding expected frequencies from Table B (circled values) and place them in the column labeled *E*.
3. Subtract the numbers in the *E* column from the corresponding numbers in the *O* column and place the answer in the $(O - E)$ column.
4. Square each number in the $(O - E)$ column and put the results in the column labeled $(O - E)^2$.
5. Divide the numbers in the $(O - E)^2$ column by their *E* value and put the results in the column labeled $(O - E)^2/E$.
6. Find chi square (II). Sum the numbers found in step 5; that is, sum the numbers in the column labeled $(O - E)^2/E$. Add $1.00 + .64 + .07 + 1.33 + .90 + .09$. Write the sum, 4.03, in the blank.

$\chi^2 = 4.03$

7. Find degrees of freedom (*df*). Referring back to Table E, use the formula (rows − 1) × (columns − 1) to compute the degrees of freedom. Subtract 1 from the number of rows $(3 - 1)$ and subtract 1 from the number of columns $(2 - 1)$; then take these values and multiply them together (2×1). Write 2 in the blank.

$df = 2$

8. Find the table value. Use the *df* found in step 7 to enter Table E. Run your fingers across the row until you are under the predetermined level of significance (.05). Record the value found in this table; write 5.99 in the blank.

$T = 5.99$

9. If your chi-square value (4.03) is equal to or greater than the table value (5.99), reject the null hypothesis; if not, write *do not reject* in the blank.

Do not reject

For this problem there was not a significant difference in the way the three instructors graded their classes. Now try your hand at a similar problem.

Problem

A sociology study compared three groups in their responses to one question: "Are you happier now than you were four years ago?" Group A was a professional group, Group B a blue collar group, and Group C unskilled laborers. The frequencies of response in each of three categories were compared: "More," "Less," and "Same." The data are presented in Table 7-6.

Table 7-6: Responses to Happiness Question

		Response	
Group	More	Less	Same
A	30	11	12
B	15	30	20
C	10	10	10

The *null hypothesis* states there is no significant difference among the groups in their response to the question. The *alternative hypothesis* states the three groups are different. Set your level of significance at .01 and find out if there is a significant difference among the three groups in their response to this question. In computing the expected frequencies, round out to the nearest whole number.

Answer

The value found in the table is 13.28 ($df = 4$). Reject the null hypothesis, because the chi-square value equals 15.03, and this is greater than the table value, 13.28. The three groups are not the same in their response to the question.

Table 7-7: Contingency Table

		Response	
Group	More	Less	Same
A	$\dfrac{53 \times 55}{148} = 20$	$\dfrac{51 \times 53}{148} = 18$	$\dfrac{42 \times 53}{148} = 15$
B	$\dfrac{65 \times 55}{148} = 24$	$\dfrac{51 \times 65}{148} = 22$	$\dfrac{42 \times 65}{148} = 18$
C	$\dfrac{30 \times 55}{148} = 11$	$\dfrac{51 \times 30}{148} = 10$	$\dfrac{42 \times 30}{148} = 9$

Table 7-8: Computation of the Chi Square

	O	E	$(O-E)$	$(O-E)^2$	$\dfrac{(O-E)^2}{E}$
Group A more	30	20	10	100	5.00
Group B more	15	24	−9	81	3.38
Group C more	10	11	−1	1	.09
Group A less	11	18	−7	49	2.72
Group B less	30	22	8	64	2.91
Group C less	10	10	0	0	.00
Group A same	12	15	−3	9	.60
Group B same	20	18	2	4	.22
Group C same	10	9	1	1	.11

$$\chi^2 = 15.03$$

The steps used in the chi-square (II) test may be summarized as follows.

Chi-Square (II)
Summary

1. Set up a contingency table to find the expected frequencies.
2. Use Formula 7-2 to find the chi-square value:

$$\chi^2 = \Sigma \frac{(O - E)^2}{E}$$

3. Find *df*. Use the formula: (rows − 1) × (columns − 1).
4. Find the table value; consult Table E.
5. If your chi-square value is equal to or greater than the table value, reject the null hypothesis.

In the play in Chapter 5 Max found a chi-square value equal to 13.08. This was a chi-square (II) problem. Max's work is shown below.

	Alive	*Dead*
Vial water	25	25
Clear water	42	8

Contingency table

$\frac{50 \times 67}{100} = 33.50$	$\frac{50 \times 33}{100} = 16.50$	50
$\frac{50 \times 67}{100} = 33.50$	$\frac{50 \times 33}{100} = 16.50$	50
67	33	100

O	E	$(O - E)$	$(O - E)^2$	$\dfrac{(O - E)^2}{E}$
25	33.50	−8.50	72.25	2.16
25	16.50	8.50	72.25	4.38
42	33.50	8.50	72.25	2.16
8	16.50	−8.50	72.25	4.38

$$\chi^2 = 13.08$$

$$\chi^2 = \Sigma \frac{(O - E)^2}{E}$$
$$= 2.16 + 4.38 + 2.16 + 4.38$$
$$= 13.08$$

McNEMAR TEST

The McNemar test is used for before and after research designs. It is used with matched pairs or when a subject is his own control. The purpose is to determine the significance of the observed change. The requirements are listed below.

McNemar	**1.** Nominal data
Requirements	**2.** Two groups
	3. Related groups
	4. Expected frequencies five or more
	5. Two-tail test only

The following example will illustrate when to use the McNemar test.

A survey of 100 voters was taken before an advertising campaign; 20 of these individuals were for a bond issue and 80 were against it. After the advertising campaign these same people were again polled, but now 60 were for the bond issue and only 40 were against it. Were these changes in attitude significant?

These individuals' responses can be recorded in four possible ways, as shown in Table 7-9.

Table 7-9: Ways of Recording Results

	Before campaign	*After campaign*
1. Individual 1	For	For
2. Individual 2	Against	Against
3. Individual 3	For	Against
4. Individual 4	Against	For

Looking at these possibilities, you can see that an individual could have been for the bond issue before the advertising campaign and still for it after the campaign. An individual could have been against the bond issue before the advertising campaign and still against it after the campaign. These types of individuals represent no change, and they are disregarded when using the McNemar test; the test focuses on individuals such as 3 and 4, who represent change. Individuals such as 3 change from being for the bond issue to being against it, and individuals such as 4 change from being against the bond issue to being for it. Change in one direction will henceforth be designated as *A,* and change in the opposite direction as *D*. For the example above, the individuals who were for the bond issue and changed to being against are designated as *A*. Individuals who were against the bond issue and changed to being for it are designated as *D*.

Formula 7-3 is used to ascertain if there is a significant change.

| **Formula 7-3** | *McNemar Test* |
| | $$\chi^2 = \frac{(|A - D| - 1)^2}{A + D}$$ |

Let us apply this formula to Situation IX in Chapter 6 and see if there was a significant change.

Situation

A political science student wanted to find out if moving from a rural to an urban area affected a person's voting preference. He randomly selected 27 new residents on their first day of arrival in Chicago and categorized them as Democrat or Republican. He then observed these same new residents one year later, after each had been exposed to the influences of the big city, and made the same categorization of the data. He recorded this information in Table 7-10.

Table 7-10: Voting Preferences of Urban Newcomers

First day	After one year	
	Democrats	Republicans
Republicans	15	4
Democrats	3	5

In the upper left-hand corner of the table the number 15 represents the individuals who changed from Republicans to Democrats. In the upper right-hand square the number 4 represents the individuals who remained Republicans. In the lower left-hand square the number 3 represents the individuals who remained Democrats. Finally, in the lower right-hand square the number 5 represents the individuals who changed from Democrats to Republicans. Since the political science student is interested only in those individuals who changed, he shades the squares in the table that represent no change. Next he designates those individuals who change from Republican to Democrat as *A* and those who change from Democrat to Republican as *D*. The value for *A* in this case is 15 and for *D* is 5.

We are now ready to use the McNemar test to see if the changes from one political party to another are significant. The *null hypothesis* states there is no significant difference in the political attitude of the two groups. The *alternative hypothesis* states the two groups are different in their political attitude. We will set the level of significance at .05. A two-tail test is used.

The symbols you will encounter in learning about the McNemar test are explained below.

Symbol	Meaning
A	Number of individuals changing in one direction (Republican to Democrat)
D	Number of individuals changing in the opposite direction from A (Democrat to Republican)
E	Expected number of individuals under the null hypothesis $\frac{1}{2}(A + D)$
df	Degrees of freedom is always 1 for the McNemar test

PROCEDURE

Directions for Setting Up the McNemar Worksheet

$A = \underline{15}$

$D = \underline{5}$

$A - D = \underline{10}$

$|A - D| - 1 = \underline{9}$

$(|A - D| - 1)^2$

$= \underline{81}$

$(A + D) = \underline{20}$

$\chi^2 = \underline{4.05}$

1. Record the number you designate for A, 15, in the blank.
2. Record the number you designate as D, 5, in the blank.
3. Find $A - D$. Subtract the number found in step 2 (5) from the number found in step 1 (15). Write 10 in the blank.
4. Find $|A - D| - 1$. Subtract one[16] from the value you found in step 3 (10 − 1). Write 9 in the blank.
5. Find $(|A - D| - 1)^2$. Square the value found in step 4 (9^2). Write 81 in the blank.
6. Find $(A + D)$. Take the number found in step 1 (15) and add it to the number found in step 2 (5). Write 20 in the blank.
7. Find $(|A - D| - 1)^2 / (A + D)$. Divide the number found in step 5 (81) by the number found in step 6 (20). Write 4.05 in the blank.
8. Find the table value. Enter Table E (the sampling distribution for chi square) with one degree of freedom.[17] Run your fingers across the page until you are at your predetermined level of significance (.05). Write the table value you find (3.84) in the blank.
9. If your value found in step 7 (4.05) is equal to or greater than the table value (3.84), reject the null hypothesis. Write *reject* in the blank.

Table value
$= \underline{3.84}$

reject

In this situation you rejected the null hypothesis and said there was a significant difference in the changes from one political party to another. We can conclude that the voting preferences changed significantly.

---

[16] Subtract one from the value disregarding its sign.

[17] For the McNemar test the degrees of freedom is always one.

As you can see, the McNemar test is very easy to use. However, before you can legitimately use it, your data must have five or more expected frequencies. The expected frequencies are found by adding $A + D$ and then dividing by two. The formula is $E = \frac{1}{2}(A + D)$. In the problem the expected frequencies would equal ten $[(15 + 5)/2]$. Because the expected frequencies were five or more, it was all right to use the McNemar test. If they had been less than five, this test would not have been appropriate.

Now let's see if you can do a problem on your own.

Problem   Sue took a random sample of 40 people and recorded whether they were for or against pay toilets. She then showed them some films against pay toilets. One month later she recorded their position on this issue. Those people who changed from for to against she designated as A. Those who changed from against to for she designated as D. Those people who did not change, she ignored. The results are shown in Table 7-11.

Table 7-11: Attitudes toward Pay Toilets

Before film	After film	
	Against	For
For	12	13
Against	10	5

The 12 represents those who were for pay toilets and changed to against. The 5 represents those who were against and changed to for. The numbers 13 and 10 represent no change. The *null hypothesis* states that the people's attitudes toward pay toilets remain the same. The *alternative hypothesis* states that the people's attitudes toward pay toilets are different. (A two-tail test.)

Set a .01 level of significance and answer these questions:

1. Do your data have five or more expected frequencies?
2. What are the results when you use your statistical test?
3. Did these individuals' attitudes change significantly?

Answers   1. Your data have an $E = 8.5$ $[E = \frac{1}{2}(A + D) = 17/2$ or $8.5]$. Since 8.5 is over 5, you can use the McNemar test.

2. The results are that $\chi^2 = 2.12$:

$$\chi^2 = \frac{(|A - D| - 1)^2}{A + D}$$

$$\chi^2 = \frac{(|12 - 5| - 1)^2}{12 + 5}$$

$$\chi^2 = \frac{(7 - 1)^2}{17}$$

$$\chi^2 = \frac{(6)^2}{17}$$

$$\chi^2 = \frac{36}{17} = 2.12$$

The null hypothesis was not rejected.

3. There is not a significant difference. The film did not seem to affect the attitudes of people regarding pay toilets. The value found in the table is 6.64. You cannot reject the null hypothesis, because chi square equals 2.12, and this is not equal to or greater than the table value.

The steps in the use of the McNemar test may be summarized as follows:

McNemar Test Summary

1. Determine the expected frequencies using the formula $E = \frac{1}{2}(A + D)$. If the expected frequencies are less than five, use another test.
2. If the expected frequencies are five or larger, use Formula 7-3,

$$\chi^2 = \frac{(|A - D| - 1)^2}{(A + D)}.$$

3. Degrees of frequency is always one.
4. Enter Table E, sampling distribution for chi square.
5. If your chi-square value is equal to or greater than the table value, reject the null hypothesis.

COCHRAN Q TEST

The McNemar test for two related groups can be extended to more than two groups. This extension is called the Cochran Q test. It is a method for testing whether three or more matched sets of frequencies differ significantly among each other. The matching can be on relevant features of different people, or the same person can be used under different conditions. Each type of matching will be shown in the examples that follow. The first example matches men on their ability to install glass and then assigns them to three groups. The second example has each buyer shown each calculator, exposing the same person to three different conditions; in a sense he is in three different groups.

Scores for the Cochran Q test can take only two values: 0 or 1. The 1 represents values that are recorded as positive, while the 0 represents values that are negative.

The requirements for the Cochran Q test are as follows:

Cochran Q Requirements

1. Nominal data
2. Three or more groups
3. Related groups
4. Data in frequency form
5. Two-tail test only

The Cochran Q formula is

Formula 7-4

Cochran Q Test

$$Q = \frac{(k-1)\ (k \Sigma C^2 - T^2)}{kT - \Sigma R^2}$$

The symbols in the formula have the following meanings:

Symbol	Meaning
k	Number of groups
R	Row totals
C	Column totals
T	Grand total (sum of R or sum of C)

We are ready now to use the Cochran Q on Situation VI, Chapter 6.

Situation

An efficiency expert who devised three new methods to install glass in cars wanted to find out which method was easiest. He matched three groups of men on the basis of their ability to install glass.[18] Each man was matched with two other men whose performance was as close as possible to his in installing glass. Then

---

[18] These groups are related; this is the signal to use the Cochran Q rather than the chi square.

a man from each matched triplet was assigned to a group. This procedure continued until 30 men were assigned among three groups. Group One was then shown Method I, Group Two was shown Method II, and Group Three was shown Method III. Each man was asked to write 1 if he felt his method was easy and 0 if he felt his method was hard. The data were set up in a worksheet, allowing one row for each set of three matched workers. Since there were 30 men, there were ten rows. Read the directions below the worksheet and see if you can follow the steps. The *null hypothesis* states there is no significant difference among the three groups in their perceptions. The *alternative hypothesis* states the groups are different in their perceptions. The level of significance for this situation is set at .05.

PROCEDURE

Directions for Setting Up a Worksheet for Cochran Q

Set	Method I	Method II	Method III	R	R^2
1	1	1	1	3	9
2	0	1	1	2	4
3	0	0	0	0	0
4	1	1	1	3	9
5	0	0	0	0	0
6	1	0	1	2	4
7	0	0	1	1	1
8	1	0	1	2	4
9	1	0	1	2	4
10	0	0	1	1	1
C	5	3	8	$T = 16$	$\Sigma R^2 = 36$
C^2	25	9	64	$\Sigma C^2 = 98$	$T^2 = 256$

$k = 3$

1. Record the data as 1 or 0. Assign 1 for easy, 0 for hard.
2. Find k. Record the number of groups in the blank for k. Record 3.
3. Find the row totals. Add up the numbers in each row and place their sum on the dashed line to the right of each row. For example, the first row total is found by adding $1 + 1 + 1$, and its sum, 3, is placed on the dashed line.

4. Find R^2. Square each number found in step 2 and put it in the column labeled R^2.

5. Find ΣR^2. Add all the numbers in the column headed R^2. Write their sum opposite the $\Sigma R^2 = \underline{\hspace{1cm}}$. Add $9 + 4 + 0 + \cdots + 1$ and write 36 opposite $\Sigma R^2 = \underline{\hspace{1cm}}$.

6. Find the column totals. Add the numbers in each column and place their sum on the dashed line underneath each column. For example, for the numbers in the first column the total is found by adding $1 + 0 + 0 + 1 + \cdots + 0$, and its sum, 5, is placed on the dashed line.

7. Find the grand total (T). Add all the scores in the row headed C. Write their sum in the box opposite the $T = \underline{\hspace{1cm}}.$[19] Add $5 + 3 + 8$ and record 16.

8. Find T^2. Square the number found in step 7. Write the answer in the box opposite the $T^2 = \underline{\hspace{1cm}}$.

9. Find C^2. Square each number in the C row and write it underneath in the row headed C^2.

10. Find the ΣC^2. Add all the numbers in the row headed C^2. Write their sum opposite the $\Sigma C^2 = \underline{\hspace{1cm}}$. Add $25 + 9 + 64$ and write 98.

Substitutions

Using the worksheet, we are ready to substitute the numbers found in steps 1 through 10. These substitutions will be made in the Cochran Q formula

$$Q = \frac{(k - 1)(k \Sigma C^2 - T^2)}{kT - \Sigma R^2}$$

A. Substitute the number of groups (3) for (k)

$$Q = \frac{(3 - 1)(3 \Sigma C^2 - T^2)}{(3)T - \Sigma R^2}$$

B. Substitute the number 98 for ΣC^2 and substitute the number 256 for T^2

$$Q = \frac{(3 - 1)(3 \times 98 - 256)}{(3)T - \Sigma R^2}$$

C. Substitute the number 16 for T and the number 36 for ΣR^2

$$Q = \frac{(3 - 1)(3 \times 98 - 256)}{3 \times 16 - 36}$$

[19] The grand total is also found by adding all the numbers in the fourth column labeled R. This can serve as a check on your work.

Solving the Formula

Now we can solve the Cochran Q formula, performing the following computations:

A. For the numerator perform all the multiplications: multiply 3 times 98 (294). For the denominator multiply 3 times 16 (48)

$$Q = \frac{(3-1)(294-256)}{48-36}$$

B. Perform all the subtractions. Subtract 1 from 3 (2). Subtract 256 from 294 (38) and subtract 36 from 48 (12)

$$Q = \frac{(2)(38)}{12}$$

C. Multiply 2 times 38

$$Q = \frac{76}{12}$$

D. Divide 76 by 12 (6.33)

$$Q = 6.33$$

E. Place Cochran Q in a solution box

$$\boxed{Q = 6.33}$$

Statistical Decision

$df = 2$

1. Find the degrees of freedom. Use the formula $(k-1)$. Subtract 1 from the number of groups (3). Write 2 in the blank.
2. Find the table value. Enter the sampling distribution for chi square, Table E, with the proper degrees of freedom (2). Run your fingers across the row until you are at the predetermined level of significance (.05). Record the table value (5.99) in the blank.

Table value
= 5.99

3. Record your decision. If your calculated Q found in the solution box (6.33) is equal to or greater than the table value found here under statistical decision, reject the null hypothesis; otherwise do not reject. Record *reject* in the blank.

reject

In this problem it appears there was a significant difference in the methods that were tried.

Now that you feel secure in working through a problem, try one on your own.

Problem   A manufacturer of calculators shows three of his latest models (A, B, and C) to ten buyers from neighboring retail stores, eight of whom place orders (marked 1) as follows:

Orders for Calculators

Buyer	A	B	C	R	R²
1	1	1	1	– – –	– – –
2	0	1	1	– – –	– – –
3	0	1	1	– – –	– – –
4	0	0	1	– – –	– – –
5	0	0	1	– – –	– – –
6	0	0	1	– – –	– – –
7	0	0	1	– – –	– – –
8	0	0	1	– – –	– – –
9	0	0	0	– – –	– – –
10	0	0	0	– – –	– – –
C	– – –	– – –	– – –	$T =$	$\Sigma R^2 =$
C²	– – –	– – –	– – –	$\Sigma C^2 =$	$T^2 =$
					$k =$ ___

Is there a statistically significant difference in the demand for the three types of calculators? The *null hypothesis* states that the demand for the calculators is the same. The *alternative hypothesis* states the demand for the calculators is different. The predetermined level of significance for this problem is .05.[20]

Answer   The value found in the table is 5.99. The null hypothesis is rejected, because the Q value, 11.14, is much higher than the table value. The demand for the calculators is different.

$$Q = \frac{(k-1)(k \Sigma C^2 - T^2)}{kT - \Sigma R^2}$$

$$= \frac{(3-1)(3 \times 74 - 144)}{3 \times 12 - 22}$$

$$= \frac{(2)(222 - 144)}{36 - 22}$$

$$= \frac{(2)78}{14}$$

$$= \frac{156}{14}$$

$$\boxed{Q = 11.14}$$

[20] Note all three calculators are tried on each member of the group; that is why the groups are related.

The procedure used for the Cochran Q test may be summarized as follows.

Summary for Cochran Q Test	1. Assign a 1 or 0 to the data. 2. Use Formula 7-4 to determine Q: $$Q = \frac{(k-1)(k \Sigma C^2 - T^2)}{kT - \Sigma R^2}$$ 3. Degrees of freedom equals $k - 1$. 4. Find the table value by using Table E. 5. If your calculated Q is equal to or greater than your table value, reject the null hypothesis.

SUMMARY

We are almost at the end of Chapter 7. We reached the tests we discussed by traveling on Nominal avenue. We discussed five widely used nominal tests.

The binomial test is useful when you have a very small sample with only two categories. The chi square, however, has many more applications. We discussed two types of chi square, chi square (I) and chi square (II). This test is so versatile it can be used with any number of independent groups. The reader was cautioned not to be fooled by its versatility and to pay close attention to its restrictions.

Finally, the McNemar and Cochran Q tests were explained. The McNemar test is used for two related groups; its extension, the Cochran Q, is used for three or more related groups.

In discussing these five tests we noted many points of distinction. Flowchart II (p. 206) summarizes what has been discussed. Use it as a reference to help you make a quick decision in choosing a nominal test.

SELF-TEST FOR MASTERY

If you have trouble working a problem, reread the explanation on the page listed.

Directions: Read each test situation carefully. Answer its multiple-choice questions by underlining the correct answer. Then place the boldface letter for the underlined answer on the dashed line below the mystery picture. Carry over your partial answer from one picture to the next, adding to it as you go. When you have answered the questions to all five situations, you will have a description of what the mystery drawing is. Question 1 has been done for you in Situation I.

Flowchart II: Nominal Tests

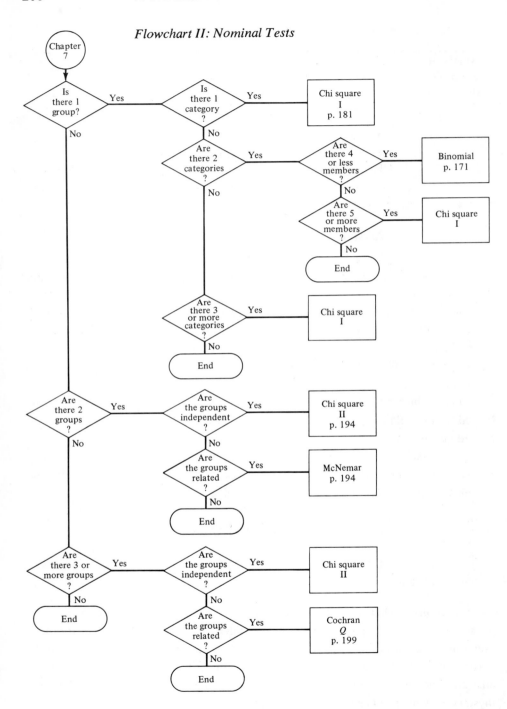

Situation I. A school superintendent was studying the teacher absentee rate for the first week in June. He wanted to know if the absenteeism for that week was the same for each day. The *null hypothesis* states that the absentee rate for that week is the same for each day. The *alternative* hypothesis states that the absentee rate is different. Help the superintendent find his answer by testing the null hypothesis at the .01 level of significance. The table gives the data you need to answer the multiple-choice questions.

Absenteeism in School for Week of June 1

	Mon.	Tues.	Wed.	Thurs.	Fri.
Number of teachers absent	30	10	10	15	35

p. 181 **1.** Which test would you use: a chi square (I) **A**, binomial **T**, chi square (II) **B**, McNemar **V**, Cochran Q **C**?

p. 185 **2.** Solve the problem using the proper test. What is the result of your calculation: 31.33 **b**, 27.50 **f**, 20.22 **t**, 2.33 **l**, 3.99 **d**?

p. 186 **3.** At the .01 level of significance do not reject **a**, reject **i**, the null hypothesis.

p. 181 **4.** What kind of test does the situation warrant: one group, one category **e**; one group, five categories **s**; one group, two categories **r**; two related groups **t**; two independent groups **l**?

Situation II. Ellery feels that his recipe for chocolate cake is first-rate. He randomly selects eight cooks and has them try his new creation, then asks them by secret ballot to rate his cake as first-rate or deficient. He thinks that the majority of the cooks will decide it is first-rate. The *null hypothesis* states that there will be an equal number of people favoring the cake as opposed to it. The *alternative hypothesis* states that more people will think the cake is first-rate. (This is a one-tail test.) The level of significance is set at .10. The results show that six of the cooks think the cake is first-rate. Is this a sufficient number to say the cake has the support of the majority of cooks?

p. 171 **1.** Which test would you use: a chi square (I) **t**, Cochran *Q* **l**, McNemar **r**, binomial **h**, chi square (II) **s**?

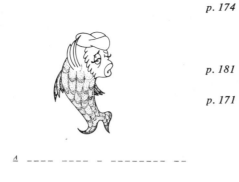

p. 174 **2.** Solve the problem using the proper test. What is the result of your calculation: .145 **w**, .356 **t**, .001 **l**, .333 **d**, .067 **m?**

p. 181 **3.** At the .10 level of significance do not reject **i**, reject **a**, the null hypothesis.

p. 171 **4.** What kind of test does the situation warrant: one group, one category **s**; one group, two categories, large expected frequencies **r**; one group, two categories, small expected frequencies **t**; three groups, independent **h**; one group, three categories **w?**

A ____ ____ _ _____ __

Situation III. Paul, a psychotherapist, wanted to show his students the easiest method to reduce anxiety level. He had three possible ways of accomplishing this, but his students might not find them equally easy to understand. He explained each method to his class of 12 pupils and then asked them to write down which of the three methods they had understood. Paul analyzed the results immediately. Six had understood method X, ten had understood method Y, and five had understood method Z. The *null hypothesis* states that the three methods are the same in difficulty. The *alternative hypothesis* states that the three methods are different in difficulty. The results are entered in the table below. When a person understood the method, it was entered in the table as 1. When a person did not understand, it was entered as 0.

Method	Student											
	1	2	3	4	5	6	7	8	9	10	11	12
X	1	1	0	1	1	1	0	0	0	0	0	0
Y	0	1	1	1	1	1	1	1	1	1	1	0
Z	1	0	1	0	1	1	0	1	0	0	0	0

p. 199 **1.** Which test would you use: chi square (I) **w**, McNemar **r**, chi square (II) **s**, Cochran *Q* **h**, McNemar **t?**

p. 201 **2.** Solve the problem using the proper test. What is the result of your calculation: 9.0 **t**, 6.9 **r**, 7.8 **l**, 5.6 **a**, 2.35 **k?**

p. 203 **3.** At the .01 level of significance, accept **h**, reject **i**, the null hypothesis.

p. 200 **4.** What kind of test does the situation warrant: three group, independent **t**,

A ____ ____ _ _____ __

three group, related **a,** two group, related **b,** two group, independent **c,** one group, one category **d?**

Situation IV. A researcher asked a sample of 40 people whether they thought teachers had a right to strike, and he recorded their responses. Three years later the same group of people were asked the same question and their responses were recorded. The data appear in the following table.

	Present	
Three years ago	*No*	*Yes*
Yes	10	10
No	14	6

The *null hypothesis* states that the opinions of the two groups are the same. The *alternative hypothesis* states that the two groups are not the same in their opinion on striking.

p. 194   **1.** Which test would you use: chi square (I) **e,** chi square (II) **o,** Cochran *Q* **u,** McNemar **n,** binomial **i?**

p. 197   **2.** Solve the problem using the proper test. What is the result of your calculation: 3.11 **r,** 4.22 **s,** .33 **w,** 5.32 **l,** .56 **g?**

p. 197   **3.** At the .05 level of significance would you accept **o,** reject **d,** the null hypothesis?

p. 195   **4.** What kind of test does the situation warrant: two group, related **v,** two group, independent **r,** one group, two categories, large expected frequencies **s,** three group, independent **e,** three group, related **l?**

Situation V. A survey was done of lawyers in a large city. These lawyers were divided into three groups on the basis of their grades in law school and their income in practice ten years after their graduation. Using a .05 level of significance see if there is a relationship between grades and income. The *null hypothesis* states that the three groups are the same. The *alternative hypothesis* states that the three groups are different. The data are recorded in the table below.

	Income		
Grades	*High*	*Average*	*Low*
High	10	15	4
Average	30	40	26
Low	7	11	10

p. 189   **1.** Which test would you use: chi square (II) **e**, McNemar **r**, Cochran *Q* **c**, chi square (I) **b**, binomial **t?**

p. 190   **2.** Solve the problem using the proper test. What is the result of your calculation: 21.55 **e**, 18.33 **s**, 2.48 **a**, 4.32 **r**, 13.56 **o?**

p. 189   **3.** What kind of test does the situation warrant: three group, related **?**, three group, independent **!**, two group, related **.**, two group, independent **:**, one group, one category **-.**

p. 192   **4.** At the .05 level of significance did you accept **!**, or reject **.**, the null hypothesis?

ANSWERS TO SELF-TEST

<u>A fish with a hangover!!</u>

Score yourself by adding up the points for each correct answer and write the total in the Evaluation form.

Evaluation

Situations correct	*Instructions*
4–5	Proceed to the next chapter
3	Review trouble spots
0–2	Reread the chapter

ORDINAL
TESTS

8

Figure 8-1: Ordinal Tests

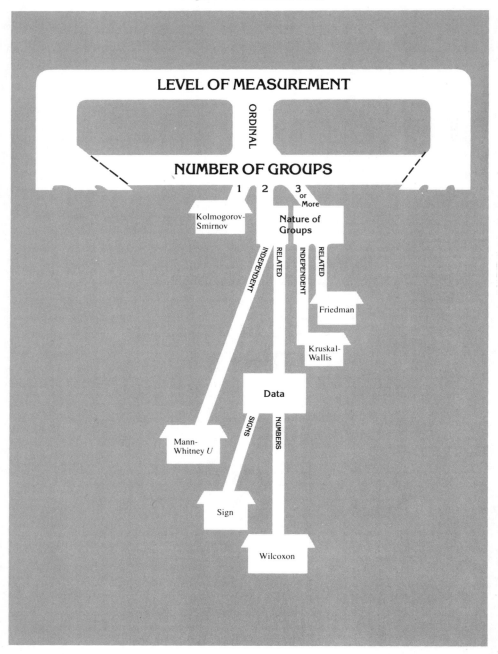

Chapter 8 deals with statistical tests originating from Ordinal avenue on the map (Figure 8-1). Each test will be discussed in the following manner:

1. Its purpose will be explained.
2. Its requirements will be listed.
3. A situation that warrants its use will be described.
4. The reader will be shown an easy-to-follow procedure to solve the formula for the statistical test.
5. A practice problem will be provided.
6. The procedure will be summarized.

In this chapter we will discuss the following tests; Kolmogorov-Smirnov, Mann-Whitney *U*, sign, Wilcoxon, Kruskal-Wallis, and Friedman.

KOLMOGOROV-SMIRNOV TEST

The Kolmogorov-Smirnov is an ordinal test used with one-group samples. The researcher uses it to find out whether a distribution of observations is significantly different from a theoretical distribution. The test compares the cumulative distribution of the observed scores and the cumulative distribution of the expected scores. The point where the two distributions show the largest divergence is then determined. Next the researcher refers to the sampling distribution to determine whether this divergence is the result of chance or a real difference. Do the scores in these two distributions come from the same population? The requirements for the Kolmogorov-Smirnov test are as follows:

Kolmogorov-Smirnov Test	1. Ordinal data 2. One group 3. Simple random sample

The formula for the Kolmogorov-Smirnov test is:

Formula 8-1	*Kolmogorov-Smirnov Test* $$D = \frac{LD}{N}$$

The symbols you will encounter in learning about the Kolmogorov-Smirnov test are listed and explained below.

Symbol	Meaning
LD	Large difference
N	Number of individuals in the sample
O	Number of individuals observed
E	Numbers of individuals you would expect in the sample
OC	Observed cumulative distribution
EC	Expected cumulative distribution
f	Frequency of scores

In the definitions of *OC* and *EC* we notice the terms *cumulative distribution*. Before you can use the Kolmogorov-Smirnov test, you must know how to create a cumulative distribution.

How to Form a Cumulative Distribution

Once you know how to form a cumulative distribution, you can use this knowledge in forming both the observed and expected cumulative distributions for the Kolmogorov-Smirnov test. A cumulative distribution that has already been created is shown in Table 8-1.

Table 8-1: Cumulative Distribution

Rank	Frequency	Cumulative distribution	Addition work
1	1	17	$5 + 6 + 2 + 3 + 1 = 17$
2	3	16	$5 + 6 + 2 + 3 = 16$
3	2	13	$5 + 6 + 2 = 13$
4	6	11	$5 + 6 = 11$
5	5	5	5

Next to each rank is a frequency which tells you the number of scores at each rank. The frequency column is used to form the cumulative distribution column by a series of additions on the scores.

1. The bottom frequency is taken from the frequency column and rewritten in the cumulative distribution column.
2. Next a series of additions are performed on the frequency column to create the cumulative distribution. The work is shown to the right of the table.

In effect you are adding each number in the frequency column to the numbers it has below it to form the cumulative distribution column. You begin with 5; since there is no number below it, you rewrite the 5 in the cumulative distribution column opposite the 5 in the frequency column. The next number is 6; since there is a 5 below it, you add 5 + 6 and write 11 in the cumulative distribution column opposite the 6 in the frequency column. The next number is 2, which has 5 and 6 below it; you add 5 + 6 + 2 and place 13 in the cumulative distribution column opposite the 2 in the frequency column. This procedure continues for the remaining numbers in the frequency column. If you have completed your cumulative distribution column correctly, its top number equals the sum of the scores in the frequency column. In this example the sum of the scores in the frequency column equals 1 + 3 + 2 + 6 + 5 or 17, and the top number in the cumulative distribution column is 17.

Exercise   Use the following series of frequencies to form a cumulative distribution.

Rank	Frequencies	Cumulative distribution	Addition work
1	1		
2	5		
3	3		
4	8		
5	4		
6	2		
7	3		

Answer

Rank	Fre-quencies	Cumula-tive distribu-tion	Addition work
1	1	26	3 + 2 + 4 + 8 + 3 + 5 + 1 = 26
2	5	25	3 + 2 + 4 + 8 + 3 + 5 = 25
3	3	20	3 + 2 + 4 + 8 + 3 = 20
4	8	17	3 + 2 + 4 + 8 = 17
5	4	9	3 + 2 + 4 = 9
6	2	5	3 + 2 = 5
7	3	3	3

Now let's take a situation involving the Kolmogorov-Smirnov test and use it to reach a decision about the dryness of wine. We shall use Situation X, The Wine Merchant, from Chapter 6.

Situation

Alfredo, a wine expert, wants to determine if the choice of wine is determined by its dryness. He arranges to have five different varieties of white wine placed before ten randomly selected wine buyers. The wines range from very dry, ranked 1, to extremely sweet, ranked 5. Each customer is then offered a choice among the five different types of wines; the customers' selections are shown in Table 8-2.

Table 8-2: Wine Selected by Customers

Rank	1	2	3	4	5
Customer choice	2	2	5	0	1

The *null hypothesis* states that there is no significant difference in the wine preferred. The *alternative hypothesis* states there is a significant difference in the wine preferred. The level of significance is set at .01; a two-tail test is used. We will use the Kolmogorov-Smirnov test to find out if there is a significant difference in the customer's choice of wine. Our worksheet is shown below, followed by the directions for setting it up.

PROCEDURE

The Kolmogorov-Smirnov Test Worksheet

PART I

Wine ranks	O	OC	E	EC
5	1	10	2	10
4	0	9	2	8
3	5	9	2	6
2	2	4	2	4
1	2	2	2	2

PART II

Wine ranks	OC	EC	OC − EC
5	10	10	0
4	9	8	1
3	9	6	3
2	4	4	0
1	2	2	0

Directions

PART I

1. Write down the observed scores in the column labeled O.
2. Add the numbers in the observed column and put the sum in the blank. Add $2 + 2 + 5 + 0 + 1$. Write 10 in the blank.
3. Form the OC column (observed cumulative distribution). Starting with the bottom number of the observed column, form a cumulative distribution. Record these numbers in the OC column.
4. Find the expected frequencies. Write down the expected scores in the column labeled E. The expected frequencies are found by the formula $E = N/k$: the number in the group divided by the number of categories.[1] That is, 10 divided by 5 equals 2; write the number 2 for each rank.
5. Form the EC column (expected cumulative distribution). Starting with the bottom number of the expected column, form a cumulative distribution. Record these numbers in the EC column.

$N = \underline{10}$

PART II

6. Recopy the OC and EC columns (steps 3 and 5) in Part II of the worksheet. Be sure to place each number opposite its proper position. For example, the OC number of 2 is placed opposite the wine rank of 1.
7. Form the $OC - EC$ column. Subtract the numbers in the EC column from those in the OC column and record the answers in the column labeled $OC - EC$. For example, starting at the top of the OC and EC columns, $10 - 10$ is equal to 0, and this 0 is written in the $OC - EC$ column.
8. Find LD. Look at the numbers in the $OC - EC$ column and take the largest number, whether positive or negative (the absolute value).[2] In effect you ignore the plus or minus sign. Write the number, 3, in the blank.

$LD = \underline{3}$

---

[1] Refer to Chapter 7 for a more complete explanation of how to find the expected frequencies.

[2] The *absolute value* of a number is its numerical value, disregarding its sign. Obviously a positive number is always greater than a negative number. For example, .0001 is greater than $-10,000,000$. However, when you want the number with the largest *absolute* value, you ignore the sign, and in this case you take 10,000,000.

Substitute and Solve

Make the appropriate substitutions by replacing each step with its corresponding number.

$$9. \quad D = \frac{LD}{N}$$

$$10. \quad D = \frac{\text{step 8}}{\text{step 2}}$$

$$11. \quad D = \frac{3}{10}$$

Solve the formula by changing this fraction to a decimal. Divide 3 by 10 and write the answer, .30, in a box.

12. $\boxed{D = .30}$

Statistical Decision

$D = .30$

13. Take the answer enclosed in the box in step 12 and write it in the blank.

14. Find the table value. Enter Table I (two-tail probabilities).[3] Run your finger down the N column until you are at your value for N, in this case 10. Run your fingers across this row until you are under the predetermined level of significance, .01. The value found in the table is .486; place this number for table value in the blank.

Table
value $= .486$

15. If the absolute value found for D (.30) is equal to or greater than the table value found in step 14 (.486), reject the null hypothesis. If it is not, do not reject the null hypothesis. Write *do not reject* in the blank.

do not reject

In Situation X there was no reason to believe there was a significant difference in the preference for wines. We were unable to reject the null hypothesis.

Now let us solve a practice problem and see if you understand the Kolmogorov-Smirnov test.

Problem

Mrs. Martinez, the research consultant for Super Cereal, wants to see if the hardness of cereal affects a child's choice. To test this hypothesis she arranges to have eight different cereals placed before 16 children. The cereals range from a very soft-chewing one, ranked 1, to an extremely hard-chewing one, ranked 8. The

---

[3] The Kolmogorov-Smirnov test is a two-tail test except under very special circumstances (Goodman, 1954).

children are then asked to choose their favorite cereal; their selections are shown in Table 8-3.

Table 8-3: Children's Choice of Cereal

Rank	1	2	3	4	5	6	7	8
Number of children	1	0	1	4	6	3	1	0

The *null hypothesis* states there is no significant difference in the children's preference for cereal. The *alternative hypothesis* states there is a difference in children's preference for cereal; the cereals are not all alike. The level of significance is set at .05. A two-tail test is used.

Answer

The null hypothesis is not rejected. The table value is .328. The value for *D*, .25, is less than the table value of .328; therefore you do not reject the null hypothesis. The hardness of cereal does not seem to affect a child's preference.

Rank	OC	EC	D
8	16	16	0
7	16	14	2
6	15	12	3
5	12	10	2
4	6	8	−2
3	2	6	−4
2	1	4	−3
1	1	2	−1

$$D = \frac{LD}{N} = \frac{4}{16} = .25$$

The procedure used for the Kolmogorov-Smirnov test is summarized below.

Summary of the Procedure for the Kolmogorov-Smirnov Test

1. Form the *OC* and *EC* columns.
2. Arrange the scores in the *OC* and *EC* columns so they are at the right rank.
3. Use Formula 8-1 to find *D*: $D = LD/N$.
4. Next refer to Table I to find the table value for a two-tail test at the appropriate level of significance.
5. If your *D*'s absolute value is equal to or greater than the table value, reject the null hypothesis in favor of the alternative hypothesis.

THE MANN-WHITNEY U TEST

Before we discuss the Mann-Whitney *U* test, you need to know how to rank data. Many of the tests you will be discussing rank their scores, and so you must be familiar with this procedure.

How to Rank

Ranking is the assigning of numbers to people or things. The numbers are assigned from lowest to highest or vice versa. For example, the 15 entries in a cake-baking contest could be assigned their ranks from lowest to highest; the rank of 1 would be considered the best cake, and the rank of 2 the second best, the rank of 3 the third best, and so on, with 15 being in last place. In other situations, such as the ranking of gem hardness, the ranks are assigned from highest to lowest; the rank of 1 is given to the least hard gem, the rank of 2 to a little harder gem, and the rank of 10 to the hardest gem, the diamond. There are many uses of ranking in everyday life, such as for beauty contests, art show competitions, student teaching, the Olympics, tennis tournaments, and consumer products. The ranking that will concern us in this text is the ranking of scores.

When we rank scores, we will rank them from lowest to highest. Suppose we have the following six scores: 16, 11, 17, 8, 14 and 10; we rank them as follows:

1. First we place these numbers in order from lowest to highest: 8, 10, 11, 14, 16, 17.
2. Next we assign each value a rank number. The smallest 8, is assigned a 1; next 10 is assigned a 2; next 11 is assigned a 3; and so forth until the largest, 17, is assigned a 6. The results of this ranking are shown in the following chart.

Rank	1	2	3	4	5	6
Scores	8	10	11	14	16	17

Problem   Now try your hand and rank the following nine scores: 10, 8, 19, 20, 30, 6, 2, 7, and 3.

Answer   Nine ranks are assigned:

Rank	1	2	3	4	5	6	7	8	9
Scores	2	3	6	7	8	10	19	20	30

Probably everyone did this perfectly. The only problem when people rank scores seems to occur when numbers are tied. If you are asked to rank 8, 5, 3, 3, and 2, you will note two numbers are tied for the same rank: there are two 3's. You handle the tie by assigning each tied value the average rank of the rank positions they occupy. Let's see how this works out. First we order the numbers: 2, 3, 3, 5, 8. Now we assign ranks. The number 2 is given a rank of 1. Since the two 3's occupy rank positions 2 and 3, we find the average rank by adding these two rank positions together and dividing by the number of rank positions involved, in this case 2. That is, $(2 + 3)/2 = 2.5$. After you give the 3's each the rank of 2.5, you assign the next number the rank of 4 and finally assign 8 the rank of 5. The chart below summarizes the results.

Rank	1	2.5	2.5	4	5
Scores	2	3	3	5	8

Let's look at a final example of tied ranks. The numbers have been ordered, and the assigning of ranks is shown in the chart that follows.

Rank	1	2	3	4	5.5	5.5	7	9	9	9	11
Scores	40	44	46	47	56	56	60	62	62	62	64

Assigning the first four ranks is a straightforward procedure. The rank of 1 is assigned to the 40, the rank of 2 to the 44, the rank of 3 to the 46, and the rank of 4 to the 47. At this point a tie occurs; there are two 56's in rank positions 5 and 6. We find the average rank: $(5 + 6)/2 = 5.5$, and we write this rank in the rank position for each number. Since the 5 and 6 rank positions are taken care of, we resume with rank 7 and place this above the number 60. Next we encounter three 62's, which are in rank positions 8, 9, and 10. We assign each a rank of 9, since

$$\frac{8 + 9 + 10}{3} = \frac{27}{3} = 9$$

Finally, we resume with rank position 11 and assign it to 64.

To make sure you really understand a difficult ranking assignment, solve the practice problem.

Problem   Rank the following numbers from 1 to 14: 6, 3, 9, 41, 7, 8, 5, 7, 10, 11, 25, 25, 44, 25.

Answer

Rank	1	2	3	4.5	4.5	6	7	8	9	11	11	11	13	14
Score	3	5	6	7	7	8	9	10	11	25	25	25	41	44

Use of the Mann-Whitney U Test

The Mann-Whitney U can be applied when you have two independent, randomly selected groups of unequal sizes. It tests whether two independently drawn samples have been drawn from the same population. Do the scores from one sample significantly differ from those of the other sample, so that we can conclude each sample represents a different population, or is the difference due to the luck of the draw? In the latter case we would conclude that, though the samples may differ, they represent the same population.

The requirements for the Mann-Whitney U are as follows:

Mann-Whitney U Requirements	**1.** Ordinal data. **2.** Two groups. **3.** Independently drawn samples. **4.** Data in ranks. **5.** Simple random samples. **6.** Sample size can be different for two groups.

Let us take a situation where the Mann-Whitney test is appropriate and follow it through.

Situation

For our example let's take the situation found in Chapter 6, Rate a Teacher. Martin wanted to find out if there was a difference in the way two groups of student teachers rated an experienced teacher. He randomly selected two groups of prospective student teachers; the experimental group (seven students) took a special teacher training course, the control group (nine students) took the regular

Table 8-4: Teacher Effectiveness Ratings

Experimental group scores	Control group scores
10	15
13	17
3	20
18	19
5	22
11	30
2	29
	4
	3

course in student teaching. At the end of the semester each group was shown a video-tape of a teacher presenting material in front of a classroom and was asked to give him a total score of from 1 to 30, depending on his fulfilling certain enumerated criteria. The *null hypothesis* states the two groups are the same in the scores they give the experienced teacher. The *alternative hypothesis* states the two groups are different in the scores they give the experienced teacher. The ratings are shown in Table 8-4.

The Mann-Whitney U test is used to see if there is a significant difference in the way the two groups rated the teacher. We will set the level of significance at .05 and use a two-tail test. The formulas used in the computation of U are as follows:

Formula 8-2   *Mann-Whitney U*

$$U_1 = n_1 n_2 + \frac{n_1(n_1 + 1)}{2} - \Sigma R_1$$

Formula 8-3   *Mann-Whitney U*

$$U_2 = n_1 n_2 - U_1$$

The reason that two formulas are necessary is that we need to find the smaller U of the two. Since we are dealing with two populations, usually of different sizes, it stands to reason the two formulas will give different values of U. We perform both tests for U, and whichever happens to be smaller is used as our U value. Don't worry if you don't understand these formulas now; just look at them.

The symbols we use for computing and understanding the formulas are explained below.

Symbol	Meaning
n_1	Size of the smaller group[4]
n_2	Size of the larger group
N	Total number in both groups $(n_1 + n_2)$
ΣR_1	Sum of the ranks in group one
ΣR_2	Sum of the ranks in group two

PROCEDURE

We are ready to use the Mann-Whitney U test to find out if there is a significant difference between the two groups rating the teacher. A worksheet is shown next, followed by directions for setting it up.

---

[4] Use the smaller group regardless of whether it is the control or experimental group.

Worksheet for the Mann-Whitney U

RANKING GRID

Rank	1	2.5	2.5	4	5	6	7	8
Score	2	3	3	4	5	10	11	13

Rank	9	10	11	12	13	14	15	16
Score	15	17	18	19	20	22	29	30

COMPUTATIONAL TABLE

Experimental group		Control group	
n_1	R_1	n_2	R_2
10	6	15	9
13	8	17	10
3	2.5	20	13
18	11	19	12
5	5	22	14
11	7	30	16
2	1	29	15
	$\Sigma R_1 = \overline{40.5}$	4	4
		3	2.5
			$\Sigma R_2 = \overline{95.5}$
$n_1 = \underline{7}$		$n_2 = \underline{9}$	$N = \underline{16}$

Directions for Setting Up the Mann-Whitney U Worksheet

1. Combine the scores of *both groups* by arranging them from lowest to highest along the bottom half of the ranking grid, labeled "Scores."
2. Next, following the ranking procedure you just learned, put in the rank for each score along the top half of the grid, labeled "Rank."
3. In the computational table, write the scores of the individuals in the smaller group in the column labeled n_1.
4. In the computational table, write the scores of the individuals in the larger group in the column labeled n_2.
5. Complete the R_1 and R_2 columns in the computational table. Using the ranking grid, write the proper rank opposite its score in the R_1 or R_2 column (or in both columns when tied). For example, the score of 10 in the n_1 column should have the rank of 6 placed opposite it in the R_1 column, and the score of 15 in the n_2 column should have a rank of 9 placed opposite it in the R_2 column.

6. Find the ΣR_1. Add all the numbers in the R_1 column. Write their sum opposite $\Sigma R_1 =$ _____. Write 40.5 in this blank.
7. Find the ΣR_2. Add all the numbers in the R_2 column. Write their sum opposite the $\Sigma R_2 =$ _____. Write 95.5 in this blank.[5]
8. Find n_1. Count the number of individuals in the group labeled n_1. Write the number opposite the $n_1 =$ _____. Write 7 in the blank.
9. Find n_2. Count the number of individuals in the group labeled n_2. Write the number opposite the $n_2 =$ _____. Write 9 in the blank.
10. Find N. Add the numbers found for n_1 and n_2. Write their sum opposite the $N =$ _____. Write 16 in the blank.

Solving the Formulas

We are ready to make substitutions, using the numbers found in steps 1 through 9.

Substitute and solve the formula for U_1, Formula 8-2:

$$U_1 = n_1 n_2 + \frac{n_1(n_1 + 1)}{2} - \Sigma R_1$$

A. Substitute the number 7 for every n_1, substitute the number 9 for n_2, and substitute the number 40.5 for ΣR_1.

$$U_1 = (7)(9) + \frac{(7)(7 + 1)}{2} - 40.5$$

B. Add the numbers in the parentheses first. Add $7 + 1$ to get 8.

$$U_1 = 7(9) + \frac{(7)(8)}{2} - 40.5$$

C. Perform all the multiplications. Multiply 7 times 9 to get 63; multiply 7 times 8 to get 56.

$$U_1 = 63 + \frac{56}{2} - 40.5$$

D. Divide 56 by 2 to get 28.

$$U_1 = 63 + 28 - 40.5$$

[5] As a check to make sure you ranked these numbers correctly, use the formula $\Sigma R_1 + \Sigma R_2 = N[(N + 1)/2]$. In this example the ΣR_1 was 40.5, the ΣR_2 was 95.5, and the N was 16. Substituting in the formula, you have $40.5 + 95.5 = 16[(16 + 1)/2]$, or $136 = 136$.

E. Add $63 + 28$ to get 91.

   $U_1 = 91 - 40.5$

F. Subtract 40.5 from 91 and enclose the answer, 50.5, in a box.

   $$\boxed{U_1 = 50.5}$$

Substitute and solve the formula for U_2, Formula 8-3:

   $U_2 = n_1 n_2 - U_1$

A. Substitute the number 7 for n_1, the number 9 for n_2, and the number 50.5 for U_1.

   $U_2 = (7)(9) - 50.5$

B. Multiply 7 times 9 to get 63.

   $U_2 = 63 - 50.5$

C. Subtract 50.5 from 63 and enclose the answer, 12.5, in a box.

   $$\boxed{U_2 = 12.5}$$

Statistical Decision

$U = \underline{12.5}$

1. Look at the answers for U_1 (50.5) and for U_2 (12.5). Record the smaller value in the blank opposite $U = $ _____. Write 12.5.

2. Find the table value for U. Refer to Table J. There are four tables, giving the significance levels of .001, .01, .025, and .05 for a one-tail test and .002, .02, .05, and .10 for a two-tail test. Since this problem is a two-tail test at the .05 level of significance, refer to the appropriate table. Run your fingers down the extreme left column of the table until you find your n_1 (7). Next run your fingers across this row until you are under your n_2 (9). Record your table value in the blank to the left. Write 12 in this blank.

$T = \underline{12}$

3. If the value found in step 1 (12.5) is *equal to or smaller than* the table value found in step 2 (12), reject the null hypothesis. If this is not the case, do not reject the null hypothesis. Write *do not reject* in the blank to the left.

do not reject

The null hypothesis states that the two groups are the same in their ratings of this teacher. There is not sufficient evidence to warrant the rejection of this hypothesis.

Tables to Use for the Mann-Whitney U

When n_2 is between 9 and 20, you use Table J. The problem just given illustrates the use of this table.

When n_2 is 8 or less, you use the same formula in solving for U but refer to Table K. Table K has six separate tables on two pages for values of n_2 from 3 to 8. The researcher selects the table that is labeled with the correct n_2 value.

For example, if you have $n_1 = 5$, $n_2 = 5$, and $U = 6$ at the .05 level of significance, you look these values up in the table with the n_2 value of 5. The researcher finds his U of 6 in the left-hand column in this table. He runs his fingers across this row until he is under the n_1 of 5. Where these two points intersect, the exact probability of .111 is found. This table value tells you that if your U is equal to 6, it has a .111 probability of occurring. The researcher rejects the null hypothesis if this probability is equal to or less than his predetermined level of significance. His decision in this case would be to fail to reject the null hypothesis, since the table value, .111, is greater than his .05 level of significance. The K tables show probabilities that are one-tail; for two-tail probabilities simply double the values found in the table. For our example we would multiply .111 × 2.

When n_2 is larger than 20, you have to carry out some further calculations. In this case you use your value of U to compute the value of z given by Formula 8-4.

Formula 8-4   *Mann-Whitney U* (when n_2 is larger than 20)

$$z = \frac{U + \dfrac{1}{2} - \dfrac{n_1 n_2}{2}}{\sqrt{\dfrac{n_1 n_2 (n_1 + n_2 + 1)}{12}}}$$

The sampling distribution for z is approaching the normal distribution, so you now refer to Table D after you find z. Reject the null hypothesis if the probability for z is equal to or less than the predetermined level of significance. The one-tail probabilities are given in this table; for two-tail probabilities double the table values.

Now let us see if you can solve a practice problem by using the Mann-Whitney U and referring to the right table.

Problem   A horse trainer is training 20 randomly chosen horses to obey certain commands. The trainer is using two different techniques, the reward method (I) on 11 horses and the no-reward method (II) on nine horses. The table below shows the number of sessions needed for the horse to obey a command. Rank these data.

Scores I	23	27	34	28	31	47	39	41	43	47	31
Scores II	40	43	23	31	32	33	42	35	31		

The *null hypothesis* states there is no significant difference between the two groups of horses. The *alternative hypothesis* states there is a difference between the two groups of horses.

Does the trainer have evidence that one method is significantly different than the other? The level of significance is set at .10, and it is a two-tailed test.

Answer $U = 48.$

Rank	1.5	1.5	3	4	6.5	6.5	6.5	6.5	9	10
Score	23	23	27	28	31	31	31	31	32	33

Rank	11	12	13	14	15	16	17.5	17.5	19.5	19.5
Score	34	35	39	40	41	42	43	43	47	47

$$U_1 = n_1 n_2 + \frac{n_1(n_1 + 1)}{2} - \Sigma R_1 \qquad U_2 = n_1 n_2 - U_1$$
$$= (9)(11) - 51 = 48$$
$$= (9)(11) + \frac{9(9 + 1)}{2} - 93 \qquad U_2 = 48$$
$$= 99 + 45 - 93 = 51$$
$$U_1 = 51$$

The table value of 27 for a two-tail test is found in Table J. Since the U of 48 is not equal to or less than the table value of 27, the null hypothesis is not rejected.

The procedure used for the Mann-Whitney U is summarized below.

Summary of Procedure for the Mann-Whitney U	1. Designate the smaller sample size as n_1 and the larger sample size as n_2.

Summary of Procedure for the Mann-Whitney *U*

1. Designate the smaller sample size as n_1 and the larger sample size as n_2.
2. Rank all the scores regardless of group together.
3. Determine the value of U using Formulas 8-2 and 8-3.

$$U_1 = n_1 n_2 \frac{n_1(n_1 + 1)}{2} - \Sigma R_1 \qquad U_2 = n_1 n_2 - U_1$$

4. Refer to the appropriate table, depending upon your sample size.

(a) Refer to Table K if n_2 is 8 or less. Reject the null hypothesis if the probability found for U is equal to or less than the predetermined level of significance. One-tail probabilities are given in the table. If you want two-tail probabilities, double the table values.

(b) Refer to Table J if n_2 is between 9 and 20. The significance levels are given for one- and two-tail tests. Reject the null hypothesis only if the value found for U is *equal to or smaller than* the table value.

(c) Refer to Table D if n_2 is larger than 20. In this case use your value for U to compute the value of z given by Formula 8-4.

$$z = \frac{U + \dfrac{1}{2} - \dfrac{n_1 n_2}{2}}{\sqrt{\dfrac{n_1 n_2 (n_1 + n_2 + 1)}{12}}}$$

Reject the null hypothesis if the probability for z is equal to or less than the predetermined level of significance. The one-tail probabilities are given in this table; for two-tail probabilities double the table values.

Comment about the Mann-Whitney U

The Mann-Whitney U test, a nonparametric test, is often used as a substitute for the t-test,[6] a parametric test. This test is used when the t-test's assumptions appear to be in doubt—for example, when the shape of the distribution does not appear to be normal and the level of measurement is ordinal. The Mann-Whitney U is an easy-to-apply nonparametric test.

SIGN TEST

In Chapter 7 you studied the binomial test. You used the binomial distribution to test different hypotheses. Now we are going to study the sign test, which is based on the binomial distribution. When the sample size in our experiment is 25 or smaller, we will evaluate the results by using the binomial distribution as the sampling distribution.

[6] The t-test will be discussed at greater length in Chapter 9.

The sign test measures the significance of the difference between two treatment conditions. It is used with two groups that are matched. You choose this test when you are concerned with the direction of differences, which you indicate by a plus or a minus sign. In using the sign test you analyze every matched pair's scores, recording whether the sign of the difference between a pair is negative or positive. If the scores of a pair are the same, you disregard that pair. The pertinent requirement for this test is that each pair is matched on the important variable that you are studying. For example, high-school children may be matched on their ability to shoot baskets, if you are concerned about basket-shooting ability.

The requirements for the sign test are as follows:

Sign Test Requirements	**1.** Ordinal data **2.** Two-group test **3.** Related groups **4.** When a pair of observations are tied, neither is used **5.** Plus and minus signs are used to indicate differences

Let's take a situation where the sign test is appropriate and follow it through.

Situation

Ms. Iris O'Connor wanted to find out if her new weight-reducing plan guaranteed that a person would lose weight in three weeks' time. She randomly selected ten people and weighed them. She had them follow her plan for three weeks, and then she weighed them again. Next she took each pair of scores and evaluated them as plus and minus. A plus indicates the person lost weight and a minus indicates the person gained weight. Under the null hypothesis you would expect as many

Table 8-5: Results from a Three-Week Reducing Plan

Subject	Weight before (kg)	Weight after (kg)
1. Mr. Gomez	63	50
2. Mr. Polansky	106	90
3. Ms. Tsai	52	72
4. Mrs. Garcia	65	65
5. Mr. Goldblatt	90	82
6. Mr. Trujillo	50	60
7. Mr. Ching	82	80
8. Mr. Espinosa	87	85
9. Mrs. Youngblood	88	90
10. Mrs. Yancy	75	79

plus signs as minus signs. That is, about half of the signs would be plus and half would be minus. The *null hypothesis* states the median of differences is equal to 0. That is, as many people gained weight as lost weight using Ms. O'Connor's plan. Since she feels her plan will work, she states as her *alternative hypothesis* that the median of the differences is positive. In doing this, she is predicting that there will be more plus signs and fewer minus signs. Whenever we make a prediction about the direction of the difference before we collect the data, we use a one-tail test. Ms. O'Connor then sets a .05 level of significance. The data are shown in Table 8-5.

What we are trying to find out for this problem is if there are more plus than minus signs. If there are an equal number of plus and minus signs, the weight-reduction plan is not effective. The symbols to be used have the following meanings:

Symbol	Meaning
x	The number of pluses or the number of minuses, whichever is less
N	Total number of pluses and minuses in the group

The frequency of occurrence of a particular plus or minus sign can be determined by looking at Table H, The Binomial Distribution, when p and q both are equal to 1/2. The procedure for using the sign test is quite simple.

PROCEDURE

Directions for Setting Up a Worksheet for the Sign Test

We are now ready to quickly solve the weight-reducing problem using the sign test. We will set up a worksheet and look up the proper value in Table H.

Worksheet

Subject	Weight before (kg)	Weight after (kg)	Sign
1. Mr. Gomez	63	50	+
2. Mr. Polansky	106	90	+
3. Ms. Tsai	52	72	−
4. Mrs. Garcia	65	65	0
5. Mr. Goldblatt	90	82	+
6. Mr. Trujillo	50	60	−
7. Mr. Ching	82	80	+
8. Mr. Espinosa	87	85	+
9. Mrs. Youngblood	88	90	−
10. Mrs. Yancy	75	79	−

Follow these simple directions and you will find out if Iris has an effective weight-reducing plan.

1. For your sign column. Examine each pair of scores, putting a plus when the score in the left column is higher than the score in the right column. This would mean the person lost weight. For example, Mr. Gomez's score of 63 (left column) is higher than his score of 50 (right column); therefore a plus is put in the sign column. Put a minus in the sign column when the score in the left column is lower than the score in the right column. This would mean the person gained weight. Ms. Tsai's score of 52 (left column) is lower than her score of 72 (right column); therefore a minus sign is put in the sign column. Finally, put a zero when the pair of scores are equal. Mrs. Garcia's score in the left column is 65 and her score in the right column is 65; therefore a zero is placed in the sign column.

2. Find x. Count the number of pluses in the sign column (5). Then count the number of minuses (4). Record the number that is smaller in the blank to the left. Record 4 in this blank.[7]

$\underline{x = 4}$

3. Find N. Count the total number of pluses and minuses, disregarding zeroes. Record this number in the blank to the left. Write 9.

$\underline{N = 9}$

4. Find the table value.[8] Enter Table H and run your finger down the N column until you are at your N value (step 3); then run your fingers across this row until you are under the value for x (step 2). Write the table value in the blank to the left. Write .500.

table value
$\underline{= .500}$

5. Statistical decision. If your table value (.500) is equal to or less than the level of significance (.05), reject the null hypothesis. If your table value is more than the level of significance, do not reject the null hypothesis. Record *do not reject*.

$\underline{\text{do not reject}}$

In this instance about as many people gained weight as lost it. Ms. O'Connor's plan did not result in people's significantly losing weight. We were not able to reject

[7] Note that since Ms. O'Connor is predicting more plus signs, there should be fewer minus signs. There are in fact fewer minus signs. Now she must determine if the number of pairs that have a minus sign (4) is significantly different from the number of pairs that have a plus sign (5). However, let's pretend the direction of the difference was not as predicted; instead, there were fewer plus signs at the end of the experiment. Even though this difference might appear significant, the researchers must overlook it when a one-tail test is used.

[8] You predicted there would be fewer minus signs, and there were; you are now trying to find out the probability of this occurrence.

the null hypothesis. Table H gives you the one-tail probabilities. However, if you had not specified before gathering your data the direction of the differences, you would need two-tail probabilities. If you double the values found in Table H, you will have your two-tail probabilities.

Comments about the Sign Test

The major weakness of the sign test is it does not use all the information given, so if possible a parametric test should be used. Notice in this problem you were ignoring the size of the differences in weight. An advantage of this test is that it is easy to use.

When the sample size is larger than 25, the normal distribution approximates the binomial sampling distribution, and Formula 8-5 is used:

Formula 8-5   *Sign Test* (sample size larger than 25)

$$z = \frac{(x \pm .5) - \frac{1}{2}N}{\frac{1}{2}\sqrt{N}}$$

Table D is used for interpretation.

The question asked in the foregoing problem could be put another way: what is the probability of getting four heads out of nine tosses of a coin? (The tie score is regarded as a coin that is not counted in the sample.) In other words, this is a binomial problem and the formula $\binom{N}{x} P^x Q^{N-x}$ can be used to solve it. The calculation of this problem is shown in Table 8-6. Adding the individual probabilities, $.246 + .164 + .070 + .018 + .002$, you get an answer of .500, the same answer you found for the sign test by going directly to Table H.

Table 8-6: Computation of Binomial Probabilities

Probability of 4 heads out of 9:	$p(4) = \binom{9}{4}\left(\frac{1}{2}\right)^4 \left(\frac{1}{2}\right)^5 = .246$
Probability of 3 heads out of 9:	$p(3) = \binom{9}{3}\left(\frac{1}{2}\right)^3 \left(\frac{1}{2}\right)^6 = .164$
Probability of 2 heads out of 9:	$p(2) = \binom{9}{2}\left(\frac{1}{2}\right)^2 \left(\frac{1}{2}\right)^7 = .070$
Probability of 1 head out of 9:	$p(1) = \binom{9}{1}\left(\frac{1}{2}\right)^1 \left(\frac{1}{2}\right)^8 = .018$
Probability of 0 heads out of 9:	$p(0) = \binom{9}{0}\left(\frac{1}{2}\right)^0 \left(\frac{1}{2}\right)^9 = .002$

Using Table H and the worksheet, solve the following practice sign problem.

Problem.   George Whitecloud, a restaurant owner, wants to find out if Alpha Pie is better than Beta Pie, so that he can decide which brand to order for his restaurant. He matches samples of pie on color and texture. He randomly selects 11 adults, blindfolds them, and tells them to rate the two brands of pie on a continuum from 1 to 5. A 5 indicates a fantastic piece of pie, a 1 indicates a mediocre piece. Since the rating system is not perfect and there is really no way of determining how much better a 2-rated piece of pie is than a 1-rated piece, the sign test is used. Mr. Whitecloud records the scores; then he takes each pair and evaluates them as plus and minus. A plus indicates the Alpha Pie is better and a minus indicates the Beta Pie is better. Under the *null hypothesis* there is no significant difference in the ranking of the pies. That is, there should be the same number of plus and minus signs. Since Mr. Whitecloud feels that the Alpha Pie will be preferred over the Beta Pie, he states as his *alternative hypothesis* that the Alpha Pie is preferred over the Beta Pie. Thus he expects fewer minus signs, because there will be more plus signs in favor of the Alpha Pie. Since he is predicting the direction of the difference, a one-tail test is appropriate. He sets a .05 level of significance. The data are shown in the accompanying table.

Rating of Alpha and Beta Apple Pies

Rater	Alpha	Beta	Sign
John Eberhard	1	3	−
Ted Amos	5	1	+
Sue Russell	3	1	+
Lil Tamurka	2	1	+
Susan O'Brien	2	2	0
Martin Zuccaro	4	1	+
Marilyn Schuber	5	3	+
Ed Gond	4	1	+
Gloria Tang	2	1	+
Sam Miller	5	1	+
Barbara Kennedy	4	2	+

Answer   The sign that occurred fewer times was minus; there was one negative sign. The table value is .011. Since .011 is less than the level of significance of .05, you can reject the null hypothesis in favor of the alternative hypothesis. The Alpha brand is preferred over the Beta brand of apple pie. For this problem $x = 1$ and

$N = 10$. If George Whitecloud had not predicted the direction of the difference, he would have used a two-tail test. For example, for his alternative hypothesis he might have stated there is a difference between Alpha and Beta pie. Since this alternative hypothesis does not predict the direction of the difference, he would use a two-tail test. He would still use Table H; however, since the table values are one-tail probabilities, he would find the two-tail probabilities by doubling the values found in the table. In this case, $.011 \times 2 = .022$.

The procedure you just learned in using the sign test is summarized below:

Steps in Using the Sign Test	1. Evaluate each pair of scores as negative or positive.
	2. Determine x, the number of pluses or the number of minuses, whichever is less.
	3. Determine N by counting the number of plus and minus signs, disregarding zeroes.
	4. Consult a table to determine the probability under the null hypothesis.

(a) If N is 25 or less, refer to Table H. Table H gives you one-tail probabilities associated with a number as small as the value of x. For a two-tail test double the values shown in Table H. If the probability found in Table H is equal to or less than your level of significance, reject the null hypothesis.

(b) If N is larger than 25, refer to Table D. Find x, then compute the value of Z using Formula 8-5.

$$z = \frac{(x \pm .5) - \frac{1}{2}N}{\frac{1}{2}\sqrt{N}}$$

Next refer to Table D. If the value found in the table is equal or less than your level of significance, reject the null hypothesis in favor of the alternative hypothesis. These are one-tail probabilities; if you want two-tail probabilities, simply double the value shown in the table.

WILCOXON SIGNED-RANKS TEST

The Wilcoxon test compares the distributions of two related groups. The groups are related in one of two ways:

1. The same people have been tested under two different conditions.
2. Pairs of individuals have been matched on the same basis before being tested.

The purpose of this test is to determine whether the differences between the groups favor one group over the other.

The sign test, which you have just read about, concerns itself with only the direction of the differences between the pairs; it does not consider the size of the differences. All we recorded by using a plus or a minus sign for each matched pair of scores for the sign test was whether one of the pairs was larger or smaller; we did not record how large or small this difference was. We were not interested that there was a 13-point spread between the scores of 63 and 50. The sign test did not use all the information that was available. However, the Wilcoxon concerns itself not only with the direction of the differences, but also with their size. It makes a distinction between these differences by ranking them.

The requirements of the Wilcoxon signed-ranks test are as follows:

Wilcoxon Signed-Ranks Test	1. Ordinal data 2. Two groups 3. Related groups 4. Ranked data

Situation

Returning to Chapter 6 and Situation VIII, the Dancing Coach, we will solve this problem using the Wilcoxon test. Pete Finely, a choreographer, has to choose between two dancing coaches who have opposite approaches. He decides to do a little study to help him decide. He auditions 20 dancers and then matches them on their ability to do certain routines. One person from each matched pair is assigned at random to one of the two dancing coaches. For 60 hours each coach teaches the dancers the same new routines. At the end of this time the dancers are

Table 8-7: Ratings on Dancers Doing Routines Taught by Coaches A and B

Pair	Coach A	Coach B
A	30	20
B	10	5
C	29	24
D	20	18
E	16	20
F	23	23
G	21	16
H	26	25
I	23	20
J	23	20

tested and rated from 1 to 30 on their ability to do the new routine. The results are expressed in Table 8-7.

Do the results indicate a significant difference between the two groups of dancers, or could the difference have arisen from chance alone? Since Pete just wants to know if there is a significant difference in effectiveness between the two groups, he uses a two-tail test. He tests his hypothesis at .05. The *null hypothesis* states there is no significant difference between Coach A's group and Coach B's group. The *alternative hypothesis* states there is a significant difference between Coach A's group and Coach B's group.

Symbol	Meaning
N	Number of matched pairs, excluding those with a deviation (D) of zero
T	The smaller value for either $\Sigma\,R^+$ or $\Sigma\,R^-$

PROCEDURE

Directions for Setting Up a Worksheet for the Wilcoxon

We will now set up a worksheet. Be careful to follow the directions for forming the columns.

Wilcoxon Worksheet

COMPUTATIONAL TABLE

Pair	Coach A, column 1	Coach B, column 2	D	R	R^+	R^-
A	30	20	10	9	9	
B	10	5	5	7	7	
C	29	24	5	7	7	
D	20	18	2	2	2	
E	16	20	−4	−5		−5
F	23	23	-0̶			
G	21	16	5	7	7	
H	26	25	1	1	1	
I	23	20	3	3.5	3.5	
J	23	20	3	3.5	3.5	

$$N = 9 \qquad \Sigma\,R^+ = 40.0 \quad \Sigma\,R^- = 5$$
$$T = 5$$

RANKING GRID

Rank	1	2	3.5	3.5	5	7	7	7	9
D scores	1	2	3	3	4	5	5	5	10

The scores in this grid are taken from column D in the computational table.

Directions for Using This Worksheet

1. Form columns 1 and 2. Put the scores from one group in column 1 and put the scores from the corresponding members of the matched pairs of dancers in column 2.
2. Form column *D*. Subtract each number found in column 2 from its corresponding number in column 1. Place the results in column *D*.[9] For example, for pair A a score of 20 is subtracted from a score of 30, giving an answer of 10 to be placed in column *D*.
3. Find *N*. Ignore all the zero values in the *D* column by putting a line through them. Count the number of *D*'s that are not zeroes and record this number opposite the *N* = ___. Write 9 in the blank.

$N = \underline{9}$

4. Using the ranking grid. Rank all the values not crossed out in the *D* column. When you rank, for the time being, ignore the plus and minus signs.
5. Form the *R* column. Transpose the ranks from the ranking grid to the *R* column. For example, a *D* score of 10 is given a rank of 9. Next place the correct sign in front of the number in this column by looking at the *D* column. For instance, the rank for pair E is −5, because there is a minus sign in the *D* column.
6. Form the *R*⁺ column. Using the *R* column, put all the positive numbers in a column labeled *R*⁺. You put 9, 7, 7, 2, 7, 1, 3.5, and 3.5 in this column.
7. Find the Σ *R*⁺. Add all the numbers in the *R*⁺ column and place the answer opposite the Σ *R*⁺ = ___. Write 40 in the blank.

$\Sigma R^+ = \underline{40}$

8. Form the *R*⁻ column. Using the *R* column, put all the negative numbers in the column labeled *R*⁻. You put −5 in this column.
9. Find the Σ *R*⁻. Add all the numbers in the *R*⁻ column and place the answer opposite the Σ *R*⁻ = ___. Write −5 in the blank.[10]

$\Sigma R^- = \underline{-5}$

10. Find *T*. Compare the answers found for step 7 and step 9. Record the smaller number (absolute value), disregarding the sign, as *T*. Place the answer opposite the *T* = ___. Write 5 in the blank.

$T = \underline{5}$

---

[9] If the number in column 1 is smaller than the number in column 2, put a minus sign in front of the answer.

[10] A check to see if your values for the Σ *R*⁺ and Σ *R*⁻ are correct is: $\Sigma R^+ + \Sigma R^- = \frac{1}{2}n(n+1)$. For this problem $40 + 5 = \frac{1}{2} \cdot 9(9+1)$, which equals 45.

Statistical Decision

table value
= <u>6</u>

11. Find the table value. Refer to Table L. Enter this table by running your fingers down the N column until you stop at the proper value for N (9). Next run your fingers across that row until you are under the predetermined level of significance and proper tail (.05 and two-tail). Write the number you find as your table value. Write 6 in the blank.
12. If the T value you found in step 10 (5) is equal to or less than the table value found in step 11, the null hypothesis is rejected. If the T value is more than the table value, do not reject the null hypothesis. Since the T value of 5 is less than the table value of 6, you write *reject* in the blank to the left.

reject

The null hypothesis was rejected in favor of the alternative hypothesis. In this situation there was reason to believe the two groups were different in their ability to do dance routines.

Next try a practice problem to see if you understand how to use this test.

Problem

Manuel wants to find out if talking to plants has an effect. He buys two sets of identical plants, sets up two identical rooms, and assigns one plant from each matched pair to a room. For the next two months the two groups of plants are given the same treatment except one group is talked to for 25 minutes a day. At the end of the experiment an expert is called in to rate the plants for health, using a rating scale of 1 to 25. The results are recorded in the accompanying table.

Plants Rated on Scale of 1 to 25 for Healthiest

Pairs	Talking treatment	Nontalking treatment
A	20	21
B	24	21
C	8	5
D	9	6
E	5	7
F	4	6
G	9	3
H	3	10

The *null hypothesis* states that there is no significant difference in the health of the two groups of plants. As his *alternative hypothesis* Manuel states that the health of the two groups of plants will be different. He sets his level of significance at .05.

Since his alternative hypothesis is nondirectional, he uses a two-tail test.

Answer   The T value is equal to 14. In this case we do not reject the null hypothesis. The value found in the table is 4. Since the T value of 14 is higher than the table value, we cannot reject the null hypothesis. $\Sigma R^+ = 22.0$ and $\Sigma R^- = 14$. The plants from both groups are the same.

We have given examples of two-tail tests. If you want to use the Wilcoxon for a one-tail test, it is a relatively easy matter. In the preceding practice problem if Manuel believes the plants he talks to will be healthier, he might state this as his alternative hypothesis. He is predicting in advance the direction of the differences. Since he feels the plants he talks to will do better, he has predicted the sign of the smaller sum of the ranks to be negative $(-)$, since the sign of the larger sum of the ranks would have to be in favor of the talked-to plants. In this situation the sign of the smaller sum of the ranks turned out to be negative. Remember, the T of 14 came from the negative sum of the ranks. Manuel now refers to Table L, which is adapted for use for one-tail as well as two-tail tests. At the .05 level of significance, using a one-tail test, the table value is 6. Manuel is still unable to reject the null hypothesis that the two groups of plants are the same.

Sample Sizes Larger Than 25

When you have a sample size larger than 25, you cannot use Table L. In such instances, your T is almost normally distributed. When this is the case, you proceed as before to find T. That is, you find the sum of the smaller ranks. After you find T, you use Formula 8-6 and refer to Table D to evaluate the results.

Formula 8-6   *Wilcoxon Test* (sample size larger than 25)

$$z = \frac{T - \frac{N(N+1)}{4}}{\sqrt{\frac{N(N+1)(2N+1)}{24}}}$$

Let us take the previous situation involving plants, increasing the size of our sample to 26. We will use a one-tail test, predicting the sign of the smaller ranks to be minus. In this case let's say we found $T = 51$, and the sign of the smaller sum of the ranks was minus. We now substitute in the formula, and the problem looks like this:

$$z = \frac{51 - \dfrac{26(26+1)}{4}}{\sqrt{\dfrac{26(26+1)((2)26+1)}{24}}}$$

$$= \frac{51 - \dfrac{26(27)}{4}}{\sqrt{\dfrac{(26)(27)(53)}{24}}}$$

$$= \frac{51 - 175.5}{\sqrt{1550.25}}$$

$$= \frac{-124.5}{39.37}$$

$$= -3.2$$

Table D shows us that a z value as extreme as -3.2 has a one-tail probability of occurring of .0007. Since this is less than .05, we reject the null hypothesis in favor of the alternative, which says the plants who are talked to are healthier. For a two-tail test you simply double the probabilities, shown in Table D. The steps in using the Wilcoxon test are summarized in the box.

Summary of the Procedure for Using the Wilcoxon Test

1. Determine T, using the procedure given. That is, determine the smaller of the sum of the ranks.
2. Determine N, which is the total number of d's having a sign.
3. Refer to the appropriate table.
   (a) If N is 25 or less, refer to Table L. If the value of T is equal to or less than the one given in the table for a pre-determined level of significance, reject the null hypothesis.
   (b) If N is larger than 25, find T; then compute the value of z, using Formula 8-6, and refer to Table D. (If the probability you obtain is equal to or less than your pre-determined level of significance, reject the null hypothesis.) For a two-tail test you double the probability shown in the table.

KRUSKAL-WALLIS TEST

The Kruskal-Wallis test is similar to the Mann-Whitney U test. The Mann-Whitney U compared two groups, whereas the Kruskal-Wallis compares three or more groups. The researcher wants to know if the difference among the groups he is studying is due to sampling error or is a real difference. The Kruskal-Wallis test determines if there is a difference by finding out if the sums of the ranks for each of its groups differ significantly from each other. A significant value of H implies that the medians of the distribution are not the same. When using the Kruskal-Wallis test, the researcher does not have to be concerned about whether he is using a one- or two-tail test. His only concern is whether there is a difference.

The requirements for using this test are as follows:

Kruskal-Wallis	1. Ordinal level
Requirements	2. Three or more groups
	3. Independent groups
	4. Simple random sample

Let us look now at a situation in which the Kruskal-Wallis test is appropriate.

Situation

A consumer bureau is rating the fried chicken of four frozen-food companies on a scale of 1 to 20. They want to find out whether or not the chicken of these companies differs in overall quality. Table 8-8 gives the ratings for the four companies.

Table 8-8: Ratings of Fried Chicken for Four Frozen-food Companies

Group A	Group B	Group C	Group D
2	18	18	4
2	19	15	1
5	16	17	3
6	20	12	8
10	12	14	7
13	18	12	8
		11	9

The consumer bureau sets a .05 level of significance. The null hypothesis states there is no significant difference among the products of the four companies. The alternative hypothesis states there is a difference. Use the Kruskal-Wallis test, Formula 8-7, on these data.

Formula 8-7   *Kruskal-Wallis Test*

$$H = \frac{12}{N(N+1)} \left[\frac{(\Sigma R_1)^2}{n_1} + \frac{(\Sigma R_2)^2}{n_2} + \frac{(\Sigma R_3)^2}{n_3} + \dots + \frac{(\Sigma R_k)^2}{n_k} \right] - 3(N+1)$$

The meanings of the terms used in this formula are as follows:

Symbol	Meaning
N	Total number of subjects $(n_1 + n_2 + n_3 + \dots)$
$(\Sigma R_1)^2, (\Sigma R_2)^2, (\Sigma R_3)^2, \dots$	Sum of the ranks for Group 1 squared, sum of the ranks for Group 2 squared, sum of the ranks for Group 3 squared, and so on.
$n_1, n_2, n_3, \dots$	Number of subjects in Group 1, number of subjects in Group 2, number of subjects in Group 3, and so on.
$df = k - 1$	Degrees of freedom, equal to the number of groups minus one.

PROCEDURE

Directions for Setting Up the Worksheet for the Kruskal-Wallis

We are now ready to use our formula for the Kruskal-Wallis and find out if there is a difference in the ratings of Groups A, B, C, and D. There are four parts to solving this problem. In part I you will set up a worksheet; in part II you will follow the directions in order to form the columns on the worksheet. When you reach part III you will be able to substitute and solve the formula. In part IV you will reach a statistical decision.

Part I: Setting Up a Worksheet

We will now set up a worksheet; follow the directions to form the columns, and solve the formula.

Worksheet for the Kruskal-Wallis

RANKING GRID

Rank	1	2.5	2.5	4	5	6	7	8	9.5	9.5	11	12	13
Scores	1	2	2	3	4	5	6	7	8	8	9	10	11
Rank	15	15	15	17	18	19	20	21	23	23	23	25	26
Scores	12	12	12	13	14	15	16	17	18	18	18	19	20

COMPUTATIONAL WORKSHEET

Group A scores	R_1	Group B scores	R_2	Group C scores	R_3	Group D scores	R_4
2	2.5	18	23	18	23	4	5
2	2.5	19	25	15	19	1	1
5	6	16	20	17	21	3	4
6	7	20	26	12	15	8	9.5
10	12	12	15	14	18	7	8
13	17	18	23	12	15	8	9.5
				11	13	9	11

$$\Sigma R_1 = 47.0 \qquad \Sigma R_2 = 132 \qquad \Sigma R_3 = 124 \qquad \Sigma R_4 = 48.0$$

$$\boxed{(\Sigma R_1)^2 = 2209} \quad \boxed{(\Sigma R_2)^2 = 17{,}424} \quad \boxed{(\Sigma R_3)^2 = 15{,}376} \quad \boxed{(\Sigma R_4)^2 = 2304}$$

$$n_1 = \underline{6} \qquad n_2 = \underline{6} \qquad n_3 = \underline{7} \qquad n_4 = \underline{7}$$

$$N = 26$$

Part II: Forming the Columns

1. Rank all the scores together, using the ranking grid. As a refresher, if you are having problems, refer back to the beginning of this chapter.
2. Form the R_1, R_2, R_3, and R_4 columns. Take the ranks from the ranking grid and write them in their respective columns. For example, the rank of 2.5 is written twice in the R_1 column opposite both scores of 2. The rank of 23 is written three times, two times in the R_2 column opposite both scores of 18 and once in the R_3 column opposite the score of 18.
3. Find the ΣR_1, ΣR_2, ΣR_3, and ΣR_4. Find the ΣR_1 by adding the numbers in the R_1 column. You add $2.5 + 2.5 + 6 + 7 + 12 + 17$ and place their sum opposite the $\Sigma R_1 = $ _____. Write 47. Find the ΣR_2, ΣR_3, and ΣR_4 by repeating the procedure used to find the ΣR_1.
4. Find the $(\Sigma R_1)^2$, $(\Sigma R_2)^2$, $(\Sigma R_3)^2$, and $(\Sigma R_4)^2$. Find the $(\Sigma R_1)^2$ by squaring the number found for ΣR_1. You square 47 and write 2209 opposite the $(\Sigma R_1)^2 = $ _____. Find the $(\Sigma R_2)^2$, $(\Sigma R_3)^2$, and $(\Sigma R_4)^2$ by repeating this procedure. Square the values found for ΣR_2 (132), ΣR_3 (124), and ΣR_4 (48) and place their answers in the correct boxes.
5. Find n_1, n_2, n_3, n_4. Find n_1 by counting the number of subjects for Group A. Write the answer opposite the $n_1 = $ _____. Write 6. Find n_2, n_3, n_4 by repeating the same procedure.
6. Find N. Add the numbers found for n_1, n_2, n_3, and n_4. Add $6 + 6 + 7 + 7$ and write 26 opposite the $N = $ _____ in the triangle.[11]

[11] At this point check to see if you did the ranking correctly: add

Part III: Substituting and Solving the Formula

$$H = \frac{12}{N(N+1)} \left[\frac{(\Sigma R_1)^2}{n_1} + \frac{(\Sigma R_2)^2}{n_2} + \frac{(\Sigma R_3)^2}{n_3} + \frac{(\Sigma R_4)^2}{n_4} + \cdots + \frac{(\Sigma R_k)^2}{n_k} \right] - 3(N+1)$$

7. Substitute the number found for N, which was placed in the triangle. Wherever there is an N, write the number 26 in the formula:

$$H = \frac{12}{26(26+1)} \left[\frac{(\Sigma R_1)^2}{n_1} + \frac{(\Sigma R_2)^2}{n_2} + \frac{(\Sigma R_3)^2}{n_3} + \frac{(\Sigma R_4)^2}{n_4} + \cdots + \frac{(\Sigma R_k)^2}{n_k} \right] - 3(26+1)$$

8. Substitute the values found in the boxes (step 4) for $(\Sigma R_1)^2$, $(\Sigma R_2)^2$, $(\Sigma R_3)^2$, and $(\Sigma R_4)^2$. Write 2209 for $(\Sigma R_1)^2$, 17,424 for $(\Sigma R_2)^2$, 15,376 for $(\Sigma R_3)^2$, and 2304 for $(\Sigma R_4)^2$.

$$H = \frac{12}{26(26+1)} \left[\frac{2209}{n_1} + \frac{17,424}{n_2} + \frac{15,376}{n_3} + \frac{2304}{n_4} \right] - 3(26+1)$$

9. Finally, substitute the values found for n_1, n_2, n_3, and n_4. Write 6 for n_1, 6 for n_2, 7 for n_3, and 7 for n_4.

$$H = \frac{12}{26(26+1)} \left[\frac{2209}{6} + \frac{17,424}{6} + \frac{15,376}{7} + \frac{2304}{7} \right] - 3(26+1)$$

10. Solve this formula by dealing with the numbers in the brackets first. Divide each numerator by its denominator. Divide 2209 by 6 (368.17); divide 17,424 by 6 (2904); divide 15,376 by 7 (2196.57); and divide 2304 by 7 (329.14).

$$H = \frac{12}{26(26+1)} [368.17 + 2904 + 2196.57 + 329.14] - 3(26+1)$$

the numbers found for ΣR_1, ΣR_2, ΣR_3, and ΣR_4; if their sum equals $N(N+1)/2$, you have done the work correctly. For this example $47 + 132 + 124 + 48$ should equal $26(26+1)/2$. It equals 351.

11. Add the numbers in the brackets together and put a bracket around the answer. Add $368.17 + 2904 + 2196.57 + 329.14$; put a bracket around the answer, 5797.88.

$$H = \frac{12}{26(26+1)} [5797.88] - 3(26+1)$$

12. Solve the numbers in parentheses. Since the numbers in parentheses are the same, add $26 + 1$ and write the answer, 27, in both parentheses.

$$H = \frac{12}{26(27)} 5797.88 - 3(27)$$

13. Perform all multiplications. Multiply 26 times 27 (702); multiply 12 times 5797.88 (69,574.56); multiply three times 27 (81).

$$H = \frac{69,574.56}{702} - 81$$

14. Perform all divisions. Divide 69,574.56 by 702 (99.11).

$$H = 99.11 - 81$$

15. Perform the remaining subtraction. Subtract 81 from 99.11 (18.11).

$$H = 18.11$$

16. Enclose the answer for H in a box.

$$\boxed{H = 18.11}$$

Part IV: Reaching a Statistical Decision

Fill in the blanks in the left-hand column.

1. Find df. The degrees of freedom for the Kruskal-Wallis is $k - 1$. Subtract 1 from the number of groups (4). Write 3 in the blank.

$df = \underline{3}$

2. Record H. Take the value found in step 14 (18.11) and write it in the blank. Write 18.11.

$H = \underline{18.11}$

3. Find the table value. Use the chi-square table, Table E. Run your fingers down the df column until you are at the df found in step 1 (3). Next run your fingers across this row until you are under your predetermined level of significance (.05). Record the value you find in the table. Write 7.82 in the blank.

table
value $= \underline{7.82}$

4. If the value you have found for H (18.11) is equal to or greater than the table value (7.82), reject the null hypothesis; if not, do not reject. Write *reject* in the blank to the left.

reject

For this problem there was a significant difference in the way the chicken was rated. The frozen-food companies' products are not the same. In effect, what does this result really tell you? It just implies the groups are different. Without an application of a significance test for multiple comparison, it is impossible to say more than that the groups appear to be different. The Kruskal-Wallis test simply provides you with an over-all result; it does not make these specific comparisons between the groups. Since it might be important to locate the specific differences, see the multiple-comparisons procedure designed by Ryan (1960).

Before trying a practice problem for the Kruskal-Wallis, let's discuss what to do when the sample sizes are small.

Tables to Use for the Kruskal-Wallis Test When Sample Sizes Are Small

For almost all cases consult Table E with $k - 1$ degrees of freedom. However, when your sample sizes are five or less and there are only three groups, your distribution does not approximate the chi square. Only in this case do you use special tables that Kruskal and Wallis devised. You follow the identical procedure for finding H, but instead of referring to the chi-square table, as we did before, you refer to the set of tables of exact probabilities. This entire set is called Table M.

Table M has combinations of different group sizes from one to five. It is divided into three columns: sample sizes, H values, and probabilities.

Let's demonstrate how to use this table with an $n_1 = 5$, $n_2 = 4$, and $n_3 = 4$, a computed H of 4.65, and a .05 level of significance. First find the right group sizes for n_1, n_2, and n_3 in the sample-size column. In this case you find the numbers 5, 4, 4. Starting at these numbers you run across this row into the next column, the H column. Now you have to choose among the six numbers listed in this cluster. You go down this column until you find a value that comes closest to your H value of 4.65 without exceeding it. The value that fits this description is 4.6187. Next find the number directly across from this value in the next column, the probability column. The number you find in this case is .100. This tells you that an H of 4.6187 occurs 10 percent of the time. Since your H is 4.65, it occurs less than .100 of the time. However, your *H* of 4.65 does not have .05 probability of occurring, because it does not equal or exceed the *H* of 5.6176 in the table. Since your probability of .10 is not smaller than your .05 level of significance, you cannot reject the null hypothesis.

Now try a problem using this table.

Problem   Level of significance for this problem is set at .01; $H = 6.87$; $n_1 = 5$, $n_2 = 2$, $n_3 = 2$.

Answer   Reject the null hypothesis, since an *H* of 6.87 comes closest to 6.533, and the probability of occurrence of this value is .008, which is less than your level of significance of .01. Since 6.87 is more than 6.533, the probability of its occurring would be less than .008.

Now you are ready to solve a practice problem using the Kruskal-Wallis test. First find *H*; then decide on Table E or Table M.

Problem   Returning to Situation IV, The Bubble Gum Children, solve this problem using the Kruskal-Wallis test. Maria wants to find out if the three groups of children differ in their bubble-blowing ability. The children are rated on a scale from 1 to 9. The data are shown again in the accompanying table. Set a .01 level of significance and find out if a significant difference exists among the three groups. The *null hypothesis* states that the three groups are the same in their ability to blow bubbles. The *alternative hypothesis* states that the three groups are different.

Ratings on Bubble-Blowing Ability for Three Groups of Children

Brand A	Brand B	Brand C
3	1	9
5	2	8
7	4	9
6		

Answer   You reject the null hypothesis. Your *H* value, 7.32, exceeds the table value, 6.7455, which has a probability of occurring of .010. Your *H* value of 7.32 is more than 6.7455, so the probability of its occurring would be less than .01. The three groups of children are different in their bubble-blowing ability.

Ranking Grid

Rank	1	2	3	4	5	6	7	8	9.5	9.5
Score	1	2	3	4	5	6	7	8	9	9

The Effect of Ties

When the number of ties is large, H will be a little smaller than it should be. There is a correction for ties that makes it easier to reject the null hypothesis. If you do not correct for ties, your rejection of the null hypothesis will be harder, and your test is more conservative. We shall not deal with this correction formula, because it has little effect on the value of H unless the number of ties is extreme (Hays, 1973).[12]

The steps involved in using the Kruskal-Wallis test are summarized below.

Procedure for Using the Kruskal-Wallis Test

1. Use Formula 8-7 to find H.
2. Refer to the appropriate table, depending upon the number of groups you have and your sample size.
   (a) If there are three groups and if n_1 and n_2 and n_3 are equal to or less than five, consult Table M. Reject the null hypothesis if your value for H has a probability of occurring that is equal to or less than your level of significance.
   (b) If you do not have three groups and if n_1 and n_2 and n_3 are not equal to or less than five, consult Table E and use $k - 1$ as your degrees of freedom. Reject the null hypothesis if your value for H is equal to or greater than your table value.

FRIEDMAN TEST

The Friedman test is useful when we want to test the null hypothesis that many groups have been drawn from the same population. The Friedman is an extension of the previously discussed Wilcoxon test. The Wilcoxon, as you remember, can be used with only two groups, while the Friedman can be used with three or more groups. Like the Wilcoxon, the Friedman uses related or matched groups. Either these groups are matched on the basis of some variable, or the same subjects are used for different treatments. Since the Friedman uses groups that are

[12] Refer to Siegel (1956) for the formula and a complete treatment of correction for ties.

matched, there are the same number of subjects in each sample. The requirements for the Friedman test are as follows:

Friedman Test Requirements	**1.** Ordinal data.
	2. Three or more groups.
	3. Related groups.
	4. Sample drawn at random from matched scores.

Let us look at a situation for which the Friedman test is appropriate.

Situation

Gloria Leone, a specialist in making bread, was best at nut bread, plain white bread, raisin bread, and cinnamon bread. She wanted to know if her breads were regarded as equal in overall quality. She felt that they would be regarded as different in their overall quality. She gave samples of her bread to a team of experts who rated them on a scale from 1 to 30. The ratings are shown in Table 8-9.

Table 8-9: Ratings of Four Types of Bread

Experts	*Nut*	*White*	*Raisin*	*Cinnamon*
A	27	25	30	20
B	16	10	15	15
C	20	24	25	21
D	27	23	25	26
E	18	22	21	16
F	21	15	17	20

Notice that each row[13] in this table is a matched group of subjects. In this case the match is that the same person takes all four treatments. The *null hypothesis* states that there is no significant difference in the overall ratings of the four types of bread. The *alternative hypothesis* states that the ratings of the four types of bread are different. The level of significance is set at .01. The Friedman formula used on these data is given below:

Formula 8-8	*Friedman Test*

$$\chi_r^2 = \frac{12}{Nk(k+1)} [\Sigma R_i^2] - 3N(k+1)$$

[13] Remember that the rows run horizontally across the page and the columns run vertically like the columns holding up the roof of a Greek temple.

The terms to be used in this formula are:

Symbol	Meaning
k	Number of columns
N	Number of rows
ΣR_i^2	Sum of the squared rank sums
$df = k - 1$	Degrees of freedom, equal to the number of columns minus one.

PROCEDURE

Directions for Setting Up the Friedman Worksheet

We are now ready to use our formula for the Friedman and find out if there is a significant difference between the breads in the situation just presented.

In order to solve the Friedman formula, you change the scores to ranks and work only with these ranks. Table 8-9 shows the original scores given to the four different kinds of bread by the six experts. Rank the scores in each row (NOT by columns) and place the results in another table, which here is labeled 8-10. Table 8-10 is actually the worksheet you use to solve the formula. You will use it to find the numbers in your formula, then substitute these numbers in the formula and solve it. Finally, you will reach a statistical decision.

We begin by looking at Table 8-9 and ranking the scores for *each row* (NOT by columns). Record the ranks with the corresponding rows in Table 8-10. For example, take the top row, which shows the scores given by expert A: 27, 25, 30, and 20.

Table 8-10: Ranked Scores

Experts	R_1 Nut	R_2 White	R_3 Raisin	R_4 Cinnamon
A	3	2	4	1
B	4	1	2.5	2.5
C	1	3	4	2
D	3	1	2	4
E	2	4	3	1
F	4	1	2	3
	$\Sigma R_1 = \overline{17}$	$\Sigma R_2 = \overline{12}$	$\Sigma R_3 = \overline{17.5}$	$\Sigma R_4 = \overline{13.5}$
	$\Sigma R_1^2 = 289$	$\Sigma R_2^2 = 144$	$\Sigma R_3^2 = 306.25$	$\Sigma R_4^2 = 182.25$

$$\Sigma R_i^2 = 921.50$$

Ranking from lowest to highest, the score of 20 is ranked 1, the score of 25 is ranked 2, 27 is ranked 3, and 30, the highest score, is ranked 4. These rankings appear in the top row of Table 8-10 as the ranked scores of expert A.

Expert B's scores form the second row of Table 8-9: 16, 10, 15, and 15. Looking at Table 8-10, you will notice that 10, the lowest score, receives a rank of 1, and 16, the highest score, receives a rank of 4. Each score of 15 is given a rank of 2.5, because they are tied scores. This procedure is followed for the remaining four rows. When Table 8-10 is completed, you follow the directions below.

Directions for Working with Table 8-10

1. Find the sum of each column. For example, the sum of R_1 is found by adding $3 + 4 + 1 + 3 + 2 + 4$ and putting its sum, 17, opposite the $\Sigma\ R_1$. Now repeat the same procedure to find the sums of the remaining columns, $\Sigma\ R_2$, $\Sigma\ R_3$, and $\Sigma\ R_4$.
2. Square the sum of each column, as found in step 1. For example, the square of the sum of R_1 is 17×17 or 289. Place this answer opposite the $\Sigma\ R_1^2$ in the box. Repeat the same procedure to find the square of sums of the remaining columns, $\Sigma\ R_2^2$, $\Sigma\ R_3^2$, and $\Sigma\ R_4^2$. Place these answers in the correct boxes.
3. Sum the values found in step 2—the numbers in boxes— and place this answer in the octagon opposite the $\Sigma\ R_i^2$. Write 921.50. Also write this answer in the blank to the left.

$\Sigma\ R_i^2 = \underline{921.50}$

4. Find k. Count the number of columns in Table 8-9 and record the answer. Write 4 in the blank to the left.

$k = \underline{4}$

5. Find N. Count the number of rows and record it. Write 6 in the blank to the left.[14]

$N = \underline{6}$

Substitute in the Formula

Make the appropriate substitutions by replacing each step with its corresponding number.

$$\chi_r^2 = \frac{12}{Nk(k+1)}\ [\Sigma\ R_i^2] - 3N(k+1)$$

$$= \frac{12}{(\text{step 5}) \times (\text{step 4})(\text{step 4} + 1)}$$
$$\times [\text{step 3}] - 3 \times \text{step 5} (\text{step 4} + 1)$$

[14] Check your calculations by seeing if the sum of the ranks $(\Sigma\ R^1 + \Sigma\ R^2 + \Sigma\ R^3 + \Sigma\ R^4 = \frac{1}{2}Nk(k+1))$. In this problem that would mean $17 + 12 + 17.5 + 13.5 = \frac{1}{2}6(4)(4+1)$, which equals 60.

$$= \frac{12}{6 \times 4(4+1)} [921.50] - 3 \times 6(4+1)$$

Solving the Formula

$$\chi_r^2 = \frac{12}{6 \times 4(4+1)} [921.50] - 3 \times 6(4+1)$$

Perform the operations in the parentheses first. Since the numbers in parentheses are the same, write the answer, 5, in both parentheses.

$$\chi_r^2 = \frac{12}{6 \times 4(5)} [921.50] - 3 \times 6(5)$$

Perform all the multiplications. Starting at the left, multiply 6 times 4 times 5 (120); multiply 12 times 921.50 (11,058); and multiply 3 times 6 times 5 (90).

$$\chi_r^2 = \frac{11,058}{120} - 90$$

Perform the division. Divide 11,058 by 120 (92.15).

$$\chi_r^2 = 92.15 - 90$$

Perform the remaining subtraction. Subtract 90 from 92.15 (2.15), and place the results for Friedman in a circle.

$$\chi_r^2 = 2.15$$

Statistical Decision

$\chi_r^2 = \underline{2.15}$

$df = \underline{3}$

$T = \underline{11.34}$

$\underline{\text{do not reject}}$

6. Take the answer enclosed in a circle above and write it in the blank to the left.
7. Find your degrees of freedom. Use the formula $df = k - 1$. Subtract 1 from your number of columns $(4 - 1)$. Write 3 in this blank.
8. Find the table value. Use the df found in step 8 to enter Table E. Run your fingers across the row until you are under your predetermined level of significance (.01). Record the value found in this table. Write 11.34 in the blank to the left.
9. If your value for the Friedman (2.15) is equal to or greater than the table value (11.34), reject the null hypothesis; if not, write *do not reject* in the blank.

In this situation there was no reason to doubt that Gloria's theory regarding her bread was inaccurate. The null hypothesis was not rejected. The results show that there appears to be no difference among the ratings of the four different types of bread. Notice the higher the value found for χ_r^2, the greater your chances of rejecting the null hypothesis. The Friedman test is analyzed by using the chi-square distribution. Note if you had rejected the null hypothesis, all you could say was that the ratings of the four types of bread are different. The remarks concerning the Kruskal-Wallis test on page 247 apply here. Without the application of a significance test for multiple comparisons it is impossible to say any more than that the groups appear to be different. The Friedman test just indicates a significant difference between the whole set of groups. To carry the analysis further, you make individual comparisons by any one of these multiple-comparison techniques.

A discussion of the theory underlying these multiple-comparison tests is found in Wilcoxon and Wilcox (1964, pp. 9–12).

Small Sample Sizes

When you have three columns with two to nine rows or when you have four columns with two to four rows, you use Table N which consists of tables of exact probabilities. In these cases you do not use the chi-square distribution to analyze your results.

Table N is very simple to use. Let's pretend that your value for the Friedman (χ_r^2) is 7.0, you have a row size of three and a column or group size of four, and your predetermined level of significance is .01. First you find the page with the correct column size—in this case the one that has a $k = 4$ at the top. Second, you look on this page until you find your row size. In this instance it is labeled $N = 3$. The $N = 3$ column is divided into two parts, χ_r^2 and p. This is the section of the table we will be using. You now determine the probability of the occurrence of your χ_r^2 of 7.0 by starting at the top of the χ_r^2 column and running your fingers down this column until you find a number that is equal to or comes closest to the number you found for your χ_r^2 (7.0) without exceeding this number. Put your finger on 7.0. Next, look at the number directly next to it, in the p column, and you will find the 7.0's probability of occurrence, which is .054. If the probability is equal to or less than your predetermined level of significance (.01), reject the null hypothesis. Since .054 is not less than .01, you are not able to reject the null hypothesis. The four groups appear to be the same.

Now try the following problem, using Table N.

Problem $k = 3, N = 4, \chi_r^2 = 6.9$, level of significance $= .05$

Answer   Reject the null hypothesis, because the probability of $\chi_r^2 = 6.9$ is less than .042, which is less than the .05 level of significance. The χ_r^2 value in the table is 6.5.

Problem   Now let's return to Situation II, The Beau Brummel Professors, and solve the problem. Tom, Phil, and John were having a contest to see who wore the most fashionable attire. They matched their prospective students ahead of time on the basis of socioeconomic level and grades, and they randomly assigned the members of each matched triplet to a classroom. The students were then asked to fill out a questionnaire on their professors. The highest possible score attainable was a 25. The predetermined level of significance was set at .01. The *null hypothesis* states that there is no significant difference between the classes in their ratings of the professors. The *alternative hypothesis* states that the professors are not the same. The results are shown in the accompanying table.

The Dress Ratings

Matched triplet	Tom	Phil	John
A	20	25	10
B	21	24	15
C	22	20	16
D	18	20	22
E	16	20	25
F	16	20	25
G	14	23	15
H	17	24	13
I	14	23	13
J	18	22	10

Answer   The value found in Table E is 9.21. The null hypothesis is not rejected, because the χ_r^2 value of 5.4 is not higher than the table value.

$$\chi_r^2 = \frac{12}{Nk(k+1)} [\Sigma R_i^2] - 3N(k+1)$$

$$= \frac{12}{(10)(3)(3+1)} [1254] - 3(10)(3+1)$$

$$= 5.4$$

The procedure you just learned in using the Friedman test is summarized below:

Steps in Using the Friedman Test

1. Rank the scores in each row.
2. Use Formula 8-8 to find χ_r^2.
3. Refer to the appropriate table, depending upon the number of rows and columns in your sample.
   (a) When you have three columns with two to nine rows or four columns with two to four rows, use Table N. Reject the null hypothesis if your χ_r^2 value has a probability of occurring that is equal to or less than your level of significance.
   (b) If you do *not* have three columns with two to nine rows or four columns with two to four rows, consult Table E. Use a $df = k - 1$. Reject the null hypothesis if your value for the Friedman is equal to or greater than the table value.

SUMMARY

The tests that we have discussed in Chapter 8 were reached by traveling on Ordinal avenue. We talked about six ordinal tests.

The Kolmogorov-Smirnov test is especially useful when you have a small sample and only one group.

The Mann-Whitney U test is used with two independent groups.

The sign test is used with two groups, but these groups are related. The sign test measures only the direction of a difference and not its magnitude.

The Wilcoxon test uses two related groups. This test, unlike the sign test, measures the magnitude of differences as well as the direction.

The Kruskal-Wallis test handles three or more independent groups.

Finally, the Friedman test handles three or more related groups.

Quite a lot of information was presented on these six tests, and many distinctions were made between the types of situations in which a particular test is appropriate. So that these distinctions do not become blurred, Flowchart III summarizes everything you have learned about choosing ordinal tests.

In conclusion, you have covered a variety of ordinal tests to use in your research. In deciding which one of the six tests is best, you can use your statistical map or Flowchart III. These devices will help you choose the test that will do the best job for the situation.

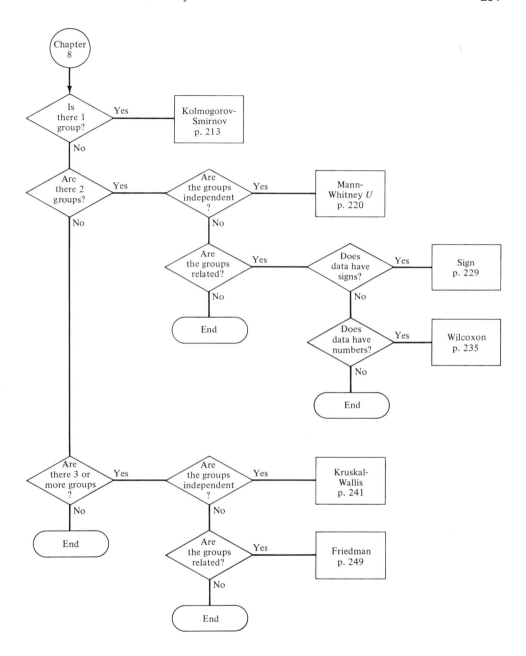

Flowchart III: Ordinal Tests

SELF-TEST FOR MASTERY

If you have trouble working a problem, reread the explanation on the page listed.

In the left-hand column of problems 1 through 7 are the descriptions of statistical tests, and in the right-hand column are the names of statistical tests. Match each description with the appropriate statistical test. When you find a match, write the italicized word following the name of the statistical test in the proper answer blank below the riddle. The first one has been done for you. When you have matched the remaining six items you will have answered the riddle.

p. 212

Find the Right Test

1. Nominal, two related groups
2. Two related groups, ordinal, measures direction and magnitude
3. Ordinal, two related groups, measures direction only
4. Ordinal, two independent groups
5. Ordinal, four independent groups
6. Ordinal, one group
7. Ordinal, four related groups

Wilcoxon   *you*
McNemar   *Because*
Mann-Whitney U *your*
Kolmogorov-Smirnov   *in*
Friedman   *it*
Kruskal-Wallis   *foot*
Cochran Q *he*
Chi square   *mouth*
Sign   *put*

Riddle:

Why do you always make a mistake when you put on your shoe?

Answer:

Because

1	2	3	4	5	6	7

Problems 8 to 13 consist of six situations. Read each situation and answer the three questions that follow it.

8. *Situation I: The Talkative Monkeys.* A scientist was interested in monkeys' ability to learn sign language. He matched 30 monkeys three at a time according to their ability to

learn. He then assigned a monkey from each matched triplet to a group. These monkeys were trained under three different types of reinforcement labeled I, II, and III. Although the 30 monkeys received the same amount of reinforcement, the way it was administered was different. After this training the monkeys were rated on their ability to follow commands. The results are shown in the table.

Matched triplet	Types of reinforcement		
	I	*II*	*III*
A	1	8	10
B	6	7	3
C	4	1	2
D	3	5	8
E	7	4	3
F	10	8	6
G	8	9	10
H	7	8	9
I	9	6	7
J	7	5	3

The *null hypothesis* states that the type of reinforcement has no effect on the monkeys. The *alternative hypothesis* states the type of reinforcement affects the monkeys. The level of significance is set at .01.

p. 249
p. 251
p. 253

  (a) What test should you use? _____
  (b) Use the test and record the results. _____
  (c) Should you accept or reject the null hypothesis? Circle the right answer.
  (d) Do you feel this example made a monkey out of you?

9. *Situation II: The Ambitious Salesman.* A market analyst drew a random sample of nine dress salesmen from one sales territory and a random sample of eight salesmen from another sales territory of her company. She wanted to compare their sales records for the month of August. The dollar sales for these salesmen are listed in the accompanying table. Rank these values and see if there is a significant difference in the two groups. Set a .05 level of significance. The *null hypothesis* states there is no significant difference between the two groups of salesmen. The *alternative hypothesis* states the two groups of salesmen are different.

*Selling Record of Two Groups of Salesmen
for the Month of August*

Group I	Group II
$ 400	$ 500
680	634
780	800
1340	1400
2331	2134
6789	7341
8789	9345
9752	8723
8435	

p. 222   (a) What test should you use? _____
p. 223   (b) Use the test and record the results. _____
p. 226   (c) Should you accept or reject the null hypothesis? Circle
             the right answer.

10. *Situation III: The Rock and Roll Singers.* Three rock and
     roll singers were arguing over how much emotional response
     they elicited from their audience during a performance.
     They decided to have independent experts rate them on
     five of their concert performances. The scores for each rock
     and roll singer are shown in the table below.

The Rock and Roll Singers' Ranks for Five Performances

Elvis Jennings	Dino Lorenzo	Alice Fisher
34	37	26
25	23	31
20	22	27
24	28	29
32	21	33

The *null hypothesis* states the three singers' ratings are
the same. The *alternative hypothesis* states the ratings are
different. Set the level of significance at .05.

p. 241   (a) What test should you use? _____
p. 243   (b) Use the test and record the results. _____
p. 246   (c) Should you accept or reject the null hypothesis? Circle
             the right answer.

11. *Situation IV: The Hardworking Students.* Mr. McNemar was very interested in the study habits of his students as compared to Ms. Gonzales' students. The *null hypothesis* states that the two classes are the same. The *alternative hypothesis* states that the two classes are different. Mr. McNemar matched 24 students on the basis of their grades and assigned one member of each matched pair to a class. At the end of the semester he recorded in the table below how many hours a week they studied.

Class Study Hours Per Week for 24 Students

Mr. McNemar	Ms. Gonzales	Sign
22	22	0
26	25	+
21	18	+
23	27	−
20	10	+
5	2	+
7	3	+
11	8	+
9	4	+
11	16	−
23	30	−
12	15	−

Mr. McNemar examined the data in the table and then recorded a plus when the student studied more than the corresponding student in Ms. Gonzales' class and a minus when the student studied less than the corresponding student in Ms. Gonzales' class. The level of significance is set at .05.

p. 229
(a) What test should you use? _____

p. 231
(b) Use the test and record the results. _____

p. 232
(c) Should you accept or reject the null hypothesis? Circle the right answer.

12. *Situation V: The Wonderful Hand Lotion.* A chemist had discovered a marvelous hand lotion. However, before it could be marketed, he wanted to know if it worked well on dry dishpan hands. He took a random sample of nine people suffering from dry hands. In each case he determined the amount of dryness of the person's hands both before and after using the lotion. The results are shown in the table below.

Hand Lotion Results

Person	Before	After
1	55	70
2	75	40
3	40	3
4	60	4
5	30	15
6	20	10
7	20	20
8	40	23
9	25	18

The *null hypothesis* states that the hand lotion has no effect on the people. The *alternative hypothesis* states that there is a difference after the hand lotion is used. The level of significance was set at .01.

p. 235
(a) What test should you use? _____

p. 237
(b) Use the test and record the results. _____

p. 239
(c) Should you accept or reject the null hypothesis? Circle the right answer.

13. *Situation VI: The Brown Candy.* A candy researcher is interested in seeing if the choice of candy is determined by color. To test this hypothesis she arranges to have six different shades of brown candy placed before 12 randomly selected children. The candy ranges from a very light chocolate, ranked as 1, to an extremely dark chocolate, ranked as 6. Each child is offered a choice among the six different pieces of candy. The candy selected by the children is shown in the chart below.

Ranking of Six Different Colors of Candy

Ranks	1	2	3	4	5	6
Children's choice	5	3	2	1	1	0

The *null hypothesis* states that the number of times the candy in each rank will be chosen will be the same. The *alternative hypothesis* states that the number of times candy in each rank will be chosen will be different. The level of significance is set at .05.

p. 213
(a) What test should you use? _____

p. 216
(b) Use the test and record the results. _____

p. 218
(c) Should you accept or reject the null hypothesis? Circle the right answer.

ANSWERS TO SELF-TEST

Score yourself by adding up the points for each correct answer and write the total in the Evaluation form.

Problems 1-7: answer the riddle

1 point each

Because	you	put	your	foot	in	it
1	2	3	4	5	6	7

5 points   **8.** (a) Friedman

10 points   (b) $\chi_r^2 = .2$

$$\chi_r^2 = \frac{12}{10 \times 3(3+1)}[1202] - 3 \times 10(3+1)$$

Rank check: $\Sigma R_1 + \Sigma R_2 + \Sigma R_3 = \frac{1}{2}Nk(k+1)$

$$21 + 19 + 20 = \frac{1}{2}(10)(3)(3+1)$$
$$60 = 60$$

5 points   (c) Do not reject. The table value is 9.21, and .2 is less than 9.21.

5 points   **9.** (a) Mann-Whitney U

10 points   (b) $U = 34$

$$U_1 = (8)(9) + (8)\frac{8+1}{12} - 70$$
$$U_1 = 38$$
$$U_2 = (8)(9) - 38$$
$$U_2 = 34$$

Rank check: $U_1 + U_2 = n_1 n_2$
$$38 + 34 = (8)(9)$$
$$72 = 72$$

5 points   (c) Do not reject the null hypothesis. The table value is 15, and 34 is more than 15.

5 points   **10.** (a) Kruskal-Wallis

10 points   (b) $H = 1.34$

$$H = \frac{12}{15(15+1)}\frac{1444}{5} + \frac{1089}{5} + \frac{2401}{5} - 3(15+1)$$

Rank check: $\Sigma R_1 + \Sigma R_2 + \Sigma R_3 = \frac{N(N+1)}{2}$

$$38 + 33 + 49 = \frac{15(15+1)}{2}$$
$$120 = 120$$

5 points   (c) Do not reject the null hypothesis. Use Table M for small sample sizes. Since the H of 1.34 does not have a probability of occurrence less than your level of significance of .05, you cannot reject the null hypothesis. In order to have a value that is significant you must have an *H* over 5.6600.

11. (a) Sign test

5 points

(b) $x = 4, N = 11$

10 points

(c) Do not reject the null hypothesis, since the table value, .548, is greater than the level of significance. This is a two-tail test; $2 \times .274 = .548$, the table value.

5 points

12. (a) Wilcoxon

5 points

(b) $T = 3.5$. This is a two-tail test. $N = 8$

10 points

Check: $\Sigma R^+ + \Sigma R^- = \frac{1}{2}n(n + 1)$

$$32.5 + 3.5 = \frac{1}{2} \cdot 8(8 + 1)$$
$$36 = 36$$

Rank	1	2	3.5	3.5	5	6	7	8
Score	7	10	15	15	17	35	37	56

(c) Do not reject the null hypothesis, because your *T* of 3.5 is more than the table value, which is zero.

5 points

13. (a) Kolmogorov-Smirnov

5 points

(b) $D = .33$

10 points

$$D = \frac{LD}{N} \text{ or } \frac{4}{12}$$

(c) Do not reject the null hypothesis, because .33 is not greater than the table value of .375.

5 points

Evaluation

Rating	Evaluation
126	You are absolutely perfect.
100–125	Review.
51–99	Restudy this chapter thoroughly.
50 or less	Please get some outside help, but do not give up hope.
10 or less	Everybody is beautiful in some way.

INTERVAL
TESTS

9

Figure 9-1: Interval Tests

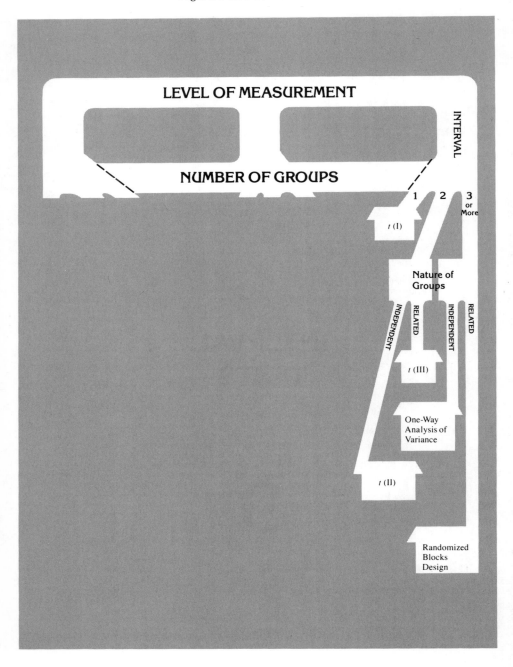

Chapter 9 deals with statistical tests originating from Interval avenue on the map. Each will be discussed in the following manner:

1. Its purpose will be explained.
2. Its requirements will be listed.
3. A situation that warrants its use will be described.
4. The reader will be shown an easy-to-follow procedure to solve the formula for the test.
5. A practice problem will be provided.
6. The procedure will be summarized.

In this chapter we will discuss the following tests; *t* (I),[1] *t* (II), *t* (III), and the one-way analysis of variance. In our discussion of the one-way analysis of variance, we will show you how to use the Scheffé test in order to test for comparisons between means.

The *t*-test, often referred to as Student's *t* or the *t*-ratio, was described first in 1908 in an article in *Biometrika* by William S. Gosset, who wrote under the pseudonym of "Student." Gosset, a 32-year-old chemist, was a consultant for the Guinness Brewery in Ireland.[2] In doing his research he discovered the *t*-distribution, which permitted him to test hypotheses with small samples when the population had a normal distribution, the population mean was assumed, and the population standard deviation was unknown.

In the majority of small practical research problems a knowledge of the standard deviation is not available. If previous experience does not supply the standard deviation, one uses the *t*. In using the *t* to test a hypothesis, you calculate the *t* and then refer to a *t* table to determine the probability for this statistic.

t-TEST (I)

The *t*-test (I) is used with one-group samples where the population has a normal distribution. For example, suppose a population is assumed to have a mean of 1.85 meters and it has a normal distribution. We then reach into this

---

[1] The author has taken certain liberties in this book. The *t*-ratio will be known as *t* (I), *t* (II), and *t* (III). When the *t* is used with one group it is referred to as *t* (I); with two independent groups, as *t* (II); and with two related groups, as *t* (III).

[2] The Guinness Brewery did not allow its employees to publish. However, Gosset did publish his statistical findings under the nom de plume of "Student" (Walker, 1969).

population, pull out a sample, compute its mean, and compare its mean to the population mean of 1.85 meters by using the *t*-test (I). If the difference between the sample mean and the assumed population mean is too large, then the assumption that the population mean is 1.85 meters is rejected.

The requirements for the *t*-test (I) are as follows:

t-Test (I) Requirements	**1.** At least the interval level of measurement **2.** Random sample **3.** Sample drawn from a population that has a normal distribution

The formula for the *t*-test (I) is $(\overline{X} - \mu)/s\overline{X}$—that is, the sample means minus the population mean divided by the standard error of the mean. Using the formula for *t* does not require skills beyond what you already have learned. In effect you are calculating a mean, a standard deviation, and a standard error of the mean. In Chapter 3 you learned how to figure means; in Chapter 4 you learned how to find standard deviations and standard errors of means. By using these three formulas, you can compute a *t* for any group of scores. To shorten this task, a formula that combines all the components is used:

Formula 9-1   *t-Test (I)*

$$t = \frac{\overline{X} - \mu}{\sqrt{\dfrac{\Sigma X^2 - \dfrac{(\Sigma X)^2}{N}}{N(N-1)}}}$$

The symbols you will encounter in learning about *t* (I) are explained below:

Symbol	Meaning
$\overline{X}$	Sample mean
μ	Population mean
ΣX^2	Square each score, then find the sum of the squares
N	Count the number of scores
$(\Sigma X)^2$	Square the sum of the scores
$df = N - 1$	Degrees of freedom, number of scores minus one

We are now ready to use the *t*-test (I) on a practical problem.

Situation

The space academy is entering a new and difficult program in space exploration, and the director is concerned about his astronauts' ability. Last year the mean score on the flight survival test was shown to be 6. The standard deviation for the scores is unknown. The director wants to test the hypothesis that the average score of his present class of astronauts on the flight survival test is better than 6. He feels that they are a very bright group and therefore their mean score should be greater than 6. The director draws a random sample of 14 people from the population of astronauts at large and records their scores. The scores are shown in Table 9-1.

Table 9-1: Astronaut Scores on Flight Survival Test

Individual scores													
5	6	7	8	9	10	8	7	9	8	12	11	4	8

The *null hypothesis* states that the mean of the population is 6. The director thinks his astronauts are better than the average. He states a directional *alternative hypothesis* that the mean of the population is greater than 6. The level of significance is set at .05 and a one-tail test is used. We shall analyze these data using a *t*-test (I). A worksheet with directions follows.

PROCEDURE

Worksheet for t-Test (I)

X	X^2
5	25
6	36
7	49
8	64
9	81
10	100
8	64
7	49
9	81
8	64
12	144
11	121
4	16
8	64
$\Sigma X = 112$	$\Sigma X^2 = 958$

Directions for Using the Worksheet for *t* (I)

Follow the directions to form the columns and find the values.

$\Sigma X = \underline{112}$

$N = \underline{14}$

$\bar{X} = \underline{8}$

$\Sigma X^2 = \underline{958}$

$\mu = \underline{6}$

1. Find the ΣX. Add the scores in the column labeled X. Add $5 + 6 + 7 + 9 + \cdots + 8$. Write the sum opposite the ΣX in the blank to the left. Write 112.
2. Find N. Count the number of scores in the X column. Write this number opposite the N in the blank to the left. Write 14.
3. Find the mean, $\bar{X}$. Divide the ΣX (step 1) by N (step 2) and write the answer in the blank to the left. Divide 112 by 14 and write 8.
4. Form the X^2 column. Square each score in the X column and write its answer in the column headed X^2. For example, 5 squared is 5×5, and the answer is 25, written opposite the 5 in the X^2 column.
5. Find the ΣX^2. Add all the numbers in the column headed X^2. Write their sum opposite the ΣX^2 in the blank to the left. Add $25 + 36 + 49 + 64 + 81 + \cdots + 64$ and write their sum, 958, in this blank.
6. Record the population mean, which was given. Write 6 opposite the μ in the blank to the left.

Substitutions

7. We are ready to make our step-by-step substitutions using the numbers in the left-hand column of the direction sheet.

$$t = \frac{\bar{X} - \mu}{\sqrt{\dfrac{\Sigma X^2 - \dfrac{(\Sigma X)^2}{N}}{N(N - 1)}}}$$

(a) Substitute the number 8 for the $\bar{X}$. Substitute the number 6 for the μ.

$$t = \frac{8 - 6}{\sqrt{\dfrac{\Sigma X^2 - \dfrac{(\Sigma X)^2}{N}}{N(N - 1)}}}$$

(b) Substitute the number (958) for ΣX^2, substitute the number 112 for (ΣX), and substitute the number 14 for every N.

$$t = \frac{8 - 6}{\sqrt{\dfrac{958 - \dfrac{(112)^2}{14}}{14(14 - 1)}}}$$

Solving the Formula

Now we can solve the formula.

8. We solve the numbers in the numerator first. We subtract the 6 from the 8, leaving 2.

$$t = \frac{2}{\sqrt{\dfrac{958 - \dfrac{(112)^2}{14}}{14(14 - 1)}}}$$

9. We next solve the numbers inside the square-root sign.
   (a) Square the 112 (112 × 112), which equals 12,544.

$$t = \frac{2}{\sqrt{\dfrac{958 - \dfrac{12,544}{14}}{14(14 - 1)}}}$$

   (b) Divide the 12,544 by 14, which equals 896.

$$t = \frac{2}{\sqrt{\dfrac{958 - 896}{14(14 - 1)}}}$$

   (c) Subtract the 958 from 896, leaving 62.

$$t = \frac{2}{\sqrt{\dfrac{62}{14(14 - 1)}}}$$

10. Again we work inside the square-root sign.
    (a) Subtract 1 from 14, which equals 13.

$$t = \frac{2}{\sqrt{\dfrac{62}{14(13)}}}$$

    (b) Multiply this 13 times the 14, which gives 182.

$$t = \frac{2}{\sqrt{\frac{62}{182}}}$$

11. Again looking at the remaining numbers in the square root.
    (a) Divide the 62 by 182, which equals .34.

$$t = \frac{2}{\sqrt{.34}}$$

    (b) Find the square root of .34, which is .58.

$$t = \frac{2}{.58}$$

12. Find t. Divide 2 by .58, which equals 3.45. Put this answer in the box.

$$\boxed{t = 3.45}$$

Statistical Decision

1. Find the *df*. The degrees of freedom are $N - 1$. Subtract 1 from the number of scores (14); write the answer, 13, in the blank to the left.

$df = \underline{13}$

2. Record the boxed t value (step 12) in the blank to the left. Write 3.45.

$t = \underline{3.45}$

3. Find the table value. Use the t-distribution, Table O. Run your fingers down the *df* column until you are at the *df* found in step 1. Next run your fingers across this row until you are under predetermined level of significance (.05).[3] Record the value found in the table. Write 1.771 in the blank to the left.

table
value $= \underline{1.771}$

4. If the value you found for t (3.45) is equal to or greater than the table value (1.771), reject the null hypothesis; if not, do not reject. Write *reject* in the blank to the left.

$\underline{reject}$

For this problem the population mean was not 6. You reject the null hypothesis in favor of the alternative hypothesis. The mean of this group of astronauts was larger than the assumed population mean of 6.

Now see if you can solve a practice problem.

Problem   A marine biologist, Anita Vacaro, wants to test the hypothesis that the mean vocabulary score for a population of dolphins is 3. The standard deviation for the scores is unknown. She draws a

[3] Note that this is a one-tail test. So be sure you are under the proper column.

random sample of 15 dolphins from the population and records their vocabulary scores. The results are shown below.

Dolphin Vocabulary Scores

Scores	5	7	6	5	3	4	6	8	10	11	9	7	7	5	3

The *null hypothesis* states that the population mean of the dolphins is 3. However, Ms. Vacaro thinks that this is not the case. She states as her *alternative hypothesis* that the population mean is not 3. She uses a two-tail test, because the alternative hypothesis is nondirectional. She sets a .05 level of significance.

Answer

$t = 5.48$. Reject the null hypothesis because the t is equal to 5.48 and this is greater than the table value of 2.145. The alternative hypothesis proposed by Ms. Vacaro seems to be true. That is, the mean of the sample is significantly different from the assumed population mean of 3.

$$t = \frac{\bar{X} - \mu}{\sqrt{\dfrac{\Sigma X^2 - \dfrac{(\Sigma X)^2}{N}}{N(N-1)}}} = \frac{6.4 - 3}{\sqrt{\dfrac{694 - \dfrac{(96)^2}{15}}{15(15-1)}}} = \frac{3.4}{\sqrt{\dfrac{694 - 614.4}{15(14)}}}$$

$$= \frac{3.4}{\sqrt{\dfrac{79.6}{210}}} = \frac{3.4}{\sqrt{.38}} = \frac{3.4}{.62}$$

$$\boxed{t = 5.48}$$

The procedure you just learned for using the *t*-test (I) is summarized below.

Steps in Using the *t*-Test (I)

1. Use Formula 9-1 to find t (I):

$$t = \frac{\bar{X} - \mu}{\sqrt{\dfrac{\Sigma X^2 - \dfrac{(\Sigma X)^2}{N}}{N(N-1)}}}$$

2. Next refer to Table O to find the table value for a one-tail or a two-tail test. Use $N - 1$ as your degrees of freedom.
3. If your value for t is equal to or greater than the table value, reject the null hypothesis in favor of the alternative hypothesis.

Comments about the t-Distribution

The distribution for the *t* is very similar to the normal curve; that is, it is symmetrical with a mean of 0 and a standard deviation slightly more than 1. However, the *t* curve is more peaked than the normal curve. Furthermore, the *t* is not just one distribution, like the normal curve, but many distributions. Each of these distributions looks different, depending upon its degrees of freedom. Figure 9-2 shows three examples of the *t* curve with different degrees of freedom.

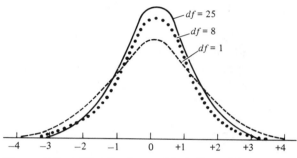

Figure 9-2: t-Distributions with 1, 8, and 25

Notice that the larger your degrees of freedom, the more your *t* resembles the normal curve. When the number in your sample is equal to or greater than 100, the normal curve may be substituted for the *t*-distribution.

Because the *t* is composed of so many distributions, tables for the *t* include these distributions. The *t* table is given in this book in abbreviated form, because you would need a volume to show the different distributions for the *t*. Table O of the Appendix gives selected percentage points of the *t* distribution along with their respective degrees of freedom.

t-TEST (II)

The *t*-test (II) concerns itself with two groups. These groups are independent (see Chapter 6); that is, an individual in one group cannot be in any way related to an individual in the other group. The purpose of the *t* (II), or *t*-ratio as it is called, is to determine whether the mean of one group is significantly different from the mean of the other group. The requirements of the *t* (II) are as follows:

_t_-Test (II) **Requirements**	1. The two groups are independent. 2. Measurement is at least at the interval level. 3. The populations are both normally distributed. 4. The populations have the same variances.[4] 5. The samples are drawn at random.

Importance of Requirements 3 and 4

Requirement 3 states that the two populations should be normally distributed. A severe departure from normality seems to have little effect on the conclusions when sample sizes are 30 or more. Of course, the results would be more accurate if the distribution were normal. In reality you can violate this assumption and not worry about it as long as your samples are not extremely small (Hays, 1973).

Requirement 4 (homogeneity of variance) states that the populations should have the same variances. When the populations do not have the same variances and the sample sizes are equal, there is little effect on the conclusions reached by the *t*-test. However, when the sample sizes are extremely small and of unequal sizes, there is an effect on the *t*-ratio. One way to handle this problem is to avoid using samples of unequal sizes. However, if this is not possible, and if the situation warrants it, use a nonparametric test instead of a *t*. If these two solutions are not feasible, the only other possibility is to use a computational formula that computes the standard error of each sample separately and use a corrected number for your degrees of freedom.

Formula for t-Test (II)

The best formula to use for the *t*-test (II) is the following:

Formula 9-2   *t-Test (II)*

$$\frac{\overline{X}_1 - \overline{X}_2}{\sqrt{\dfrac{\left[\Sigma\, X_1{}^2 - \dfrac{(\Sigma\, X_1)^2}{N_1}\right] + \left[\Sigma\, X_2{}^2 - \dfrac{(\Sigma\, X_2)^2}{N_2}\right]}{N_1 + N_2 - 2} \cdot \left(\dfrac{N_1 + N_2}{N_1 \cdot N_2}\right)}}$$

[4] Older statistics books and articles suggest that a test of homogeneity of variance be carried out before it is permissible to use a *t*-ratio. However, many modern statisticians feel that such a test is not worth the time and effort. Where these tests for homogeneity of variance are most needed—on small samples with unequal sizes—they are the least effective (Hayes, 1973).

The numerator is the actual difference between the means, whereas the denominator is an estimate of the standard error of the difference between the means. The denominator is an estimate of the variability of the difference between the means of the two samples. When you use this formula you are dividing the observed differences (numerator) by the variation of differences (denominator) that can be expected due to chance. If there is no significant difference between the groups, the ratio will be equal to zero. The further the ratio goes from zero, the more likely it is that there is a real difference between the groups.

The formula for t (II) looks very complicated, but these symbols are in fact old friends. Their meanings are given below.

Symbol	Meaning
$\bar{X}_1$	Mean of Group I [5]
ΣX_1^2	Square the individual scores for Group I and then find the sum
$(\Sigma X_1)^2$	Sum the individual scores for Group I and then square the sum
N_1	Count the number of subjects in Group I
$df = N_1 + N_2 - 2$	Degrees of freedom, the number of subjects in Group I plus the number of subjects in Group II minus 2

We will now use the t-test (II) on a practical problem.

Situation

The Sharp Clinic deals solely with football patients recovering from a delicate knee cartilage operation. Alfred Enos, one of the physical therapists,

Table 9-2: Recovery Time in Months

Group I, X_1	Group II, X_2
7	2
8	4
8	3
9	5
6	2
8	9
4	5
7	6
6	3
3	

[5] The meanings of the symbols for Group II are the same as for Group I.

has developed a postoperative treatment that he thinks would speed recovery of these players. The clinic's director takes an interest and instructs Alfred to do a study to see if his technique is better than the standard procedures they are now using. Alfred randomly selects two groups of patients from the clinic. Group I is to receive the usual treatment, while Group II is to receive Alfred's experimental treatment. The amount of time it takes each member to recover is recorded. During the experiment one of the members of Group II has a heart attack and dies; his score is not recorded. The results of the study are shown in Table 9-2.

The *null hypothesis* states there is no significant difference between the two groups of football players. Alfred feels that his postoperative treatment is better than the standard treatment. Therefore, the *alternative hypothesis* states that Group II will recover faster than Group I. A one-tail test is used. The level of significance is set at .05. The *t*-test (II) is used to analyze these data.

PROCEDURE

Directions for Setting Up a Worksheet for *t* (II)

We are now ready to use the formula for *t* (II) and find out if there is a significant difference between the two sample means. The worksheet for *t* (II) follows.

Worksheet

GROUP I		GROUP II	
X_1	$X_1{}^2$	X_2	$X_2{}^2$
7	49	2	4
8	64	4	16
8	64	3	9
9	81	5	25
6	36	2	4
8	64	9	81
4	16	5	25
7	49	6	36
6	36	3	9
3	9		

A. $\Sigma X_1 = 66$ D. $\Sigma X_1{}^2 = 468$ E. $\Sigma X_2 = 39$ H. $\Sigma X_2{}^2 = 209$

B. $N_1 = 10$ F. $N_2 = 9$

C. $\bar{X}_1 = 6.6$ G. $\bar{X}_2 = 4.3$

Directions for Using the Worksheet for *t* (II)

Follow the directions for forming the columns and finding the values. Record the answers on the worksheet.

DIRECTIONS FOR GROUP I

1. Find $\Sigma\, X_1$. Add the scores in the column labeled X_1. Add $7 + 8 + 8 + 9 + \cdots + 3$. Write the sum, 66, in box A.
2. Find N_1. Count the number of scores in the X_1 column. Write this number, 10, in box B.
3. Find the $\bar{X}$ for Group I. Divide the $\Sigma\, X_1$ (66) by N_1 (10) and write 6.6 in box C.
4. Form the $X_1{}^2$ column. Square each score in the X_1 column and write its answer in the column headed $X_1{}^2$. For example, 7 squared is 49, and 49 is written in the $X_1{}^2$ column opposite the 7.
5. Find the $\Sigma\, X_1{}^2$. Add all the numbers in the column headed $X_1{}^2$, $49 + 64 + 64 + 81 + 36 + \cdots + 9$; write their sum, 468, opposite the $\Sigma\, X_1{}^2 =$ in box D.

DIRECTIONS FOR GROUP II

Repeat steps 1 through 5 for Group II to find the numbers to be placed in boxes E, F, G, and H. Find the $\Sigma\, X_2$ and write it in box E; find N_2 and write it in box F; find the mean, $\bar{X}_2$, for Group II, and write its value in box G; form column $X_2{}^2$ and find the $\Sigma\, X_2{}^2$ and write its sum in box H.

Substitutions

We are ready to substitute the numbers in boxes A through D for Group I. These numbers are found on the worksheet. The substitutions will be made in the following formula:

$$t = \frac{\bar{X}_1 - \bar{X}_2}{\sqrt{\frac{\left[\Sigma\, X_1{}^2 - \frac{(\Sigma\, X_1)^2}{N_1}\right] + \left[\Sigma\, X_2{}^2 - \frac{(\Sigma\, X_2)^2}{N_2}\right]}{N_1 + N_2 - 2} \cdot \left(\frac{N_1 + N_2}{N_1 \cdot N_2}\right)}}$$

6. Substitute the number found in box C (6.6) for $\bar{X}_1$; substitute the number found in box D (468) for $\Sigma\, X_1{}^2$; substitute the number found in box A (66) for $\Sigma\, X_1$; substitute the number found in box B (10) for every N_1.

$$t = \frac{6.6 - \overline{X}_2}{\sqrt{\frac{\left[468 - \frac{(66)^2}{10}\right] + \left[\Sigma X_2{}^2 - \frac{(\Sigma X_2)^2}{N_2}\right]}{10 + N_2 - 2} \cdot \left(\frac{10 + N_2}{10 \cdot N_2}\right)}}$$

7. We are ready to substitute the numbers in boxes E through H for Group II. These numbers are found on the worksheet. Substitute the number found in box G (4.3) for $\overline{X}_2$; substitute the number found in box H (209) for $\Sigma X_2{}^2$; substitute the number found in box E (39) for ΣX_2; substitute the number found in box F (9) for every N_2.

$$t = \frac{6.6 - 4.3}{\sqrt{\frac{\left[468 - \frac{(66)^2}{10}\right] + \left[209 - \frac{(39)^2}{9}\right]}{10 + 9 - 2} \cdot \left(\frac{10 + 9}{10 \cdot 9}\right)}}$$

Solving the Formula

We are about to solve the following problem:

$$t = \frac{6.6 - 4.3}{\sqrt{\frac{\left[468 - \frac{(66)^2}{10}\right] + \left[209 - \frac{(39)^2}{9}\right]}{10 + 9 - 2} \cdot \left(\frac{10 + 9}{10 \cdot 9}\right)}}$$

8. First do a series of computations inside the square-root sign. In the brackets on the left, square 66, divide by 10, and then subtract from 468. That is, $(66)^2 = 4356$; $4356/10 = 435.6$; and $468 - 435.6 = 32.40$. Repeat the same steps for the numbers in the brackets at the right. That is, $(39)^2 = 1521$; $1521/9 = 169$; and $209 - 169 = 40$.

$$t = \frac{6.6 - 4.3}{\sqrt{\frac{[32.40] + [40]}{(10 + 9 - 2)} \cdot \left(\frac{10 + 9}{10 \cdot 9}\right)}}$$

9. Work with the numbers in the brackets and parentheses.
   (a) Add $32.40 + 40$, which equals 72.40; add $10 + 9$, then subtract 2 from the answer: $10 + 9 = 19$, $19 - 2 = 17$; next add $10 + 9$, which equals 19; and finally multiply 10 times 9, which equals 90.

$$t = \frac{6.6 - 4.3}{\sqrt{\frac{[72.40]}{17} \times \left(\frac{19}{90}\right)}}$$

(b) Divide 72.40 by 17, which equals 4.26;[6] divide 19 by 90, which equals .21.

$$t = \frac{6.6 - 4.3}{\sqrt{4.26 \times .21}}$$

(c) Multiply 4.26 by .21, then find its square root:
4.26 × .21 = .89, $\sqrt{.89}$ = .94

$$t = \frac{6.6 - 4.3}{.94}$$

10. Subtract the means in the numerator: 6.6 − 4.30 = 2.30. Divide your numerator by your denominator: 2.30 ÷ .94 = 2.45. The answer, 2.45, is placed in the box.

$$t = \frac{2.30}{.94}, \qquad \boxed{t = 2.45}$$

Statistical Decision

1. Find the *df*. The degrees of freedom for the *t* (II) is $N_1 + N_2 - 2$. In the present example add the value for N_1 (10) and the value for N_2(9), then subtract 2: 10 + 9 = 19, 19 − 2 = 17. Write 17 in the blank to the left.

df = <u>17</u>
t = <u>2.45</u>

2. Record the boxed *t* value (2.45) in the blank to the left.
3. Find the table value. Use the *t*-distribution, Table O. Run your fingers down the *df* column until you are at the *df* found in step 1. Next run your fingers across this row until you are under your predetermined level of significance (.05) and proper tail (one-tail). Record the value found in the table. Write 1.740 in the blank to the left.

table value
= <u>1.740</u>

4. If your absolute value found for *t* (2.45) is equal to or greater than the table value (1.740), reject the null hypothesis; if not, do not reject.[7] Write *reject* in the blank to the left.

<u>reject</u>

The results show that there is a significant difference between the two sample means. Apparently, Alfred has developed an effective postoperative treatment. The alternative hypothesis that Group II will recover faster is probably true.

[6] The numbers inside the square-root sign are carried to the hundredths place.

[7] You are predicting that Group II will recover faster than Group I; therefore, in order to use this table, the mean of Group II must be lower than the mean of Group I. If the reverse were true, even though there might be significance you would ignore it, because you would have been wrong in your prediction.

In Chapter 6 we had a problem involving the *t* (II) called The Dedicated Researcher. See if you can solve this problem now as your practice problem.

Problem

A researcher who is working with autistic children is interested in determining the effects of two new teaching methods. He compares two groups on a reading achievement test. The results are shown in the accompanying table.

Reading Achievement Scores for Two Groups of Autistic Children

Method A, Group I	Method B, Group II
2	3
3	3
2	2
1	1
1	1
2	2
3	3
2	2
2	3
	4

Find out if there is a significant difference between the two groups by comparing the reading achievement scores. The *null hypothesis* states there is no significant difference between the two groups. The *alternative hypothesis* states the two groups are different. Use a .01 level of significance and a two-tail test.

Answer

$t = -1.03$. Do not reject the null hypothesis, because the *t* is equal to -1.03, and this is not greater than the table value of 2.898. There appears to be no significant difference between the two groups.

$$t = \frac{\bar{X}_1 - \bar{X}_2}{\sqrt{\frac{\left[\Sigma X_1{}^2 - \frac{(\Sigma X_1)^2}{N_1}\right] + \left[\Sigma X_2{}^2 - \frac{(\Sigma X_2)^2}{N_2}\right]}{(N_1 + N_2 - 2)} \cdot \left(\frac{N_1 + N_2}{N_1 \cdot N_2}\right)}}$$

$$= \frac{2.0 - 2.4}{\sqrt{\frac{\left[40 - \frac{(18)^2}{9}\right] + \left[66 - \frac{(24)^2}{10}\right]}{(9 + 10 - 2)} \cdot \left(\frac{9 + 10}{9 \cdot 10}\right)}}$$

$$= \frac{-.40}{\sqrt{\frac{[4.00] + [8.40]}{17} \cdot \left(\frac{19}{90}\right)}}$$

$$= \frac{-.40}{\sqrt{\frac{12.40}{17} \cdot (.21)}} = \frac{-.40}{\sqrt{\frac{2.60}{17}}} = \frac{-.40}{\sqrt{.15}} = \frac{-.40}{.39} = -1.03$$

The procedure you have learned for using the t-test (II) may be summarized as follows:

Steps in Using the t-Test (II)

1. Use Formula 9-2 to find t (II).

$$\frac{\bar{X}_1 - \bar{X}_2}{\sqrt{\frac{\left[\Sigma X_1{}^2 - \frac{(\Sigma X_1)^2}{N_1}\right] + \left[\Sigma X_2{}^2 - \frac{(\Sigma X_2)^2}{N_2}\right]}{(N_1 + N_2 - 2)} \cdot \left(\frac{N_1 + N_2}{N_1 \cdot N_2}\right)}}$$

2. Next refer to Table O to find the table value for a one-tail or a two-tail test. Use $N_1 + N_2 - 2$ as your degrees of freedom.
3. If your absolute value for t is equal to or greater than the table value, reject the null hypothesis in favor of the alternative hypothesis.

---

t-TEST (III)

The t-test (III) is also used with two groups. This test's concern is to find out if the mean of one group is actually different from the mean of the other group. The difference between the t-test (II) and the t-test (III) has to do with the nature of the two groups. The t-test (III) is used only in cases where the two groups are related. When we talk about related groups, we mean groups that are matched on some variable or in which the subjects are used more than once. (See Chapter 6 for a more detailed explanation.) The requirements for the t-test (III) are as follows:

---

t-Test (III) Requirements

1. Two groups related.
2. At least interval level of measurement.
3. Populations both normally distributed.
4. Populations having the same variances.
5. Samples drawn at random.

The formula used to evaluate whether the difference between these two groups is significant is different from the one used for the *t* (II). You compute the differences between each pair of scores and then use this difference to estimate the population standard error of the difference.

Formula 9-3   *t-Test (III)*

$$t = \frac{\overline{D}}{\sqrt{\dfrac{\Sigma D^2 - \dfrac{(\Sigma D)^2}{N}}{N(N - 1)}}}$$

The symbols and their meanings are listed below:

Symbol	Meaning
$\overline{D}$	Mean of the difference
ΣD^2	Square the differences, then find the sum
$(\Sigma D)^2$	Sum the differences, then square the sum
N	Number of pairs of scores

We will now use the *t*-test (III) on a sample problem.

Situation

The chairperson of an anthropology department was being pressured by the academic dean to use computer technology as an integral part of the instructional program. The dean wanted the anthropology department to purchase some software for the existing computers. The chairperson felt that this was an unnecessary expense, because the lecture method of instruction was just as effective. In order to help him decide whether or not to buy the new software, the chairperson performed a study comparing computer-based instruction to lecture instruction. He used ten pairs of sophomore anthropology majors who had been matched according to a number of factors that could influence learning of anthropology, such as age, sex, grade-point average, and college entrance exam scores. Then one member of the pair was assigned to Group I and the other was assigned to Group II. As a result of his matching he had two groups that were equivalent on the above factors. Group I then was exposed to concepts in anthropology using computer-based instruction, while Group II was exposed to the identical concepts using the lecture approach. At the end of the course a final test was given to the students in both groups. The results are shown in Table 9-3.

*Table 9-3: Anthropology Exam Scores of Students Exposed
to Two Different Teaching Methods*

Computer-Based Method, Group I	Lecture Method, Group II
8	10
15	20
10	15
18	10
11	11
10	20
22	12
20	15
15	8
15	10

PROCEDURE

The *null hypothesis* states there is no significant difference between the two instructional approaches. The department chairperson has a preference for the lecture method, so he states as the *alternative hypothesis* that the lecture method is better than the computer-based method of instruction. The level of significance is set at .05, and a one-tail test is used.

Directions for Setting Up a Worksheet for t (III)

We are now ready to use the formula for t (III) and find out if there is a significant difference between the two methods of instruction.

Worksheet

Pair	Group I, computer-based	Group II, lecture	D	D^2
A	8	10	−2	4
B	15	20	−5	25
C	10	15	−5	25
D	18	10	8	64
E	11	11	0	0
F	10	20	−10	100
G	22	12	10	100
H	20	15	5	25
I	15	8	7	49
J	15	10	5	25

D. $N = 10$

C. $\Sigma D = 13$ B. $\Sigma D^2 = 417$

A. $\bar{D} = 1.3$

WORKING BOX FOR FINDING THE ΣD

+ *nos.*	− *nos.*
8	−2
10	−5
5	−5
7	−10
5	−22
35	

$$\Sigma\,(+\text{ nos.}) = 35$$
$$\Sigma\,(-\text{ nos.}) = -22$$
$$\Sigma D = 13$$

Directions for Using the Worksheet for t (III)

Follow the directions for forming the columns and finding the values. Record your answers on the worksheet.

1. Put the scores for each pair down on the worksheet. Make sure that the scores for each pair are placed next to one another. For example, for pair A the score for the person in Group I is 8, and this number is placed next to the score for his matched partner in Group II, whose score is 10.
2. Form column D. Find the difference between each pair of scores and write that number in the column labeled D. For example, 8 minus 10 equals −2, and the −2 is placed in the D column.
3. Find the $\Sigma\,D$. Using the workbox, find the algebraic sum of the D column. Add together the positive numbers first: $8 + 10 + 5 + 7 + 5 = 35$. Next, add the negative numbers: $(-2) + (-5) + (-5) + (-10) = -22$. Finally, adding these two sums, $35 + (-22)$, results in a $\Sigma\,D$ equal to 13. Write this 13 opposite the $\Sigma\,D$ in box C.
4. Find N. Count the number of pairs of scores. Write the number 10 opposite the N in box D.
5. Find the mean of D, $\bar{D}$. Divide the $\Sigma\,D$ (13) by N (10) and write the number 1.3 opposite the $\bar{D}$ in box A.
6. Form the D^2 column. Square each score in the D column and write its answer in the column headed D^2. For example, −2 squared is 4, and this 4 is written in the D^2 column opposite the −2.
7. Find the $\Sigma\,D^2$. Add all the numbers in the column headed D^2, $4 + 25 + 25 + 64 + \cdots + 25$, and write their sum, 417, opposite the $\Sigma\,D^2$ in box B.

Substitutions

8. We are ready to make our substitutions, using the numbers in boxes A through D on the worksheet.

$$t = \frac{\bar{D}}{\sqrt{\dfrac{\Sigma D^2 - \dfrac{(\Sigma D)^2}{N}}{N(N-1)}}}$$

Substitute the number found in box A (1.3) for $\bar{D}$; substitute the number found in box B (417) for ΣD^2; substitute the number found in box C (13) for ΣD; substitute the number found in box D (10) for every N.

$$t = \frac{1.3}{\sqrt{\dfrac{417 - \dfrac{(13)^2}{10}}{10(10-1)}}}$$

Solving the Problem

9. We are about to solve the problem.
   (a) Working inside the square-root sign, square 13, divide it by 10, then subtract that from 417: $(13)^2 = 169$; $169/10 = 16.9$, and then $417 - 16.9 = 400.1$.

$$t = \frac{1.3}{\sqrt{\dfrac{400.1}{10(10-1)}}}$$

   (b) Next, working below the line, subtract 1 from 10 and then multiply this number by 10: $10 - 1 = 9$; $9 \times 10 = 90$.

$$t = \frac{1.3}{\sqrt{\dfrac{400.1}{90}}}$$

10. (a) Divide 400.1 by 90, which equals 4.44.[8]

$$t = \frac{1.3}{\sqrt{4.45}}$$

   (b) Find the square root of 4.45, which equals 2.11.

$$t = \frac{1.3}{2.11}$$

   (c) Divide 1.3 by 2.11, which equals .62. Put this answer opposite the t.

$$\boxed{t = .62}$$

[8] Carry to the hundredths place.

Statistical Decision

1. Find *df*. The degrees of freedom from *t* (III) is $N - 1$. In the present example N is the number of pairs of scores. Subtract 1 from 10 (N) and write 9 in the blank to the left.

df = 9

2. Record the box *t* value (step 10) in the blank to the left opposite the *t*. Write .62.

t = .62

3. Find the table value. Use the *t*-distribution, Table O. Run your fingers down the *df* column until you are at the *df* found in step 1. Next run your fingers across the row until you are under your predetermined level of significance, .05, and proper tail (one-tail). Record the value found in table; write 1.833 in the blank to the left.

table value = 1.833

4. If the absolute value found for *t* (.62) is equal to or greater than the table value (1.833), reject the null hypothesis; if not, write *do not reject* in the blank to the left.

do not reject

In this problem there was no significant difference between the two sample means. Apparently, the computer based-method of instruction was as effective as the lecture method.

As our next practice problem let us solve Situation XII, The Long-Ball Hitters, from Chapter 6.

Problem

A high-school physical education instructor wanted to compare the effectiveness of two methods of instruction on home-run hitting. He paired individuals on home-run-hitting ability by assigning one member of each matched pair to Group A and the other member to Group B. Group A received batting practice for six weeks from a pitching machine, while Group B received batting practice for six weeks from major-league sluggers. At the end of the instruction each individual was given a slugging test, and the distance he hit the long ball is recorded. The results are shown in the accompanying table.

Long-Ball Hitters' Scores (in Meters)

Group A	Group B
76	120
90	130
100	130
75	140
120	140
100	135
70	140

Find out if there is a significant difference between the two groups. The *null hypothesis* states there will be no significant difference between the two sample means. The *alternative hypothesis* states that Group B will hit further than Group A. Use a .05 level of significance and a one-tail test.

Answer $t = 6.32$. Reject the null hypothesis, because the t is equal to -6.32 and this is greater than the table value of 1.943 (one-tail). The alternative hypothesis proposed by the coach seems to be true. Group B seems more effective in hitting the long ball than Group A.

$$t = \cfrac{\bar{D}}{\sqrt{\cfrac{\Sigma D^2 - \cfrac{(\Sigma D)^2}{N}}{N(N-1)}}} = \cfrac{-43.43}{\sqrt{\cfrac{15,186 - \cfrac{(304)^2}{7}}{7(7-1)}}}$$

$$= \cfrac{-43.43}{\sqrt{\cfrac{15,186 - 13,202.29}{42}}}$$

$$= \cfrac{-43.43}{\sqrt{\cfrac{1983.71}{42}}} = \cfrac{-43.43}{\sqrt{47.23}} = \cfrac{-43.43}{6.87}$$

$$t = -6.32$$

The procedure you have learned for using the t (III) is summarized below.

Steps in Using the *t*-Test (III)

1. Put the scores for each pair next to one another on the worksheet.
2. Use Formula 9-3 to find t (III):

$$t = \cfrac{\bar{D}}{\sqrt{\cfrac{\Sigma D^2 - \cfrac{(\Sigma D)^2}{N}}{N(N-1)}}}$$

3. Next refer to Table O to find the table value for a one-tail or a two-tail test. Use $N - 1$ as your degrees of freedom.
4. If your value for t is equal to or greater than the table value, reject the null hypothesis in favor of the alternative hypothesis.

In the practice problem above you were concerned with whether two groups differed significantly with respect to their ability to hit the long ball. You used the *t*-test to find out if there was a significant difference between these groups. Problems of this type arise frequently in statistical work. You often want to see if one group is better than another after using some product. However, often three groups or more are involved in your study. A researcher might be looking at six groups after field-testing different instructional material. In this case it is *not* efficient to compare groups two at a time. If you chose to use the *t*-test on these six groups, you would have to make 15 separate comparisons. Furthermore, doing 15 *t*-tests instead of one increases your chances of incorrectly rejecting the null hypothesis. The test used in order to solve the problem of testing three or more groups simultaneously is the analysis of variance.

ONE-WAY ANALYSIS OF VARIANCE

The *analysis of variance* (*ANOVA*), called the *F*-test or *F*-ratio, was developed by R. A. Fisher and his associates in England. The test bears Fisher's initial. This test treats a wide variety of situations, but in this chapter we will discuss only the one-way analysis of variance.

The *one-way analysis of variance* is used when you have three or more independent groups and only one independent variable. It tests the significance of the difference among the means of these groups simultaneously. The purpose of the one-way analysis of variance is to find out if the variance among the means of the groups is a function of chance alone. The requirements of the test are as follows:

One-Way Analysis of Variance Requirements	1. Population normally distributed. 2. Variances equal.[9] 3. Three or more independent groups. 4. Individuals of the sample randomly drawn from the population. 5. At least interval level of measurement.

Let's look at a situation that would involve the one-way analysis of variance.

Situation

An experimenter wanted to compare the effectiveness of three different types of rewards on the teaching of children with special learning problems.

[9] Modern statisticians feel that using a test of homogeneity of variances before using an analysis of variance is of little utility. You should forget about using this variance test and just use the analysis of variance, especially when your sample sizes are equal (Hays, 1973).

Table 9-4: Scores on Addition Problems
Using Different Rewards

Group I	Group II	Group III
4	2	2
2	1	1
1	4	6
5	7	4
2	5	7

Fifteen children age nine were randomly assigned to three independent groups. Each child was shown ten cards bearing an addition problem, together with three answer cards for each problem card. The child was to correctly match each addition problem with the correct answer card. Whenever a correct match occurred, the experimenter rewarded the child. In Group I the child was given hard candy, in Group II, praise, and in Group III, chips that let him select his own prize in a fish bowl. The experimenter recorded the score for each child in Table 9-4.

The *null hypothesis* states there is no significant difference between the three groups.[10] The *alternative hypothesis* states the three groups are different. The level of significance is set at .05.

The Rationale behind Finding F-Ratio

Let's just look at the scores in Table 9-4. We see that the three groups differ two ways:

1. The groups differ from each other.
2. The individuals differ within each group.

These sources of variation are important when we are computing an analysis of variance. The difference between the groups represents the experimental treatment and/or just the variation due to chance. The variation of the individuals within the groups reflects the difference among people, and this is considered the error term. In order to calculate an *F*-ratio, you must find these two variances[11]—the variance

---

[10] Grammatically the term *among groups* would be correct, but the term *between groups* is used in the literature.

[11] See Chapter 4 for a complete discussion of variance.

between the groups and the variance within the groups. The variance between the groups is called the *mean square between* (MS_B), and the variance within the groups is called the *mean square within* (MS_W). After you have found these variances, their relationship to each other gives you the F-ratio.

Formula 9-4 *F-Ratio*

$$F = \frac{MS_B}{MS_W}$$

When the null hypothesis is not rejected, F has a value close to one. However, when the null hypothesis is rejected, the value for F is much larger than one. For example, the null hypothesis would be true if the variances were practically the same —say 7/6; the F-ratio would then equal 1.17. There would be no difference between the three groups. However, suppose the between-group variance were very large and the within-group variance very small—for instance, 18/1; the F-ratio would then equal 18. Since 18 is much larger than 1, it appears the groups are very different.

Calculating these variances is not any more complicated than calculating any variance.[12] For example, to find the variance between groups you find the sum of the squares for the differences between groups, next the degrees of freedom of the groups. Finally you divide the first of these values by the second to obtain the between-groups variance.

PROCEDURE

The computational procedures for finding the one-way analysis of variance are summarized in Table 9.5 (p. 292).

To handle these calculations it is best to use a hand calculator. The calculations are simplified in a three-part worksheet. Part I will calculate the between-groups sum of squares and its degrees of freedom. Part II will calculate the total sum of squares and its degrees of freedom. Part III will show you how to use the values you calculated to find the rest of the numbers in the table. You will find the between-group variance (MS_B) and the within-group variance (MS_W) and arrive at an F-ratio. From this F-ratio you will be able to reach a statistical decision.

[12] In Chapter 4 you found the variance of one group by finding the sum of the squares of the group and dividing it by the number of subjects in the group.

Table 9-5: Computational Procedures for the One-Way Analysis of Variance

Source of variation	Sum of squares (SS)	Degrees of freedom (df)	Mean square (MS)	F
Between groups	$\dfrac{(\Sigma X_1)^2}{n_1} + \dfrac{(\Sigma X_2)^2}{n_2}$ $+ \cdots + \dfrac{(\Sigma X_k)^2}{n_k} - \dfrac{(\Sigma X)^2}{N}$	$k - 1$	$\dfrac{\text{Between } SS}{\text{Between } df}$	$\dfrac{MS \text{ between}}{MS \text{ within}}$
Within groups	Total SS minus between SS[13]	Total df minus between df	$\dfrac{\text{Within } SS}{\text{Within } df}$	
Total	$\Sigma X^2 - \dfrac{(\Sigma X)^2}{N}$	$N - 1$		

Directions for Part I

Follow the directions and fill in the correct answers in the summary table on the worksheet.

1. Find ΣX_1. Add the numbers for Group I, $4 + 2 + 1 + 5 + 2$, and place their sum, 14, opposite ΣX_1. Repeat the same procedure for ΣX_2 and ΣX_3.
2. Find ΣX. Find the sum of $\Sigma X_1 + \Sigma X_2 + \Sigma X_3$; add $14 + 19 + 20$ and place 53 opposite ΣX in box A on the worksheet.
3. Find n_1. Count the number in Group I and record 5 opposite n_1. Repeat the same procedure for Group II and Group III.
4. Find N. Find the sum of $n_1 + n_2 + n_3$ and place it in box B. Add $5 + 5 + 5$ and record 15 opposite N.
5. Find the correction term, $(\Sigma X)^2/N$. Square the number in box A (53), then divide this by the number in box B (15): $53 \times 53 = 2809$; $2809/15 = 187.27$. Write 187.27 in box C.
6. Find the between-group sum of squares (between SS). Substitute in the formula, using the numbers on the worksheet in Part I. For ΣX_1 substitute 14; for ΣX_2 substitute 19; for ΣX_3 substitute 20. For n_1 substitute 5, for n_2 substitute 5, and for n_3 substitute 5. For $(\Sigma X)^2/N$ substitute the correction term found in box C, 187.27. Solve the formula,[14] then put the answer, 4.13, in the summary table.

[13] This is a shortcut method for finding the within-group sum of squares; the long computational formula is

$$\Sigma X_1^2 - \frac{(\Sigma X_1)^2}{n_1} + \Sigma X_2^2 - \frac{(\Sigma X_2)^2}{n_2} + \cdots + \Sigma X_k^2 - \frac{(\Sigma X_k)^2}{n_k}$$

[14] If you are unclear on procedure, refer to Chapter 1.

Part I   Worksheet

SUMMARY TABLE

Source of variations	Sum of squares (SS)	Degrees of freedom (df)	Mean square (MS)	F
Between groups	4.13	2		
Within groups				
Total				

Group I, X_1	Group II, X_2	Group III, X_3	
4	2	2	
2	1	1	
1	4	6	
5	7	4	
2	5	7	
$\Sigma X_1 = 14$	$\Sigma X_2 = 19$	$\Sigma X_3 = 20$	**A. $\Sigma X = 53$**
$n_1 = 5$	$n_2 = 5$	$n_3 = 5$	**B. $N = 15$**

BETWEEN-GROUPS SUM OF SQUARES:

$$\frac{(\Sigma X_1)^2}{n_1} + \frac{(\Sigma X_2)^2}{n_2} + \frac{(\Sigma X_3)^2}{n_3} - \frac{(\Sigma X)^2}{N}$$

$$= \frac{(14)^2}{5} + \frac{(19)^2}{5} + \frac{(20)^2}{5} - 187.27$$

$$= 4.13$$

C. Correction term
$$\frac{(\Sigma X)^2}{N} = 187.27$$

BETWEEN-GROUPS DEGREES OF FREEDOM:

$$k - 1 = 3 - 1 = 2$$

7. Find the between-group df, $k - 1$. Subtract 1 from the number of groups: $3 - 1 = 2$. Write 2 in the summary table.

Directions for Part II

1. Rewrite the scores for Group I, Group II, and Group III, rewrite the correction term (box C), and rewrite box B.
2. Form the X_1^2 column. Square each score in the X_1 column and write its answer in the column labeled X_1^2. For example, 4 squared is 16, and 16 is written opposite the 4 in the column labeled X_1^2. Repeat the same procedure for the scores in Groups II and III.

3. Find ΣX_1^2. Add all the numbers in the column headed X_1^2. Write their sum opposite ΣX_1^2. Add $16 + 4 + 1 + 25 + 4$ and write their sum, 50, on the worksheet. Repeat the same procedure for ΣX_2^2 and ΣX_3^2.

4. Find ΣX^2. Add the $\Sigma X_1^2 + \Sigma X_2^2 + \Sigma X_3^2$ and write this answer opposite ΣX^2 in box D. Add $50 + 95 + 106$ and write 251 in box D.

5. Find the total sum of squares, $\Sigma X^2 - (\Sigma X)^2/N$. Substitute in the formula, using the numbers in box D and box C. Substitute 251 for ΣX^2; substitute 187.27 for $(\Sigma X)^2/N$. Solve the formula and write the answer, 63.73, in the summary table.

6. Find the total degrees of freedom, $N - 1$. Subtract 1 from the number of people in the sample (box B). Subtract 1 from 15 and write 14 in the summary table.

Part II   Worksheet

SUMMARY TABLE

Source of variation	Sum of squares (SS)	Degrees of freedom (df)	Mean square (MS)	F
Between groups				
Within groups				
Total	63.73	14		

Group I		Group II		Group III		
X_1	X_1^2	X_2	X_2^2	X_3	X_3^2	B. $N = 15$
4	16	2	4	2	4	
2	4	1	1	1	1	
1	1	4	16	6	36	
5	25	7	49	4	16	
2	4	5	25	7	49	
	$\Sigma X_1^2 = 50$		$\Sigma X_2^2 = 95$		$\Sigma X_3^2 = 106$	

C. Correction term
$$\frac{(\Sigma X)^2}{N} = 187.27$$

D. $\Sigma X^2 = 251$

TOTAL SUM OF SQUARES:

$$\Sigma X^2 - \frac{(\Sigma X)^2}{N} = 251 - 187.27 = 63.73$$

TOTAL DEGREES OF FREEDOM:

$$N - 1 = 15 - 1 = 14$$

Directions for Part III

We will use the numbers in the summary table to find *F* and reach a statistical decision.

Part III   Worksheet
SUMMARY TABLE

Source of variation	Sum of squares (SS)	Degrees of freedom (df)	Mean square (MS)	F	Probability
Between groups	4.13	2	2.07	.42	(n.s.)
Within groups	59.60	12	4.97		
Total	63.73	14			

1. Find the within-groups sum of squares. Subtract the between-groups sum of squares from the total sum of squares and put the difference in the table. Subtract 4.13 from 63.73 and write 59.60 as the within-groups sum of squares.
2. Find the within-groups degrees of freedom. Subtract the between-groups degrees of freedom from the total degrees of freedom and put the difference in the table.[15] Subtract 2 from 14 and write 12 as the within-groups degrees of freedom.
3. Find the between-groups mean square. Divide the between-groups sum of squares by the between-groups degrees of freedom. Divide 4.13 by 2 and write 2.07 in the box for the between-groups mean square.
4. Find the within-groups mean square. Divide the within-groups sum of squares by the within-groups degrees of freedom. Divide 59.60 by 12 and write 4.97 in the box for the within-groups mean square.
5. Find *F*. Divide the between-groups mean square (2.07) by the within-groups mean square (4.97) and write the answer, .42, for *F*.

$F = \underline{.42}$

6. Find your table value. Enter Table P using the degrees of freedom found for the between-groups (2) and for the within-groups (12). Run your fingers down the *df* column until you are at the within-groups *df*, which is 12. Next run your fingers across this row until you are underneath your between-groups *df*, which is 2. At this point you will find two numbers, a boldface number and a lightface number. The boldface number is

[15] You can find the within-groups degrees of freedom by using the formula $N - k$. N represents the total number of subjects and k the number of groups or treatments. In this problem $N = 15$ and $k = 3$; therefore $15 - 3 = 12$, your within-groups degrees of freedom.

table
value = 3.88

do not reject

for a .01 level of significance and the lightface number for a .05 level of significance. Since your predetermined level of significance was .05, your table value is 3.88. Record that in the blank to the left.

7. If the value you found for F (.42) is equal to or greater than the table value (3.88), reject the null hypothesis. If not, write *do not reject* in the blank to the left and write n.s. in the table, which means nonsignificant.

There is no significant difference between the three groups of children. Math skill is not affected by which reinforcement is used. The fact that the null hypothesis is not rejected tells us that the children in the three groups can be treated as a group of 15 from a single population.

For our practice problem let's return to Chapter 6, Situation VII, Professor X's Discovery.

Problem

Professor X had discovered a new serum, which would increase a person's speed when running. The Summer Olympics was approaching and the professor wanted to test his serum. He randomly assigned 20 individuals who were competing in the 32-kilometer race to four groups, five subjects in each group. Each group received a different gram dosage of the serum, and each person in the group then ran the 32-kilometer race. The time each person required to run the race is shown in the accompanying table.[16]

Find out if there is a significant difference between the four groups. The *null hypothesis* states there will be no significant difference between the sample means. The *alternative hypothesis* states that the four groups are different. Use a .01 level of significance.

Number of Minutes Required to Run the 32-Kilometer Race

Group A	Group B	Group C	Group D
6	5	4	2
6	3	4	2
6	4	4	2
7	4	3	1
7	4	3	1

Answer

$F = 55.43$. Reject the null hypothesis, because the F of 55.43 is greater than the table value of 5.29. On the basis that the null

---

[16] This situation is a hyperbole. To run 32 km in one minute would be to exceed the speed of sound.

hypothesis is probably false, the inference is made that the alternative hypothesis is probably true: the groups are different. The expression $p < .01$ is written in the probability column in the summary table to show that the probability of the variation's occurring by chance is one or fewer out of a hundred.

SUMMARY TABLE

Source of variation	Sum of squares (SS)	Degrees of freedom (df)	Mean square (MS)	F	Probability
Between groups	58.20	3	19.40		
Within groups	5.60	16	.35	55.43	$p < .01$
Total	63.80	19			

The procedure for finding the analysis of variance is summarized below.

Steps Used to Find the Analysis of Variance	**1.** Use this summary table to find *F*, which is MS_B/MS_W.

Source of variations	Sum of squares (SS)	Degrees of freedom (df)	Mean square (MS)	F
Between groups				
Within groups				
Total				

2. Use Table P to find your table value, using the degrees of freedom for the between-groups $(k - 1)$ and the within-groups degrees of freedom $(N - k)$ to enter the table. Your table value is the lightface number if you have a .05 level of significance and the boldface number if you have a .01 level of significance.

3. If your value for *F* is equal to or greater than the table value, reject the null hypothesis in favor of the alternative hypothesis.

In this practice problem there was a significant difference between the groups. However, the one-way analysis of variances told you only that the groups were different. It did not tell you which pair of groups had differences that were significant and which pair had differences that were not significant. For example, Group A may be significantly different from Group B and from Group C, but Group B and Group C may not be significantly different from each other. In order to find out which means are significantly larger than other means, you must use a significance test.

SCHEFFÉ TEST

The test you will learn how to use is the Scheffé. It is easy to compute and conservative, and your comparisons do not have to be planned in advance. Referring back to your practice problem, you would make six different comparisons to find out which groups have means that are significantly different.[17] The means you would compare are:

1. Group A versus Group B
2. Group A versus Group C
3. Group A versus Group D
4. Group B versus Group C
5. Group B versus Group D
6. Group C versus Group D

When you use the Scheffé, you compute a separate F for every comparison, using the following formula:

Formula 9-5   *Scheffé Test*

$$F = \frac{(\bar{X}_1 - \bar{X}_2)^2}{MS_W \left(\dfrac{n_1 + n_2}{n_1 n_2} \right) (k - 1)}$$

After this F is computed, you compare it to the table value you found when you did your analysis of variance. If the F is equal to or greater than the table value, it is considered significant.

To demonstrate how this works, we will use the Scheffé to find out if the mean in Group A is significantly greater than the mean for Group B (comparison 1). We will use a direction sheet to do this problem.

Scheffé Direction Sheet

This direction sheet has a summary chart that you fill in as you follow the directions.

---

[17] A simple formula to use to determine mathematically how many comparisons are possible, taking two groups at a time, is $k(k - 1)/2$, where k is the number of groups. In this example there are four groups; therefore, we can make $4(4 - 1)/2 = 4(3)/2 = 12/2$ or 6 comparisons.

Summary Chart

Group A $\bar{X}_1 = 6.40$
Group B $\bar{X}_2 = 4.00$
$MS_W = .35$
$n_1 = 5$
$n_2 = 5$
$k - 1 = 3$
$T = 5.29$

1. Find the mean of Group A.[18] Write the answer, 6.40, oppo-site the $\bar{X}_1$ in the summary chart.
2. Find the mean of Group B. Write the answer, 4.00, opposite the $\bar{X}_2$ in the summary chart.
3. Find the MS_W. Look at the analysis of variance summary table that you did for your practice problem. Under the source of variation column find the within groups, then run your fingers across this row until you are under the mean-square heading. The number you find here is the mean square within. Write this number, .35, opposite MS_W.
4. Find n_1 and n_2. Refer back to your original data. Count the number of people in Group A and record this number, 5, as n_1. Count the number of people in Group B and record this number, 5, as n_2.
5. Find $k - 1$. Look at your analysis of variance summary table and record the number you found for the between-groups de-grees of freedom. Write 3 opposite the $k - 1$.
6. Find the table value. Rewrite the table value you found for your practice problem opposite T. Write 5.29.

Now, using this summary chart, you are ready to substitute in the formula:

$$F = \frac{(\bar{X}_1 - \bar{X}_2)^2}{MS_W \left(\dfrac{n_1 + n_2}{n_1 n_2} \right) (k - 1)}$$

7. Substitute 6.40 for $\bar{X}_1$, 4.0 for $\bar{X}_2$, .35 for MS_W, 5 for n_1, 5 for n_2, and 3 for $k - 1$.

$$F = \frac{(6.40 - 4.00)^2}{.35 \left(\dfrac{5 + 5}{(5)(5)} \right) (3)}$$

---

[18] It does not matter which group becomes $\bar{X}_1$.

8. Solve the problem, following the arithmetic rules of order. Enclose your answer for F in a box.

$$F = \frac{(2.40)^2}{.35 \; \dfrac{10}{25} \; (3)} = \frac{5.76}{.35(.40)(3)} = \frac{5.76}{.42}$$

$$\boxed{F = 13.71}$$

9. Look at the F you found in step 8 (13.71). If it is equal to or more than the table value shown in the summary chart, these two groups are significantly different. Since 13.71 is greater than the table value, 5.29, you can say Group A and Group B are different.

Problem　　　　As practice find out if the mean of Group B and the mean of Group C are significantly different.

Answer　　　　$F = .38$. Group B and Group C are not different from each other, because the F of .38 is not equal to or greater than the table value of 5.29.

Summary Chart

Group B $\overline{X}_1 = 4.0$
Group C $\overline{X}_2 = 3.60$
　　$MS_W = .35$
　　　$n_1 = 5$
　　　$n_2 = 5$
　$k - 1 = 3$
　　　$T = 5.29$

SUMMARY

In this chapter we have discussed a few parametric tests. These tests have stringent assumptions that the nonparametric tests do not possess.[19]

The first test mentioned was the *t*-ratio. We talked about three applications of the *t*, which we labeled as *t*-test (I), *t*-test (II), and *t*-test (III). The *t*-test (I) was used with one group, the *t*-test (II) with two independent groups, and the *t*-test (III) with two related groups.

After a rather complete discourse on the *t* we turned our attention to the *F*-ratio. We were concerned only with one application, the one-way analysis of variance. This test is used with three or more independent groups and concerns itself with only

[19] Chapter 6 provides a more complete discussion of the parametric and nonparametric tests.

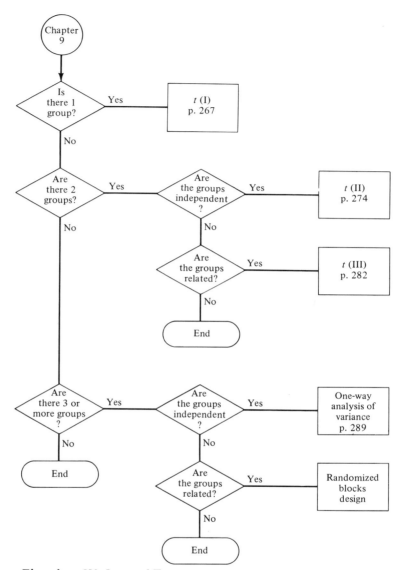

Flowchart IV: Interval Tests

one variable. After a thorough grounding in the rationale and statistical procedure used to compute this F, we learned how to apply the Scheffé significance test.

Many distinctions were made in terms of the types of data or situation in which a particular test is appropriate. Flowchart IV displays these delineations.

As a prompt review, let's see how well you do on this self-test for mastery. Please allow for rounding error.

SELF-TEST FOR MASTERY

If you have trouble working a problem, reread the explanation on the page listed.

1. An investigator for a television repair company wanted to test the effectiveness of its three new television repair schools. He randomly selected five pupils from each school's six-month training program and gave them a standardized test. The results are shown below.

Group A	Group B	Group C
2	2	6
1	2	5
2	3	5
3	2	5
2	3	6

The null hypothesis states that the three groups are the same. The alternative hypothesis states that the three groups are different. The level of significance is set at .05.

p. 291
(a) Use the one-way analysis of variance and find F.

p. 295
(b) Do you reject the null hypothesis?

p. 298
(c) Use the Scheffé to see if Group A is significantly different from Group B.

2. A group of ten students were given a test on multiplication and their scores were recorded. Two days later the same group retook this multiplication test, but this time the psychometrist induced anxiety before and during the exam. The results from both exams are shown in the following table.

Before scores	After scores
10	8
9	7
8	5
7	8
8	6
10	5
10	5
10	8
10	6
9	5

The null hypothesis states that the two groups are the same. The alternative hypothesis states that the two groups are different. The level of significance is set at .01. Use a two-tail test.

p. 284
(a) Use the *t*-test (III) and record the results.

p. 287
(b) Do you reject the null hypothesis?

3. A class of ten children are tested in math and their scores are shown. Test the hypothesis that the population mean is equal to 6, using the *t* distribution.

Class's scores, X
9
9
5
6
7
5
6
7
10
10

The null hypothesis states that the mean of the population is 6. The alternative hypothesis states that the sample mean is not equal to 6. The level of significance is set at .01. Use a two-tail test.

p. 270
(a) Use the *t*-test (I) and record the results.

p. 272
(b) Do you reject the null hypothesis?

4. Two randomly selected groups of students took a statistics test. One group was rewarded before the test and promised an even bigger reward after it, while the other group was given nothing. The table below gives the scores of the members of the two independent groups. The null hypothesis states there is no difference between the two groups. The alternative hypothesis states the two groups are different. The level of significance is set at .01. Use a two-tail test.

Rewarded group	Nonrewarded group
10	13
5	14
4	10
3	5
8	7

p. 277
(a) Use the *t* (II) and record the results.

p. 280
(b) Do you reject the null hypothesis?

ANSWERS TO SELF-TEST

Score yourself by adding up the points for each correct answer and write the total in the Evaluation form.

1. The table value is 3.88.

15 points (a) $F = 46.62$.

5 points (b) Reject the null hypothesis.

15 points (c) Group A and Group B are not significantly different.

Summary Chart

Group A $\overline{X}_1 = 2$
Group B $\overline{X}_2 = 2.4$
$MS_W = .37$
$n_1 = 5$
$n_2 = 5$
$k - 1 = 2$
$T = 3.88$

2. The table value is 3.250.

15 points (a) $t = 4.91$.

5 points (b) Reject the null hypothesis.

3. The table value is 3.250.

15 points (a) $t = 2.26$.

5 points (b) Do not reject the null hypothesis.

4. The table value is 3.355.

15 points (a) $t = -1.77$.

5 points (b) Do not reject the null hypothesis.

Evaluation

Rating	Evaluation
95	You are exceptional
85	You are doing okay
70	You are being careless
65 or less	Reread the chapter; quitting is not for you

CORRELATION

10

For our closing chapter we will discuss correlation. In the process you will learn what correlation is, how to construct a scattergram, and how to interpret it. A good portion of the chapter will be devoted to three correlational techniques, the Pearson product-moment coefficient, the Spearman rank coefficient, and the contingency coefficient. Each technique will be discussed in the following manner:

1. Its rationale will be explained.
2. Its requirements will be listed.
3. A situation that warrants its use will be described.
4. You will learn how to compute it, and a practice problem will be presented.
5. The procedure will be summarized.

To complete this chapter you will take a final self-test for mastery.

WHAT IS CORRELATION?

When a researcher wants to find out the degree to which two variables are related, he is asking a correlation question. For example, he may have evidence that smoking and cancer are related, as are height and weight or high-school grades and college grades or athletic ability and academic performance. But he may want to know more than the fact that these relationships exist. He may want to know how closely the two variables are related to one another. This is very much like family relationships. You may have two first cousins, which obviously means that they are related to you. But you may feel a lot closer to one than to the other. The relationship with one is stronger than with the other. It is this strength or closeness of the relationship that we are talking about when we say that *the correlation coefficient measures the degree of relationship*. In measuring the degree of relationship, the correlation coefficient also gives us evidence as to whether or not a relationship does exist between two variables.

As an example, let us take the relationship between high-school grades and college grades. We are interested in finding out whether these two variables are related to one another. So we use a correlation-coefficient formula to measure the degree of relationship between the two, on the basis of which we determine both whether a relationship does exist and how close it is. For this study we look at a small random selection of college graduates. We record their grade-point average (GPA) in both high school and college. The data are shown in Table 10-1.

Looking at these data, we are curious about the relationship that exists between the two variables. To attempt to discover what the form of this relationship might be, we plot these pair of scores on a graph called a *scattergram*. We represent each pair

Table 10-1: Ten Students' High-School and College GPA's

Student	High-School GPA	College GPA
A	3.8	3.7
B	3.5	3.3
C	3.3	3.1
D	3.1	3.1
E	2.9	2.7
F	2.7	2.5
G	2.2	2.5
H	2.2	2.0
I	2.0	1.8
J	2.0	1.6

of scores by one point. By looking at this scattergram, we can get an idea whether a strong relationship exists between the two variables and, if so, whether the relationship may be treated as linear—that is, whether the values plotted on the graph tend to scatter along a straight line. This information is important to us if we are going to use a technique such as the Pearson product-moment, which only can be used when the data are linear. To begin, let's learn how to construct a scattergram.

How to Construct a Scattergram

Let's draw a scattergram using a piece of graph paper. We draw a vertical axis on this paper and label it Y. Perpendicular to this vertical axis we construct a horizontal axis, which we label X. Using the data in Table 10-1, let the Y axis be the college GPA and the X axis be the high-school GPA. The college GPA's range from 1.6 to 3.7, so the Y axis must include at least this range of scores. We allow a small margin at each end of the range; that is why the numbers on the Y axis of our graph range from 1.4 to 3.8. These numbers are placed at an equal distance on a series of equally spaced marks which increase by .10. Likewise the X axis, the high-school GPA, is labeled so that the scores from 2.0 to 3.8 can be included. The numbers on the X axis range from 1.8 to 4.0. After the axes are drawn and labeled, one dot is used to represent each person's pair of scores. For example, to locate student A's two scores, you plot the dot by first locating his high-school GPA of 3.8. To do this you run your fingers horizontally on the X axis until you come to 3.8. At this point you change direction and go up this line on the graph until you find his college GPA of 3.7; here you stop and make a dot. A rule of thumb for placing a dot is *across then up*. For this example the across score is 3.8 and the up score is 3.7. Student A's dot has been plotted on the scattergram, Figure 10-1.

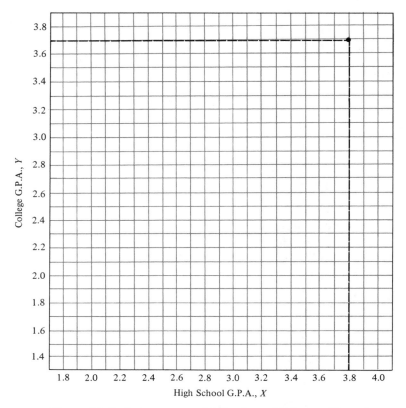

Figure 10-1: Scattergram with Student A's Scores Plotted

Exercise   Before continuing, plot the pairs of scores found in Table 10-1
                    on a scattergram.

Answer   See the figure on page 309.

Let's look at this plotted scattergram and see what we can learn from it. Notice
that large values for X seem to be associated with large values of Y. For instance,
student A received a 3.8 on his high-school GPA and a 3.7 on his college GPA. The
trend of this diagram seems to be a straight line. We look to see if the dots appear to
be scattered on both sides of a curve or whether they appear to be scattered on both
sides of a straight line. In this picture it appears they are scattered along a straight
line. If the correlation had been perfect, all the dots would form a straight line.

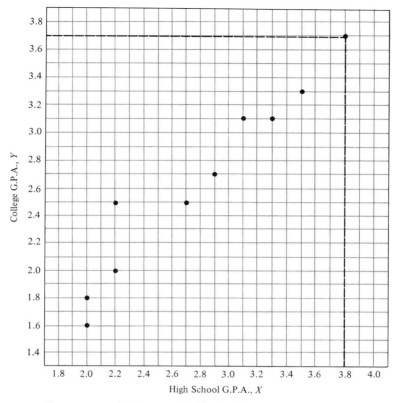

Scattergram for Data in Table 10-1

A Perfect Positive Correlation

Figure 10-2 shows a perfect positive relationship. On this scattergram for every increase of 2 on the X variable there is an increase of 1 on the Y variable. When one variable increases, the other variable increases. This relationship is considered positive because the variables increase in the same direction together. In this situation if a person is high on one variable he is high on the other; moreover, if a person is low on one variable he is low on the other. This situation is considered a perfect relationship because this exact relationship is maintained. That is, person A was best on the X variable and he was also the best on the Y variable. Person B was second best on the X variable and he was also second best on the Y variable. This pattern continues down to person G, who did the poorest on the X variable and also did poorest on the Y variable. When these pairs of scores were plotted, they formed

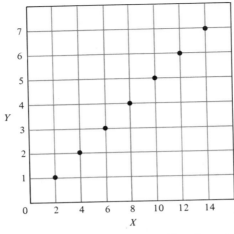

Figure 10-2: A Scattergram Showing a Correlation of +1.00

Person	X	Y
A	14	7
B	12	6
C	10	5
D	8	4
E	6	3
F	4	2
G	2	1

a straight line. Notice this straight line runs from the lower left-hand corner to the upper right-hand corner. Using the scores in the table in Figure 10-2, this correlation when computed is equal to +1.00.

A Perfect Negative Correlation

Figure 10-3 shows a perfect negative relationship. On this diagram for every increase of 2 on the X variable there is a decrease of 1 on the Y

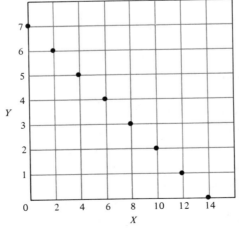

Person	X	Y
A	14	0
B	12	1
C	10	2
D	8	3
E	6	4
F	4	5
G	2	6

Figure 10-3: A Scattergram Showing a Correlation of −1.00

variable. There is a definite relationship here, which is different from the perfect positive relationship. This time when one variable increases, the other decreases. It is considered a negative relationship because the better you are on the X variable the worse you are on the Y variable. It is considered perfect because this relationship is maintained throughout. Person A has the highest score on the X variable and the lowest score on the Y variable. Person B has the second highest score on the X variable and the second lowest score on the Y variable. When these scores are plotted, they form a straight line, running from the upper left-hand corner to the lower right-hand corner. Using the scores in the table in Figure 10-3, this correlation when computed equals -1.00.

Notice that a positive or negative sign refers to the direction of the relationship. The sign has nothing to do with the strength, which is given by the numerical value of the correlation coefficient. It would be wonderful if all relationships that you plotted were perfect. However, since this almost is never the case, you will more than likely have a scattergram that resembles Figure 10-1. In cases where there is no relationship between the two variables, you may have a scattergram such as Figure 10-4, which shows zero correlation.[1] Looking at the data in such cases shows that no pat-

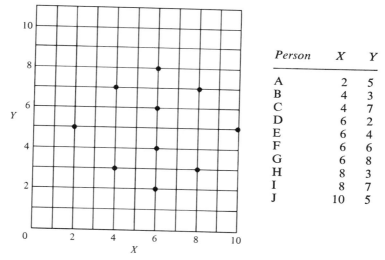

Person	X	Y
A	2	5
B	4	3
C	4	7
D	6	2
E	6	4
F	6	6
G	6	8
H	8	3
I	8	7
J	10	5

Figure 10-4: A Scattergram Having a Zero Correlation

[1] It is possible to have a very strong relationship between the variables and still have a correlation of zero; however, this relationship would clearly not be linear.

tern exists. Knowing that the *X* variable is large tells you nothing about whether the *Y* variable is large. Using the scores found in the table in Figure 10-4, this correlation when computed equals zero.

In summary, the scattergram is constructed to give you a rough estimate of the strength, direction, and form of the relationship.

How do we choose a correlation technique? We choose on the basis of the situation that is being examined and the data's level of measurement. In this chapter we will discuss three techniques,[2] of which two are nonparametric and one is parametric. These procedures are most often found in beginning statistics books, and each serves a different level of measurement, as illustrated by the following chart.

Level of measurement	Correlational technique	Kind
Nominal	Contingency coefficient	Nonparametric
Ordinal	Spearman rank	Nonparametric
Interval	Pearson product-moment	Parametric

After we choose a correlation technique, we use it to compute a number called a *coefficient of correlation*. This number tells us the exact strength and direction of the relationship between the two sets of scores.

We begin our discussion with the Pearson product-moment coefficient of correlation.

PEARSON PRODUCT-MOMENT COEFFICIENT

The *Pearson product-moment coefficient of correlation* or the *Pearson r,* as it is sometimes called, was derived by the English statistician Karl Pearson. It is the most popular measure of correlation for measuring the linear relationship between two numerically valued random variables. In order to use this parametric measure, we assume the scores on each variable come from a normally distributed population. The requirements for the Pearson *r* are as follows:

Pearson *r* **Requirements**	1. Relationship is linear.
	2. Scores of the population form a normal distribution curve.
	3. Scattergram is homoscedastic.
	4. Scores are at interval level of measurement.[3]

---

[2] We will deal with correlational techniques that involve only two variables.

[3] Refer to Chapter 2 for a discussion of the requirement of interval level of measurement.

Discussion of the Requirements

Requirement 1 assumes linearity. That is, the values for X and Y tend to scatter along a straight line, instead of a curved line. Figure 10-5 shows a

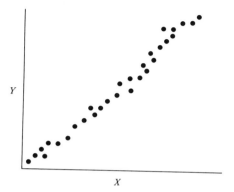

Figure 10-5: Linear Scattering

drawing of points that tend to be plotted along a straight line. Scores in reading might be represented on the X variable and scores in math on the Y variable. An interpretation of this illustration might be that individuals who score high in reading tend to score high in math.

A curvilinear relationship occurs when X and Y scores tend to fall along a

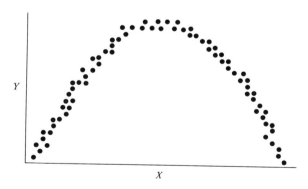

Figure 10-6: Curvilinear Scattering

curved line. Figure 10-6 illustrates this type of relationship. The scores in this case might represent age on the X variable and strength on the Y variable. An interpretation of this picture might be that as a person's age increases, his physical strength increases (dots going up), until he reaches adulthood where things stabilize; then, as he approaches old age, his strength decreases (dots going down).

The best way to determine whether the variables you are studying are linear is to draw and inspect a scattergram. If the points seem to fall along a straight line as in Figure 10-6, you can assume linearity.[4]

Requirement 2 has to do with normality. The shape of both distributions should be similar. If one distribution is skewed and the Pearson r is used as a measure, it will underestimate the relationship between the variables.

Requirement 3 concerns *homoscedasticity*. You determine this by drawing and inspecting a scattergram. In order for it to be homoscedastic, the distance of the dots must be nearly the same on both sides of the line. Figure 10-7 shows a homoscedastic relationship.

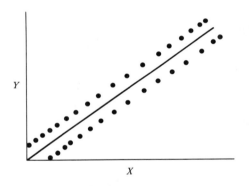

Figure 10-7: Homoscedasticity

If the dots are not at nearly the same distance on both sides of the line, you might get a nonhomoscedastic relationship, which looks like Figure 10-8. The points are close together in the lower part of the drawing but farther apart in the upper right. The Pearson r in this instance would underestimate the more scattered region of the drawing.

There are more sophisticated methods to determine homoscedastic relationships, but they are beyond this text.

[4] If you are unclear about the nature of the scattergram, you may test for linearity using a procedure described in Dixon and Massey (1957), pp. 197–198.

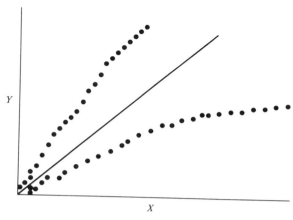

Figure 10-8: Nonhomoscedasticity

What Is the Pearson r?

The Pearson r is simply the mean of the z-score products, or $r = \Sigma\, z_x z_y / N$. To compute r you do nothing new. You convert every X-score value and every Y-score value to a z score. Then you multiply each z score of X by its z score of Y. You sum the products and divide by the number of pairs. The Pearson r then shows you the extent to which individuals have the same position on these two variables. Because you change both sets of scores to z scores, you do not have to worry that the variables are not measured on the same type of scale. In other words, you can correlate weight with height. Looking at this formula and understanding what it means helps one to understand the concept of correlation. However, using this formula to compute r is computationally a pain in the neck. Can you imagine the time and effort it would take to convert every X score and Y score to a z score? Needless to say, it makes life easier to know that other formulas have been derived from this basic definitional formula. One of the easiest to use is given below:

Formula 10-1   *Pearson r Coefficient*

$$r = \frac{N \Sigma\, XY - (\Sigma\, X)(\Sigma\, Y)}{\sqrt{[N \Sigma\, X^2 - (\Sigma\, X)^2][N \Sigma\, Y^2 - (\Sigma\, Y)^2]}}$$

The terms used in this formula have the following meanings:

Symbol	Meaning
ΣXY	Multiply each X by its Y, then sum the results
N	Number of pairs
ΣX	Sum of the X scores
ΣY	Sum of the Y scores
ΣX^2	Square the X scores, then sum the results
ΣY^2	Square the Y scores, then sum the results

Let's take a situation where we should use the Pearson r and demonstrate how to compute it.

Situation

A psychometrist wanted to test the hypothesis that the longer it takes individuals to complete a math problem-solving test, the lower their score will be on that test. She randomly selected seven individuals and measured them on these two variables. She recorded their test scores and the number of hours it took to complete the test. The results are shown in Table 10-2.

Table 10-2: Individual Scores on Math Test and Number of Hours Taken to Complete the Test

Individual	Score, X	Hours, Y
A	3	5
B	4	5
C	4	4
D	5	3
E	7	2
F	8	2
G	10	1

She then set a .05 level of significance. The *null hypothesis* states there is no correlation between these two variables. The *alternative hypothesis* is one-tail and states there will be a negative relationship between the two variables. Let us compute the Pearson r and see if the null hypothesis should be rejected.

PROCEDURE

Directions for Setting Up a Worksheet for the Pearson r

We shall set up a worksheet and follow the directions for forming the columns and solving the psychometrist's problem.

Pearson Product-Moment Coefficient Worksheet

PART I

Individual	Score, X	Hours, Y	XY
A	3	5	15
B	4	5	20
C	4	4	16
D	5	3	15
E	7	2	14
F	8	2	16
G	10	1	10

$N = 7$ $\Sigma XY = 106$

PART II

Individual	Score, X	X^2	Hours, Y	Y^2
A	3	9	5	25
B	4	16	5	25
C	4	16	4	16
D	5	25	3	9
E	7	49	2	4
F	8	64	2	4
G	10	100	1	1
	$\Sigma X = 41$	$\Sigma X^2 = 279$	$\Sigma Y = 22$	$\Sigma Y^2 = 84$

Directions for Using the Worksheet

PART I

1. Find N. Count the number of individuals in the study. Write 7 opposite N.
2. Form the XY column. Multiply each X score by its corresponding Y score and place the answer in the column labeled XY. For example, individual A's X score of 3 is multiplied by his Y score of 5, and 15 is written in the XY column.
3. Find ΣXY. Add the numbers in the XY column and put the answer opposite ΣXY. Add $15 + 20 + 16 + \cdots + 10$ and put the answer, 106, opposite ΣXY.

PART II

4. In Part II of the worksheet rewrite the X and Y columns from Part I.
5. Find ΣX. Add all the scores in the X column, $3 + 4 + 4 + \cdots + 10$, and put the sum, 41, opposite ΣX.

6. Form the X^2 column. Square each score in the X column and record the answer in the column labeled X^2. For example, individual A's X score of 3 is squared and 9 is written in the X^2 column.

7. Find $\Sigma\,X^2$. Add the scores in the X^2 column, $9 + 16 + 16 + \cdots + 100$, and record the sum, 279, opposite $\Sigma\,X^2$.

8. Find $\Sigma\,Y$. Add all the scores in the Y column, $5 + 5 + 4 + \cdots + 1$, and put their sum, 22, opposite $\Sigma\,Y$.

9. Form the Y^2 column. Square each score in the Y column and record the answer in the column labeled Y^2. For example, individual A's score, 5, is squared, and 25 is written in the Y^2 column.

10. Find $\Sigma\,Y^2$. Add the scores in the Y^2 column, $25 + 25 + \cdots + 1$, and write their sum, 84, opposite the $\Sigma\,Y^2$.

Substituting in the Formula

Using Part I and Part II of the worksheet, we will substitute in the formula:

$$r = \frac{N\,\Sigma\,XY - (\Sigma\,X)(\Sigma\,Y)}{\sqrt{[N\,\Sigma\,X^2 - (\Sigma\,X)^2][N\,\Sigma\,Y^2 - (\Sigma\,Y)^2]}}$$

11. Substitute 7 for every N; substitute 106 for the $\Sigma\,XY$; substitute 41 for every $\Sigma\,X$; substitute 22 for every $\Sigma\,Y$; substitute 279 for the $\Sigma\,X^2$; and substitute 84 for the $\Sigma\,Y^2$.

$$r = \frac{(7)106 - (41)(22)}{\sqrt{[(7)279 - (41)^2][(7)84 - (22)^2]}}$$

Solving the Problem

12. First do the series of computations inside the square-root radical.

   (a) In the left-hand brackets, square 41, multiply 7 times 279, then subtract the results from each other: $(41)^2 = 1681$; $7 \times 279 = 1953$; and then $1953 - 1681 = 272$. Repeat the same steps for the numbers in the brackets at the right; that is, $(22)^2 = 484$; $7 \times 84 = 588$; $588 - 484 = 104$.

$$r = \frac{7(106) - 41(22)}{\sqrt{[272] \times [104]}}$$

   (b) Multiply the numbers in the brackets together, then

find the square root of the results. That is, $[272] \times [104] = 28{,}288$, and $\sqrt{28{,}288}$ is 168.19.

$$r = \frac{7(106) - 41(22)}{168.19}$$

(c) Working now just with the numerator, perform all multiplications, then subtract the results: $7 \times 106 = 742$; $41 \times 22 = 902$; $742 - 902 = -160$.

$$r = \frac{-160}{168.19}$$

(d) Now divide the numerator by the denominator: $-160 \div 168.19 = -.95$. Box the results.

$$\boxed{r = -.95}$$

The boxed-in value is our coefficient of correlation. We will later use this value to reach a statistical decision about the psychometrist's problem. But now let us digress for a moment to explain what this coefficient of $-.95$ is and how to interpret it.

What Is a Coefficient of Correlation?

A *coefficient of correlation* is a number that will tell you the exact strength and direction of the relationship between two variables. The Pearson r measures the degree of linear or straight-line relationship between two variables. The numbers that you can compute range from $+1.00$ through 0 to -1.00.

-1.00 0 $+1.00$

The sign of the coefficient has nothing to do with the strength of the relationship. For instance, the strength of the relationship between two variables with a coefficient of correlation of $+.85$ is identical to the strength of the relationship between two variables with a coefficient of correlation of $-.85$. The sign tells the direction of the relationship. The $+.85$ means that the two variables increase together, whereas the $-.85$ means that one variable increases while the other decreases.

How to Interpret the Pearson Product-Moment Coefficient of Correlation

A rough gauge for interpreting a coefficient of correlation is shown in Table 10-3.[5]

Table 10-3: Gauge for Interpreting Coefficient of Correlation

(a) .85 to 1.0 (or −.85 to −1.0):	High
(b) .50 to .84 (or −.50 to −.84):	Moderate
(c) 0 to .49 (or 0 to −.49):	Low

The stronger the relationship between the two variables, the closer the coefficient is to $+1.00$ or -1.00. For instance, if your two variables have a coefficient of correlation of $+.95$, this is interpreted to indicate a strong positive relationship between them. A coefficient of correlation of $-.90$ is considered a strong negative relationship between two variables. The weaker the relationship, the closer the coefficient is to zero. A correlation coefficient of zero is considered to indicate no relationship between the two variables. What conclusions can you draw from these indications? You can draw conclusions only in regard to strength and sign of relationship—not about whether one of the variables caused the other. In fact, inferring causality in some studies would be absurd. For example, if the two variables being measured were shoe size and intelligence and they correlated $+.85$, you could not say a certain shoe size causes a person to be intelligent, or vice versa.

Returning to the Pearson product-moment coefficient of correlation we just computed, $-.95$, we can see that this is a very high and negative relationship. We now want to test the significance of this r in order to reach a statistical decision about whether these two variables are associated in the population. In testing the significance of this correlation you are testing the null hypothesis, which states there is no correlation in the population.

Statistical Decision

Record the answers in the blank to the left. We are testing the statistical significance of r when N is smaller than 30.

$r = \underline{-.95}$

$df = \underline{5}$

1. Record the value found for r ($-.95$).
2. Find your df using the formula $N - 2$. Subtract 2 from 7 and write 5.

[5] You cannot apply this gauge to the contingency coefficient because it is not scaled between -1.00 and 1.00. Use this chart as a way of interpreting the Pearson product-moment coefficient of correlation and the Spearman rank coefficient of correlation.

table
value = .6694

3. Find the table value. In Table Q at your *df* of 5 run your fingers across the row until you are at the predetermined level of significance, .05, for the proper tail (one-tail); record the table value of .6694.
4. If the *r* value[6] you found, −.95, is less than the table value found in step 3 (.6694), do not reject the null hypothesis. If the *r* value is equal to or greater than the table value, reject the null hypothesis. Write *reject* in the blank to the left.

reject

For this particular problem the null hypothesis was rejected. There is a relationship between the variables. The math score and the time it took to finish the test are negatively related. The psychometrist's hypothesis that the higher a person's score on the math test, the less time it takes him to complete the test, seems to be true.

To test the statistical significance of *r* when *N* is 30 or more we compute a $z = r \sqrt{N - 1}$. For example, *r* is .60, *N* = 37, it is a one-tail test, and the level of significance is set at .05. Then $z = (.60) \sqrt{37 - 1} = (.60) \sqrt{36} = (.60)(6) = 3.6$.

1. Determine *z*'s probability by referring to Table D in the appendix. A *z* of 3.6 has a probability of .00016. For a two-tail test double the probability.
2. If the probability shown in the table is equal to or less than your level of significance, reject the null hypothesis. Since .00016 is less than .05, the null hypothesis would be rejected.

The procedure just used for the Pearson *r* is shown below.

Summary of Steps for the Pearson *r*

1. Determine *r* by the formula

$$r = \frac{N \Sigma XY - (\Sigma X)(\Sigma Y)}{\sqrt{[N \Sigma X^2 - (\Sigma X)^2][N \Sigma Y^2 - (\Sigma Y)^2]}}$$

2. Determine the statistical significance of *r* when *N* is smaller than 30.
   (a) Refer to Table Q.
   (b) Using a *df* of *N* − 2, enter Table Q.
   (c) If your *r* is equal to or greater than the table value found in Table Q, reject the null hypothesis.
3. Determine the statistical significance of *r* when *N* is 30 or larger.
   (a) Compute $z = r \sqrt{N - 1}$.
   (b) Consult Table D.
   (c) Reject the null hypothesis if your *z* value has a probability of occurring that is equal to or less than your level

[6] Use the absolute value.

of significance. For a two-tail test, double the probability shown.

By this time you should be ready to solve a practice problem.

Problem

Roger and Abdula wanted to find out if there was a correlation between the number of peanuts people ate and their weight. At a cocktail party they observed five people. They recorded their weight and how many peanuts they ate during the entire evening, as shown in Table 10-4.

The *null hypothesis* states there is no correlation between weight and peanuts consumed. The *alternative hypothesis* states that there will be a positive correlation between weight and peanut consumption. They set a .05 level of significance and used a one-tail test.

Table 10-4: Weight and Number of Peanuts Consumed

Individual	Weight (lb)	Peanuts
A	115	20
B	101	11
C	110	15
D	105	14
E	103	13

Shortcut in Computing the Pearson r

Since the numbers are quite large in this problem, it would be best to use a coding technique. Simply select a convenient number and subtract it from each score for X or Y or both; then compute r. There is no need to uncode these values, because the value for r is not affected if we take either X or Y or both and add, subtract, multiply, or divide by a constant. In Table 10-4 code the numbers

Table 10-5: Values in Table 10-4 after Coding

Individual	X	Y
A	15	10
B	1	1
C	10	5
D	5	4
E	3	3

for the X variable by subtracting 100 from each number and code the numbers for the Y variable by subtracting 10 from each number to get the values shown in Table 10-5.

Now solve the problem.

Answer
$$r = \frac{(5)(230) - (34)(23)}{\sqrt{[(5)360 - (34)^2][(5)151 - (23)^2]}} = +.96$$

Reject the null hypothesis, since the r value of .96 is higher than the table value of .8054. There is a high positive correlation between weight and peanuts consumed. The heavier people seem to eat more peanuts.

Additional Comments on the Interpretation of r

The Pearson r is more sensitive to the presence of a relationship than the Spearman rho or contingency coefficient. It is a coefficient that has scores from -1.00 through 0 to $+1.00$. Remember, the sign indicates the direction of the correlation and the number the magnitude of the correlation.

A word of warning about interpreting r. Even though the coefficient tells you the degree to which the variables are related, we must emphasize that this in no way implies causality. In our first example it would be ridiculous to interpret the r of $-.95$ by saying that a high score on the math test was caused by taking it fast and that a low score was caused by taking it slow. The relationship may have been to a third factor, such as IQ in math.

Another warning to the wise: the fact that r is an index of relationship does not mean it is interpreted as a percent. That is, an r of .20 does not indicate 20% agreement between the X and Y variables. Neither can you say that a correlation of .60 is twice as strong as a correlation of .30.

There are many ways of interpreting r in terms of variance, slope, and errors in prediction. The most common way is in terms of variance.

Interpreting r in Terms of Variance

Suppose we found an r of .80 between scores on a math test (X) and IQ scores (Y). We might ask then: (1) What portion of the individual differences in math scores are due to individual differences in intellectual ability? (2) What portion of the differences between the individuals are due to other factors, such as motivation, how a person felt, and grading errors? We find the answers by interpreting the *r* in terms of variance. First use the formula r^2 to find the answer to the first question. By squaring an *r* of .80 you obtain .64. This .64 equals the percentage of the variance of the *X* scores that is associated with the variance of the *Y* scores. In plain language, 64% of the variance of the math scores is accounted for by the variance of the IQ scores. The variance associated with other factors—motivation, health, and so on—(question 2) is found by subtracting .64 from 1.00. The .36 obtained is this variance. Judging from this interpretation of *r,* a correlation of .40 would seem low, because it accounts for only 16% of *Y* variance as associated with *X*. In some cases, however, this correlation could be important.

The second coefficient of correlation we will discuss is the Spearman rank, the most often used of the rank correlational techniques.

SPEARMAN RANK COEFFICIENT (rho)

Charles Spearman, a British psychologist, is given credit for the first work on the relationship between ranks. His early writings on the subject became known as Spearman's rank-order correlation.[7]

The *Spearman rank coefficient* is referred to as the *Spearman rho* because it is denoted by the Greek letter ρ. It is a nonparametric measure for use with data that are either reduced to ranks or collected in the form of ranks.

In testing the significance of this correlation you are testing the null hypothesis, which states there is zero correlation in the population. The requirements for using the Spearman rho are as follows:

Spearman Rank	**1.** Ordinal data.
Coefficient	**2.** Two variables.
Requirements	**3.** Each subject in the study ranked separately on each variable.

Let us look at a situation in which the use of the Spearman rho is appropriate.

Situation

The mayor of Alta County was curious about the annual Male Beauty Contest. The contestants were judged on five items: good looks, intelligence, talent, figure, and voice quality. The mayor wanted to find out if there was a correla-

---

[7] In reality it was Galton, not Spearman, who developed the idea of rank-order correlation, and it was Pearson who derived the formula (Walker, 1975).

Table 10-6: Results from the Alta County
Beauty Contest

Male	Looks	Talent
A	50	12
B	48	10
C	30	40
D	47	13
E	20	50
F	25	45
G	40	20

tion between two of these variables: he wanted to see if good looks was correlated with talent. After the contest he obtained the judge's scores on the seven contestants on these two variables. Each man's score on looks and talent is recorded in Table 10-6.

The *null hypothesis* states that there is no relationship between the two variables: there is no correlation between good looks and talent. The *alternative hypothesis* states that good looks and talent are related (a two-tailed test). The level of significance is set at .02. The Spearman rho is used to analyze the data.

The terms used to find the Spearman rho have the following meanings:

Symbol	Meaning
N	Number of individuals in the group
D	Difference between the ranks in the column labeled R_1 and the column labeled R_2
ΣD^2	Square each difference and then find the sum
ρ	Spearman rank coefficient

PROCEDURE

The method for finding the Spearman rho entails placing a rank next to each person on each variable. Next, determine the difference between the two ranks, square this difference, and sum all these squares, which results in a ΣD^2. Then use the ΣD^2 to substitute in the formula below:

Formula 10-2   *Spearman Rho Coefficient*

$$\rho = 1 - \frac{6 \Sigma D^2}{N(N^2 - 1)}$$

Begin now by drawing a worksheet for the data. Follow the directions given for forming the columns on this worksheet and for substituting values in the formula for the Spearman rho.

Worksheet for the Spearman Rho

PART I

Male	Looks	R_1	Talent	R_2
A	50	7	12	2
B	48	6	10	1
C	30	3	40	5
D	47	5	13	3
E	20	1	50	7
F	25	2	45	6
G	40	4	20	4

PART II

Male	R_1	R_2	D	D^2
A	7	2	5	25
B	6	1	5	25
C	3	5	−2	4
D	5	3	2	4
E	1	7	−6	36
F	2	6	−4	16
G	4	4	0	0

$N = 7$
$N^2 = 49$

$\Sigma D^2 = 110$

Directions for Using This Worksheet

The two parts to these directions coincide with the two parts on the worksheet.

PART I

1. Form the R_1 column. Rank the scores on the first variable, looks,[8] and place these ranks opposite their score in the column labeled R_1. For example, male A is given a rank of 7 on looks, which is placed in the R_1 column opposite the score of 50.

2. Form the R_2 column. Rank the scores on the second variable, talent, and place these ranks opposite their score in the column labeled R_2. For example, male A is given a rank of

[8] Follow the ranking procedure you learned in Chapter 8. Give the lowest score a rank of 1.

2 on talent, which is placed in the R_2 column opposite the score of 12.

PART II

3. Rewrite columns R_1 and R_2 in Part II of the worksheet.
4. Form the D column. Subtract the numbers found in the R_2 column from their corresponding numbers in the R_1 column. Place the results in the column labeled D. For example, male A's R_2 of 2 is subtracted from his R_1 of 7, and 5 is placed in column D.
5. Form the D^2 column. Square each number in the column labeled D and place the results in the D^2 column. For example, male A's D score is 5, and 5 squared equals 25, which is written in the D^2 column.
6. Find the ΣD^2. Add all the numbers in the D^2 column and place the answer opposite the ΣD^2. Add $25 + 25 + 4 + 4 + 36 + 16 + 0$ and write 110.
7. Find N. Count the number of individuals in the group and write the number 7 opposite the N.
8. Find N^2. Square the value found for N (7×7) and write the answer (49) opposite N^2.
9. Substitute in the formula $\rho = 1 - 6 \Sigma D^2 / [N(N^2 - 1)]$, using the answers on the worksheet. Substitute the value found in step 6 for ΣD^2; write 110. Substitute the value found in step 7 for N; write 7. Substitute the value found in step 8 for N^2; write 49.

$$\rho = 1 - \frac{6(110)}{7(49 - 1)}$$

10. Solve the problem and place the answer in the blank to the left opposite the ρ.
    (a) Perform the operations inside the parentheses first; that is, subtract 1 from 49 to get 48.

$$\rho = 1 - \frac{(6)110}{7(48)}$$

    (b) Perform all multiplications next. Multiply 6 times 110 to get 660; multiply 7 times 48 to get 336.

$$\rho = 1 - \frac{660}{336}$$

    (c) Divide 660 by 336 to get 1.96.

$$\rho = 1 - 1.96$$

$\rho = \underline{-.96}$

(d) Subtract 1.96 from 1 to get −.96.

$$\rho = -.96$$

For this problem we have a correlation of −.96.

The Spearman rank coefficient of correlation is like the Pearson product-moment coefficient of correlation in that it yields a value of +1.00 to −1.00. Table 10-3 on page 320 can be used as a rough gauge to interpret the Spearman rank as well as the Pearson. Since your coefficient of correlation was −.96, there appears to be a strong negative correlation between good looks and talent for this beauty contest. The men who were judged the best on looks were also judged the worst on talent.

We now want to test the significance of this ρ in order to reach a statistical decision. That is, does the observed value of ρ, −.96, differ from zero only by chance? The tables you consult depend upon your sample size. Let us look closely now at tables for different sample sizes.

A. Directions for Sample Sizes from 4 to 10

For the beauty contest example, where your sample size is small (7), you would do the following.

table value
= .893

1. Enter Table R. Run your fingers down the N column until you stop at the value for N (7). Next run your fingers across the row until you are under your predetermined level of significance and proper tail (.02 and two-tail). Write .893 for the table value in the blank to the left.
2. If the ρ value you found, −.96, is less than the table value found in step 1, .893, accept the null hypothesis. If the ρ value is equal to or more than the table value, reject the null hypothesis. In this example the ρ value of −.96 is more than the table value of .893, so write *reject* in the blank to the left.

reject

The null hypothesis is rejected. The alternative hypothesis seems to be true: good looks and talent are related.

B. Directions for Sample Sizes from 10 to 30

If your sample size was 12, your ρ was .75, your predetermined level of significance was .025, and a one-tail test was being used, you would do the following.

$\rho = .75$

1. Record the value found for ρ (.75) opposite the ρ.

df = 10

table value
= .5760

2. Find your *df* using the formula $N - 2$. Subtract 2 from 12 and record 10 opposite the *df*.
3. Find the table value. In Table Q at your *df* of 10 run your fingers across the row until you are at the predetermined level of significance, .025, and the proper tail (one-tail). Record the table value of .5760.
4. If the ρ value you found, .75, is less than the table value found in step 3, .5760, do not reject the null hypothesis. If the ρ value is equal to or greater than the table value, reject the null hypothesis. In this example the ρ value is more than the table value of .5760, so write *reject* in the blank to the left.

reject

C. Directions for Sample Sizes over 30

If your sample size was 37, ρ was .30, level of significance .05, and a one-tail test is being used, do the following.

1. Compute $z = \rho \sqrt{N - 1}$. That is, $z = .30 \sqrt{37 - 1} = .30 \sqrt{36} = (.30)(6) = 1.8$.
2. Determine z's probability by consulting Table D. A z of 1.8 has a probability of .0359. For a two-tail test double the probability shown in the table.
3. If the probability shown in the table is equal to or less than your level of significance, reject the null hypothesis. Since .0359 is less than .05, the null hypothesis would be rejected.

Discussion of the Spearman Rho

The Spearman rho, like the Pearson coefficient of correlation, yields a value from +1.00 to −1.00, and it is interpreted in the same way.

In calculating the Spearman, students always ask: what do you do if there are many scores tied? The answer is: nothing, if the number of ties is not too large, because the effect on the Spearman will be negligible. If the number of ties is large, however, a correction factor should be incorporated in the formula.[9]

The procedure just used for the Spearman rho is summarized below.

Summary for the Spearman Rho

1. Rank the scores on the X variable and rank the scores on the Y variable.
2. Determine rho by computing the formula

$$\rho = 1 - 6 \Sigma D^2 / [N(N^2 - 1)]$$

[9] See Siegel (1956) for a more complete treatment of ties.

3. Determine the statistical significance of rho.
   (a) If N is from 4 to 10, refer to Table R. If rho is equal to or greater than the table value, reject the null hypothesis.
   (b) If N is greater than 10, determine statistical significance by referring to Table Q with a $df = N - 2$. If ρ is equal to or greater than the table value, reject the null hypothesis.
   (c) If N is larger than 30, compute $z = \rho \sqrt{N - 1}$ and consult Table D. Determine z's probability. If the probability shown in the table is equal to or less than your level of significance, reject the null hypothesis. For a two-tail test, double the probability shown in the table.

Now see if you can use the Spearman rho to solve the practice problem.

Problem

Mr. Rodriguez, a driving instructor, wanted to see if there was a relationship between the scores earned on a simulated driver's test and the scores earned on a real driver's test. The simulated driver's test consisted of a play wheel and a video tape showing different situations, with the driver reacting by turning the wheel. The actual driver's test had the person driving an obstacle course with a real car. Mr. Rodriguez recorded the scores of 12 people who took both tests, as shown in the accompanying table.[10]

Driver's Test Scores for 12 Students

Individual	Simulated test	Actual test
A	98	95
B	55	60
C	50	45
D	87	85
E	77	75
F	89	87
G	79	75
H	98	97
I	94	92
J	83	80
K	74	71
L	73	72

The *null hypothesis* states there is no correlation between the two variables: a person's score on the simulated driver's test is not related to his real driver's test score. The *alternative hypothesis* states there is a relationship between scores on the

---

[10] These test scores are based on ordinal data.

two tests. Mr. Rodriguez uses a two-tailed test and sets the predetermined level of significance at .01.

Answer

$$\rho = 1 - \frac{(6 \Sigma D^2)}{N(N^2 - 1)} = 1 - \frac{6(3)}{12(144 - 1)}$$

$$\boxed{\rho = .99}$$

We reject the null hypothesis, since the value found for ρ (.99) is greater than the table value (.7079). There is a relationship between scores on these two tests.

The last coefficient we will discuss is the contingency coefficient.

CONTINGENCY COEFFICIENT

The *contingency coefficient* is a nonparametric measure of correlation that tells you the extent of the relationship between two sets of variables. In testing the significance of this correlation you are testing the null hypothesis, which states there is zero correlation in the population.

When we use the contingency coefficient, the data in our study must be discrete and categorical. In computing and determining the significance of the contingency coefficient we use the chi square. The contingency coefficient (C) is very different from other measures of correlation because we do not refer to the sampling distribution of C to determine significance; instead we refer to the chi-square distribution.[11] Because we use the chi square in computing and determining the significance of the contingency coefficient, we must make sure the contingency coefficient meets some of the same requirements as chi square. The requirements for the contingency coefficient are as follows:

Contingency Coefficient Requirements	**1.** Nominal data.
	2. Categorical data.
	3. Adequate sample size—no more than 20% of expected frequencies smaller than 5.
	4. Two variables.
	5. Each subject classified in one category on each variable.

[11] Mathematically it is too complex to refer to the sampling distribution of C, and the chi square provides a simpler indication of the significance of C.

Now let's look at a situation where it is appropriate to use the contingency coefficient.

Situation

A high-school teacher from Chicago wanted to see if there was a correlation between sex and choice of high-school curriculum. On the first day of school he randomly selected 75 students to participate in his experiment. Each student's sex was recorded as male or female, and his or her curriculum choice was recorded as college, general, or vocational. The results are shown in Table 10-7.

Table 10-7: Results from Teacher's Study

	Male	Female
College	20	5
General	10	15
Vocational	5	20

The *null hypothesis* states that there is no relationship between the two variables. In other words, there is no correlation between sex and curriculum choice. The *alternative hypothesis* states that sex and curriculum choice are related. The level of significance is set at .05.

PROCEDURE

Finding the contingency coefficient is easy. You begin by finding chi square. You arrange the scores in a contingency table and determine the expected frequencies for each observed frequency. Next you use Formula 7-2, $\dfrac{\Sigma(O - E)^2}{E}$, to find chi square.[12] After you have found chi square, you determine whether it is significant or not. If it is significant, there is most likely a relationship, and you compute the contingency coefficient to indicate the degree of the relationship. You find C by inserting the value you found for chi square in the formula $\sqrt{\dfrac{\chi^2}{\chi^2 + N}}$. Now by looking at C you can see the strength of the relationship between the two variables.

Returning to the teacher's problem at the high school, let's solve it by using the contingency coefficient.

[12] Refer to Chapter 7 for a complete explanation of how to find chi square.

Formula 10-3	*Contingency Coefficient*

$$C = \sqrt{\frac{\chi^2}{\chi^2 + N}}$$

Directions for Finding the Contingency Coefficient

$N = \underline{75}$

1. Find N. Record the total number of subjects in the study. Write 75 opposite the N.

2. Find chi square (χ^2). Set up your worksheet as you did in Chapter 7 and find chi square.[13] Record the answer, 18.75, opposite χ^2.

$\chi^2 = \underline{18.75}$

3. Find df. Referring back to the original data, use the formula (rows − 1) × (columns − 1) to compute the degrees of freedom. Subtract 1 from the number of rows (3 − 1) and subtract 1 from the number of columns (2 − 1), and then take these values and multiply them together (2 × 1). Write 2 in the blank.

$df = \underline{2}$

4. Find the table value by using the chi-square distribution. Enter Table E with the df found in step 3. Run your fingers across this row until you are under the predetermined level of significance (.05). Write 5.99 in the blank.

$T = \underline{5.99}$

5. Statistical decision. If your chi-square value (18.75) is equal to or greater than the table value (5.99), reject the null hypothesis; if not, accept it. Write *reject* in the blank.

For this particular problem you rejected the null hypothesis, which said that the relationship between the two variables was 0. In this problem sex and curriculum choice seem to be related. Since χ^2 resulted in significance, we will compute C to determine the magnitude of the association between the variables. Now substitute in the formula and solve for C.

<u>reject</u>

6. Substitute in the formula for C. To make the appropriate substitutions, replace each step with its corresponding number.

[13] To help you locate your mistakes quicker, the expected table should look like this:

	Male	*Female*
College	$\frac{35 \times 25}{75} = 11.67$	$\frac{40 \times 25}{75} = 13.33$
General	$\frac{35 \times 25}{75} = 11.67$	$\frac{40 \times 25}{75} = 13.33$
Vocational	$\frac{35 \times 25}{75} = 11.67$	$\frac{40 \times 25}{75} = 13.33$

$$C = \sqrt{\frac{\chi^2}{\chi^2 + N}} = \sqrt{\frac{\text{step 2}}{\text{step 2} + \text{step 1}}} = \sqrt{\frac{18.75}{18.75 + 75}}$$

7. Solve the formula for C. Perform the operations in the square root first. (a) Add the denominator: $18.75 + 75 = 93.75$. (b) Divide the numerator by the denominator: $18.75 \div 93.75 = .20$. (c) Find the square root of .20 and record the answer opposite the C.

$C = .45$

(a) $C = \sqrt{\dfrac{18.75}{93.75}}$ (b) $C = \sqrt{.20}$ (c) $C = .45$

What Does C Mean?

Does a C of .45 mean there is a weak relationship? Is this coefficient interpreted the same way as the Pearson and the Spearman? No, the contingency coefficient is not interpreted the same way as the Pearson or the Spearman. In fact, it is very unclear what a C of .45 means. In the next paragraphs you will learn what interpretation is possible for the contingency coefficient.

The contingency coefficient is different from the Pearson product-moment coefficient and the Spearman rank coefficient. These coefficients can be negative and positive and range from $+1.00$ through 0 to -1.00, whereas the contingency coefficient is never negative;[14] its minimum value is 0 and it never quite reaches 1.0. If $C = 0$, there is no relationship. C's upper limit is a function of its number of categories (rows and columns). For example, if the data you are analyzing with C are recorded in a 2×2 table, the upper limit for C is .707 or .71. If the data you are analyzing are recorded in a 4×4 table, the upper limit of C is .866 or .87. In Table 10-8 the maximum values for C for tables up to and including size 10×10 are recorded.

Upper limits for tables that have the same number of rows and columns, that is 2×2, 3×3, are determined by the formula $C = \sqrt{\dfrac{(k-1)}{k}}$, where k is the number of rows or columns. For example, for a 2×2 table size, you would have $C\sqrt{\dfrac{2-1}{2}} = \sqrt{\dfrac{1}{2}} = \sqrt{.5}$, which is .707. All upper limits for tables where the number of rows do not equal the number of columns have been determined by a procedure explained in Peters and Van Voorhis (1940, pp. 393–399).

Looking at Table 10-8, you can see that as the number of categories increases, C becomes closer to 1. In thinking about this characteristic of C you can see the dif-

[14] It is not negative by definition.

Table 10-8: Upper Limit for the Contingency Coefficient for Tables up to and Including 10 × 10

Table size	Upper limit of C	Table size	Upper limit of C	Table size	Upper limit of C
2 × 2	.707	3 × 9	.843	6 × 6	.913
2 × 3	.685	3 × 10	.846	6 × 7	.930
2 × 4	.730	4 × 4	.866	6 × 8	.936
2 × 5	.753	4 × 5	.863	6 × 9	.941
2 × 6	.765	4 × 6	.877	6 × 10	.945
2 × 7	.774	4 × 7	.888	7 × 7	.926
2 × 8	.779	4 × 8	.893	7 × 8	.947
2 × 9	.783	4 × 9	.898	7 × 9	.952
2 × 10	.786	4 × 10	.901	7 × 10	.955
3 × 3	.816	5 × 5	.894	8 × 8	.935
3 × 4	.786	5 × 6	.904	8 × 9	.957
3 × 5	.810	5 × 7	.915	8 × 10	.961
3 × 6	.824	5 × 8	.920	9 × 9	.943
3 × 7	.833	5 × 9	.925	9 × 10	.966
3 × 8	.838	5 × 10	.929	10 × 10	.949

ficulties one would have in interpreting C if it is not close to its upper limit. It has been argued that except in the 2 × 2 case the measure cannot be interpreted (Lindgren, 1976, p. 442). Because of this property C is not comparable directly with other measures of coefficient of correlation, such as the Pearson product-moment correlation.[15] C can be compared with other values of C only when they are based on tables having the same number of rows and columns. You can compare a C based on a 2 × 2 table with a C based on another 2 × 2 table. You cannot compare a C based on a 2 × 2 table with a C based on a 4 × 4 table.

To summarize, if C is equal to zero there is no relationship. If C is close to its upper limit the relationship is strong. The difficult part is what to do if C is not very close to its upper limit; what the relationship looks like then is not at all clear. Let us return to our problem where we have a $C = .45$. The upper limit of C for a 2 × 3 is .685. A C of .45 tells us little about the strength of the relationship.

As practice, see if you can use the contingency coefficient to solve the following problem.

Problem   A driving instructor wanted to find out if there was a relationship between gender and passing or failing the driver's test. She chose a random sample of 75 people and classified them as male or

[15] A tedious correction has to be made to run this type of comparison.

Contingency Table

	Pass	Fail
Male	12	27
Female	26	10

female and as pass or fail on the driver's test. The data are re-corded in the contingency table above.

The *null hypothesis* states there is no relation between gender and passing or failing the driver's test. The *alternative hypothesis* states that there is a relationship between gender and passing or failing the test. The level of significance is set at .01. Find out if there is a relationship between these two variables. Calculate the *C* to determine approximate strength of this relationship.

Answer

Reject the null hypothesis. There appears to be a relationship between sex and passing or failing the driver's test. The χ^2 value was 12.87. The table value is 6.64. We reject the null hypothesis because the chi-square value is equal to 12.87, and this is greater than the table value of 6.64. The contingency table used to figure this answer follows.

	Pass	Fail
Male	$\dfrac{38 \times 39}{75} = 19.76$	$\dfrac{37 \times 39}{75} = 19.24$
Female	$\dfrac{38 \times 36}{75} = 18.24$	$\dfrac{37 \times 36}{75} = 17.76$

The upper limit for *C* on a 2×2 table is .707. The value found for *C* is .38. A *C* of .38 tells us little about the strength of the relationship.

The procedure just used for the contingency coefficient is summarized below.

Summary for the Contingency Coefficient	1. Arrange the values in a contingency table and find the expected frequencies.
	2. Compute chi square using the formula $\dfrac{\Sigma(O - E)^2}{E}$.
	3. Test chi square's significance by looking at Table E and using

the $df = (c - 1)(r - 1)$. If the value for χ^2 is equal to or greater than the table value, reject the null hypothesis.

4. Use the value for χ^2 to compute the value for C. Use the formula

$$C = \sqrt{\frac{\chi^2}{\chi^2 + N}}$$

5. Refer to Table 10-9 for C's upper limits.

A Few Comments on the Contingency Coefficient

After reading the previous paragraphs on the contingency coefficient and the problems in interpreting it, you may wonder why one would use this measure at all. There are four reasons why you might want to use it:

1. There are no assumptions involving the nature of the variables; they can be discrete or continuous.
2. Like other nonparametric tests it involves no assumptions about the shape of the distribution.
3. It is easy to compute.
4. When no other measure is applicable usually C can be used, because of its freedom from assumptions.

SUMMARY

This chapter has explored what correlation is. The three measures of correlation discussed were the Pearson product-moment coefficient, the Spearman rank coefficient, and the contingency coefficient. These measures are used when you are exploring the relationship between two variables. The uses of these techniques and their limitations were explained in detail.

The Pearson product-moment coefficient, a parametric technique used with interval data, makes more requirements of the researcher than the two other measures, most importantly normality and homoscedasticity.

The Spearman rank, a nonparametric technique used with ordinal data, stipulates that the individuals are to be ranked in two ordered sequences.

The contingency coefficient, a nonparametric technique used with nominal data, is free from the restrictions of a parametric test.

SELF-TEST FOR MASTERY

If you have trouble working a problem, reread the explanation on the page listed.

p. 307
1. Sketch approximately the scattergram you would expect for each correlation coefficient.
(a) −.95
(b) +.98
(c) −.04

p. 309
2. What do the following correlation coefficients mean?
(a) +1.00
(b) −1.00
(c) .00

p. 311
3. The sign of the coefficient indicates _____.

p. 311
4. The size of the coefficient of correlation indicates _____.

5. *Situation I.* A stock market analyst wanted to find out if there was a relationship between the cost of meat per kilogram and the Dow-Jones Average. He selected six days at random and recorded the price of meat and the Dow-Jones Average. The results are shown in the accompanying table.

Meat Cost and Dow-Jones Average

Days	Meat cost	Dow-Jones
1	$3.45	990
2	$3.50	989
3	$3.65	958
4	$3.55	966
5	$3.44	970
6	$3.47	966

The *null hypothesis* states there is no correlation between the cost of meat and the Dow-Jones Average. The *alternative hypothesis* states there is a relationship between the cost of meat and the Dow-Jones Average. A .05 level of significance is set. A two-tail test is used. Using the data in the table, perform (a) through (f).

p. 307
(a) Do a scattergram for these data.

p. 307
(b) What does the scattergram tell you?

p. 312
(c) What are three requirements for using the Pearson product-moment coefficient of correlation?

p. 316
(d) Calculate the Pearson *r*.

p. 320
(e) Did you reject the null hypothesis?

p. 323
(f) Interpret the *r* in terms of variance.

6. *Situation II.* A psychologist, living in a rural community, wanted to see if there was a relationship between aggressiveness and psychological dependence. He randomly selected nine subjects for his study. The variable *dependence* was measured by a score the subject received on a personality scale. The variable aggressiveness was measured by a score the subject received in the performance of certain tasks. The results are recorded in the accompanying table.

Nine Students Measured on Dependence and Aggressiveness

Student	Aggressiveness	Dependence
A	100	10
B	95	20
C	80	30
D	83	35
E	70	40
F	40	50
G	30	60
H	20	55
I	10	70

The *null hypothesis* states there is no correlation between aggressiveness and dependence. The *alternative hypothesis* states there is a negative relationship between being aggressive and being dependent. A .05 level of significance is set. A one-tail test is used. Use the table and perform (a) through (d).

p. 324
p. 325
p. 328
p. 329

(a) Why should you use the Spearman rho?
(b) Calculate the Spearman rho.
(c) Did you reject the null hypothesis?
(d) Interpret the results.

7. *Situation III.* A nutritionist was curious about the relationship between passing physics and eating breakfast in the morning. She randomly selected 50 students who were taking physics. She then recorded whether they passed or failed the course and whether or not they ate breakfast. The results are shown in the accompanying table.

50 Students' Physics Grades and Breakfast Habits

	Pass	Fail
Ate breakfast	17	10
No breakfast	15	8

The *null hypothesis* states there is no correlation between eating breakfast and passing physics. The *alternative hypothesis* states there is a relationship between eating breakfast and passing physics. A .01 level of significance is set. Use the table to perform (a) through (f).

p. 331   (a) Why should you use the contingency coefficient?
p. 333   (b) Did you reject the null hypothesis?
p. 334   (c) Whatever happened, what does it mean?
p. 333   (d) Calculate C, even if it is not necessary.
p. 334   (e) What is the highest value that is possible for C?
p. 335   (f) Interpret the C you obtained.

ANSWERS TO SELF-TEST

Score yourself by adding up the points for each correct answer and write the total in the Evaluation form.

2 points each   **1.**

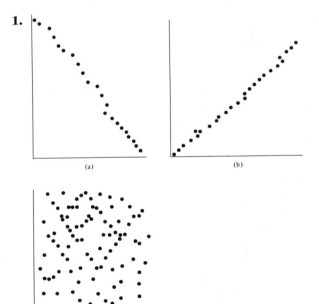

(a)   (b)

(c)

2 points each   **2.** (a) A perfect positive correlation. When one variable increases, the other variable increases.

(b) A perfect negative correlation. When one variable increases, the other variable decreases.

(c) Zero correlation. No linear relationship between the variables.

2 points   **3.** It shows direction.

2 points   **4.** The strength of the relationship between the two variables.

5. (a) A scattergram for the data.

5 points

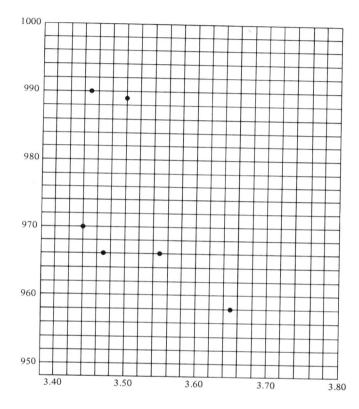

5 points   (b) The data are linear, homoscedastic, and appear to have no correlation.

5 points   (c) Interval level of measurement, linearity, and homoscedasticity.

10 points   (d) $r = \dfrac{(6)(220.82) - (3.06)(439)}{\sqrt{[(6)1.5920 - (3.06)^2][(6)32,997 - (439)^2]}}$
$= .59$

Shortcut method: 3 points subtracted from X variable and 900 subtracted from Y variable.

5 points   (e) No. This is a two-tailed alternative hypothesis. Table value is .8114.

5 points   (f) Of the variance Y, 35% can be accounted for by its correlation with X; the other 65% is explained by other factors.

5 points   **6.** (a) Ordinal data.

10 points   (b) Rho $= -.97$

5 points   (c) Yes, reject the null hypothesis. Accept the one-tailed alternative hypothesis. Table value $= .600$

5 points   (d) There is a strong negative correlation between dependency and aggressiveness.

5 points   **7.** (a) Categorical and nominal data.

5 points   (b) No, $\chi^2 = .03$. Table value $= 6.64$

5 points   (c) There is no relationship between eating breakfast and passing physics.

10 points   (d) $C = .02$

5 points   (e) $C = \sqrt{\dfrac{k-1}{k}} = \sqrt{\dfrac{2-1}{2}} = \sqrt{\dfrac{1}{2}} = .71$

5 points   (f) There is practically zero correlation, which means no relationship when interpreting C.

Evaluation

Rating	Evaluation
111	Perfect again?
96–110	Good job.
80–95	You pass.
0–79	You have your work cut out for you.

This evaluation ends the book. The appendix that follows includes a glossary of symbols, a list of formulas, references, and an index. It is up to you now to use what you've learned as you explore the frontier territory that is the social sciences.

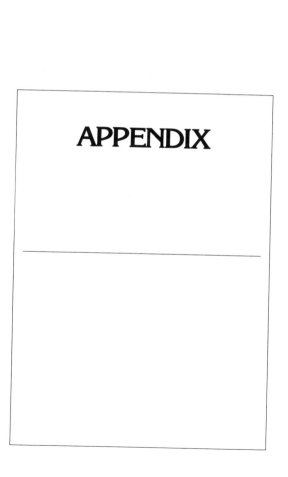

APPENDIX

Table A: Squares and Square Roots for Numbers 1 to 1000

N	N^2	$\sqrt{N}$	N	N^2	$\sqrt{N}$	N	N^2	$\sqrt{N}$	N	N^2	$\sqrt{N}$
1	1	1.0000	66	43 56	8.1240	131	1 71 61	11.4455	196	3 84 16	14.0000
2	4	1.4142	67	44 89	8.1854	132	1 74 24	11.4891	197	3 88 09	14.0357
3	9	1.7321	68	46 24	8.2462	133	1 76 89	11.5326	198	3 92 04	14.0712
4	16	2.0000	69	47 61	8.3066	134	1 79 56	11.5758	199	3 96 01	14.1067
5	25	2.2361	70	49 00	8.3666	135	1 82 25	11.6190	200	4 00 00	14.1421
6	36	2.4495	71	50 41	8.4261	136	1 84 96	11.6619	201	4 04 01	14.1774
7	49	2.6458	72	51 84	8.4853	137	1 87 69	11.7047	202	4 08 04	14.2127
8	64	2.8284	73	53 29	8.5440	138	1 90 44	11.7473	203	4 12 09	14.2478
9	81	3.0000	74	54 76	8.6023	139	1 93 21	11.7898	204	4 16 16	14.2829
10	1 00	3.1623	75	56 25	8.6603	140	1 96 00	11.8322	205	4 20 25	14.3178
11	1 21	3.3166	76	57 76	8.7178	141	1 98 81	11.8743	206	4 24 36	14.3527
12	1 44	3.4641	77	59 29	8.7750	142	2 01 64	11.9164	207	4 28 49	14.3875
13	1 69	3.6056	78	60 84	8.8318	143	2 04 49	11.9583	208	4 32 64	14.4222
14	1 96	3.7417	79	62 41	8.8882	144	2 07 36	12.0000	209	4 36 81	14.4568
15	2 25	3.8730	80	64 00	8.9443	145	2 10 25	12.0416	210	4 41 00	14.4914
16	2 56	4.0000	81	65 61	9.0000	146	2 13 16	12.0830	211	4 45 21	14.5258
17	2 89	4.1231	82	67 24	9.0554	147	2 16 09	12.1244	212	4 49 44	14.5602
18	3 24	4.2426	83	68 89	9.1104	148	2 19 04	12.1655	213	4 53 69	14.5945
19	3 61	4.3589	84	70 56	9.1652	149	2 22 01	12.2066	214	4 57 96	14.6287
20	4 00	4.4721	85	72 25	9.2195	150	2 25 00	12.2474	215	4 62 25	14.6629
21	4 41	4.5826	86	73 96	9.2736	151	2 28 01	12.2882	216	4 66 56	14.6969
22	4 84	4.6904	87	75 69	9.3274	152	2 31 04	12.3288	217	4 70 89	14.7309
23	5 29	4.7958	88	77 44	9.3808	153	2 34 09	12.3693	218	4 75 24	14.7648
24	5 76	4.8990	89	79 21	9.4340	154	2 37 16	12.4097	219	4 79 61	14.7986
25	6 25	5.0000	90	81 00	9.4868	155	2 40 25	12.4499	220	4 84 00	14.8324
26	6 76	5.0990	91	82 81	9.5394	156	2 43 36	12.4900	221	4 88 41	14.8661
27	7 29	5.1962	92	84 64	9.5917	157	2 46 49	12.5300	222	4 92 84	14.8997
28	7 84	5.2915	93	86 49	9.6437	158	2 49 64	12.5698	223	4 97 29	14.9332
29	8 41	5.3852	94	88 36	9.6954	159	2 52 81	12.6095	224	5 01 76	14.9666
30	9 00	5.4772	95	90 25	9.7468	160	2 56 00	12.6491	225	5 06 25	15.0000
31	9 61	5.5678	96	92 16	9.7980	161	2 59 21	12.6886	226	5 10 76	15.0333
32	10 24	5.6569	97	94 09	9.8489	162	2 62 44	12.7279	227	5 15 29	15.0665
33	10 89	5.7446	98	96 04	9.8995	163	2 65 69	12.7671	228	5 19 84	15.0997
34	11 56	5.8310	99	98 01	9.9499	164	2 68 96	12.8062	229	5 24 41	15.1327
35	12 25	5.9161	100	1 00 00	10.0000	165	2 72 25	12.8452	230	5 29 00	15.1658
36	12 96	6.0000	101	1 02 01	10.0499	166	2 75 56	12.8841	231	5 33 61	15.1987
37	13 69	6.0828	102	1 04 04	10.0995	167	2 78 89	12.9228	232	5 38 24	15.2315
38	14 44	6.1644	103	1 06 09	10.1489	168	2 82 24	12.9615	233	5 42 89	15.2643
39	15 21	6.2450	104	1 08 16	10.1980	169	2 85 61	13.0000	234	5 47 56	15.2971
40	16 00	6.3246	105	1 10 25	10.2470	170	2 89 00	13.0384	235	5 52 25	15.3297
41	16 81	6.4031	106	1 12 36	10.2956	171	2 92 41	13.0767	236	5 56 96	15.3623
42	17 64	6.4807	107	1 14 49	10.3441	172	2 95 84	13.1149	237	5 61 69	15.3948
43	18 49	6.5574	108	1 16 64	10.3923	173	2 99 29	13.1529	238	5 66 44	15.4272
44	19 36	6.6332	109	1 18 81	10.4403	174	3 02 76	13.1909	239	5 71 21	15.4596
45	20 25	6.7082	110	1 21 00	10.4881	175	3 06 25	13.2288	240	5 76 00	15.4919
46	21 16	6.7823	111	1 23 21	10.5357	176	3 09 76	13.2665	241	5 80 81	15.5242
47	22 09	6.8557	112	1 25 44	10.5830	177	3 13 29	13.3041	242	5 85 64	15.5563
48	23 04	6.9282	113	1 27 69	10.6301	178	3 16 84	13.3417	243	5 90 49	15.5885
49	24 01	7.0000	114	1 29 96	10.6771	179	3 20 41	13.3791	244	5 95 36	15.6205
50	25 00	7.0711	115	1 32 25	10.7238	180	3 24 00	13.4164	245	6 00 25	15.6525
51	26 01	7.1414	116	1 34 56	10.7703	181	3 27 61	13.4536	246	6 05 16	15.6844
52	27 04	7.2111	117	1 36 89	10.8167	182	3 31 24	13.4907	247	6 10 09	15.7162
53	28 09	7.2801	118	1 39 24	10.8628	183	3 34 89	13.5277	248	6 15 04	15.7480
54	29 16	7.3485	119	1 41 61	10.9087	184	3 38 56	13.5647	249	6 20 01	15.7797
55	30 25	7.4162	120	1 44 00	10.9545	185	3 42 25	13.6015	250	6 25 00	15.8114
56	31 36	7.4833	121	1 46 41	11.0000	186	3 45 96	13.6382	251	6 30 01	15.8430
57	32 49	7.5498	122	1 48 84	11.0454	187	3 49 69	13.6748	252	6 35 04	15.8745
58	33 64	7.6158	123	1 51 29	11.0905	188	3 53 44	13.7113	253	6 40 09	15.9060
59	34 81	7.6811	124	1 53 76	11.1355	189	3 57 21	13.7477	254	6 45 16	15.9374
60	36 00	7.7460	125	1 56 25	11.1803	190	3 61 00	13.7840	255	6 50 25	15.9687
61	37 21	7.8102	126	1 58 76	11.2250	191	3 64 81	13.8203	256	6 55 36	16.0000
62	38 44	7.8740	127	1 61 29	11.2694	192	3 68 64	13.8564	257	6 60 49	16.0312
63	39 69	7.9373	128	1 63 84	11.3137	193	3 72 49	13.8924	258	6 65 64	16.0624
64	40 96	8.0000	129	1 66 41	11.3578	194	3 76 36	13.9284	259	6 70 81	16.0935
65	42 25	8.0623	130	1 69 00	11.4018	195	3 80 25	13.9642	260	6 76 00	16.1245

Source: Abridged from *Fundamental Statistics in Psychology and Education*, Fifth Edition, by J. P. Guilford and Benjamin Fruchter, copyright © 1973, McGraw Hill. Used with permission of McGraw-Hill Book Company.

N	N^2	$\sqrt{N}$	N	N^2	$\sqrt{N}$	N	N^2	$\sqrt{N}$	N	N^2	$\sqrt{N}$
261	6 81 21	16.1555	336	11 28 96	18.3303	411	16 89 21	20.2731	486	23 61 96	22.0454
262	6 86 44	16.1864	337	11 35 69	18.3576	412	16 97 44	20.2978	487	23 71 69	22.0681
263	6 91 69	16.2173	338	11 42 44	18.3848	413	17 05 69	20.3224	488	23 81 44	22.0907
264	6 96 96	16.2481	339	11 49 21	18.4120	414	17 13 96	20.3470	489	23 91 21	22.1133
265	7 02 25	16.2788	340	11 56 00	18.4391	415	17 22 25	20.3715	490	24 01 00	22.1359
266	7 07 56	16.3095	341	11 62 81	18.4662	416	17 30 56	20.3961	491	24 10 81	22.1585
267	7 12 89	16.3401	342	11 69 64	18.4932	417	17 38 89	20.4206	492	24 20 64	22.1811
268	7 18 24	16.3707	343	11 76 49	18.5203	418	17 47 24	20.4450	493	24 30 49	22.2036
269	7 23 61	16.4012	344	11 83 36	18.5472	419	17 55 61	20.4695	494	24 40 36	22.2261
270	7 29 00	16.4317	345	11 90 25	18.5742	420	17 64 00	20.4939	495	24 50 25	22.2486
271	7 34 41	16.4621	346	11 97 16	18.6011	421	17 72 41	20.5183	496	24 60 16	22.2711
272	7 39 84	16.4924	347	12 04 09	18.6279	422	17 80 84	20.5426	497	24 70 09	22.2935
273	7 45 29	16.5227	348	12 11 04	18.6548	423	17 89 29	20.5670	498	24 80 04	22.3159
274	7 50 76	16.5529	349	12 18 01	18.6815	424	17 97 76	20.5913	499	24 90 01	22.3383
275	7 56 25	16.5831	350	12 25 00	18.7083	425	18 06 25	20.6155	500	25 00 00	22.3607
276	7 61 76	16.6132	351	12 32 01	18.7350	426	18 14 76	20.6398	501	25 10 01	22.3830
277	7 67 29	16.6433	352	12 39 04	18.7617	427	18 23 29	20.6640	502	25 20 04	22.4054
278	7 72 84	16.6733	353	12 46 09	18.7883	428	18 31 84	20.6882	503	25 30 09	22.4277
279	7 78 41	16.7033	354	12 53 16	18.8149	429	18 40 41	20.7123	504	25 40 16	22.4499
280	7 84 00	16.7332	355	12 60 25	18.8414	430	18 49 00	20.7364	505	25 50 25	22.4722
281	7 89 61	16.7631	356	12 67 36	18.8680	431	18 57 61	20.7605	506	25 60 36	22.4944
282	7 95 24	16.7929	357	12 74 49	18.8944	432	18 66 24	20.7846	507	25 70 49	22.5167
283	8 00 89	16.8226	358	12 81 64	18.9209	433	18 74 89	20.8087	508	25 80 64	22.5389
284	8 06 56	16.8523	359	12 88 81	18.9473	434	18 83 56	20.8327	509	25 90 81	22.5610
285	8 12 25	16.8819	360	12 96 00	18.9737	435	18 92 25	20.8567	510	26 01 00	22.5832
286	8 17 96	16.9115	361	13 03 21	19.0000	436	19 00 96	20.8806	511	26 11 21	22.6053
287	8 23 69	16.9411	362	13 10 44	19.0263	437	19 09 69	20.9045	512	26 21 44	22.6274
288	8 29 44	16.9706	363	13 17 69	19.0526	438	19 18 44	20.9284	513	26 31 69	22.6495
289	8 35 21	17.0000	364	13 24 96	19.0788	439	19 27 21	20.9523	514	26 41 96	22.6716
290	8 41 00	17.0294	365	13 32 25	19.1050	440	19 36 00	20.9762	515	26 52 25	22.6936
291	8 46 81	17.0587	366	13 39 56	19.1311	441	19 44 81	21.0000	516	26 62 56	22.7156
292	8 52 64	17.0880	367	13 46 89	19.1572	442	19 53 64	21.0238	517	26 72 89	22.7376
293	8 58 49	17.1172	368	13 54 24	19.1833	443	19 62 49	21.0476	518	26 83 24	22.7596
294	8 64 36	17.1464	369	13 61 61	19.2094	444	19 71 36	21.0713	519	26 93 61	22.7816
295	8 70 25	17.1756	370	13 69 00	19.2354	445	19 80 25	21.0950	520	27 04 00	22.8035
296	8 76 16	17.2047	371	13 76 41	19.2614	446	19 89 16	21.1187	521	27 14 41	22.8254
297	8 82 09	17.2337	372	13 83 84	19.2873	447	19 98 09	21.1424	522	27 24 84	22.8473
298	8 88 04	17.2627	373	13 91 29	19.3132	448	20 07 04	21.1660	523	27 35 29	22.8692
299	8 94 01	17.2916	374	13 98 76	19.3391	449	20 16 01	21.1896	524	27 45 76	22.8910
300	9 00 00	17.3205	375	14 06 25	19.3649	450	20 25 00	21.2132	525	27 56 25	22.9129
301	9 06 01	17.3494	376	14 13 76	19.3907	451	20 34 01	21.2368	526	27 66 76	22.9347
302	9 12 04	17.3781	377	14 21 29	19.4165	452	20 43 04	21.2603	527	27 77 29	22.9565
303	9 18 09	17.4069	378	14 28 84	19.4422	453	20 52 09	21.2838	528	27 87 84	22.9783
304	9 24 16	17.4356	379	14 36 41	19.4679	454	20 61 16	21.3073	529	27 98 41	23.0000
305	9 30 25	17.4642	380	14 44 00	19.4936	455	20 70 25	21.3307	530	28 09 00	23.0217
306	9 36 36	17.4929	381	14 51 61	19.5192	456	20 79 36	21.3542	531	28 19 61	23.0434
307	9 42 49	17.5214	382	14 59 24	19.5448	457	20 88 49	21.3776	532	28 30 24	23.0651
308	9 48 64	17.5499	383	14 66 89	19.5704	458	20 97 64	21.4009	533	28 40 89	23.0868
309	9 54 81	17.5784	384	14 74 56	19.5959	459	21 06 81	21.4243	534	28 51 56	23.1084
310	9 61 00	17.6068	385	14 82 25	19.6214	460	21 16 00	21.4476	535	28 62 25	23.1301
311	9 67 21	17.6352	386	14 89 96	19.6469	461	21 25 21	21.4709	536	28 72 96	23.1517
312	9 73 44	17.6635	387	14 97 69	19.6723	462	21 34 44	21.4942	537	28 83 69	23.1733
313	9 79 69	17.6918	388	15 05 44	19.6977	463	21 43 69	21.5174	538	28 94 44	23.1948
314	9 85 96	17.7200	389	15 13 21	19.7231	464	21 52 96	21.5407	539	29 05 21	23.2164
315	9 92 25	17.7482	390	15 21 00	19.7484	465	21 62 25	21.5639	540	29 16 00	23.2379
316	9 98 56	17.7764	391	15 28 81	19.7737	466	21 71 56	21.5870	541	29 26 81	23.2594
317	10 04 89	17.8045	392	15 36 64	19.7990	467	21 80 89	21.6102	542	29 37 64	23.2809
318	10 11 24	17.8326	393	15 44 49	19.8242	468	21 90 24	21.6333	543	29 48 49	23.3024
319	10 17 61	17.8606	394	15 52 36	19.8494	469	21 99 61	21.6564	544	29 59 36	23.3238
320	10 24 00	17.8885	395	15 60 25	19.8746	470	22 09 00	21.6795	545	29 70 25	23.3452
321	10 30 41	17.9165	396	15 68 16	19.8997	471	22 18 41	21.7025	546	29 81 16	23.3666
322	10 36 84	17.9444	397	15 76 09	19.9249	472	22 27 84	21.7256	547	29 92 09	23.3880
323	10 43 29	17.9722	398	15 84 04	19.9499	473	22 37 29	21.7486	548	30 03 04	23.4094
324	10 49 76	18.0000	399	15 92 01	19.9750	474	22 46 76	21.7715	549	30 14 01	23.4307
325	10 56 25	18.0278	400	16 00 00	20.0000	475	22 56 25	21.7945	550	30 25 00	23.4521
326	10 62 76	18.0555	401	16 08 01	20.0250	476	22 65 76	21.8174	551	30 36 01	23.4734
327	10 69 29	18.0831	402	16 16 04	20.0499	477	22 75 29	21.8403	552	30 47 04	23.4947
328	10 75 84	18.1108	403	16 24 09	20.0749	478	22 84 84	21.8632	553	30 58 09	23.5160
329	10 82 41	18.1384	404	16 32 16	20.0998	479	22 94 41	21.8861	554	30 69 16	23.5372
330	10 89 00	18.1659	405	16 40 25	20.1246	480	23 04 00	21.9089	555	30 80 25	23.5584
331	10 95 61	18.1934	406	16 48 36	20.1494	481	23 13 61	21.9317	556	30 91 36	23.5797
332	11 02 24	18.2209	407	16 56 49	20.1742	482	23 23 24	21.9545	557	31 02 49	23.6008
333	11 08 89	18.2483	408	16 64 64	20.1990	483	23 32 89	21.9773	558	31 13 64	23.6220
334	11 15 56	18.2757	409	16 72 81	20.2237	484	23 42 56	22.0000	559	31 24 81	23.6432
335	11 22 25	18.3030	410	16 81 00	20.2485	485	23 52 25	22.0227	560	31 36 00	23.6643

N	N²	√N	N	N²	√N	N	N²	√N	N	N²	√N
561	31 47 21	23.6854	636	40 44 96	25.2190	711	50 55 21	26.6646	786	61 77 96	28.0357
562	31 58 44	23.7065	637	40 57 69	25.2389	712	50 69 44	26.6833	787	61 93 69	28.0535
563	31 69 69	23.7276	638	40 70 44	25.2587	713	50 83 69	26.7021	788	62 09 44	28.0713
564	31 80 96	23.7487	639	40 83 21	25.2784	714	50 97 96	26.7208	789	62 25 21	28.0891
565	31 92 25	23.7697	640	40 96 00	25.2982	715	51 12 25	26.7395	790	62 41 00	28.1069
566	32 03 56	23.7908	641	41 08 81	25.3180	716	51 26 56	26.7582	791	62 56 81	28.1247
567	32 14 89	23.8118	642	41 21 64	25.3377	717	51 40 89	26.7769	792	62 72 64	28.1425
568	32 26 24	23.8328	643	41 34 49	25.3574	718	51 55 24	26.7955	793	62 88 49	28.1603
569	32 37 61	23.8537	644	41 47 36	25.3772	719	51 69 61	26.8142	794	63 04 36	28.1780
570	32 49 00	23.8747	645	41 60 25	25.3969	720	51 84 00	26.8328	795	63 20 25	28.1957
571	32 60 41	23.8956	646	41 73 16	25.4165	721	51 98 41	26.8514	796	63 36 16	28.2135
572	32 71 84	23.9165	647	41 86 09	25.4362	722	52 12 84	26.8701	797	63 52 09	28.2312
573	32 83 29	23.9374	648	41 99 04	25.4558	723	52 27 29	26.8887	798	63 68 04	28.2489
574	32 94 76	23.9583	649	42 12 01	25.4775	724	52 41 76	26.9072	799	63 84 01	28.2666
575	33 06 25	23.9792	650	42 25 00	25.4951	725	52 56 25	26.9258	800	64 00 00	28.2843
576	33 17 76	24.0000	651	42 38 01	25.5147	726	52 70 76	26.9444	801	64 16 01	28.3019
577	33 29 29	24.0208	652	42 51 04	25.5343	727	52 85 29	26.9629	802	64 32 04	28.3196
578	33 40 84	24.0416	653	42 64 09	25.5539	728	52 99 84	26.9815	803	64 48 09	28.3373
579	33 52 41	24.0624	654	42 77 16	25.5734	729	53 14 41	27.0000	804	64 64 16	28.3549
580	33 64 00	24.0832	655	42 90 25	25.5930	730	53 29 00	27.0185	805	64 80 25	28.3725
581	33 75 61	24.1039	656	43 03 36	25.6125	731	53 43 61	27.0370	806	64 96 36	28.3901
582	33 87 24	24.1247	657	43 16 49	25.6320	732	53 58 24	27.0555	807	65 12 49	28.4077
583	33 98 89	24.1454	658	43 29 64	25.6515	733	53 72 89	27.0740	808	65 28 64	28.4253
584	34 10 56	24.1661	659	43 42 81	25.6710	734	53 87 56	27.0924	809	65 44 81	28.4429
585	34 22 25	24.1868	660	43 56 00	25.6905	735	54 02 25	27.1109	810	65 61 00	28.4605
586	34 33 96	24.2074	661	43 69 21	25.7099	736	54 16 96	27.1293	811	65 77 21	28.4781
587	34 45 69	24.2281	662	43 82 44	25.7294	737	54 31 69	27.1477	812	65 93 44	28.4956
588	34 57 44	24.2487	663	43 95 69	25.7488	738	54 46 44	27.1662	813	66 09 69	28.5132
589	34 69 21	24.2693	664	44 08 96	25.7682	739	54 61 21	27.1846	814	66 25 96	28.5307
590	34 81 00	24.2899	665	44 22 25	25.7876	740	54 76 00	27.2029	815	66 42 25	28.5482
591	34 92 81	24.3105	666	44 35 56	25.8070	741	54 90 81	27.2213	816	66 58 56	28.5657
592	35 04 64	24.3311	667	44 48 89	25.8263	742	55 05 64	27.2397	817	66 74 89	28.5832
593	35 16 49	24.3516	668	44 62 24	25.8457	743	55 20 49	27.2580	818	66 91 24	28.6007
594	35 28 36	24.3721	669	44 75 61	25.8650	744	55 35 36	27.2764	819	67 07 61	28.6182
595	35 40 25	24.3926	670	44 89 00	25.8844	745	55 50 25	27.2947	820	67 24 00	28.6356
596	35 52 16	24.4131	671	45 02 41	25.9037	746	55 65 16	27.3130	821	67 40 41	28.6531
597	35 64 09	24.4336	672	45 15 84	25.9230	747	55 80 09	27.3313	822	67 56 84	28.6705
598	35 76 04	24.4540	673	45 29 29	25.9422	748	55 95 04	27.3496	823	67 73 29	28.6880
599	35 88 01	24.4745	674	45 42 76	25.9615	749	56 10 01	27.3679	824	67 89 76	28.7054
600	36 00 00	24.4949	675	45 56 25	25.9808	750	56 25 00	27.3861	825	68 06 25	28.7228
601	36 12 01	24.5153	676	45 69 76	26.0000	751	56 40 01	27.4044	826	68 22 76	28.7402
602	36 24 04	24.5357	677	45 83 29	26.0192	752	56 55 04	27.4226	827	68 39 29	28.7576
603	36 36 09	24.5561	678	45 96 84	26.0384	753	56 70 09	27.4408	828	68 55 84	28.7750
604	36 48 16	24.5764	679	46 10 41	26.0576	754	56 85 16	27.4591	829	68 72 41	28.7924
605	36 60 25	24.5967	680	46 24 00	26.0768	755	57 00 25	27.4773	830	68 89 00	28.8097
606	36 72 36	24.6171	681	46 37 61	26.0960	756	57 15 36	27.4955	831	69 05 61	28.8271
607	36 84 49	24.6374	682	46 51 24	26.1151	757	57 30 49	27.5136	832	69 22 24	28.8444
608	36 96 64	24.6577	683	46 64 89	26.1343	758	57 45 64	27.5318	833	69 38 89	28.8617
609	37 08 81	24.6779	684	46 78 56	26.1534	759	57 60 81	27.5500	834	69 55 56	28.8791
610	37 21 00	24.6982	685	46 92 25	26.1725	760	57 76 00	27.5681	835	69 72 25	28.8964
611	37 33 21	24.7184	686	47 05 96	26.1916	761	57 91 21	27.5862	836	69 88 96	28.9137
612	37 45 44	24.7386	687	47 19 69	26.2107	762	58 06 44	27.6043	837	70 05 69	28.9310
613	37 57 69	24.7588	688	47 33 44	26.2298	763	58 21 69	27.6225	838	70 22 44	28.9482
614	37 69 96	24.7790	689	47 47 21	26.2488	764	58 36 96	27.6405	839	70 39 21	28.9655
615	37 82 25	24.7992	690	47 61 00	26.2679	765	58 52 25	27.6586	840	70 56 00	28.9828
616	37 94 56	24.8193	691	47 74 81	26.2869	766	58 67 56	27.6767	841	70 72 81	29.0000
617	38 06 89	24.8395	692	47 88 64	26.3059	767	58 82 89	27.6948	842	70 89 64	29.0172
618	38 19 24	24.8596	693	48 02 49	26.3249	768	58 98 24	27.7128	843	71 06 49	29.0345
619	38 31 61	24.8797	694	48 16 36	26.3439	769	59 13 61	27.7308	844	71 23 36	29.0517
620	38 44 00	24.8998	695	48 30 25	26.3629	770	59 29 00	27.7489	845	71 40 25	29.0689
621	38 56 41	24.9199	696	48 44 16	26.3818	771	59 44 41	27.7669	846	71 57 16	29.0861
622	38 68 84	24.9399	697	48 58 09	26.4008	772	59 59 84	27.7849	847	71 74 09	29.1033
623	38 81 29	24.9600	698	48 72 04	26.4197	773	59 75 29	27.8029	848	71 91 04	29.1204
624	38 93 76	24.9800	699	48 86 01	26.4386	774	59 90 76	27.8209	849	72 08 01	29.1376
625	39 06 25	25.0000	700	49 00 00	26.4575	775	60 06 25	27.8388	850	72 25 00	29.1548
626	39 18 76	25.0200	701	49 14 01	26.4764	776	60 21 76	27.8568	851	72 42 01	29.1719
627	39 31 29	25.0400	702	49 28 04	26.4953	777	60 37 29	27.8747	852	72 59 04	29.1890
628	39 43 84	25.0599	703	49 42 09	26.5141	778	60 52 84	27.8927	853	72 76 09	29.2062
629	39 56 41	25.0799	704	49 56 16	26.5330	779	60 68 41	27.9106	854	72 93 16	29.2233
630	39 69 00	25.0998	705	49 70 25	26.5518	780	60 84 00	27.9285	855	73 10 25	29.2404
631	39 81 61	25.1197	706	49 84 36	26.5707	781	60 99 61	27.9464	856	73 27 36	29.2575
632	39 94 24	25.1396	707	49 98 49	26.5895	782	61 15 24	27.9643	857	73 44 49	29.2746
633	40 06 89	25.1595	708	50 12 64	26.6083	783	61 30 89	27.9821	858	73 61 64	29.2916
634	40 19 56	25.1794	709	50 26 81	26.6271	784	61 46 56	28.0000	859	73 78 81	29.3087
635	40 32 25	25.1992	710	50 41 00	26.6458	785	61 62 25	28.0179	860	73 96 00	29.3258

N	N²	√N	N	N²	√N	N	N²	√N	N	N²	√N
861	74 13 21	29.3428	896	80 28 16	29.9333	931	86 67 61	30.5123	966	93 31 56	31.0805
862	74 30 44	29.3598	897	80 46 09	29.9500	932	86 86 24	30.5287	967	93 50 89	31.0966
863	74 47 69	29.3769	898	80 64 04	29.9666	933	87 04 89	30.5450	968	93 70 24	31.1127
864	74 64 96	29.3939	899	80 82 01	29.9833	934	87 23 56	30.5614	969	93 89 61	31.1288
865	74 82 25	29.4109	900	81 00 00	30.0000	935	87 42 25	30.5778	970	94 09 00	31.1448
866	74 99 56	29.4279	901	81 18 01	30.0167	936	87 60 96	30.5941	971	94 28 41	31.1609
867	75 16 89	29.4449	902	81 36 04	30.0333	937	87 79 69	30.6105	972	94 47 84	31.1769
868	75 34 24	29.4618	903	81 54 09	30.0500	938	87 98 44	30.6268	973	94 67 29	31.1929
869	75 51 61	29.4788	904	81 72 16	30.0666	939	88 17 21	30.6431	974	94 86 76	31.2090
870	75 69 00	29.4958	905	81 90 25	30.0832	940	88 36 00	30.6594	975	95 06 25	31.2250
871	75 86 41	29.5127	906	82 08 36	30.0998	941	88 54 81	30.6757	976	95 25 76	31.2410
872	76 03 84	29.5296	907	82 26 49	30.1164	942	88 73 64	30.6920	977	95 45 29	31.2570
873	76 21 29	29.5466	908	82 44 64	30.1330	943	88 92 49	30.7083	978	95 64 84	31.2730
874	76 38 76	29.5635	909	82 62 81	30.1496	944	89 11 36	30.7246	979	95 84 41	31.2890
875	76 56 25	29.5804	910	82 81 00	30.1662	945	89 30 25	30.7409	980	96 04 00	31.3050
876	76 73 76	29.5973	911	82 99 21	30.1828	946	89 49 16	30.7571	981	96 23 61	31.3209
877	76 91 29	29.6142	912	83 17 44	30.1993	947	89 68 09	30.7734	982	96 43 24	31.3369
878	77 08 84	29.6311	913	83 35 69	30.2159	948	89 87 04	30.7896	983	96 62 89	31.3528
879	77 26 41	29.6479	914	83 53 96	30.2324	949	90 06 01	30.8058	984	96 82 56	31.3688
880	77 44 00	29.6648	915	83 72 25	30.2490	950	90 25 00	30.8221	985	97 02 25	31.3847
881	77 61 61	29.6816	916	83 90 56	30.2655	951	90 44 01	30.8383	986	97 21 96	31.4006
882	77 79 24	29.6985	917	84 08 89	30.2820	952	90 63 04	30.8545	987	97 41 69	31.4166
883	77 96 89	29.7153	918	84 27 24	30.2985	953	90 82 09	30.8707	988	97 61 44	31.4325
884	78 14 56	29.7321	919	84 45 61	30.3150	954	91 01 16	30.8869	989	97 81 21	31.4484
885	78 32 25	29.7489	920	84 64 00	30.3315	955	91 20 25	30.9031	990	98 01 00	31.4643
886	78 49 96	29.7658	921	84 82 41	30.3480	956	91 39 36	30.9192	991	98 20 81	31.4802
887	78 67 69	29.7825	922	85 00 84	30.3645	957	91 58 49	30.9354	992	98 40 64	31.4960
888	78 85 44	29.7993	923	85 19 29	30.3809	958	91 77 64	30.9516	993	98 60 49	31.5119
889	79 03 21	29.8161	924	85 37 76	30.3974	959	91 96 81	30.9677	994	98 80 36	31.5278
890	79 21 00	29.8329	925	85 56 25	30.4138	960	92 16 00	30.9839	995	99 00 25	31.5436
891	79 38 81	29.8496	926	85 74 76	30.4302	961	92 35 21	31.0000	996	99 20 16	31.5595
892	79 56 64	29.8664	927	85 93 29	30.4467	962	92 54 44	31.0161	997	99 40 09	31.5753
893	79 74 49	29.8831	928	86 11 84	30.4631	963	92 73 69	31.0322	998	99 60 04	31.5911
894	79 92 36	29.8998	929	86 30 41	30.4795	964	92 92 96	31.0483	999	99 80 01	31.6070
895	80 10 25	29.9166	930	86 49 00	30.4959	965	93 12 25	31.0644	1,000	1 00 00 00	31.6228

Table B: Random Numbers

03 47 43 73 86	36 96 47 36 61	46 98 63 71 62	33 26 16 80 45	60 11 14 10 95
97 74 24 67 62	42 81 14 57 20	42 53 32 37 32	27 07 36 07 51	24 51 79 89 73
16 76 62 27 66	56 50 26 71 07	32 90 79 78 53	13 55 38 58 59	88 97 54 14 10
12 56 85 99 26	96 96 68 27 31	05 03 72 93 15	57 12 10 14 21	88 26 49 81 76
55 59 56 35 64	38 54 82 46 22	31 62 43 09 90	06 18 44 32 53	23 83 01 30 30
16 22 77 94 39	49 54 43 54 82	17 37 93 23 78	87 35 20 96 43	84 26 34 91 64
84 42 17 53 31	57 24 55 06 88	77 04 74 47 67	21 76 33 50 25	83 92 12 06 76
63 01 63 78 59	16 95 55 67 19	98 10 50 71 75	12 86 73 58 07	44 39 52 38 79
33 21 12 34 29	78 64 56 07 82	52 42 07 44 38	15 51 00 13 42	99 66 02 79 54
57 60 86 32 44	09 47 27 96 54	49 17 46 09 62	90 52 84 77 27	08 02 73 43 28
18 18 07 92 46	44 17 16 58 09	79 83 86 19 62	06 76 50 03 10	55 23 64 05 05
26 62 38 97 75	84 16 07 44 99	83 11 46 32 24	20 14 85 88 45	10 93 72 88 71
23 42 40 64 74	82 97 77 77 81	07 45 32 14 08	32 98 94 07 72	93 85 79 10 75
52 36 28 19 95	50 92 26 11 97	00 56 76 31 38	80 22 02 53 53	86 60 42 04 53
37 85 94 35 12	83 39 50 08 30	42 34 07 96 88	54 42 06 87 98	35 85 29 48 39
70 29 17 12 13	40 33 20 38 26	13 89 51 03 74	17 76 37 13 04	07 74 21 19 30
56 62 18 37 35	96 83 50 87 75	97 12 25 93 47	70 33 24 03 54	97 77 46 44 80
99 49 57 22 77	88 42 95 45 72	16 64 36 16 00	04 43 18 66 79	94 77 24 21 90
16 08 15 04 72	33 27 14 34 09	45 59 34 68 49	12 72 07 34 45	99 27 72 95 14
31 16 93 32 43	50 27 89 87 19	20 15 37 00 49	52 85 66 60 44	38 68 88 11 80
68 34 30 13 70	55 74 30 77 40	44 22 78 84 26	04 33 46 09 52	68 07 97 06 57
74 57 25 65 76	59 29 97 68 60	71 91 38 67 54	13 58 18 24 76	15 54 55 95 52
27 42 37 86 53	48 55 90 65 72	96 57 69 36 10	96 46 92 42 45	97 60 49 04 91
00 39 68 29 61	66 37 32 20 30	77 84 57 03 29	10 45 65 04 26	11 04 96 67 24
29 94 98 94 24	68 49 69 10 82	53 75 91 93 30	34 25 20 57 27	40 48 73 51 92
16 90 82 66 59	83 62 64 11 12	67 19 00 71 74	60 47 21 29 68	02 02 37 03 31
11 27 94 75 06	06 09 19 74 66	02 94 37 34 02	76 70 90 30 86	38 45 94 30 38
35 24 10 16 20	33 32 51 26 38	79 78 45 04 91	16 92 53 56 16	02 75 50 95 98
38 23 16 86 38	42 38 97 01 50	87 75 66 81 41	40 01 74 91 62	48 51 84 08 32
31 96 25 91 47	96 44 33 49 13	34 86 82 53 91	00 52 43 48 85	27 55 26 89 62
56 67 40 67 14	64 05 71 95 86	11 05 65 09 68	76 83 20 37 90	57 16 00 11 66
14 90 84 45 11	75 73 88 05 90	52 27 41 14 86	22 98 12 22 08	07 52 74 95 80
68 05 51 18 00	33 96 02 75 19	07 60 62 93 55	59 33 82 43 90	49 37 38 44 59
20 46 78 73 90	97 51 40 14 02	04 02 33 31 08	39 54 16 49 36	47 95 93 13 30
64 19 58 97 79	15 06 15 93 20	01 90 10 75 06	40 78 78 89 62	02 67 74 17 33
05 26 93 70 60	22 35 85 15 13	92 03 51 59 77	59 56 78 06 83	52 91 05 70 74
07 97 10 88 23	09 98 42 99 64	61 71 62 99 15	06 51 29 16 93	58 05 77 09 51
68 71 86 85 85	54 87 66 47 54	73 32 08 11 12	44 95 92 63 16	29 56 24 29 48
26 99 61 65 53	58 37 78 80 70	42 10 50 67 42	32 17 55 85 74	94 44 67 16 94
14 65 52 68 75	87 59 36 22 41	26 78 63 06 55	13 08 27 01 50	15 29 39 39 43
17 53 77 58 71	71 41 61 50 72	12 41 94 96 26	44 95 27 36 99	02 96 74 30 83
90 26 59 21 19	23 52 23 33 12	96 93 02 18 39	07 02 18 36 07	25 99 32 70 23
41 23 52 55 99	31 04 49 69 96	10 47 48 45 88	13 41 43 89 20	97 17 14 49 17
60 20 50 81 69	31 99 73 68 68	35 81 33 03 76	24 30 12 48 60	18 99 10 72 34
91 25 38 05 90	94 58 28 41 36	45 37 59 03 09	90 35 57 29 12	82 62 54 65 60
34 50 57 74 37	98 80 33 00 91	09 77 93 19 82	74 94 80 04 04	45 07 31 66 49
85 22 04 39 43	73 81 53 94 79	33 62 46 86 28	08 31 54 46 31	53 94 13 38 47
09 79 13 77 48	73 82 97 22 21	05 03 27 24 83	72 89 44 05 60	35 80 39 94 88
88 75 80 18 14	22 95 75 42 49	39 32 82 22 49	02 48 07 70 37	16 04 61 67 87
90 96 23 70 00	39 00 03 06 90	55 85 78 38 36	94 37 30 69 32	90 89 00 76 33

Source: Table B is taken from Table XXXIII: Random Numbers (I) and (III), of Fisher and Yates: *Statistical Tables for Biological, Agricultural and Medical Research*, published by Longman Group Ltd., London (previously published by Oliver and Boyd, Edinburgh), and by permission of the authors and publishers.

```
22 17 68 05 84    68 95 23 92 35    87 02 22 57 51    61 09 43 95 06    58 24 82 03 47
19 36 27 59 46    13 79 93 37 55    39 77 32 77 09    85 52 05 30 62    47 83 51 62 74
16 77 23 02 77    09 61 87 25 21    28 06 24 25 93    16 71 13 59 78    23 05 47 47 25
78 43 76 71 61    20 44 90 32 64    97 67 63 99 61    46 38 03 93 22    69 81 21 99 21
03 28 28 26 08    73 37 32 04 05    69 30 16 09 05    88 69 58 28 99    35 07 44 75 47

93 22 53 64 39    07 10 63 76 35    87 03 04 79 88    08 13 13 85 51    55 34 57 72 69
78 76 58 54 74    92 38 70 96 92    52 06 79 79 45    82 63 18 27 44    69 66 92 19 09
23 68 35 26 00    99 53 93 61 28    52 70 05 48 34    56 65 05 61 86    90 92 10 70 80
15 39 25 70 99    93 86 52 77 65    15 33 59 05 28    22 87 26 07 47    86 96 98 29 06
58 71 96 30 24    18 46 23 34 27    85 13 99 24 44    49 18 09 79 49    74 16 32 23 02

57 35 27 33 72    24 53 63 94 09    41 10 76 47 91    44 04 95 49 66    39 60 04 59 81
48 50 86 54 48    22 06 34 72 52    82 21 15 65 20    33 29 94 71 11    15 91 29 12 03
61 96 48 95 03    07 16 39 33 66    98 56 10 56 79    77 21 30 27 12    90 49 22 23 62
36 93 89 41 26    29 70 83 63 51    99 74 20 52 36    87 09 41 15 09    98 60 16 03 03
18 87 00 42 31    57 90 12 02 07    23 47 37 17 31    54 08 01 88 63    39 41 88 92 10

88 56 53 27 59    33 35 72 67 47    77 34 55 45 70    08 18 27 38 90    16 95 86 70 75
09 72 95 84 29    49 41 31 06 70    42 38 06 45 18    64 84 73 31 65    52 53 37 97 15
12 96 88 17 31    65 19 69 02 83    60 75 86 90 68    24 64 19 35 51    56 61 87 39 12
85 94 57 24 16    92 09 84 38 76    22 00 27 69 85    29 81 94 78 70    21 94 47 90 12
38 64 43 59 98    98 77 87 68 07    91 51 67 62 44    40 98 05 93 78    23 32 65 41 18

53 44 09 42 72    00 41 86 79 79    68 47 22 00 20    35 55 31 51 51    00 83 63 22 55
40 76 66 26 84    57 99 99 90 37    36 63 32 08 58    37 40 13 68 97    87 64 81 07 83
02 17 79 18 05    12 59 52 57 02    22 07 90 47 03    28 14 11 30 79    20 69 22 40 98
95 17 82 06 53    31 51 10 96 46    92 06 88 07 77    56 11 50 81 69    40 23 72 51 39
35 76 22 42 92    96 11 83 44 80    34 68 35 48 77    33 42 40 90 60    73 96 53 97 86

26 29 13 56 41    85 47 04 66 08    34 72 57 59 13    82 43 80 46 15    38 26 61 70 04
77 80 20 75 82    72 82 32 99 90    63 95 73 76 63    89 73 44 99 05    48 67 26 43 18
46 40 66 44 52    91 36 74 43 53    30 82 13 54 00    78 45 63 98 35    55 03 36 67 68
37 56 08 18 09    77 53 84 46 47    31 91 18 95 58    24 16 74 11 53    44 10 13 85 57
61 65 61 68 66    37 27 47 39 19    84 83 70 07 48    53 21 40 06 71    95 06 79 88 54

93 43 69 64 07    34 18 04 52 35    56 27 09 24 86    61 85 53 83 45    19 90 70 99 00
21 96 60 12 99    11 20 99 45 18    48 13 93 55 34    18 37 79 49 90    65 97 38 20 46
95 20 47 97 97    27 37 83 28 71    00 06 41 41 74    45 89 09 39 84    51 67 11 52 49
97 86 21 78 73    10 65 81 92 59    58 76 17 14 97    04 76 62 16 17    17 95 70 45 80
69 92 06 34 13    59 71 74 17 32    27 55 10 24 19    23 71 82 13 74    63 52 52 01 41

04 31 17 21 56    33 73 99 19 87    26 72 39 27 67    53 77 57 68 93    60 61 97 22 61
61 06 98 03 91    87 14 77 43 96    43 00 65 98 50    45 60 33 01 07    98 99 46 50 47
85 93 85 86 88    72 87 08 62 40    16 06 10 89 20    23 21 34 74 97    76 38 03 29 63
21 74 32 47 45    73 96 07 94 52    09 65 90 77 47    25 76 16 19 33    53 05 70 53 30
15 69 53 82 80    79 96 23 53 10    65 39 07 16 29    45 33 02 43 70    02 87 40 41 45

02 89 08 04 49    20 21 14 68 86    87 63 93 95 17    11 29 01 95 80    35 14 97 35 33
87 18 15 89 79    85 43 01 72 73    08 61 74 51 69    89 74 39 82 15    94 51 33 41 67
98 83 71 94 22    59 97 50 99 52    08 52 85 08 40    87 80 61 65 31    91 51 80 32 44
10 08 58 21 66    72 68 49 29 31    89 85 84 46 06    59 73 19 85 23    65 09 29 75 63
47 90 56 10 08    88 02 84 27 83    42 29 72 23 19    66 56 45 65 79    20 71 53 20 25

22 85 61 68 90    49 64 92 85 44    16 40 12 89 88    50 14 49 81 06    01 82 77 45 12
67 80 43 79 33    12 83 11 41 16    25 58 19 68 70    77 02 54 00 52    53 43 37 15 26
27 62 50 96 72    79 44 61 40 15    14 53 40 65 39    27 31 58 50 28    11 39 03 34 25
33 78 80 87 15    38 30 06 38 21    14 47 47 07 26    54 96 87 53 32    40 36 40 96 76
13 13 92 66 99    47 24 49 57 74    32 25 43 62 17    10 97 11 69 84    99 63 22 32 98
```

Table C: Areas of a Standard Normal Distribution

An entry in the table is the proportion under the entire curve which is between $z = 0$ and a positive value of z. Areas for negative values of z are obtained by symmetry.

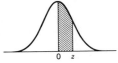

z	.00	.01	.02	.03	.04	.05	.06	.07	.08	.09
0.0	.0000	.0040	.0080	.0120	.0160	.0199	.0239	.0279	.0319	.0359
0.1	.0398	.0438	.0478	.0517	.0557	.0596	.0636	.0675	.0714	.0753
0.2	.0793	.0832	.0871	.0910	.0948	.0987	.1026	.1064	.1103	.1141
0.3	.1179	.1217	.1255	.1293	.1331	.1368	.1406	.1443	.1480	.1517
0.4	.1554	.1591	.1628	.1664	.1700	.1736	.1772	.1808	.1844	.1879
0.5	.1915	.1950	.1985	.2019	.2054	.2088	.2123	.2157	.2190	.2224
0.6	.2257	.2291	.2324	.2357	.2389	.2422	.2454	.2486	.2517	.2549
0.7	.2580	.2611	.2642	.2673	.2703	.2734	.2764	.2794	.2823	.2852
0.8	.2881	.2910	.2939	.2967	.2995	.3023	.3051	.3078	.3106	.3133
0.9	.3159	.3186	.3212	.3238	.3264	.3289	.3315	.3340	.3365	.3389
1.0	.3413	.3438	.3461	.3485	.3508	.3531	.3554	.3577	.3599	.3621
1.1	.3643	.3665	.3686	.3708	.3729	.3749	.3770	.3790	.3810	.3830
1.2	.3849	.3869	.3888	.3907	.3925	.3944	.3962	.3980	.3997	.4015
1.3	.4032	.4049	.4066	.4082	.4099	.4115	.4131	.4147	.4162	.4177
1.4	.4192	.4207	.4222	.4236	.4251	.4265	.4279	.4292	.4306	.4319
1.5	.4332	.4345	.4357	.4370	.4382	.4394	.4406	.4418	.4429	.4441
1.6	.4452	.4463	.4474	.4484	.4495	.4505	.4515	.4525	.4535	.4545
1.7	.4554	.4564	.4573	.4582	.4591	.4599	.4608	.4616	.4625	.4633
1.8	.4641	.4649	.4656	.4664	.4671	.4678	.4686	.4693	.4699	.4706
1.9	.4713	.4719	.4726	.4732	.4738	.4744	.4750	.4756	.4761	.4767
2.0	.4772	.4778	.4783	.4788	.4793	.4798	.4803	.4808	.4812	.4817
2.1	.4821	.4826	.4830	.4834	.4838	.4842	.4846	.4850	.4854	.4857
2.2	.4861	.4864	.4868	.4871	.4875	.4878	.4881	.4884	.4887	.4890
2.3	.4893	.4896	.4898	.4901	.4904	.4906	.4909	.4911	.4913	.4916
2.4	.4918	.4920	.4922	.4925	.4927	.4929	.4931	.4932	.4934	.4936
2.5	.4938	.4940	.4941	.4943	.4945	.4946	.4948	.4949	.4951	.4952
2.6	.4953	.4955	.4956	.4957	.4959	.4960	.4961	.4962	.4963	.4964
2.7	.4965	.4966	.4967	.4968	.4969	.4970	.4971	.4972	.4973	.4974
2.8	.4974	.4975	.4976	.4977	.4977	.4978	.4979	.4979	.4980	.4981
2.9	.4981	.4982	.4982	.4983	.4984	.4984	.4985	.4985	.4986	.4986
3.0	.4987	.4987	.4987	.4988	.4988	.4989	.4989	.4989	.4990	.4990

Source: Reproduced from *Elementary Statistics,* Fourth Edition, by Paul G. Hoel, copyright © 1976, John Wiley & Sons, Inc. Reprinted by permission of John Wiley & Sons, Inc.

Table D: Probabilities Associated with Values as Extreme as the Observed Values of z in the Normal Distribution

The body of the table gives one-tailed probabilities under H_0 of z. The left-hand marginal column gives various values of z to one decimal place. The top row gives various values to the second decimal place. Thus, for example, the one-tailed p of $z \geq .11$ or $z \leq -.11$ is $p = .4562$.

z	.00	.01	.02	.03	.04	.05	.06	.07	.08	.09
.0	.5000	.4960	.4920	.4880	.4840	.4801	.4761	.4721	.4681	.4641
.1	.4602	.4562	.4522	.4483	.4443	.4404	.4364	.4325	.4286	.4247
.2	.4207	.4168	.4129	.4090	.4052	.4013	.3974	.3936	.3897	.3859
.3	.3821	.3783	.3745	.3707	.3669	.3632	.3594	.3557	.3520	.3483
.4	.3446	.3409	.3372	.3336	.3300	.3264	.3228	.3192	.3156	.3121
.5	.3085	.3050	.3015	.2981	.2946	.2912	.2877	.2843	.2810	.2776
.6	.2743	.2709	.2676	.2643	.2611	.2578	.2546	.2514	.2483	.2451
.7	.2420	.2389	.2358	.2327	.2296	.2266	.2236	.2206	.2177	.2148
.8	.2119	.2090	.2061	.2033	.2005	.1977	.1949	.1922	.1894	.1867
.9	.1841	.1814	.1788	.1762	.1736	.1711	.1685	.1660	.1635	.1611
1.0	.1587	.1562	.1539	.1515	.1492	.1469	.1446	.1423	.1401	.1379
1.1	.1357	.1335	.1314	.1292	.1271	.1251	.1230	.1210	.1190	.1170
1.2	.1151	.1131	.1112	.1093	.1075	.1056	.1038	.1020	.1003	.0985
1.3	.0968	.0951	.0934	.0918	.0901	.0885	.0869	.0853	.0838	.0823
1.4	.0808	.0793	.0778	.0764	.0749	.0735	.0721	.0708	.0694	.0681
1.5	.0668	.0655	.0643	.0630	.0618	.0606	.0594	.0582	.0571	.0559
1.6	.0548	.0537	.0526	.0516	.0505	.0495	.0485	.0475	.0465	.0455
1.7	.0446	.0436	.0427	.0418	.0409	.0401	.0392	.0384	.0375	.0367
1.8	.0359	.0351	.0344	.0336	.0329	.0322	.0314	.0307	.0301	.0294
1.9	.0287	.0281	.0274	.0268	.0262	.0256	.0250	.0244	.0239	.0233
2.0	.0228	.0222	.0217	.0212	.0207	.0202	.0197	.0192	.0188	.0183
2.1	.0179	.0174	.0170	.0166	.0162	.0158	.0154	.0150	.0146	.0143
2.2	.0139	.0136	.0132	.0129	.0125	.0122	.0119	.0116	.0113	.0110
2.3	.0107	.0104	.0102	.0099	.0096	.0094	.0091	.0089	.0087	.0084
2.4	.0082	.0080	.0078	.0075	.0073	.0071	.0069	.0068	.0066	.0064
2.5	.0062	.0060	.0059	.0057	.0055	.0054	.0052	.0051	.0049	.0048
2.6	.0047	.0045	.0044	.0043	.0041	.0040	.0039	.0038	.0037	.0036
2.7	.0035	.0034	.0033	.0032	.0031	.0030	.0029	.0028	.0027	.0026
2.8	.0026	.0025	.0024	.0023	.0023	.0022	.0021	.0021	.0020	.0019
2.9	.0019	.0018	.0018	.0017	.0016	.0016	.0015	.0015	.0014	.0014
3.0	.0013	.0013	.0013	.0012	.0012	.0011	.0011	.0011	.0010	.0010
3.1	.0010	.0009	.0009	.0009	.0008	.0008	.0008	.0008	.0007	.0007
3.2	.0007									
3.3	.0005									
3.4	.0003									
3.5	.00023									
3.6	.00016									
3.7	.00011									
3.8	.00007									
3.9	.00005									
4.0	.00003									

Source: Reprinted from *Nonparametric Statistics for the Behavioral Sciences* by Sidney Siegel. Copyright © 1956, McGraw-Hill. Used with permission of McGraw-Hill Book Company.

Table E: Critical Values of Chi Square

df	.99	.98	.95	.90	.80	.70	.50	.30	.20	.10	.05	.02	.01	.001
1	.0002	.0006	.0039	.016	.064	.15	.46	1.07	1.64	2.71	3.84	5.41	6.64	10.83
2	.02	.04	.10	.21	.45	.71	1.39	2.41	3.22	4.60	5.99	7.82	9.21	13.82
3	.12	.18	.35	.58	1.00	1.42	2.37	3.66	4.64	6.25	7.82	9.84	11.34	16.27
4	.30	.43	.71	1.06	1.65	2.20	3.36	4.88	5.99	7.78	9.49	11.67	13.28	18.47
5	.55	.75	1.14	1.61	2.34	3.00	4.35	6.06	7.29	9.24	11.07	13.39	15.09	20.52
6	.87	1.13	1.64	2.20	3.07	3.83	5.35	7.23	8.56	10.64	12.59	15.03	16.81	22.46
7	1.24	1.56	2.17	2.83	3.82	4.67	6.35	8.38	9.80	12.02	14.07	16.62	18.48	24.32
8	1.65	2.03	2.73	3.49	4.59	5.53	7.34	9.52	11.03	13.36	15.51	18.17	20.09	26.12
9	2.09	2.53	3.32	4.17	5.38	6.39	8.34	10.66	12.24	14.68	16.92	19.68	21.67	27.88
10	2.56	3.06	3.94	4.86	6.18	7.27	9.34	11.78	13.44	15.99	18.31	21.16	23.21	29.59
11	3.05	3.61	4.58	5.58	6.99	8.15	10.34	12.90	14.63	17.28	19.68	22.62	24.72	31.26
12	3.57	4.18	5.23	6.30	7.81	9.03	11.34	14.01	15.81	18.55	21.03	24.05	26.22	32.91
13	4.11	4.76	5.89	7.04	8.63	9.93	12.34	15.12	16.98	19.81	22.36	25.47	27.69	34.53
14	4.66	5.37	6.57	7.79	9.47	10.82	13.34	16.22	18.15	21.06	23.68	26.87	29.14	36.12
15	5.23	5.98	7.26	8.55	10.31	11.72	14.34	17.32	19.31	22.31	25.00	28.26	30.58	37.70
16	5.81	6.61	7.96	9.31	11.15	12.62	15.34	18.42	20.46	23.54	26.30	29.63	32.00	39.25
17	6.41	7.26	8.67	10.08	12.00	13.53	16.34	19.51	21.62	24.77	27.59	31.00	33.41	40.79
18	7.02	7.91	9.39	10.86	12.86	14.44	17.34	20.60	22.76	25.99	28.87	32.35	34.80	42.31
19	7.63	8.57	10.12	11.65	13.72	15.35	18.34	21.69	23.90	27.20	30.14	33.69	36.19	43.82
20	8.26	9.24	10.85	12.44	14.58	16.27	19.34	22.78	25.04	28.41	31.41	35.02	37.57	45.32
21	8.90	9.92	11.59	13.24	15.44	17.18	20.34	23.86	26.17	29.62	32.67	36.34	38.93	46.80
22	9.54	10.60	12.34	14.04	16.31	18.10	21.34	24.94	27.30	30.81	33.92	37.66	40.29	48.27
23	10.20	11.29	13.09	14.85	17.19	19.02	22.34	26.02	28.43	32.01	35.17	38.97	41.64	49.73
24	10.86	11.99	13.85	15.66	18.06	19.94	23.34	27.10	29.55	33.20	36.42	40.27	42.98	51.18
25	11.52	12.70	14.61	16.47	18.94	20.87	24.34	28.17	30.68	34.38	37.65	41.57	44.31	52.62
26	12.20	13.41	15.38	17.29	19.82	21.79	25.34	29.25	31.80	35.56	38.88	42.86	45.64	54.05
27	12.88	14.12	16.15	18.11	20.70	22.72	26.34	30.32	32.91	36.74	40.11	44.14	46.96	55.48
28	13.56	14.85	16.93	18.94	21.59	23.65	27.34	31.39	34.03	37.92	41.34	45.42	48.28	56.89
29	14.26	15.57	17.71	19.77	22.48	24.58	28.34	32.46	35.14	39.09	42.56	46.69	49.59	58.30
30	14.95	16.31	18.49	20.60	23.36	25.51	29.34	33.53	36.25	40.26	43.77	47.96	50.89	59.70

Source: Table E is taken from Table IV: Distribution of χ^2, of Fisher and Yates: *Statistical Tables for Biological, Agricultural and Medical Research,* published by Longman Group Ltd., London (previously published by Oliver and Boyd, Edinburgh), and by permission of the authors and publishers.

Table F: Factorials for Numbers 0 to 20

N	N!
0	1
1	1
2	2
3	6
4	24
5	120
6	720
7	5040
8	40320
9	362880
10	3628800
11	39916800
12	479001600
13	6227020800
14	87178291200
15	1307674368000
16	20922789888000
17	355687428096000
18	6402373705728000
19	121645100408832000
20	2432902008176640000

Table G: Binomial Coefficients for Numbers 0 to 25 $\dfrac{N!}{x!(N-x)!}$

N \ x	0	1	2	3	4	5	6	7	8	9	10
0	1										
1	1	1									
2	1	2	1								
3	1	3	3	1							
4	1	4	6	4	1						
5	1	5	10	10	5	1					
6	1	6	15	20	15	6	1				
7	1	7	21	35	35	21	7	1			
8	1	8	28	56	70	56	28	8	1		
9	1	9	36	84	126	126	84	36	9	1	
10	1	10	45	120	210	252	210	120	45	10	1
11	1	11	55	165	330	462	462	330	165	55	11
12	1	12	66	220	495	792	924	792	495	220	66
13	1	13	78	286	715	1287	1716	1716	1287	715	286
14	1	14	91	364	1001	2002	3003	3432	3003	2002	1001
15	1	15	105	455	1365	3003	5005	6435	6435	5005	3003
16	1	16	120	560	1820	4368	8008	11440	12870	11440	8008
17	1	17	136	680	2380	6188	12376	19448	24310	24310	19448
18	1	18	153	816	3060	8568	18564	31824	43758	48620	43758
19	1	19	171	969	3876	11628	27132	50388	75582	92378	92378
20	1	20	190	1140	4845	15504	38760	77520	125970	167960	184756
21	1	21	210	1330	5985	20349	54264	116280	203490	293930	352716
22	1	22	231	1540	7315	26334	74613	170544	319770	314279	646646
23	1	23	253	1771	8855	33649	100947	245157	490314	634049	960925
24	1	24	276	2024	10626	42504	134596	346104	735471	1124363	1594974
25	1	25	300	2300	12650	53130	177100	480700	1081575	1859834	2719337

Table H: Probabilities Associated with Values as Small as the Observed Values of x for the Binomial Test

N	0	1	2	3	4	5	6	7	8	9	10	11	12	13	14	15
5	031	188	500	812	969	*										
6	016	109	344	656	891	984	*									
7	008	062	227	500	773	938	992	*								
8	004	035	145	363	637	855	965	996	*							
9	002	020	090	254	500	746	910	980	998	*						
10	001	011	055	172	377	623	828	945	989	999	*					
11		006	033	113	274	500	726	887	967	994	*	*				
12		003	019	073	194	387	613	806	927	981	997	*	*			
13		002	011	046	133	291	500	709	867	954	989	998	*	*		
14		001	006	029	090	212	395	605	788	910	971	994	999	*	*	
15			004	018	059	151	304	500	696	849	941	982	996	*	*	*
16			002	011	038	105	227	402	598	773	895	962	989	998	*	*
17			001	006	025	072	166	315	500	685	834	928	975	994	999	*
18			001	004	015	048	119	240	407	593	760	881	952	985	996	999
19				002	010	032	084	180	324	500	676	820	916	968	990	998
20				001	006	021	058	132	252	412	588	748	868	942	979	994
21				001	004	013	039	095	192	332	500	668	808	905	961	987
22					002	008	026	067	143	262	416	584	738	857	933	974
23					001	005	017	047	105	202	339	500	661	798	895	953
24					001	003	011	032	076	154	271	419	581	729	846	924
25						002	007	022	054	115	212	345	500	655	788	885

Source: Adapted from *Statistical Inference* by Helen M. Walker and Joseph Lev. Copyright © 1953. Adapted by permission of Holt, Rinehart and Winston, Inc., now Holt, Rinehart and Winston, CBS, Inc.

Note: To save space the decimal points in the probabilities are omitted.

* 1.0 or approximately 1.0.

Table I: Critical Values of D for the Kolmogorov-Smirnov Test

Sample Size (N)	Significance Level				
	.20	.15	.10	.05	.01
1	.900	.925	.950	.975	.995
2	.684	.726	.776	.842	.929
3	.565	.597	.642	.708	.829
4	.494	.525	.564	.624	.734
5	.446	.474	.510	.563	.669
6	.410	.436	.470	.521	.618
7	.381	.405	.438	.486	.577
8	.358	.381	.411	.457	.543
9	.339	.360	.388	.432	.514
10	.322	.342	.368	.409	.486
11	.307	.326	.352	.391	.468
12	.295	.313	.338	.375	.450
13	.284	.302	.325	.361	.433
14	.274	.292	.314	.349	.418
15	.266	.283	.304	.338	.404
16	.258	.274	.295	.328	.391
17	.250	.266	.286	.318	.380
18.	.244	.259	.278	.309	.370
19	.237	.252	.272	.301	.361
20	.231	.246	.264	.294	.352
25	.21	.22	.24	.264	.32
30	.19	.20	.22	.242	.29
35	.18	.19	.21	.23	.27
Over 35	$\dfrac{1.07}{\sqrt{N}}$	$\dfrac{1.14}{\sqrt{N}}$	$\dfrac{1.22}{\sqrt{N}}$	$\dfrac{1.36}{\sqrt{N}}$	$\dfrac{1.63}{\sqrt{N}}$

Source: Reprinted with permission from *Basic Statistical Tables,* 1971. Copyright The Chemical Rubber Co., CRC Press, Inc.

Table J: Critical Values of U in the Mann-Whitney Test When n Is between 9 and 20

Critical Values of U for a One-tailed Test at α = .001 or for a Two-tailed Test at α = .002

n_1 \ n_2	9	10	11	12	13	14	15	16	17	18	19	20
1												
2												
3								0	0	0	0	0
4		0	0	0	1	1	1	2	2	3	3	3
5	1	1	2	2	3	3	4	5	5	6	7	7
6	2	3	4	4	5	6	7	8	9	10	11	12
7	3	5	6	7	8	9	10	11	13	14	15	16
8	5	6	8	9	11	12	14	15	17	18	20	21
9	7	8	10	12	14	15	17	19	21	23	25	26
10	8	10	12	14	17	19	21	23	25	27	29	32
11	10	12	15	17	20	22	24	27	29	32	34	37
12	12	14	17	20	23	25	28	31	34	37	40	42
13	14	17	20	23	26	29	32	35	38	42	45	48
14	15	19	22	25	29	32	36	39	43	46	50	54
15	17	21	24	28	32	36	40	43	47	51	55	59
16	19	23	27	31	35	39	43	48	52	56	60	65
17	21	25	29	34	38	43	47	52	57	61	66	70
18	23	27	32	37	42	46	51	56	61	66	71	76
19	25	29	34	40	45	50	55	60	66	71	77	82
20	26	32	37	42	48	54	59	65	70	76	82	88

Critical Values of U for a One-tailed Test at α = .01 or for a Two-tailed Test at α = .02

n_1 \ n_2	9	10	11	12	13	14	15	16	17	18	19	20
1												
2					0	0	0	0	0	0	1	1
3	1	1	1	2	2	2	3	3	4	4	4	5
4	3	3	4	5	5	6	7	7	8	9	9	10
5	5	6	7	8	9	10	11	12	13	14	15	16
6	7	8	9	11	12	13	15	16	18	19	20	22
7	9	11	12	14	16	17	19	21	23	24	26	28
8	11	13	15	17	20	22	24	26	28	30	32	34
9	14	16	18	21	23	26	28	31	33	36	38	40
10	16	19	22	24	27	30	33	36	38	41	44	47
11	18	22	25	28	31	34	37	41	44	47	50	53
12	21	24	28	31	35	38	42	46	49	53	56	60
13	23	27	31	35	39	43	47	51	55	59	63	67
14	26	30	34	38	43	47	51	56	60	65	69	73
15	28	33	37	42	47	51	56	61	66	70	75	80
16	31	36	41	46	51	56	61	66	71	76	82	87
17	33	38	44	49	55	60	66	71	77	82	88	93
18	36	41	47	53	59	65	70	76	82	88	94	100
19	38	44	50	56	63	69	75	82	88	94	101	107
20	40	47	53	60	67	73	80	87	93	100	107	114

Source: Reprinted with permission from *Basic Statistical Tables,* 1971. Copyright The Chemical Rubber Co., CRC Press, Inc.

Critical Values of U for a One-tailed Test at $\alpha = .025$ or for a Two-tailed Test at $\alpha = .05$

n_1 \ n_2	9	10	11	12	13	14	15	16	17	18	19	20
1									2	2	2	2
2	0	0	0	1	1	1	1	1	2	2	2	8
3	2	3	3	4	4	5	5	6	6	7	7	8
4	4	5	6	7	8	9	10	11	11	12	13	13
5	7	8	9	11	12	13	14	15	17	18	19	20
6	10	11	13	14	16	17	19	21	22	24	25	27
7	12	14	16	18	20	22	24	26	28	30	32	34
8	15	17	19	22	24	26	29	31	34	36	38	41
9	17	20	23	26	28	31	34	37	39	42	45	48
10	20	23	26	29	33	36	39	42	45	48	52	55
11	23	26	30	33	37	40	44	47	51	55	58	62
12	26	29	33	37	41	45	49	53	57	61	65	69
13	28	33	37	41	45	50	54	59	63	67	72	76
14	31	36	40	45	50	55	59	64	67	74	78	83
15	34	39	44	49	54	59	64	70	75	80	85	90
16	37	42	47	53	59	64	70	75	81	86	92	98
17	39	45	51	57	63	67	75	81	87	93	99	105
18	42	48	55	61	67	74	80	86	93	99	106	112
19	45	52	58	65	72	78	85	92	99	106	113	119
20	48	55	62	69	76	83	90	98	105	112	119	127

Critical Values of U for a One-tailed Test at $\alpha = .05$ or for a Two-tailed Test at $\alpha = .10$

n_1 \ n_2	9	10	11	12	13	14	15	16	17	18	19	20
1											0	0
2	1	1	1	2	2	2	3	3	3	4	4	4
3	3	4	5	5	6	7	7	8	9	9	10	11
4	6	7	8	9	10	11	12	14	15	16	17	18
5	9	11	12	13	15	16	18	19	20	22	23	25
6	12	14	16	17	19	21	23	25	26	28	30	32
7	15	17	19	21	24	26	28	30	33	35	37	39
8	18	20	23	26	28	31	33	36	39	41	44	47
9	21	24	27	30	33	36	39	42	45	48	51	54
10	24	27	31	34	37	41	44	48	51	55	58	62
11	27	31	34	38	42	46	50	54	57	61	65	69
12	30	34	38	42	47	51	55	60	64	68	72	77
13	33	37	42	47	51	56	61	65	70	75	80	84
14	36	41	46	51	56	61	66	71	77	82	87	92
15	39	44	50	55	61	66	72	77	83	88	94	100
16	42	48	54	60	65	71	77	83	89	95	101	107
17	45	51	57	64	70	77	83	89	96	102	109	115
18	48	55	61	68	75	82	88	95	102	109	116	123
19	51	58	65	72	80	87	94	101	109	116	123	130
20	54	62	69	77	84	92	100	107	115	123	130	138

$n_2 = 3$

U \ n_1	1	2	3
0	.250	.100	.050
1	.500	.200	.100
2	.750	.400	.200
3		.600	.350
4			.500
5			.650

$n_2 = 4$

U \ n_1	1	2	3	4
0	.200	.067	.028	.014
1	.400	.133	.057	.029
2	.600	.267	.114	.057
3		.400	.200	.100
4		.600	.314	.171
5			.429	.243
6			.571	.343
7				.443
8				.557

$n_2 = 5$

U \ n_1	1	2	3	4	5
0	.167	.047	.018	.008	.004
1	.333	.095	.036	.016	.008
2	.500	.190	.071	.032	.016
3	.667	.286	.125	.056	.028
4		.429	.196	.095	.048
5		.571	.286	.143	.075
6			.393	.206	.111
7			.500	.278	.155
8			.607	.365	.210
9				.452	.274
10				.548	.345
11					.421
12					.500
13					.579

$n_2 = 6$

U \ n_1	1	2	3	4	5	6
0	.143	.036	.012	.005	.002	.001
1	.286	.071	.024	.010	.004	.002
2	.428	.143	.048	.019	.009	.004
3	.571	.214	.083	.033	.015	.008
4		.321	.131	.057	.026	.013
5		.429	.190	.086	.041	.021
6		.571	.274	.129	.063	.032
7			.357	.176	.089	.047
8			.452	.238	.123	.066
9			.548	.305	.165	.090
10				.381	.214	.120
11				.457	.268	.155
12				.545	.331	.197
13					.396	.242
14					.465	.294
15					.535	.350
16						.409
17						.469
18						.531

Source: Reprinted with permission from *Basic Statistical Tables,* 1971. Copyright The Chemical Rubber Co., CRC Press, Inc.

$n_2 = 7$

n_1 U	1	2	3	4	5	6	7
0	.125	.028	.008	.003	.001	.001	.000
1	.250	.056	.017	.006	.003	.001	.001
2	.375	.111	.033	.012	.005	.002	.001
3	.500	.167	.058	.021	.009	.004	.002
4	.625	.250	.092	.036	.015	.007	.003
5		.333	.133	.055	.024	.011	.006
6		.444	.192	.082	.037	.017	.009
7		.556	.258	.115	.053	.026	.013
8			.333	.158	.074	.037	.019
9			.417	.206	.101	.051	.027
10			.500	.264	.134	.069	.036
11			.583	.324	.172	.090	.049
12				.394	.216	.117	.064
13				.464	.265	.147	.082
14				.538	.319	.183	.104
15					.378	.223	.130
16					.438	.267	.159
17					.500	.314	.191
18					.562	.365	.228
19						.418	.267
20						.473	.310
21						.527	.355
22							.402
23							.451
24							.500
25							.549

$n_2 = 8$

n_1 U	1	2	3	4	5	6	7	8	t	Normal
0	.111	.022	.006	.002	.001	.000	.000	.000	3.308	.001
1	.222	.044	.012	.004	.002	.001	.000	.000	3.203	.001
2	.333	.089	.024	.008	.003	.001	.001	.000	3.098	.001
3	.444	.133	.042	.014	.005	.002	.001	.001	2.993	.001
4	.556	.200	.067	.024	.009	.004	.002	.001	2.888	.002
5		.267	.097	.036	.015	.006	.003	.001	2.783	.003
6		.356	.139	.055	.023	.010	.005	.002	2.678	.004
7		.444	.188	.077	.033	.015	.007	.003	2.573	.005
8		.556	.248	.107	.047	.021	.010	.005	2.468	.007
9			.315	.141	.064	.030	.014	.007	2.363	.009
10			.387	.184	.085	.041	.020	.010	2.258	.012
11			.461	.230	.111	.054	.027	.014	2.153	.016
12			.539	.285	.142	.071	.036	.019	2.048	.020
13				.341	.177	.091	.047	.025	1.943	.026
14				.404	.217	.114	.060	.032	1.838	.033
15				.467	.262	.141	.076	.041	1.733	.041
16				.533	.311	.172	.095	.052	1.628	.052
17					.362	.207	.116	.065	1.523	.064
18					.416	.245	.140	.080	1.418	.078
19					.472	.286	.168	.097	1.313	.094
20					.528	.331	.198	.117	1.208	.113
21						.377	.232	.139	1.102	.135
22						.426	.268	.164	.998	.159
23						.475	.306	.191	.893	.185
24						.525	.347	.221	.788	.215
25							.389	.253	.683	.247
26							.433	.287	.578	.282
27							.478	.323	.473	.318
28							.522	.360	.368	.356
29								.399	.263	.396
30								.439	.158	.437
31								.480	.052	.481
32								.520		

Table L: Critical Values of T for the Wilcoxon Test

N	Level of significance for one-tail test			
	.05	.025	.01	.005
	Level of significance for two-tail test			
	.10	.05	.02	.01
6	2	1	—	—
7	4	2	0	—
8	6	4	2	0
9	8	6	3	2
10	11	8	5	3
11	14	11	7	5
12	17	14	10	7
13	21	17	13	10
14	26	21	16	13
15	30	25	20	16
16	36	30	24	19
17	41	35	28	23
18	47	40	33	28
19	54	46	38	32
20	60	52	43	37
21	68	59	49	43
22	75	66	56	49
23	83	73	62	55
24	92	81	69	61
25	101	90	77	68

Source: Adapted with permission from *Basic Statistical Tables,* 1971. Copyright The Chemical Rubber Co., CRC Press, Inc.

Table M: Probabilities Associated with Values as Large as the Observed Values of H in the Kruskal-Wallis Test

Sample sizes			H	p	Sample sizes			H	p
n_1	n_2	n_3			n_1	n_2	n_3		
2	1	1	2.7000	.500	4	3	2	6.4444	.008
								6.3000	.011
2	2	1	3.6000	.200				5.4444	.046
								5.4000	.051
2	2	2	4.5714	.067				4.5111	.098
			3.7143	.200				4.4444	.102
3	1	1	3.2000	.300	4	3	3	6.7455	.010
								6.7091	.013
3	2	1	4.2857	.100				5.7909	.046
			3.8571	.133				5.7273	.050
								4.7091	.092
3	2	2	5.3572	.029				4.7000	.101
			4.7143	.048					
			4.5000	.067	4	4	1	6.6667	.010
			4.4643	.105				6.1667	.022
								4.9667	.048
3	3	1	5.1429	.043				4.8667	.054
			4.5714	.100				4.1667	.082
			4.0000	.129				4.0667	.102
3	3	2	6.2500	.011	4	4	2	7.0364	.006
			5.3611	.032				6.8727	.011
			5.1389	.061				5.4545	.046
			4.5556	.100				5.2364	.052
			4.2500	.121				4.5545	.098
								4.4455	.103
3	3	3	7.2000	.004					
			6.4889	.011	4	4	3	7.1439	.010
			5.6889	.029				7.1364	.011
			5.6000	.050				5.5985	.049
			5.0667	.086				5.5758	.051
			4.6222	.100				4.5455	.099
								4.4773	.102
4	1	1	3.5714	.200					
					4	4	4	7.6538	.008
4	2	1	4.8214	.057				7.5385	.011
			4.5000	.076				5.6923	.049
			4.0179	.114				5.6538	.054
								4.6539	.097
4	2	2	6.0000	.014				4.5001	.104
			5.3333	.033					
			5.1250	.052	5	1	1	3.8571	.143
			4.4583	.100					
			4.1667	.105	5	2	1	5.2500	.036
								5.0000	.048
4	3	1	5.8333	.021				4.4500	.071
			5.2083	.050				4.2000	.095
			5.0000	.057				4.0500	.119
			4.0556	.093					
			3.8889	.129					

Source: Reprinted with permission from *Basic Statistical Tables*, 1971. Copyright The Chemical Rubber Co., CRC Press, Inc.

Sample sizes			H	p	Sample sizes			H	p
n_1	n_2	n_3			n_1	n_2	n_3		
5	2	2	6.5333	.008				5.6308	.050
			6.1333	.013				4.5487	.099
			5.1600	.034				4.5231	.103
			5.0400	.056					
			4.3733	.090	5	4	4	7.7604	.009
			4.2933	.122				7.7440	.011
								5.6571	.049
5	3	1	6.4000	.012				5.6176	.050
			4.9600	.048				4.6187	.100
			4.8711	.052				4.5527	.102
			4.0178	.095					
			3.8400	.123	5	5	1	7.3091	.009
								6.8364	.011
5	3	2	6.9091	.009				5.1273	.046
			6.8218	.010				4.9091	.053
			5.2509	.049				4.1091	.086
			5.1055	.052				4.0364	.105
			4.6509	.091					
			4.4945	.101	5	5	2	7.3385	.010
								7.2692	.010
5	3	3	7.0788	.009				5.3385	.047
			6.9818	.011				5.2462	.051
			5.6485	.049				4.6231	.097
			5.5152	.051				4.5077	.100
			4.5333	.097					
			4.4121	.109	5	5	3	7.5780	.010
								7.5429	.010
5	4	1	6.9545	.008				5.7055	.046
			6.8400	.011				5.6264	.051
			4.9855	.044				4.5451	.100
			4.8600	.056				4.5363	.102
			3.9873	.098					
			3.9600	.102	5	5	4	7.8229	.010
								7.7914	.010
5	4	2	7.2045	.009				5.6657	.049
			7.1182	.010				5.6429	.050
			5.2727	.049				4.5229	.099
			5.2682	.050				4.5200	.101
			4.5409	.098					
			4.5182	.101	5	5	5	8.0000	.009
								7.9800	.010
5	4	3	7.4449	.010				5.7800	.049
			7.3949	.011				5.6600	.051
			5.6564	.049				4.5600	.100
								4.5000	.102

Table N: Probabilities Associated with Values as Large as the Observed Values of χ_r^2 in the Friedman Test

$$k = 3$$

$N = 2$		$N = 3$		$N = 4$		$N = 5$	
χ_r^2	p	χ_r^2	p	χ_r^2	p	χ_r^2	p
0	1.000	.000	1.000	.0	1.000	.0	1.000
1	.833	.667	.944	.5	.931	.4	.954
3	.500	2.000	.528	1.5	.653	1.2	.691
4	.167	2.667	.361	2.0	.431	1.6	.522
		4.667	.194	3.5	.273	2.8	.367
		6.000	.028	4.5	.125	3.6	.182
				6.0	.069	4.8	.124
				6.5	.042	5.2	.093
				8.0	.0046	6.4	.039
						7.6	.024
						8.4	.0085
						10.0	.00077

$N = 6$		$N = 7$		$N = 8$		$N = 9$	
χ_r^2	p	χ_r^2	p	χ_r^2	p	χ_r^2	p
.00	1.000	.000	1.000	.00	1.000	.000	1.000
.33	.956	.286	.964	.25	.967	.222	.971
1.00	.740	.857	.768	.75	.794	.667	.814
1.33	.570	1.143	.620	1.00	.654	.889	.865
2.33	.430	2.000	.486	1.75	.531	1.556	.569
3.00	.252	2.571	.305	2.25	.355	2.000	.398
4.00	.184	3.429	.237	3.00	.285	2.667	.328
4.33	.142	3.714	.192	3.25	.236	2.889	.278
5.33	.072	4.571	.112	4.00	.149	3.556	.187
6.33	.052	5.429	.085	4.75	.120	4.222	.154
7.00	.029	6.000	.052	5.25	.079	4.667	.107
8.33	.012	7.143	.027	6.25	.047	5.556	.069
9.00	.0081	7.714	.021	6.75	.038	6.000	.057
9.33	.0055	8.000	.016	7.00	.030	6.222	.048
10.33	.0017	8.857	.0084	7.75	.018	6.889	.031
12.00	.00013	10.286	.0036	9.00	.0099	8.000	.019
		10.571	.0027	9.25	.0080	8.222	.016
		11.143	.0012	9.75	.0048	8.667	.010
		12.286	.00032	10.75	.0024	9.556	.0060
		14.000	.000021	12.00	.0011	10.667	.0035
				12.25	.00086	10.889	.0029
				13.00	.00026	11.556	.0013
				14.25	.000061	12.667	.00066
				16.00	.0000036	13.556	.00035
						14.000	.00020
						14.222	.000097
						14.889	.000054
						16.222	.000011
						18.000	.0000006

Source: Adapted from Milton Friedman, "The Use of Ranks to Avoid the Assumption of Normality Implicit in the Analysis of Variance," *Journal of the American Statistical Association*, Vol. 32, p. 688, 1937.

$$k = 4$$

χ_r^2	p	χ_r^2	p	χ_r^2	p	χ_r^2	p
.0	1.000	.2	1.000	.0	1.000	5.7	.141
.6	.958	.6	.958	.3	.992	6.0	.105
1.2	.834	1.0	.910	.6	.928	6.3	.094
1.8	.792	1.8	.727	.9	.900	6.6	.077
2.4	.625	2.2	.608	1.2	.800	6.9	.068
3.0	.542	2.6	.524	1.5	.754	7.2	.054
3.6	.458	3.4	.446	1.8	.677	7.5	.052
4.2	.375	3.8	.342	2.1	.649	7.8	.036
4.8	.208	4.2	.300	2.4	.524	8.1	.033
5.4	.167	5.0	.207	2.7	.508	8.4	.019
6.0	.042	5.4	.175	3.0	.432	8.7	.014
		5.8	.148	3.3	.389	9.3	.012
		6.6	.075	3.6	.355	9.6	.0069
		7.0	.054	3.9	.324	9.9	.0062
		7.4	.033	4.5	.242	10.2	.0027
		8.2	.017	4.8	.200	10.8	.0016
		9.0	.0017	5.1	.190	11.1	.00094
				5.4	.158	12.0	.000072

The column groups above are headed, left to right: $N = 2$, $N = 3$, and $N = 4$.

Table O: Critical Values of t

df	Level of significance for a one-tail test				
	.05	.025	.01	.005	.0005
	Level of significance for a two-tail test				
	.10	.05	.02	.01	.001
1	6·314	12·706	31·821	63·657	636·619
2	2·920	4·303	6·965	9·925	31·598
3	2·353	3·182	4·541	5·841	12·924
4	2·132	2·776	3·747	4·604	8·610
5	2·015	2·571	3·365	4·032	6·869
6	1·943	2·447	3·143	3·707	5·959
7	1·895	2·365	2·998	3·499	5·408
8	1·860	2·306	2·896	3·355	5·041
9	1·833	2·262	2·821	3·250	4·781
10	1·812	2·228	2·764	3·169	4·587
11	1·796	2·201	2·718	3·106	4·437
12	1·782	2·179	2·681	3·055	4·318
13	1·771	2·160	2·650	3·012	4·221
14	1·761	2·145	2·624	2·977	4·140
15	1·753	2·131	2·602	2·947	4·073
16	1·746	2·120	2·583	2·921	4·015
17	1·740	2·110	2·567	2·898	3·965
18	1·734	2·101	2·552	2·878	3·922
19	1·729	2·093	2·539	2·861	3·883
20	1·725	2·086	2·528	2·845	3·850
21	1·721	2·080	2·518	2·831	3·819
22	1·717	2·074	2·508	2·819	3·792
23	1·714	2·069	2·500	2·807	3·767
24	1·711	2·064	2·492	2·797	3·745
25	1·708	2·060	2·485	2·787	3·725
26	1·706	2·056	2·479	2·779	3·707
27	1·703	2·052	2·473	2·771	3·690
28	1·701	2·048	2·467	2·763	3·674
29	1·699	2·045	2·462	2·756	3·659
30	1·697	2·042	2·457	2·750	3·646
40	1·684	2·021	2·423	2·704	3·551
60	1·671	2·000	2·390	2·660	3·460
120	1·658	1·980	2·358	2·617	3·373
∞	1·645	1·960	2·326	2·576	3·291

Source: Table O is taken from Table III: Distribution of *t*, of Fisher and Yates: *Statistical Tables for Biological, Agricultural and Medical Research,* published by Longman Group Ltd., London (previously published by Oliver and Boyd, Edinburgh), and by permission of the authors and publishers.

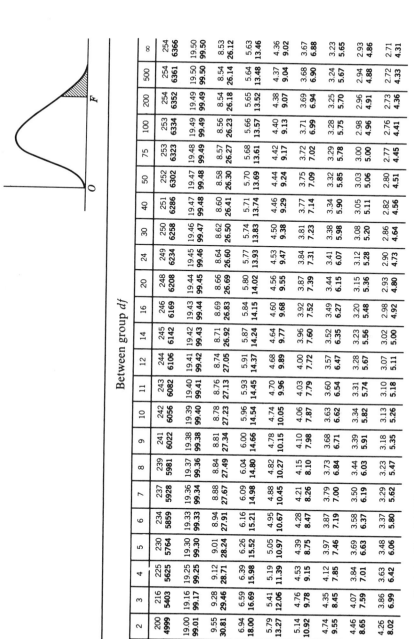

Between group df

Within group df	1	2	3	4	5	6	7	8	9	10	11	12	14	16	20	24	30	40	50	75	100	200	500	∞
1	161 **4052**	200 **4999**	216 **5403**	225 **5625**	230 **5764**	234 **5859**	237 **5928**	239 **5981**	241 **6022**	242 **6056**	243 **6082**	244 **6106**	245 **6142**	246 **6169**	248 **6208**	249 **6234**	250 **6258**	251 **6286**	252 **6302**	253 **6323**	253 **6334**	254 **6352**	254 **6361**	254 **6366**
2	18.51 **98.49**	19.00 **99.01**	19.16 **99.17**	19.25 **99.25**	19.30 **99.30**	19.33 **99.33**	19.36 **99.34**	19.37 **99.36**	19.38 **99.38**	19.39 **99.40**	19.40 **99.41**	19.41 **99.42**	19.42 **99.43**	19.43 **99.44**	19.44 **99.45**	19.45 **99.46**	19.46 **99.47**	19.47 **99.48**	19.47 **99.48**	19.48 **99.49**	19.49 **99.49**	19.49 **99.49**	19.50 **99.50**	19.50 **99.50**
3	10.13 **34.12**	9.55 **30.81**	9.28 **29.46**	9.12 **28.71**	9.01 **28.24**	8.94 **27.91**	8.88 **27.67**	8.84 **27.49**	8.81 **27.34**	8.78 **27.23**	8.76 **27.13**	8.74 **27.05**	8.71 **26.92**	8.69 **26.83**	8.66 **26.69**	8.64 **26.60**	8.62 **26.50**	8.60 **26.41**	8.58 **26.30**	8.57 **26.27**	8.56 **26.23**	8.54 **26.18**	8.54 **26.14**	8.53 **26.12**
4	7.71 **21.20**	6.94 **18.00**	6.59 **16.69**	6.39 **15.98**	6.26 **15.52**	6.16 **15.21**	6.09 **14.98**	6.04 **14.80**	6.00 **14.66**	5.96 **14.54**	5.93 **14.45**	5.91 **14.37**	5.87 **14.24**	5.84 **14.15**	5.80 **14.02**	5.77 **13.93**	5.74 **13.83**	5.71 **13.74**	5.70 **13.69**	5.68 **13.61**	5.66 **13.57**	5.65 **13.52**	5.64 **13.48**	5.63 **13.46**
5	6.61 **16.26**	5.79 **13.27**	5.41 **12.06**	5.19 **11.39**	5.05 **10.97**	4.95 **10.67**	4.88 **10.45**	4.82 **10.27**	4.78 **10.15**	4.74 **10.05**	4.70 **9.96**	4.68 **9.89**	4.64 **9.77**	4.60 **9.68**	4.56 **9.55**	4.53 **9.47**	4.50 **9.38**	4.46 **9.29**	4.44 **9.24**	4.42 **9.17**	4.40 **9.13**	4.38 **9.07**	4.37 **9.04**	4.36 **9.02**
6	5.99 **13.74**	5.14 **10.92**	4.76 **9.78**	4.53 **9.15**	4.39 **8.75**	4.28 **8.47**	4.21 **8.26**	4.15 **8.10**	4.10 **7.98**	4.06 **7.87**	4.03 **7.79**	4.00 **7.72**	3.96 **7.60**	3.92 **7.52**	3.87 **7.39**	3.84 **7.31**	3.81 **7.23**	3.77 **7.14**	3.75 **7.09**	3.72 **7.02**	3.71 **6.99**	3.69 **6.94**	3.68 **6.90**	3.67 **6.88**
7	5.59 **12.25**	4.74 **9.55**	4.35 **8.45**	4.12 **7.85**	3.97 **7.46**	3.87 **7.19**	3.79 **7.00**	3.73 **6.84**	3.68 **6.71**	3.63 **6.62**	3.60 **6.54**	3.57 **6.47**	3.52 **6.35**	3.49 **6.27**	3.44 **6.15**	3.41 **6.07**	3.38 **5.98**	3.34 **5.90**	3.32 **5.85**	3.29 **5.78**	3.28 **5.75**	3.25 **5.70**	3.24 **5.67**	3.23 **5.65**
8	5.32 **11.26**	4.46 **8.65**	4.07 **7.59**	3.84 **7.01**	3.69 **6.63**	3.58 **6.37**	3.50 **6.19**	3.44 **6.03**	3.39 **5.91**	3.34 **5.82**	3.31 **5.74**	3.28 **5.67**	3.23 **5.56**	3.20 **5.48**	3.15 **5.36**	3.12 **5.28**	3.08 **5.20**	3.05 **5.11**	3.03 **5.06**	3.00 **5.00**	2.98 **4.96**	2.96 **4.91**	2.94 **4.88**	2.93 **4.86**
9	5.12 **10.56**	4.26 **8.02**	3.86 **6.99**	3.63 **6.42**	3.48 **6.06**	3.37 **5.80**	3.29 **5.62**	3.23 **5.47**	3.18 **5.35**	3.13 **5.26**	3.10 **5.18**	3.07 **5.11**	3.02 **5.00**	2.98 **4.92**	2.93 **4.80**	2.90 **4.73**	2.86 **4.64**	2.82 **4.56**	2.80 **4.51**	2.77 **4.45**	2.76 **4.41**	2.73 **4.36**	2.72 **4.33**	2.71 **4.31**

Source: Elementary Statistics, Fourth Edition, by Paul G. Hoel, copyright © 1976, John Wiley & Sons, Inc. Reprinted by permission of John Wiley & Sons, Inc.

Between group *df*

Within group *df*	1	2	3	4	5	6	7	8	9	10	11	12	14	16	20	24	30	40	50	75	100	200	500	∞
10	4.96 / 10.04	4.10 / 7.56	3.71 / 6.55	3.48 / 5.99	3.33 / 5.64	3.22 / 5.39	3.14 / 5.21	3.07 / 5.06	3.02 / 4.95	2.97 / 4.85	2.94 / 4.78	2.91 / 4.71	2.86 / 4.60	2.82 / 4.52	2.77 / 4.41	2.74 / 4.33	2.70 / 4.25	2.67 / 4.17	2.64 / 4.12	2.61 / 4.05	2.59 / 4.01	2.56 / 3.96	2.55 / 3.93	2.54 / 3.91
11	4.84 / 9.65	3.98 / 7.20	3.59 / 6.22	3.36 / 5.67	3.20 / 5.32	3.09 / 5.07	3.01 / 4.88	2.95 / 4.74	2.90 / 4.63	2.86 / 4.54	2.82 / 4.46	2.79 / 4.40	2.74 / 4.29	2.70 / 4.21	2.65 / 4.10	2.61 / 4.02	2.57 / 3.94	2.53 / 3.86	2.50 / 3.80	2.47 / 3.74	2.45 / 3.70	2.42 / 3.66	2.41 / 3.62	2.40 / 3.60
12	4.75 / 9.33	3.88 / 6.93	3.49 / 5.95	3.26 / 5.41	3.11 / 5.06	3.00 / 4.82	2.92 / 4.65	2.85 / 4.50	2.80 / 4.39	2.76 / 4.30	2.72 / 4.22	2.69 / 4.16	2.64 / 4.05	2.60 / 3.98	2.54 / 3.86	2.50 / 3.78	2.46 / 3.70	2.42 / 3.61	2.40 / 3.56	2.36 / 3.49	2.35 / 3.46	2.32 / 3.41	2.31 / 3.38	2.30 / 3.36
13	4.67 / 9.07	3.80 / 6.70	3.41 / 5.74	3.18 / 5.20	3.02 / 4.86	2.92 / 4.62	2.84 / 4.44	2.77 / 4.30	2.72 / 4.19	2.67 / 4.10	2.63 / 4.02	2.60 / 3.96	2.55 / 3.85	2.51 / 3.78	2.46 / 3.67	2.42 / 3.59	2.38 / 3.51	2.34 / 3.42	2.32 / 3.37	2.28 / 3.30	2.26 / 3.27	2.24 / 3.21	2.22 / 3.18	2.21 / 3.16
14	4.60 / 8.86	3.74 / 6.51	3.34 / 5.56	3.11 / 5.03	2.96 / 4.69	2.85 / 4.46	2.77 / 4.28	2.70 / 4.14	2.65 / 4.03	2.60 / 3.94	2.56 / 3.86	2.53 / 3.80	2.48 / 3.70	2.44 / 3.62	2.39 / 3.51	2.35 / 3.43	2.31 / 3.34	2.27 / 3.26	2.24 / 3.21	2.21 / 3.14	2.19 / 3.11	2.16 / 3.06	2.14 / 3.02	2.13 / 3.00
15	4.54 / 8.68	3.68 / 6.36	3.29 / 5.42	3.06 / 4.89	2.90 / 4.56	2.79 / 4.32	2.70 / 4.14	2.64 / 4.00	2.59 / 3.89	2.55 / 3.80	2.51 / 3.73	2.48 / 3.67	2.43 / 3.56	2.39 / 3.48	2.33 / 3.36	2.29 / 3.29	2.25 / 3.20	2.21 / 3.12	2.18 / 3.07	2.15 / 3.00	2.12 / 2.97	2.10 / 2.92	2.08 / 2.89	2.07 / 2.87
16	4.49 / 8.53	3.63 / 6.23	3.24 / 5.29	3.01 / 4.77	2.85 / 4.44	2.74 / 4.20	2.66 / 4.03	2.59 / 3.89	2.54 / 3.78	2.49 / 3.69	2.45 / 3.61	2.42 / 3.55	2.37 / 3.45	2.33 / 3.37	2.28 / 3.25	2.24 / 3.18	2.20 / 3.10	2.16 / 3.01	2.13 / 2.96	2.09 / 2.89	2.07 / 2.86	2.04 / 2.80	2.02 / 2.77	2.01 / 2.75
17	4.45 / 8.40	3.59 / 6.11	3.20 / 5.18	2.96 / 4.67	2.81 / 4.34	2.70 / 4.10	2.62 / 3.93	2.55 / 3.79	2.50 / 3.68	2.45 / 3.59	2.41 / 3.52	2.38 / 3.45	2.33 / 3.35	2.29 / 3.27	2.23 / 3.16	2.19 / 3.08	2.15 / 3.00	2.11 / 2.92	2.08 / 2.86	2.04 / 2.79	2.02 / 2.76	1.99 / 2.70	1.97 / 2.67	1.96 / 2.65
18	4.41 / 8.28	3.55 / 6.01	3.16 / 5.09	2.93 / 4.58	2.77 / 4.25	2.66 / 4.01	2.58 / 3.85	2.51 / 3.71	2.46 / 3.60	2.41 / 3.51	2.37 / 3.44	2.34 / 3.37	2.29 / 3.27	2.25 / 3.19	2.19 / 3.07	2.15 / 3.00	2.11 / 2.91	2.07 / 2.83	2.04 / 2.78	2.00 / 2.71	1.98 / 2.68	1.95 / 2.62	1.93 / 2.59	1.92 / 2.57
19	4.38 / 8.18	3.52 / 5.93	3.13 / 5.01	2.90 / 4.50	2.74 / 4.17	2.63 / 3.94	2.55 / 3.77	2.48 / 3.63	2.43 / 3.52	2.38 / 3.43	2.34 / 3.36	2.31 / 3.30	2.26 / 3.19	2.21 / 3.12	2.15 / 3.00	2.11 / 2.92	2.07 / 2.84	2.02 / 2.76	2.00 / 2.70	1.96 / 2.63	1.94 / 2.60	1.91 / 2.54	1.90 / 2.51	1.88 / 2.49
20	4.35 / 8.10	3.49 / 5.85	3.10 / 4.94	2.87 / 4.43	2.71 / 4.10	2.60 / 3.87	2.52 / 3.71	2.45 / 3.56	2.40 / 3.45	2.35 / 3.37	2.31 / 3.30	2.28 / 3.23	2.23 / 3.13	2.18 / 3.05	2.12 / 2.94	2.08 / 2.86	2.04 / 2.77	1.99 / 2.69	1.96 / 2.63	1.92 / 2.56	1.90 / 2.53	1.87 / 2.47	1.85 / 2.44	1.84 / 2.42
21	4.32 / 8.02	3.47 / 5.78	3.07 / 4.87	2.84 / 4.37	2.68 / 4.04	2.57 / 3.81	2.49 / 3.65	2.42 / 3.51	2.37 / 3.40	2.32 / 3.31	2.28 / 3.24	2.25 / 3.17	2.20 / 3.07	2.15 / 2.99	2.09 / 2.88	2.05 / 2.80	2.00 / 2.72	1.96 / 2.63	1.93 / 2.58	1.89 / 2.51	1.87 / 2.47	1.84 / 2.42	1.82 / 2.38	1.81 / 2.36
22	4.30 / 7.94	3.44 / 5.72	3.05 / 4.82	2.82 / 4.31	2.66 / 3.99	2.55 / 3.76	2.47 / 3.59	2.40 / 3.45	2.35 / 3.35	2.30 / 3.26	2.26 / 3.18	2.23 / 3.12	2.18 / 3.02	2.13 / 2.94	2.07 / 2.83	2.03 / 2.75	1.98 / 2.67	1.93 / 2.58	1.91 / 2.53	1.87 / 2.46	1.84 / 2.42	1.81 / 2.37	1.80 / 2.33	1.78 / 2.31
23	4.28 / 7.88	3.42 / 5.66	3.03 / 4.76	2.80 / 4.26	2.64 / 3.94	2.53 / 3.71	2.45 / 3.54	2.38 / 3.41	2.32 / 3.30	2.28 / 3.21	2.24 / 3.14	2.20 / 3.07	2.14 / 2.97	2.10 / 2.89	2.04 / 2.78	2.00 / 2.70	1.96 / 2.62	1.91 / 2.53	1.88 / 2.48	1.84 / 2.41	1.82 / 2.37	1.79 / 2.32	1.77 / 2.28	1.76 / 2.26
24	4.26 / 7.82	3.40 / 5.61	3.01 / 4.72	2.78 / 4.22	2.62 / 3.90	2.51 / 3.67	2.43 / 3.50	2.36 / 3.36	2.30 / 3.25	2.26 / 3.17	2.22 / 3.09	2.18 / 3.03	2.13 / 2.93	2.09 / 2.85	2.02 / 2.74	1.98 / 2.66	1.94 / 2.58	1.89 / 2.49	1.86 / 2.44	1.82 / 2.36	1.80 / 2.33	1.76 / 2.27	1.74 / 2.23	1.73 / 2.21

Between group *df*

Within group *df*	1	2	3	4	5	6	7	8	9	10	11	12	14	16	20	24	30	40	50	75	100	200	500	∞
25	4.24 / 7.77	3.38 / 5.57	2.99 / 4.68	2.76 / 4.18	2.60 / 3.86	2.49 / 3.63	2.41 / 3.46	2.34 / 3.32	2.28 / 3.21	2.24 / 3.13	2.20 / 3.05	2.16 / 2.99	2.11 / 2.89	2.06 / 2.81	2.00 / 2.70	1.96 / 2.62	1.92 / 2.54	1.87 / 2.45	1.84 / 2.40	1.80 / 2.32	1.77 / 2.29	1.74 / 2.23	1.72 / 2.19	1.71 / 2.17
26	4.22 / 7.72	3.37 / 5.53	2.89 / 4.64	2.74 / 4.14	2.59 / 3.82	2.47 / 3.59	2.39 / 3.42	2.32 / 3.29	2.27 / 3.17	2.22 / 3.09	2.18 / 3.02	2.15 / 2.96	2.10 / 2.86	2.05 / 2.77	1.99 / 2.66	1.95 / 2.58	1.90 / 2.50	1.85 / 2.41	1.82 / 2.36	1.78 / 2.28	1.76 / 2.25	1.72 / 2.19	1.70 / 2.15	1.69 / 2.13
27	4.21 / 7.68	3.35 / 5.49	2.96 / 4.60	2.73 / 4.11	2.57 / 3.79	2.46 / 3.56	2.37 / 3.39	2.30 / 3.26	2.25 / 3.14	2.20 / 3.06	2.16 / 2.98	2.13 / 2.93	2.08 / 2.83	2.03 / 2.74	1.97 / 2.63	1.93 / 2.55	1.88 / 2.47	1.84 / 2.38	1.80 / 2.33	1.76 / 2.25	1.74 / 2.21	1.71 / 2.16	1.68 / 2.12	1.67 / 2.10
28	4.20 / 7.64	3.34 / 5.45	2.95 / 4.57	2.71 / 4.07	2.56 / 3.76	2.44 / 3.53	2.36 / 3.36	2.29 / 3.23	2.24 / 3.11	2.19 / 3.03	2.15 / 2.95	2.12 / 2.90	2.06 / 2.80	2.02 / 2.71	1.96 / 2.60	1.91 / 2.52	1.87 / 2.44	1.81 / 2.35	1.78 / 2.30	1.75 / 2.22	1.72 / 2.18	1.69 / 2.13	1.67 / 2.09	1.65 / 2.06
29	4.18 / 7.60	3.33 / 5.52	2.93 / 4.54	2.70 / 4.04	2.54 / 3.73	2.43 / 3.50	2.35 / 3.33	2.28 / 3.20	2.22 / 3.08	2.18 / 3.00	2.14 / 2.92	2.10 / 2.87	2.05 / 2.77	2.00 / 2.68	1.94 / 2.57	1.90 / 2.49	1.85 / 2.41	1.80 / 2.32	1.77 / 2.27	1.73 / 2.19	1.71 / 2.15	1.68 / 2.10	1.65 / 2.06	1.64 / 2.03
30	4.17 / 7.56	3.32 / 5.39	2.92 / 4.51	2.69 / 4.02	2.53 / 3.70	2.42 / 3.47	2.34 / 3.30	2.27 / 3.17	2.21 / 3.06	2.16 / 2.98	2.12 / 2.90	2.09 / 2.84	2.04 / 2.74	1.99 / 2.66	1.93 / 2.55	1.89 / 2.47	1.84 / 2.38	1.79 / 2.29	1.76 / 2.24	1.72 / 2.16	1.69 / 2.13	1.66 / 2.07	1.64 / 2.03	1.62 / 2.01
32	4.15 / 7.50	3.30 / 5.34	2.90 / 4.46	2.67 / 3.97	2.51 / 3.66	2.40 / 3.42	2.32 / 3.25	2.25 / 3.12	2.19 / 3.01	2.14 / 2.94	2.10 / 2.86	2.07 / 2.80	2.02 / 2.70	1.97 / 2.62	1.91 / 2.51	1.86 / 2.42	1.82 / 2.34	1.76 / 2.25	1.74 / 2.20	1.69 / 2.12	1.67 / 2.08	1.64 / 2.02	1.61 / 1.98	1.59 / 1.96
34	4.13 / 7.44	3.28 / 5.29	2.88 / 4.42	2.65 / 3.93	2.49 / 3.61	2.38 / 3.38	2.30 / 3.21	2.23 / 3.08	2.17 / 2.97	2.12 / 2.89	2.08 / 2.82	2.05 / 2.76	2.00 / 2.66	1.95 / 2.58	1.89 / 2.47	1.84 / 2.38	1.80 / 2.30	1.74 / 2.21	1.71 / 2.15	1.67 / 2.08	1.64 / 2.04	1.61 / 1.98	1.59 / 1.94	1.57 / 1.91
36	4.11 / 7.39	3.26 / 5.25	2.86 / 4.38	2.63 / 3.89	2.48 / 3.58	2.36 / 3.35	2.28 / 3.18	2.21 / 3.04	2.15 / 2.94	2.10 / 2.86	2.06 / 2.78	2.03 / 2.72	1.98 / 2.62	1.93 / 2.54	1.87 / 2.43	1.82 / 2.35	1.78 / 2.26	1.72 / 2.17	1.69 / 2.12	1.65 / 2.04	1.62 / 2.00	1.59 / 1.94	1.56 / 1.90	1.55 / 1.87
38	4.10 / 7.35	3.25 / 5.21	2.85 / 4.34	2.62 / 3.86	2.46 / 3.54	2.35 / 3.32	2.26 / 3.15	2.19 / 3.02	2.14 / 2.91	2.09 / 2.82	2.05 / 2.75	2.02 / 2.69	1.96 / 2.59	1.92 / 2.51	1.85 / 2.40	1.80 / 2.32	1.76 / 2.22	1.71 / 2.14	1.67 / 2.08	1.63 / 2.00	1.60 / 1.97	1.57 / 1.90	1.54 / 1.86	1.53 / 1.84
40	4.08 / 7.31	3.23 / 5.18	2.84 / 4.31	2.61 / 3.83	2.45 / 3.51	2.34 / 3.29	2.25 / 3.12	2.18 / 2.99	2.12 / 2.88	2.07 / 2.80	2.04 / 2.73	2.00 / 2.66	1.95 / 2.56	1.90 / 2.49	1.84 / 2.37	1.79 / 2.29	1.74 / 2.20	1.69 / 2.11	1.66 / 2.05	1.61 / 1.97	1.59 / 1.94	1.55 / 1.88	1.53 / 1.84	1.51 / 1.81
42	4.07 / 7.27	3.22 / 5.15	2.83 / 4.29	2.59 / 3.80	2.44 / 3.49	2.32 / 3.26	2.24 / 3.10	2.17 / 2.96	2.11 / 2.86	2.06 / 2.77	2.02 / 2.70	1.99 / 2.64	1.94 / 2.54	1.89 / 2.46	1.82 / 2.35	1.78 / 2.26	1.73 / 2.17	1.68 / 2.08	1.64 / 2.02	1.60 / 1.94	1.57 / 1.91	1.54 / 1.85	1.51 / 1.80	1.49 / 1.78
44	4.06 / 7.24	3.21 / 5.12	2.82 / 4.26	2.58 / 3.78	2.43 / 3.46	2.31 / 3.24	2.23 / 3.07	2.16 / 2.94	2.10 / 2.84	2.05 / 2.75	2.01 / 2.68	1.98 / 2.62	1.92 / 2.52	1.88 / 2.44	1.81 / 2.32	1.76 / 2.24	1.72 / 2.15	1.66 / 2.06	1.63 / 2.00	1.58 / 1.92	1.56 / 1.88	1.52 / 1.82	1.50 / 1.78	1.48 / 1.75
46	4.05 / 7.21	3.20 / 5.10	2.81 / 4.24	2.57 / 3.76	2.42 / 3.44	2.30 / 3.22	2.22 / 3.05	2.14 / 2.92	2.09 / 2.82	2.04 / 2.73	2.00 / 2.66	1.97 / 2.60	1.91 / 2.50	1.87 / 2.42	1.80 / 2.30	1.75 / 2.22	1.71 / 2.13	1.65 / 2.04	1.62 / 1.98	1.57 / 1.90	1.54 / 1.86	1.51 / 1.80	1.48 / 1.76	1.46 / 1.72

Between group df

Within group df	1	2	3	4	5	6	7	8	9	10	11	12	14	16	20	24	30	40	50	75	100	200	500	∞
48	4.04 / 7.19	3.19 / 5.08	2.80 / 4.22	2.56 / 3.74	2.41 / 3.42	2.30 / 3.20	2.21 / 3.04	2.14 / 2.90	2.08 / 2.80	2.03 / 2.71	1.99 / 2.64	1.96 / 2.58	1.90 / 2.48	1.86 / 2.40	1.79 / 2.28	1.74 / 2.20	1.70 / 2.11	1.64 / 2.02	1.61 / 1.96	1.56 / 1.88	1.53 / 1.84	1.50 / 1.78	1.47 / 1.73	1.45 / 1.70
50	4.03 / 7.17	3.18 / 5.06	2.79 / 4.20	2.56 / 3.72	2.40 / 3.41	2.29 / 3.18	2.20 / 3.02	2.13 / 2.88	2.07 / 2.78	2.02 / 2.70	1.98 / 2.62	1.95 / 2.56	1.90 / 2.46	1.85 / 2.39	1.78 / 2.26	1.74 / 2.18	1.69 / 2.10	1.63 / 2.00	1.60 / 1.94	1.55 / 1.86	1.52 / 1.82	1.48 / 1.76	1.46 / 1.71	1.44 / 1.68
55	4.02 / 7.12	3.17 / 5.01	2.78 / 4.16	2.54 / 3.68	2.38 / 3.37	2.27 / 3.15	2.18 / 2.98	2.11 / 2.85	2.05 / 2.75	2.00 / 2.66	1.97 / 2.59	1.93 / 2.53	1.88 / 2.43	1.83 / 2.35	1.76 / 2.23	1.72 / 2.15	1.67 / 2.06	1.61 / 1.96	1.58 / 1.90	1.52 / 1.82	1.50 / 1.78	1.46 / 1.71	1.43 / 1.66	1.41 / 1.64
60	4.00 / 7.08	3.15 / 4.98	2.76 / 4.13	2.52 / 3.65	2.37 / 3.34	2.25 / 3.12	2.17 / 2.95	2.10 / 2.82	2.04 / 2.72	1.99 / 2.63	1.95 / 2.56	1.92 / 2.50	1.86 / 2.40	1.81 / 2.32	1.75 / 2.20	1.70 / 2.12	1.65 / 2.03	1.59 / 1.93	1.56 / 1.87	1.50 / 1.79	1.48 / 1.74	1.44 / 1.68	1.41 / 1.63	1.39 / 1.60
65	3.99 / 7.04	3.14 / 4.95	2.75 / 4.10	2.51 / 3.62	2.36 / 3.31	2.24 / 3.09	2.15 / 2.93	2.08 / 2.79	2.02 / 2.70	1.98 / 2.61	1.94 / 2.54	1.90 / 2.47	1.85 / 2.37	1.80 / 2.30	1.73 / 2.18	1.68 / 2.09	1.63 / 2.00	1.57 / 1.90	1.54 / 1.84	1.49 / 1.76	1.46 / 1.71	1.42 / 1.64	1.39 / 1.60	1.37 / 1.56
70	3.98 / 7.01	3.13 / 4.92	2.74 / 4.08	2.50 / 3.60	2.35 / 3.29	2.23 / 3.07	2.14 / 2.91	2.07 / 2.77	2.01 / 2.67	1.97 / 2.59	1.93 / 2.51	1.89 / 2.45	1.84 / 2.35	1.79 / 2.28	1.72 / 2.15	1.67 / 2.07	1.62 / 1.98	1.56 / 1.88	1.53 / 1.82	1.47 / 1.74	1.45 / 1.69	1.40 / 1.63	1.37 / 1.56	1.35 / 1.53
80	3.96 / 6.96	3.11 / 4.88	2.72 / 4.04	2.48 / 3.56	2.33 / 3.25	2.21 / 3.04	2.12 / 2.87	2.05 / 2.74	1.99 / 2.64	1.95 / 2.55	1.91 / 2.48	1.88 / 2.41	1.82 / 2.32	1.77 / 2.24	1.70 / 2.11	1.65 / 2.03	1.60 / 1.94	1.54 / 1.84	1.51 / 1.78	1.45 / 1.70	1.42 / 1.65	1.38 / 1.57	1.35 / 1.52	1.32 / 1.49
100	3.94 / 6.90	3.09 / 4.82	2.70 / 3.98	2.46 / 3.51	2.30 / 3.20	2.19 / 2.99	2.10 / 2.82	2.03 / 2.69	1.97 / 2.59	1.92 / 2.51	1.88 / 2.43	1.85 / 2.36	1.79 / 2.26	1.75 / 2.19	1.68 / 2.06	1.63 / 1.98	1.57 / 1.89	1.51 / 1.79	1.48 / 1.73	1.42 / 1.64	1.39 / 1.59	1.34 / 1.51	1.30 / 1.46	1.28 / 1.43
125	3.92 / 6.84	3.07 / 4.78	2.68 / 3.94	2.44 / 3.47	2.29 / 3.17	2.17 / 2.95	2.08 / 2.79	2.01 / 2.65	1.95 / 2.56	1.90 / 2.47	1.86 / 2.40	1.83 / 2.33	1.77 / 2.23	1.72 / 2.15	1.65 / 2.03	1.60 / 1.94	1.55 / 1.85	1.49 / 1.75	1.45 / 1.68	1.39 / 1.59	1.36 / 1.54	1.31 / 1.46	1.27 / 1.40	1.25 / 1.37
150	3.91 / 6.81	3.06 / 4.75	2.67 / 3.91	2.43 / 3.44	2.27 / 3.13	2.16 / 2.92	2.07 / 2.76	2.00 / 2.62	1.94 / 2.53	1.89 / 2.44	1.85 / 2.37	1.82 / 2.30	1.76 / 2.20	1.71 / 2.12	1.64 / 2.00	1.59 / 1.91	1.54 / 1.83	1.47 / 1.72	1.44 / 1.66	1.37 / 1.56	1.34 / 1.51	1.29 / 1.43	1.25 / 1.37	1.22 / 1.33
200	3.89 / 6.76	3.04 / 4.71	2.65 / 3.88	2.41 / 3.41	2.26 / 3.11	2.14 / 2.90	2.05 / 2.73	1.98 / 2.60	1.92 / 2.50	1.87 / 2.41	1.83 / 2.34	1.80 / 2.28	1.74 / 2.17	1.69 / 2.09	1.62 / 1.97	1.57 / 1.88	1.52 / 1.79	1.45 / 1.69	1.42 / 1.62	1.35 / 1.53	1.32 / 1.48	1.26 / 1.39	1.22 / 1.33	1.19 / 1.28
400	3.86 / 6.70	3.02 / 4.66	2.62 / 3.83	2.39 / 3.36	2.23 / 3.06	2.12 / 2.85	2.03 / 2.69	1.96 / 2.55	1.90 / 2.46	1.85 / 2.37	1.81 / 2.29	1.78 / 2.23	1.72 / 2.12	1.67 / 2.04	1.60 / 1.92	1.54 / 1.84	1.49 / 1.74	1.42 / 1.64	1.38 / 1.57	1.32 / 1.47	1.28 / 1.42	1.22 / 1.32	1.16 / 1.24	1.13 / 1.19
1000	3.85 / 6.66	3.00 / 4.62	2.61 / 3.80	2.38 / 3.34	2.22 / 3.04	2.10 / 2.82	2.02 / 2.66	1.95 / 2.53	1.89 / 2.43	1.84 / 2.34	1.80 / 2.26	1.76 / 2.20	1.70 / 2.09	1.65 / 2.01	1.58 / 1.89	1.53 / 1.81	1.47 / 1.71	1.41 / 1.61	1.36 / 1.54	1.30 / 1.44	1.26 / 1.38	1.19 / 1.28	1.13 / 1.19	1.08 / 1.11
∞	3.84 / 6.64	2.99 / 4.60	2.60 / 3.78	2.37 / 3.32	2.21 / 3.02	2.09 / 2.80	2.01 / 2.64	1.94 / 2.51	1.88 / 2.41	1.83 / 2.32	1.79 / 2.24	1.75 / 2.18	1.69 / 2.07	1.64 / 1.99	1.57 / 1.87	1.52 / 1.79	1.46 / 1.69	1.40 / 1.59	1.35 / 1.52	1.28 / 1.41	1.24 / 1.36	1.17 / 1.25	1.11 / 1.15	1.00 / 1.00

Table Q: Critical Values for the Correlation Coefficient

	Level of significance for a one-tail test				
	.05	.025	.01	.005	.0005
	Level of significance for a two-tail test				
df	.10	.05	.02	.01	.001
1	.9877	.9969	.9995	.9999	1.0000
2	.9000	.9500	.9800	.9900	.9990
3	.8054	.8783	.9343	.9587	.9912
4	.7293	.8114	.8822	.9172	.9741
5	.6694	.7545	.8329	.8745	.9507
6	.6215	.7067	.7887	.8343	.9249
7	.5822	.6664	.7498	.7977	.8982
8	.5494	.6319	.7155	.7646	.8721
9	.5214	.6021	.6851	.7348	.8471
10	.4973	.5760	.6581	.7079	.8233
11	.4762	.5529	.6339	.6835	.8010
12	.4575	.5324	.6120	.6614	.7800
13	.4409	.5139	.5923	.6411	.7603
14	.4259	.4973	.5742	.6226	.7420
15	.4124	.4821	.5577	.6055	.7246
16	.4000	.4683	.5425	.5897	.7084
17	.3887	.4555	.5285	.5751	.6932
18	.3783	.4438	.5155	.5614	.6787
19	.3687	.4329	.5034	.5487	.6652
20	.3598	.4227	.4921	.5368	.6524
25	.3233	.3809	.4451	.4869	.5974
30	.2960	.3494	.4093	.4487	.5541
35	.2746	.3246	.3810	.4182	.5189
40	.2573	.3044	.3578	.3932	.4896
45	.2428	.2875	.3384	.3721	.4648
50	.2306	.2732	.3218	.3541	.4433
60	.2108	.2500	.2948	.3248	.4078
70	.1954	.2319	.2737	.3017	.3799
80	.1829	.2172	.2565	.2830	.3568
90	.1726	.2050	.2422	.2673	.3375
100	.1638	.1946	.2301	.2540	.3211

Source: Table Q is taken from Table VII: The Correlation Coefficient, of Fisher and Yates: *Statistical Tables for Biological, Agricultural and Medical Research,* published by Longman Group Ltd., London (previously published by Oliver and Boyd, Edinburgh), and by permission of the authors and publishers.

Table R: Critical Values for the Spearman Rank Correlation Coefficient When N Is between 4 and 10

| | Significance level for a one-tail test | |
	.05	.01
	Significance level for a two-tail test	
N	.10	.02
4	1.000	
5	.900	1.000
6	.829	.943
7	.714	.893
8	.643	.833
9	.600	.783
10	.564	.746

Source: Adapted from *Elementary Statistics,* Fourth Edition, by Paul G. Hoel, copyright © 1976, John Wiley & Sons, Inc. Reprinted by permission of John Wiley & Sons, Inc.

REFERENCES

Cochran, W.G. "Some Consequences When the Assumptions Underlying the Analysis of Variance Have Not Been Met." *Biometrics* 3(1947):22–28.

Dixon, W.J., and Massey, F.J. *Introduction to Statistical Analysis.* New York: McGraw-Hill Book Co., 1957.

Downie, N.M., and Heath, R.W. *Statistical Methods,* 4th ed. New York: Harper & Row, 1974.

Edwards, A.L. *Experimental Design in Psychological Research,* 4th ed. New York: Holt, Rinehart & Winston, 1972.

Ferguson, G.A. *Statistical Analysis in Psychology and Education,* 2nd ed. New York: McGraw-Hill Book Co., 1966.

Goodman, L.A. "Kolmogorov-Smirnov Tests for Psychological Research." *Psychological Bulletin* 51(1954):160–168.

Guilford, J.P., and Fruchter, B. *Fundamental Statistics in Psychology and Education,* 5th ed. New York: McGraw-Hill Book Co., 1973.

Hays, W.L. *Statistics for the Social Sciences,* 2nd ed. New York: Holt, Rinehart & Winston, 1973.

Hoel, P. *Elementary Statistics,* 4th ed. New York: John Wiley & Sons, 1976.

Lindgren, B.M. *Statistical Theory,* 3rd ed. New York: Macmillan, 1976.

Massey, F.J., Jr. "The Kolmogorov-Smirnov Test for Goodness of Fit." *Journal of American Statistics Association* 46(1951):68–78.

Meddis, R. *Statistical Handbook for Non-Statisticians.* London: McGraw-Hill Book Co., 1975.

Mitchell, S.H. "The Deaf Minority Group: A Study of Selected Discriminatory Factors." Unpublished doctoral dissertation, American University, 1969.

Mood, A.M. *Introduction to Theory of Statistics.* New York: McGraw-Hill Book Co., 1950.

Peters, C.C., and VanVoorhis, W.R. *Statistical Procedures and Their Mathematical Bases.* New York: McGraw-Hill Book Co., 1940.

Pirie, W.R. and Hamden, M.A. "Some Revised Continuity Corrections for Discrete Data." *Biometrics* 28(1972):693–701.

Ryan, T.A. "Significance Tests for Multiple Comparison of Proportions, Variances and Other Statistics." *Psychological Bulletin* 57, 4(1960):318–328.

Siegel, S. *Nonparametric Statistics for the Behavioral Sciences.* New York: McGraw-Hill Book Co., 1956.

Snedecor, G.W., and Cochran, W.G. *Statistical Methods,* 6th ed. Ames: Iowa State College Press, 1967.

Stevens, S.S. "Measurement, Statistics, and the Schemapiric View." *Science* 161(1968):845–856.

Walker, H.M. *Studies in the History of Statistical Method.* New York: Arno Press, 1975.

Walker, H.M., and Lev, J. *Statistical Inference.* New York: Holt, Rinehart & Winston, 1953.

Walker, H.M. and Lev, J. *Elementary Statistical Methods,* 3rd ed. New York: Holt, Rinehart and Winston, 1969.

Wilcoxon, F., and Wilcox, R. "Some Rapid Approximate Statistical Procedures." Pearl River, New York: Lederle Laboratories, 1964, pp. 9–12.

Winer, B.J. *Statistical Principles in Experimental Design,* 2nd ed. New York: McGraw-Hill Book Co., 1971.

INDEX

LIST OF FORMULAS

(continued)

8-1   *Kolmogorov-Smirnov Test*

$$D = \frac{LD}{N}$$

8-2   *Mann-Whitney U*

$$U_1 = n_1 n_2 + \frac{n_1(n_1 + 1)}{2} - \Sigma R_1$$

8-3   *Mann-Whitney U*

$$U_2 = n_1 n_2 - U_1$$

8-4   *Mann-Whitney U* (when n_2 is larger than 20)

$$z = \frac{U + \frac{1}{2} - \frac{n_1 n_2}{2}}{\sqrt{\frac{n_1 n_2 (n_1 + n_2 + 1)}{12}}}$$

8-5   *Sign Test* (sample size larger than 25)

$$z = \frac{(x \pm .5) - \frac{1}{2}N}{\frac{1}{2}\sqrt{N}}$$

8-6   *Wilcoxon Test* (sample size larger than 25)

$$z = \frac{T - \frac{N(N+1)}{4}}{\sqrt{\frac{N(N+1)(2N+1)}{24}}}$$

8-7   *Kruskal-Wallis Test*

$$H = \frac{12}{N(N+1)} \frac{(\Sigma R_1)^2}{n_1} + \frac{(\Sigma R_2)^2}{n_2} + \frac{(\Sigma R_3)^2}{n_3} + \ldots + \frac{(\Sigma R_k)^2}{n_k} - 3(N+1)$$

8-8   *Friedman Test*

$$\chi_r^2 = \frac{12}{Nk(k+1)} [\Sigma R_i^2] - 3N(k+1)$$